# HOLY MADNESS

*An Omega Book*

This New Age series of Paragon House is dedicated to classic and contemporary works about higher human development and the nature of ultimate reality. **Omega Books** encompasses the fields of mysticism and spirituality, psychic research and paranormal phenomena, the evolution of consciousness, and the human potential for self-directed growth in body, mind, and spirit.

Ask your bookseller for these other Omega Books:

SYNCHRONICITY: Science, Myth, and the Trickster
    by Allan Combs and Mark Holland

LIFECYCLES: Reincarnation and the Web of Life
    by Christopher Bache

MYSTICS, MAGICIANS, AND MEDICINE PEOPLE: Tales of a Wanderer
    by Doug Boyd

SWAMI
    by Doug Boyd

THE MEETING OF SCIENCE AND SPIRIT: Guidelines for a New Age
    by John White

KUNDALINI, EVOLUTION, AND ENLIGHTENMENT
    edited by John White

GENERAL EDITOR: John White

# HOLY MADNESS

## The Shock Tactics and Radical Teachings of Crazy-Wise Adepts, Holy Fools, and Rascal Gurus

## Georg Feuerstein

**PARAGON HOUSE**
**New York**

First edition, 1991
Published in the United States by

Paragon House
90 Fifth Avenue
New York, N.Y. 10011

Grateful acknowledgment is made to the following publishers and authors for permission to quote from copyrighted material: *The Royal Song of Sahara*, copyright © 1991 by H. V. Guenther, reproduced by permission of the author; *Finite and Infinite Games: A Vision of Life as Play and Possibility* by James P. Carse, copyright © 1986 by James P. Carse, reproduced by permission of The Free Press, a Division of Macmillan, Inc.; *The Confessions of Aleister Crowley: An Autobiography*, ed. by J. Symonds and K. Grant, copyright © 1979, reproduced by permission of Routledge, Chapman and Hall; *Songs of the Bards of Bengal* by Deben Bhattacharya, copyright © 1969 by UNESCO, reproduced by permission of Grove Weidenfeld; *Zen and the Comic Spirit* by M. Conrad Hyers, copyright © by M. Conrad Hyers, reproduced by permission of Random Century Group; *To a Dancing God* by Sam Keen, copyright © 1970 by Sam Keen, reproduced by permission of HarperCollins Publishers Inc.

*Manufactured in the United States*

*Library of Congress Cataloging-in-Publishing Data*

Feuerstein, Georg.
    Holy madness : the shock tactics and radical teachings of crazy-wise adepts, holy fools, and rascal gurus / Georg Feuerstein. — 1st ed.
        p.   cm. — (An Omega book)
    Includes bibliographical references and index.
    ISBN 1-55778-250-4 : $24.95
    1. Spiritual life.   2. Religion.   3. Gurus.   I. Title.
II. Series: Omega book (New York, N.Y.)
BL624.F478   1990
291.6—dc20                                                    90-21233
                                                                   CIP

10   9   8   7   6   5   4   3   2   1

*For Trisha, who shared over five years
the holiness and the foolishness of it all*

# CONTENTS

# ACKNOWLEDGMENTS

I would like to thank all the many friends and well-wishers who have contributed to this work in one form or another—too many to name each individually. However, I must express my heartfelt gratitude to Sidney and Jean Lanier for their warm friendship and tremendous moral support; Laurance S. Rockefeller for his personal interest in my work and his generous patronage, which enabled me to dedicate myself to this book during the fall and winter months of 1989; Ed Brennan, Jim Royster, and John White for their many constructive comments; Scott Anderson for many years of heart-searching dialogue about spiritual life, gurus, and the scientific viewpoint; Frances Vaughan, Seymore and Sylvia Borstein, and Arthur and Etta Deikman for allowing me to use them as sounding boards during a knotty phase in my thinking (and feeling) about holy madness; Roy Finch for a lively correspondence about crazy wisdom, which demonstrated to me that philosophers can raise "people" questions as well as academic issues; Ram Dass for spending an entire afternoon with me, during which we swapped stories about our respective teachers and pondered the near-imponderables of crazy wisdom; Roger Walsh for his many invaluable observations leading to an improved manuscript and for his kind foreword; Carolyn Anderson for working a copyeditor's minor miracles; Stacey Lynn for her conscientious proofreading; my wife, Trisha, for waving her magic wand of common sense and editorial skill over this manuscript, and not least for continuing to nourish my being with her love. Finally, I must record my indebtedness to Da Love-Ananda, who appears often on the following pages. Without him I would not have experienced both the advantages and what I perceive to be the drawbacks of a crazy-wisdom teaching and traditionalist *guru-yoga* in modern times. Sometimes we must criticize those who have served us the most. I do so in the certainty that the heart is always larger than the intellect.

# FOREWORD

*One of the first signs of a saint will be the fact that
other people do not know what to make of him.*[1]
Thomas Merton

There is considerable unanimity among the world's religions, and especially
among the contemplative traditions, that we have overestimated our usual
state of mind, yet greatly underestimated our potential. These traditions,
which together form the perennial philosophy, perennial wisdom, or perennial psychology, consider our usual awareness to be only semiconscious
dreams, *maya*, or a consensus trance. Yet these same traditions claim that we
are capable of escaping from this trance and of thereby realizing what has
been variously called enlightenment, liberation, salvation, *moksha*, or awakening.

Needless to say, these claims have evoked strong reactions throughout
history, especially in our own time. The most extreme reactions have involved
outright dismissal and dramatic idealization. The very possibility of
enlightenment—let alone of the existence of a realm of pure consciousness,
Mind, Spirit, or *Geist*, which enlightenment is said to reveal—has been
denied on metaphysical grounds by philosophies such as materialism, Marxism, and scientism. Likewise, claims for mystical insights and liberation have
been pathologized by perspectives such as those of psychoanalysis and what
William James called "medical materialism." In his classic *The Varieties of
Religious Experience*, James commented as follows:

> Medical materialism seems indeed a good appellation for the too simple-
> minded system of thought which we are considering. Medical material-
> ism finishes up Saint Paul by calling his vision on the road to Damascus a
> discharging lesion of the occipital cortex, he being an epileptic. It snuffs
> out Saint Teresa as an hysteric, Saint Frances of Assisi as an hereditary
> degenerate. George Fox's discontent with the shams of his age and his
> pining for spiritual veracity, it treats as a symptom of a disordered colon.
> . . . All such mental overtensions, it says, are, when you come to the
> bottom of the matter . . . due to the perverted action of various glands
> which physiology will yet discover.[2]

At the other extreme, spiritual practitioners have sometimes been idealized to the point where their humanity and fallibility are completely denied. In such cases the teacher can do no wrong and everything he or she does is interpreted as a divinely inspired infallible teaching for the benefit of others. The dangers of this attitude have been the delight of our mass media for years.

Yet on balance, while it is hard to accept spiritual figures, or even spiritual masters, as infallible, it is equally difficult to dismiss them out of hand. After all, the great saints and sages have been said to represent the highest levels of human development and to have had the greatest impact on human history. So at least said the historian Toynbee, the author Tolstoy, the philosophers Bergson, Schopenhauer, and Nietzsche, and the psychologists James, Maslow, and Wilber, among others. Said Toynbee, "Who are the greatest benefactors of the living generation of mankind? I should say: Confucius and Lao Tzu, the Buddha, the Prophets of Israel and Judah, Zoroaster, Jesus, Mohammed and Socrates."[3]

Assuming that alongside numbers of imposters true saints and sages do exist and have realized something profound about their nature and ours, how are we to understand our reactions to them? After all, in addition to inspiring literally billions of people, they have also been tortured, poisoned, crucified, and burned, often by law-abiding citizens seeking to protect society from their influence.

The question is complicated by the fact that some religious practitioners and masters have clearly seemed bizarre by conventional standards. Some appear to have deliberately flouted convention, provoked authorities, and offended their listeners. Indeed some of them have appeared so bizarre as to have been labeled by such names as holy fools, crazy-wisdom teachers, or god intoxicants.

What are we to make of these paradoxical people? Clearly, our answers have enormous implications for our understanding of human nature, potential, and pathology, of religion, enlightenment, and sainthood, and of the effects of contemplative practices. Yet these paradoxical people have been subject to almost no serious research.

Here at last is a book that studies them carefully, confronts the paradoxes they present, ranges over a broad expanse of traditions, cultures, and times, and is open to both the potentials and the pitfalls of spiritual practice. Here is a book that seeks neither to idealize nor to pathologize but rather to acknowledge and understand both the benign and the bizarre behavior of those subgroups of spiritual imposters, practitioners, and even masters who display what Georg Feuerstein calls "holy madness."

And who better to do this than Georg Feuerstein, a writer of enormous breadth of scholarship, a person acknowledged as one of the foremost authorities on Yoga, and yet more than just a scholar, a scholar and a practitioner. Feuerstein has practiced Yoga and other contemplative disciplines of which he writes and that is an important qualification. For it is becoming increasingly clear, both from a growing body of psychological and philosophical theory as well as from personal accounts, that one's intellectual understanding of contemplative practices, traditions, psychologies, and philosophies may be significantly enhanced by, and even dependent on, one's degree of personal experience with the practices. While there is much to be said for detached objectivity in many areas of research, it seems that in the study of contemplative practices and practitioners, careful objectivity may be best coupled with personal experience.

Prepare, then, to be educated, entertained, challenged, and confounded by the accounts of "holy madness" herein. For the men and women who are the subject of this book flout convention, polite behavior, and much that we traditionally hold dear, puncture our favorite images and illusions, and challenge our neat theories and conventional wisdom. This book tells us a great deal about them and thereby about ourselves.

—Roger Walsh, M.D., Ph.D.
Department of Psychiatry and Human Behavior
University of California Medical School, Irvine

# PREFACE

Our secularized world is witnessing a widespread revival of interest in the experiential, mystical dimension of religion, which can broadly be called "spirituality." Yet misunderstandings about the spiritual process in its different aspects and phases abound. In light of the media's exposure of such cults as the Rajneeshees and the Hare Krishnas over the past two decades, many people are wondering about the role that Eastern esoteric "cults" will or should play in the future of our Western civilization. These non-Christian paths are widely felt to clash with the rugged individualism and democratic value system of the Euro-American countries, and they tend to challenge the moralistic, theistic ideology of "civil religion." Yet millions of men and women have been influenced by one or another Eastern spiritual tradition, often through the medium of a charismatic teacher, called *guru* in Hinduism, *shaykh* in Sufism, *lama* in Tibetan Buddhism, *roshi* in Zen, and *zaddik* in Hasidism.

Goaded by the news media and Christian fundamentalism, the public is particularly questioning the traditional teacher-disciple relationship. Often the critics forget that discipleship has been at the core of Christianity ever since Jesus of Nazareth gathered the apostles around him.

There are many questions about spiritual teachers and discipleship that deserve to be posed and that will be addressed in this book. From the outset it must be emphasized that what is at stake in this consideration is nothing less than our conventional picture of the universe and the morality that accompanies it. The esoteric or spiritual worldview stands in sharp contrast to the consensus worldview, which is basically materialistic. The esoteric perspective represents a definition of reality that is diametrically opposed to the one by which most people live their lives in our postmodern world. Most important, the esoteric perspective also represents an alternative morality that is felt by many to be no morality at all, but rather the negation of moral values.

This difference becomes strikingly apparent when we examine the world-

wide tradition of spiritual adepts whose behavior and teaching prove shocking to ordinary moral sensibilities and challenge widely held norms of
thought and conduct. These are the crazy adepts of Tibetan Buddhism, the
eccentric teachers of Ch'an (Zen), the holy fools of Christianity and Islam, the
*avadhutas* and *bauls* of Hinduism, and the tricksters and religious clowns of
tribal traditions.

In order to teach spiritual truths, these masters often adopt quite unconventional means—certainly means that are not ordinarily associated with
holy folk. They resort to alcohol and other drugs, and they use sexuality for
instructional purposes. They do not mind either filth or excessive luxury.
Their generally outrageous behavior does not at all conform to our cherished
ideas of religiosity, morality, and sanctity. They practice the reversal of values
preached by Nietzsche, yet, like Nietzsche, they affirm the death of the
parental God who still dominates the thinking of the vast majority of people
alive today.

The various teachings of these adepts can all be brought under the convenient heading of holy madness, or crazy wisdom. Although this phenomenon
can be found in religious traditions around the world, it has been virtually
ignored by historians of religion. More important, holy madness has so far
not been recognized as a universal category of religious life. Because of this
gap in the study of religion and also because of the general lack of knowledge
about holy madness, it is impossible to talk intelligently about this phenomenon without placing it in a wider context by talking as well about the nature
of the spiritual process, charismatic teachers (gurus), authority, discipleship,
submission, freedom of will, nonverbal transmission, and the new religious
cults.

This book is the first attempt at a fuller exploration of holy madness, or
crazy wisdom, as a religious category. I draw on my indological and anthro-
pological background, as well as my reading in the psychological disciplines.
In addition, my discussion is informed by my personal spiritual practice. For
five years I learned firsthand about discipleship, participation in a spiritual
community, renunciation, service, meditation, and not least the predictably
unpredictable behavior of a crazy-wise teacher. While this experiment came
to an end several years ago, I continue to benefit from the lessons learned. I
believe that my direct exposure to the ego-grating experiences of discipleship
and crazy wisdom and to the often irrational demands of life in a gurucentric
community allow me to discuss the issues presented here in a more balanced
way. I do not write purely or even primarily as a theoretician but am passion-
ately interested in reflecting on my own experience, which obviously parallels the experience of others. Neither do I write as someone who belongs to a
specific tradition and has ideological wares to peddle or a sectarian axe to
grind.

Moreover, having gone through the experience of membership in what some would call a "new religious cult," I have little sympathy for the virulent criticism leveled against such groups by anticultists, who lean toward religious fundamentalism rather than unbiased thinking. I joined and left of my own free choice. It was not easy to remake my inner and outer life, just as it had not been easy to adapt to life in a spiritual community. Old friends and colleagues had reacted to my decision to "drop out" of the academic world with incomprehension, some even with hostility. Similarly, my former fellow disciples quite failed to understand why I had to leave. Some even reacted angrily toward me, and a few still harbor ill feelings.

In part, I left because the clash between their understanding of the spiritual process and my interpretation of it became increasingly difficult to negotiate in a peaceful manner. I never felt that my commitment to the spiritual process and my teacher in any way implied that I should become a nonentity; or that mystical ego-death means the obliteration of the personality; or that renunciation must squelch life's vibrant colors; or that mature participation in a spiritual community requires monolithic conformity and the abdication of all one's creative impulses; or that mindless submission to fellow aspirants on the path ("*the* community") is equivalent to spiritual obedience; or that faith necessarily excludes doubt; or even that obedience to one's teacher consists in the total suspension of one's innermost feelings and intuitions.

Fortunately, I had not inbibed the powerful ideology, or pseudomythology, by which closed communities tend to maintain themselves in a state of relative isolation from the world, or by which members justify their enthusiastic personality cult around the spiritual leader, which breeds only lovelessness, idolatry, narcissistic introversion, and an insidious power struggle for access to the guru.

More important, I left when I knew that I had learned whatever lessons I needed or was able to assimilate. I trusted my instincts and made myself available to new lessons. Among other things I realized that the autocratic way of teaching favored by most gurus is ultimately alien to my being. Indeed, I believe that it is alien to the being of most Westerners, and for very good psychohistorical reasons: Our postmodern world is a world of intense individualism—a fairly novel phenomenon in the history of human consciousness and culture. Many spiritual teachers—especially those from the East, where individualism has not yet made the same inroads—ignore this vital fact. They tend to treat the human personality as an illusion that must not be taken seriously. But this is a profound mistake—from both a metaphysical and a didactic point of view. The ego, the sense of being a skin-bound island, is an immediate experiential fact for everyone except the rare enlightened being. That there is a condition, namely enlightenment, in which the ego-sense is transcended is true. That this ego-transcending state is in itself desirable is also true. But this does not do away with the experience of billions of beings who are not so enlightened—myself included. Even if the ego were a hallucination, it would still hold true for the hallucinating person. This fact should always be acknowledged and respected. I believe that because of their illusionist metaphysics, most Eastern or Eastern-type traditions have on balance failed to effect deep and long-lasting transformations in their Western adherents.

Nonetheless, I look back upon my own period of discipleship with gratitude. I learned much about gurucentric spirituality, community life, and not least about myself. Some lessons were delightful, many were painful, but all were useful and fitting. I have no regrets. I realize that every spiritual approach has its advantages and drawbacks, and that everyone must locate his or her appropriate response at a given time.

For the past three years I have followed Gautama the Buddha's fine advice; applying the wisdom brought forth in me by my former teacher and others, I have exercised the virtue of self-reliance on the spiritual path. Once the spiritual process has been initiated, it assumes a life of its own, providing it continues to be consciously cultivated. The "guru" is still under my skin, and I would have it no other way. Still, there comes a time when a genuine teacher must kick a disciple out of the nest, or when a disciple must, in the words of Zen master Rinzai, kill the Buddha when he or she meets him on the road. If this move is not made when it is appropriate, a disciple merely stunts his or her own growth. As a Sufi maxim has it: "When the door is open, throw away the key." I do not wish to preclude the possibility of a lifelong teacher-disciple relationship. However, for this to make sense in the West today, the teacher must be willing and able to transcend traditional autocratic ways in favor of a more symmetric, dialectical relationship.

This volume contains my reflections on the great issues of those forms of spirituality that endeavor to communicate an essentially incommunicable realization to those who can as yet barely hear the "thunderous silence." My focus is on holy madness, which affords the most penetrating glimpse into the very heart of the spiritual process. But I have cast my net much farther afield in order to provide the essential contexts without which holy fools and crazy-wise masters would seem little more than queer personalities, somewhat amusing but perhaps mostly offensive to modern sensibilities and devoid of any educational merit.

In Part One, I introduce the reader to a great many holy fools and their often astonishing exploits in different religious traditions, past and present. These chapters contain numerous anecdotes and supply the material for my preliminary efforts at analysis in Part Three. I have dedicated an entire chapter to Da Love-Ananda, the contemporary crazy-wisdom adept whose teachings have influenced me the most. In fact, I owe a great debt to him not only for having stimulated my theoretical interest in the phenomenon of crazy wisdom—or holy madness—but, more important, for having given me the opportunity to feel its flesh-and-blood pulse. Not everything I have learned can be readily communicated on paper or even in words, but without those lessons, this book would undoubtedly have turned out far less informed and realistic. On the other side, it will become evident that my gratitude is not naively enthusiastic, for I have grave reservations about the teaching style for which Da Love-Ananda and other, similar adepts have become notorious. I am therefore obliged to temper my gratitude with honest criticism. This attitude would be an affront only in the framework of the autocratic guru-devotee relationship, which I feel to be antiquated and seldom constructive in a Western context.

In Part Two, I aim to provide a context for comprehending the crazy wise behavior of the spiritual eccentrics introduced in Part One. Thus I address various aspects of the spiritual process—the nature of spiritual practice, enlightenment, the guru's function, and the purpose and mechanics of discipleship.

Part Three is dedicated to interpreting and understanding holy madness as an important expression of the religious impulse. Here the question of morality is looked at in more detail, as is the issue of the possible psychiatric component in the behavior and realization of some crazy-wise adepts. The two most controversial aspects of Eastern spiritual traditions, for which they have come under attack, are their generally amoral metaphysics ("Reality is beyond good and evil") and the immense authority invested in the spiritual teacher ("The guru is God"). Both these aspects are starkly epitomized in the unconventional, "mad" behavior of spiritual eccentrics. Their seemingly crazy deeds have the express purpose of topsy-turvying consensus reality in order to lead to spiritual breakthroughs.

In this book I try to examine as objectively and compassionately as possible the questionable aspects of the gurucentric traditions, and holy madness in particular. Yet I also make a case for the authenticity *and* the *conditional* legitimacy of holy folly as a teaching tool. I even go as far as to speculate about the possible social and evolutionary usefulness of the crazy-wisdom approach. I am aware that in this orientation I am walking a tightrope between current criticisms of spirituality and contemporary partisans of gurucentric traditions. I hope that both camps—critics and protagonists—will find my observations not merely controversial but challenging and helpful.

This book is intended as a spiritually engaged account and critique of crazy wisdom rather than an academic exercise. Inevitably, it is also a critique of conventional religion and the pseudo-religion of scientific materialism, that is, the ideology of scientism. I am aware that my orientation will not sit well with all my readers. Some will want to see "hard proof" for certain of my assumptions and positions relative to the scientific enterprise; others will want to argue with me about the merit of conventional forms of religion. I wish to emphasize in advance that my critique is founded in the kind of radical spiritual attitude that marks genuine mysticism. I do not deny the *relative* usefulness and benevolence of science or religion. Yet I do seek to expose their inherent limitations from the vantage point of self-transcending spiritual practice.

Toward the end of his life, St. Thomas of Aquinas experienced his first mystical vision. He was so shattered by the experience that he refused to complete the work he had been doing. It seemed like so much straw to him. Well, this book too seems like straw to me. But in saying this, I am also aware that straw is not necessarily without merit: The reader can use these ruminations as fuel for his or her own spiritual flame.

—Georg Feuerstein
Northern California

# PART ONE
## THE PHENOMENON

# 1

## Holy Madness: Moderate Spiritual Eccentrics in Different Religious Traditions

### 1. The Upside Down World of Tricksters and Clowns

Holy madness, or crazy wisdom, is a radical style of teaching or demonstrating spiritual values. I use this term somewhat elastically in this book in order to highlight a range of similar approaches within the great spiritual traditions of the world. What these approaches have in common is an adept—a master, sage, saint, or holy person—who *typically* instructs others in ways that are designed to startle or shock the conventional mind. The beneficiaries of such instruction may be the adept's own disciples or they may simply be the general public. From the conventional point of view, the crazy-wise teachers are eccentrics who use their eccentricity to communicate an alternative vision to that which governs ordinary life. They are masters of inversion, proficient breakers of taboos, and lovers of surprise, contradiction, and ambiguity. They share these skills and penchants with the traditional figures of the trickster and the clown.

The trickster, who is usually male, belongs to the realm of tribal religion and mythology. He is either a god or a superhuman hero. He is a being who is very clever but unprincipled, delighting in the irrational. There is an element of malice in many trickster figures, though they are never entirely demonic. They are out to best their adversaries and spare no cunning to achieve their goal. As part of their duplicity, they often pretend to be stupid. They are generally depicted as merciless, cruel victors. At times, the trickster himself is killed in a fight, but it is always understood that he can come back to life.

The trickster is, moreover, depicted as having a voracious sexual appetite, which is often indicated by a huge penis. His character is a juxtaposition of carnality and spirituality. More than any other mythological figure, the trickster celebrates bodily existence, which includes all the many functions that civilization seeks to suppress or control. After the moment of creation, the Winnebago trickster Wakdjunkaga scattered all creatures across the earth by means of an enormous fart. His flatulence was thus essential to life on earth.

Trickster stories are thought to be told in order to amuse the audience. But they have a deeper significance. They are intended to communicate something about the chaotic, unpredictable, death-dealing aspect of Nature itself—an aspect that the encultured consciousness seeks to deny and avoid. The trickster is an embodiment of the anticultural forces that surround human society, which are kept at bay by the countless institutions that compose the skeleton of culture: rites, myths, dogmas, scientific theories, interpersonal arrangements, personal beliefs, and so on.

In his justly famous book *The Hero with a Thousand Faces*, Joseph Campbell retells a story about Edshu, the trickster-god of the Yoruba of West Africa. Edshu, the tale goes, saw two farmers dutifully plowing their fields. He immediately resolved to play a trick on them, to disrupt their seriousness. He donned a hat that sported a different color—red, white, green, and black—on each side, and walked by the fields. Later that evening, the two farmers each described their version of the stranger with the hat. One farmer insisted the hat had been red, while the other swore it had been white. Feeling certain of what they had seen, the farmers got into an argument, which soon turned into a brawl. The people separated them and dragged them before the village headman. The headman was unable to resolve the conflict, however. At that point, Edshu, who had joined the crowd, revealed his true identity. He admitted to having engineered the farmers' argument and remarked, "Spreading strife is my greatest joy."[1]

The trickster stories are a reminder to the tribal personality that death, destruction, and arbitrariness loom on the other side of magic, ritual, and tribal organization. They are also a way of dealing with the numerous societal constraints called into existence in the process of creating cultural order out of natural chaos. The stories have an archetypal appeal; they hold the listener spellbound, and even the modern reader is fascinated. We are provoked to laughter, or at least a smile, because the trickster reminds us of truths that we generally choose to forget—perhaps because we vaguely sense that there is a trickster in each of us who protests and wants to rid himself of the myriad cultural forms that keep our spontaneity carefully contained.

Carl Gustav Jung saw in the trickster a figure representative of an "earlier, rudimentary stage of consciousness."[2] Equating the trickster with the "shadow," the dark side of the personality, Jung remarked:

> He is both subhuman and superhuman, a bestial and divine being, whose chief and most alarming characteristic is his unconsciousness . . .
> The trickster is a primitive "cosmic" being of *divine-animal* nature, on the one hand superior to man because of his superhuman qualities, and on the other hand inferior to him because of his unreason and unconsciousness.[3]

Yet, the trickster is not *merely* a personification of the unconscious. We may also see in him a symbol of the intrapsychic impulse toward higher consciousness, or what Ken Wilber calls the "Atman project."[4] As such, the trickster is the mythological precursor of the crazy-wisdom guru who also sees it as his or her task to tear off all our cultural blinders and rational pretensions so that we may see reality unmasked. Speaking for Nature and the unconscious, both characters turn the conventional universe upside down and inside out. The trickster's impulse to spread "strife" is analogous to the guru's desire to disrupt the disciple's automaticities (called "culture") and to induce in him or her a state of discontent—a crisis in consciousness.

Conflict is not necessarily bad or evil. It is as much a part of social existence as is the desire for harmony and integration. We tend, however, to deny conflict in ourselves and in our environment. Therefore, we fail to appreciate that *some* conflict is positive and desirable. Zen teacher and management consultant Albert Low writes:

> Instead of suppressing conflicts, specific channels could be created to make this conflict explicit, and specific methods could be set up by which the conflict is resolved. Out of this growth could arise. Unresolved conflict, on the other hand, will lead to frustration and hostility, and this in turn will tend to emphasize individual differences, personality defects, and, consequently, bring to the fore interpersonal hostility.[5]

Although Low's words are intended primarily for the ears of management executives, they apply to a great many other situations as well. As he notes, "*To be* at all, we must be in conflict."[6] Low criticizes Arthur Koestler, for instance, who also admitted that schizophrenia (he spoke of "schizophysiology") is inherent in our nature but wanted to overcome his despair at the situation by prescribing a biochemical solution to restore "dynamic equilibrium." Low rightly points out that it is that very dynamism that negates the equilibrium; otherwise there would be mere stasis.

Low admits that there is no ultimate solution to the conflict in Nature, since without it, existence would simply blink out. However, there is a "solution," which is to arrive at a tertium. As he puts it:

> We believe that we have a world "in here." We believe the mind is separate from the body, emotions are separate from thought, and good has a reality that is distinct from bad . . . This fixation on the *reality of opposition* is our sickness, it is what a Zen Master called the "bumpkin sickness," and it can only be cured by our awakening. This is the simple, straightforward teaching of Zen—we must wake up. This does not mean that we gain some new insight, acquire some new knowledge or power. Insight, knowledge, and power are all downstream of opposition; awakening is upstream. Indeed Zen awakening is *awakening to the opposites as two valid ways of being*.[7]

The tricksters and the genuine crazy-wise adepts, or gurus, are not evil in themselves. They play tricks but all the while remain beyond the conventional sphere of good and evil. This at least is the thrust of both mythology and much of mysticism: Reality in its nakedness, whether mythologically pictured or mystically realized, transcends the moral dimension of human experience. It harbors within itself all contradictions. In it arise orchids and Venus flytraps, dolphins and sharks, real gold and fool's gold, Gandhis and Hitlers, life-giving suns and star-swallowing black holes.

Another favorite trick-playing figure is the religious or ritual clown. He must be distinguished from the circus clown, who is only a semblance of the former. The circus clown comes in two types—the white-faced clown, who is civilized, and the heavily made-up "Auguste," who is uncivilized and immoral, a trickster. The religious clown combines both these aspects within himself.

First, the word "clown" originally meant "clod" or "clot"; according to the *Oxford English Dictionary*, it made its appearance in the second half of the sixteenth century. A clown is an individual, usually a man, who gives the appearance of being dull or otherworldly but, as in the case of the trickster, possesses a good portion of wit and cunning. The ritual clown is a highly ambiguous and ambivalent figure: He, or more rarely she, is human, yet quite unlike any other human being, inhabiting the threshold between idiocy and saintliness.

The clown's liminal status is most starkly evinced in the occasional custom of treating a clown as a scapegoat, sacrificed for the weal of the larger social body during festivities celebrating seasonal change. This element of sacrifice is present also in spiritual clowns, the gurus who, having surrendered their egos, now submit their eccentric lives to spiritual seekers. They are free enough in themselves to oppose current mores and suffer the likely consequences of such opposition, which is at least social opprobrium, if not actual martyrdom.

Both the religious clown and the spiritual adept represent the *axis mundis*, the world axis, and are thus radically "concentric." Yet from the viewpoint of conventional society, they appear to be "eccentric"—out of focus, out of line, out of their rational mind. Lame Deer, a North American Indian shaman, has put it this way: "A clown in our language is called a *heyoka*. He is upside down, backward-forward, yes-and-no man, a contrarywise."[8]

The clown, like the guru, walks the fine line between transcendence and immanence, between sacredness and darkest profanity. In his excellent work *Zen and the Comic Spirit*, M. Conrad Hyers observed:

The clown in his freedom stands outside ordinary consciousness and beyond the confines of social conventions, sacred taboos, and rational enclosures. And the fool is essentially beyond the law, whether the moral law or societal law or the law of reason, which can mean not only prior to the law, or over against the law, but actually *transcending* the law. The clown and fool, by occupying an ambiguous space between the holy and the unholy, good and evil, wisdom and ignorance, reason and nonsense, are particularly suited to this task of pointing beyond all such distinctions, both backward to the time before them and forward to the time that lies after them. The clown's ability to garble all distinctions, and the fool's inability to make the proper distinctions, prevision the sage's capacity for moving beneath and beyond discrimination and duality.[9]

The clown's association with the transcendental Reality explains why he or she has traditionally been widely credited with magical powers—just as has the guru. Clowns wear masks and strange outfits, as do gurus, with astonishing skill, assuming different personae so that their disciples (and the public) can never be quite certain of "who" is confronting them. The guru may be all wise and serene one moment, only to talk animatedly or pace about agitatedly the next. He or she may respond to one disciple good-naturedly, with laughter, and a second later yell at another disciple at the top of his or her lungs.

Ritual clowns can be looked upon as institutionalized agents of antinomianism: safety valves for pent-up personal and societal energies. This function of the clown becomes especially transparent in the medieval Feast of Fools, a celebration held at the beginning of January in many European countries. This annual festivity was first clearly recorded in the latter part of the twelfth century, but it derived from much earlier customs of societal inversion, like the Roman saturnalia. These festivities provided an occasion in which the work ethic and the severity of social forms were temporarily suspended. The masses assumed the contrary behavior of the fool or clown. No establishment figure or convention, however lofty or sacred, was immune to criticism and ridicule. Even monks, nuns, and some Church notables participated in the frolicking. Not infrequently, the celebrants' gaiety degenerated into unbridled sensuality and mayhem. Riotous dancing, nudity, and sexual orgies were common. In some areas, banners embroidered with images of the male and female genitals were carried through the streets.

Understandably, the secular and ecclesial powers looked askance at the Feast of Fools. Yet, despite the Council of Basel's condemnation of the celebration in 1431, the Church failed to suppress the Feast of Fools for many centuries, just as earlier councils had failed to eradicate its antinomian precursors. It was not until the Age of Reformation in the sixteenth century that the feast began to fall into disuse. A different, more puritanical mood won out. Our modern Mardi Gras, Halloween, and New Year's Eve parties are faint and completely secularized survivals of the Feast of Fools.

Another invention of medieval Europe—the court jester or secular clown—also has antecedents in antiquity. Well-to-do Greeks and Romans employed a fool, or a buffoon, at their banquets. His task was simply to amuse. Not infrequently he did so by skillfully contradicting his employer, thus risking chastisement or possibly even his life. All clowns are great risk takers. Their way is that of the hero whose courage knows no bounds. This aspect of buffoonery is also shared by the adept-teacher who, for the sake of the enlightenment of others, is willing to go out on a limb. His or her vocation involves considerable risk, because it is in the nature of the ego to resist the guru's attempt to transform it. In particular, contemporary crazy-wisdom teachers face a constant threat of legal action instigated by disappointed and angry ex-disciples. And in truth it must be said that such suits are not always without basis—from a worldly perspective.

Despite, or perhaps because of, the violent secularism of our "post-Christian" era, we have of late witnessed a fascinating development: the emergence of Christ as harlequin. Theologian Harvey Cox, who has drawn our attention to this fact, wrote in 1970:

> The representation of Christ as a clown is still scattered and spotty. The artist Georges Rouault, drawing on his profound feel both for the microcosm of the circus and the French Catholic tradition, was perhaps the first person in modern times to make the identification explicit. But there were hints before him, and since his time the theme has become more widespread. One of the clearest instances occurred in the movie *The Parable*, produced for the Protestant pavilion at the 1966 New York World's Fair.[10]

Cox reminds us that one of the earliest representations of Christ in Christian art shows a crucified human figure sporting the head of an ass. This brings to mind that the Feast of Fools was also known as the Feast of the Ass, because during the festivities a donkey was ceremoniously led into the church, giving rise to much merriment. It is likely that the ass was understood to be a representation of Christ. We know of an early Roman graffito that depicts a donkey-headed figure on the cross—undoubtedly intended as a blasphemous portrayal of the crucified Jesus. We may further speculate that the ass symbolizes the long-suffering nature of the spiritual fool, the *passion* of Jesus the Christ. This brings us to the crazy-wisdom variant within Christendom—the tradition of the Fools for Christ's Sake.

## 2. The Fools for Christ's Sake: Folly as Virtue

"Before you are wise; after you are wise. In between you are otherwise."[11] This bon mot by the late Bhagwan Rajneesh (known as Osho in his final years) epitomizes very well the condition of the conventional mind. It is our "otherwiseness" that does not permit us to see our own cleverness as mere foolishness and to recognize the true fool as a sage from whom we can learn. For the same reason, modern Christianity has all but forgotten the tradition of the Fools for Christ's Sake. They are not even mentioned in several prominent dictionaries on theology and religion, and few scholars have bothered to investigate their fascinating history or to study their upside-down wisdom.

The once-flourishing tradition of the Fools for Christ's Sake is said to date back to the apostle Paul of Tarsus, who coined the phrase in his letter to the Corinthians (1 Cor. 4:10). In fact, it has its roots in the earlier prophetic traditions of Judaism, where, in the accusing words of the prophet Hosea (9:7), the prophet is called a fool and the man of the spirit is dismissed as a madman.

There was much elitist infighting among the Corinthians, and Paul, perhaps with doubtful modesty, pointed to himself as an example of a blabbering fool (*moros*) who could speak only of his numerous weaknesses. In his reprimanding epistle he argued that God's grace can thrive only in those who humble themselves and are consequently looked upon as fools by everyone else. "If any one among you," he wrote, "thinks that he is wise in this age, let him become a fool that he may become wise" (1 Cor. 3:18). The Christian, who believes in the crucified and risen Christ, appears to be a foolish believer in the eyes of a world that lacks faith. However, Paul insists, this very folly is true wisdom.

Paul, the former Saul, was a learned man who had given up much. He demonstrated no prudence in a worldly sense. His conversion to the new cult of Christianity was viewed by many as a sign of madness. So Paul knew what he was speaking about. But he derived strength from his faith and the fact that his guru, Jesus, had himself been accused of madness and demonic possession.

Paul was a monastic, and holy folly was from the beginning closely connected with Christian monasticism. The desert fathers of the third and fourth centuries were enthusiastic demonstrators of the foolishness of God. Many of them were unlettered but wise. A few were highly educated but pretended to be stupid because it furthered their spiritual intensity. Both the natural and the apparent ignoramus were called *idiota*—an illiterate. In some cases, the foolishness, or self-effacement, was so evident that it surprised even fellow Christians, who then named the *idiota* a "Fool for Christ's Sake." It appears that the Christian anchorites of the Middle East turned holy folly into a vocation.

In their aspiration to negate themselves, the fools were often left without any worldly possessions, throwing themselves completely on the mercy of their God. Sometimes renunciation of the ego-personality was taken to such extremes that practicing fools acquired the reputation of actually being mad. Sarapion Sindonites is reported to have sold himself to a Greek acting troupe to raise money for the poor. On one occasion, he met a female anchorite, whose renunciation he immediately tested by asking her to strip naked. The woman refused because people would be scandalized and accuse her of insanity. Sarapion, of course, knew only too well that she was right. Nonetheless, he reminded her that if she was unwilling to do his bidding, she should also not consider herself holier than others. He underscored his words by taking off his own small loincloth. Through such acts of renunciation, the fool sought to achieve greater attunement to God.[12]

In the tenth century, St. Andrew, the teacher of that Epiphanius who later became patriarch of Constantinople, voluntarily adopted the life of a seemingly insane beggar. He used to walk about naked in all seasons and sleep under the open sky with dogs. Nudity was a common way of expressing poverty and "madness," especially in Russia, where the Fools for Christ's Sake flourished for a long time, the inclement winters notwithstanding.

The true saint must be able to deal with shame and opprobrium. In fact, he is likely to seek out or create situations that will test his strength of self-abandonment. Thus in the sixth century, young Theophilius and Maria, who had been well brought up, wandered about in the guise of a comedian and a prostitute. No one knew their former identities, and, more important, no one was aware of their spiritual status, until John of Ephesus discovered them absorbed in deep prayer. Their theatrical performances earned them not only cheers but also a degree of rough handling. They had gone "underground" for the sake of their spiritual life.

Then there were fools, like St. Simeon, who displayed their simulated madness still more dramatically and at great personal risk. In the mid-sixth century, in order to curb his spiritual pride, St. Simeon left his peaceful hermitage to rejoin civilization in the role of a crazy outcast. One time he tied his cord belt to a dead dog and dragged it after him, receiving ridicule and plenty of blows. On another occasion, he went to Sunday church and extinguished the candles as the liturgy was beginning. When the faithful tried to remove him, he ran up to the pulpit and began to throw nuts at the women. More than once he ended up getting beaten bloody for his pranks. Although he fasted constantly and observed strict disciplines, he sometimes visited inns and brothels and is said to have collected money so that the prostitutes could get married. He hid his beneficent deeds well behind his craziness.

Also in the sixth century, the Christian monk Mark the Mad abandoned his eremitical existence in the desert, announcing that he had "failed" by sinning against purity. After fifteen years of living in solitude, he came to the city of Alexandria, supposedly to atone for his sins. He sustained himself by his winnings at the hippodrome and slept on the benches there. People considered him insane and mistreated him. When Daniel of Skete, another saintly person, met him, Mark went into histrionics, screaming for help. The crowd advised Daniel to ignore the madman, but the saint surprised them by saying: "You are the fools! This is the only reasonable man I have found in this city today." Mark the Mad was one of the Fools for Christ's Sake. Following the apostle Paul's advice, he chose a life that celebrated God's wisdom, which is folly to the world, and in doing so, showed the world's wisdom to be the greater folly.

Another holy fool was once asked to heal a sick child. At first he refused but then yielded to the urgent pleading of a disciple. As he and his disciple approached the child's village, they saw a large welcoming committee moving toward them. Suddenly, the anchorite stopped in his tracks, divested himself of all his clothes, and plunged into the river to take a bath. Ashamed of his teacher's bizarre behavior, the young disciple apologized to the villagers and advised them to return home since the old man had apparently lost his mind. When the anchorite emerged from the water, his disciple asked, "Why did you do that? Now everyone says you are crazy!" Whereupon the old man replied, "That's exactly what I wanted to hear."[13]

In the thirteenth century, a respected notary, Jacopone da Todi, took up the life-style of a fool after the death of his beloved wife. One day, during a celebration in the city of Todi, he was grasped by such religious fervor that he stripped off his clothes and crawled about on all fours, with a saddle strapped to his back and a bit set in his mouth. The crowd was deeply shocked at seeing a noted, "upright" citizen make such a demeaning spectacle of himself. In one of his poems, Jacopone gave vent to his desire to climb naked onto the cross and to die joyously in his savior's embrace. Yet in another poem (*Lauda LXXV*), he confessed:

> I flee the cross that devours me;
> I cannot bear its heat.
> I cannot bear so great a heat
> that the cross emanates; I flee from love.
> I find no hiding place, for I carry it in my heart,
> and the memory of it consumes me.[14]

The spirit of "meekness" and self-denial was also alive among female monastics. An early example is told in the *Lausiac History* of Palladius. According to this early fifth-century work, Abba Pitiroum once had a revelation in which he heard the voice of an angel. The angel challenged him, "You think much of yourself. Would you like to see a woman who is more pleasing to God than you are? Then go to the nunnery of Tabennisi, where you will find a woman who wears a crown." Pitiroum promptly went to the cloister and asked all the nuns to assemble before him. When he did not see one wearing a crown, he insisted that the assembly was incomplete. The sisters replied that the only nun missing was a mad woman. When they dragged her from the kitchen, Pitiroum immediately saw the light on her forehead and fell at her feet, begging her to bless him. The nun likewise fell to the ground, asking Abba Pitiroum for his blessings.

Pitiroum scolded the assembled nuns for failing to recognize the woman's sanctity, saying that they were the ones who were really mad. The sisters prostrated themselves and begged the woman fool's forgiveness for all the years of maltreatment they had meted out to her. They had beaten her, drenched her with water, and put mustard on her nose, not to mention the constant stream of verbal insults they had inflicted on her. The incident changed their attitude entirely; afterward they did their best to make amends and appropriately honor their saintly fellow sister. She endured their attentions for a few days and then secretly stole away from the cloister. Later she was canonized as St. Isidora.

The fourteenth-century Byzantine saint Sabas pretended to be deaf, dumb, and mad—a pretense that he kept up with great skill for a period of twenty years. Yet he could not escape the danger of fame. On visiting Cyprus, he reacted to the attention given to him by large crowds by suddenly sitting down on a dung heap, where he spent the remainder of the day. The emperor of Constantinople sought to persuade him to accept the office of patriarch, but Sabas refused. He refused even to be ordained as a priest. When the emperor attempted to have him ordained by stealth, Sabas fled; keen to have the saint remain, the emperor had to chase after him, beg his forgiveness, and solemnly promise to make no further attempts at interfering with Sabas's saintly ways.

The fool's utter disregard for himself is epitomized in the following anecdote about Abbot Moses, who had made folly his path to God. One day a high-placed gentleman visited the monastery and happened to run into Moses himself. Not recognizing the abbot, he asked to be shown to Moses' cell. The abbot replied, "What do you want with him? He is just a fool and a heretic!"

Whereas the Greeks gave the holy fool the name *salos*, the Russians called him *yurodivy* (plural: *yurodivye*). Of the forty-two canonized Christian saints who lived as fools, no fewer than thirty-six belong to the Russian Orthodox Church. Starting with St. Isaac Zatvornik of the eleventh century, Russia has spawned a galaxy of such spiritual madmen (as well as a few female fools). The best known and most cherished is St. Basil the Blessed (sixteenth century), who roamed the streets of Moscow as a naked vagrant. Like Jesus and the Byzantine saint Simeon (sixth century), as well as many other fools, St. Basil outraged the public by freely mixing with criminals and prostitutes. When they persecuted him, he "retaliated" by throwing stones at the windows of his righteous attackers, but shed tears at the dwellings of sinners.

The *yurodivye* were particularly prominent during the reign of Ivan IV ("the Terrible"), and one of them—the great Nicholas Salos (d. 1576)—actually met the Czar when he arrived in force to destroy the city of Pskov. After the seventeenth century, the fool gradually vanished from the religious scene in Russia, though he continued to be a character in Russian literature, as is evident, for instance, from Dostoyevski's *The Idiot*. A contemporary of Dostoyevski was the latter-day fool Alexis Bukharev (1822–1871), who, at the age of forty, abandoned his monastic vows and got married—all in order to intensify his spiritual practice and give witness to the greater wisdom of God. His laicization caused a great scandal and in one fell swoop deprived him of civic rights, academic degrees, salary, and the esteem and goodwill of his friends and neighbors.

The tradition of holy folly also thrived in the Western Church. St. Bernard of Clairvaux (eleventh century), the founder of the Cistercian order, spoke of himself as a fool and a jester. He preached that sanctification depends on participating ever more willingly in the foolishness of God and that humiliation is the best means to true humility. St. Bernard was an extremist—and this character trait distinguished the order he founded. He was a passionate visionary who had no time for mediocrity. At the same time, his folly was more sober than the "path of blame," to use the Sufi expression, chosen by some of his Greek and Russian predecessors.

From the time of St. Bernard until the early sixteenth century, the figure of the fool—both sacred and secular—played an important role in Western European culture. In the early thirteenth century, St. Francis of Assisi achieved immense popularity as a fool of God. Born into a rich merchant family, he renounced his family and inheritance and took up the life of a spiritual pilgrim, affiliating with other marginals, notably lepers and beggars. He invited public outrage by taking off all his clothes on the occasion of his second "birth," his conversion to a godly life. This happened in front of a large crowd in a public square not far from his paternal home. After a short uproar, the crowd fell silent, visibly moved by his gesture of renunciation. The bishop, who had summoned him, wept and then, embracing the young man, wrapped him in his cape.

Although St. Francis was prone to weep and grieve for the suffering of humanity and for the suffering inflicted on his beloved Lord, he was just as often heard singing and preaching merrily of God's glory. Shortly after his conversion to the life of a wandering "soldier of God," Francis encountered a band of robbers. When they realized that he had nothing to steal, they tore off his cloak and threw him into a snowdrift. After the brigands left, Francis clambered out of the ditch and, with chattering teeth, merrily burst into a song of praise.

Holy fools became rare in the seventeenth century and, with the dawning of the Age of Reason, virtually disappeared, together with saints and mystics. This was, in the words of the French historian Michel Foucault, the time of the "great confinement" in an economically troubled Europe. Madmen and vagrants were no longer tolerated.[15] They were publicly humiliated, beaten, and locked up in asylums or workhouses. The foundations for the work ethos and the spiritual impoverishment of our own era had been laid. The heroic aspiration, passion, and compassion of the holy fools are today only a faint memory.

It is tempting to characterize the holy fools of Christendom as *passive* crazy-wisdom adepts, since their madness consisted primarily in often spec-

tacular acts of self-abnegation—the practice of humility, or "meekness."
However, their folly was clearly not merely passive. First, their spiritual
fervor and extreme asceticism could not help but make an impact on their
communities, if only by provoking disapproval and mockery. Second, their
behavior, which they considered spiritually superior to that of ordinary
worldlings, was an implicit criticism of the secular life-style. Third, their
folly at times involved offensive acts that were designed to shock and provoke
a reaction. It matters little whether these tactics were intended simply to
invite greater public censure, and thus present the fool with an enhanced
opportunity for practicing humility, or whether they were intended to confront people with their own spiritual darkness. Their motives may not always
have been clear to the fools themselves. They simply did what they felt moved
to do within the logic of their chosen life. Perhaps it would be correct to say,
however, that the primary thrust of their eccentric lives was to maximize the
conditions that would allow them to demonstrate and to school themselves in
the art of what the great German mystic Meister Eckehart calls *gelâzenheit*,
"letting go." This is the same attitude that Hinduism celebrates as the "vision
of sameness" (*sama-darshana*): the capacity to regard gold bullion and a lump
of dirt with the same indifference and equanimity.

One cannot help but admire the tenacity with which the Fools for Christ's
Sake pursued their project of self-degradation. And yet their curious method
also raises a serious question: Is it possible that hidden beneath all their
humility and spiritual aspiration lay a certain self-centeredness, which permitted the manipulation and use of fellow beings as triggers of that very self-
abnegation? I am inclined to answer this question with a cautious yes. Unenlightened life *is*, after all, egoic life. That is to say, even in our religious and
spiritual projects, we cannot completely obliterate self-concern prior to enlightenment. And, I daresay few connoisseurs of the world's spiritual traditions would argue that most, if indeed any, known Fools for Christ's Sake
were representative of full-fledged enlightenment. The Fools glorified God,
the eternal Father, seeking to move into ever closer proximity to him. In fact,
many of them were ascetics rather than mystics. They certainly were masters
of what Duane Elgin calls "voluntary simplicity."[16] In terms of Hindu spirituality, they were practitioners of *samnyasa-yoga* (the path of renunciation),
*karma-yoga* (the path of good works), or *bhakti-yoga* (the path of devotion),
rather than *jnana-yoga* (the path of higher discernment and gnosis). This holds
true also of the holy fools in Islam, upon whom we focus next.

### 3. The Sufi Path of Blame

Few educated people in the West have not at least heard of the unbelievable,
humorous exploits of Mullah Nasrudin, told in countless Muslim Sufi tales.
It appears that Nasrudin was invented by Sufi teachers to conveniently make
any number of points about life, death, and the great Beyond. In the tales,

Nasrudin describes himself as being "upside down in this world." All authentic spirituality is a great reversal of ordinary values, attitudes, and actions. What the ordinary person deems to be of inestimable value (job, home, and family), the spiritual practitioner considers to be purely secondary. His or her heart is set on transcending all this, and on discovering what is truly and permanently real—call it God, Spirit, or Self. Nasrudin is a symbol for the Sufi path of inner change (*metanoia*) and reversal.

Like mainstream Christianity, Islam is grounded in a dualistic metaphysics that assumes God's creatorship but ultimate separateness from his creation. Despite this theistic worldview, the Muhammadan religion has produced a proliferative tradition of mystics, the Sufis, whose experience has outstripped the metaphysical dualism of the prophet Muhammad and his mainstream followers. As S. Spencer stated in his *Mysticism in World Religion*:

> The growth of Islamic mysticism (or Sufism) is a significant illustration of the strength of the mystical tendency in religion. On the face of it, the religion of Mohammed can scarcely be regarded as of itself providing fruitful soil for the growth of that tendency. Yet within a comparatively short time after the Prophet's death a movement arose among his followers which has given birth to some of the greatest of the mystics . . . The Sufis have traditionally looked upon Mohammed himself as the greatest of all mystics. That is not a view which critical study sustains. There is no question in his own life and teaching of any such experience as union with God. The gulf that divides man from God in his outlook is too great to admit of any such possibility. At the same time, there are elements in his attitude and teaching which contain the germ of a mystical development. Mohammed believed himself to be the recipient of a divine revelation. God (he taught) is 'nearer to man than his neck-vein'; He is 'the light of the heavens and the earth'; wherever we turn, there is His Face, which abides, resplendent with majesty and glory, when all on earth shall pass away.[17]

These almost pantheistic ideas proved to be anchor points for the mystical visionaries within Islam. They also proved to be nooses around the necks of those mystics who did not care or know how to harness their visionary enthusiasm by means of acceptably deistic language. Like the Hebrew Creator, the Muslim God is a jealous deity who will brook no creature's effort to rise above its creaturehood. Anyone claiming identity with God is not only thought to be deluded but is denounced as a blasphemous heretic. Generations of Sufis have experienced the Divine to be far more tolerant than that. Their history is one that is rich in testimony to the Truth (*al-haqq*) that dwells, as the heretic Hallaj put it, "inside this coat." "Glory be to me! How great is My Majesty!" exclaimed the ninth-century Sufi Abu Yazid ecstatically. The Sufi shaykh Shibli, a formerly high-ranking government official who had renounced his position, was once overpowered by ecstatic unification with the

Divine. He called out, "God!" A pious guardian of Islamic law reprimanded him for profaning God by uttering the divine name in public. He responded, "I am speaking and I am listening. In both worlds, who is there but I?"[18] On another occasion, Shibli was found holding a piece of wood burning at both ends. When asked what he was doing, he replied, "I am going to set Hell on fire with one end and Paradise with the other so that men may concern themselves only with God."

Such radical statements, spoken from the peak of esoteric realization, naturally sounded heretical and quite mad to the ears of exoteric Muslims. Not surprisingly, Shibli was committed to an asylum for a period of time because of his strange utterances. While he was in chains in the asylum, his Sufi companions visited him. He asked, "Who are you?" "Your friends," they replied. He threw stones at them, and they fled for safety. "Liars!" he yelled after them. "Do friends run away from friends only because of a few stones?" Perhaps Shibli felt that, despite their visit, his fellow travelers had inwardly abandoned him because of his wayward behavior and that, therefore, they had failed to understand the nature of his *unio mystica*. From the Sufi perspective, at any rate, Shibli was beyond reproach, because in the ecstatic state there is no ego to assume responsibility for what is being said and done. In his fine introductory book on Sufism, Reynold A. Nicholson mentioned a story that underscores this point:

> There was a certain dervish, a negro called Zangi Bashgirdi, who had attained to such a high degree of spirituality that the mystic dance could not be started until he came out and joined in it. One day, in the course of the *sama'*, he was seized with ecstasy, and rising into the air seated himself on a lofty arch which overlooked the dancers. In descending he leaped on to Majduddin of Baghdad, and encircled with his legs the neck of the Sheykh, who nevertheless continued to spin round in the dance, though he was a very frail and slender man, whereas the negro was tall and heavy. When the dance was finished, Majduddin said, "I did not know whether it was a negro or a sparrow on my neck." On getting off the Sheykh's shoulders, the negro bit his cheek so severely that the scar remained visible ever after. Majduddin often used to say that on the Day of Judgment he would not boast of anything except that he bore the mark of this negro's teeth on his face.[19]

In the eleventh century, the immensely popular shaykh Abu Sa'id attracted much adverse attention because he held sumptuous feasts with music and dance and thousands of burning candles. He even offended some of his fellow Sufis. The Sultan of Nishapur appointed a group of learned men to investigate this eccentric Sufi master who claimed to be an ascetic yet was indulging in one feast after another. Abu Sa'id is said to have learned about the imminent investigation through his paranormal abilities; he promptly ordered another celebration. However, when the appointed committee witnessed the shaykh's great charisma, spiritual authority, and superlative indifference to worldly things (especially to the threat they would have posed to a lesser man), they quickly dropped their investigation. For Abu Sa'id, the true saint lived an ordinary life, holding down a job and even marrying, yet never ceasing to contemplate God. Enjoyment, he felt, is not antagonistic to a saintly life. When the One is realized, everything assumes the same significance.

To express this vision of sameness, Abu Sa'id would sometimes wear woolen dress, while at other times he would don a silk gown. Like Hallaj, he declared that there was naught but Allah in the robe he was wearing. To demonstrate his claim, the shaykh—adds his hagiographer—pushed his index finger through his cloak as if there were only empty space where his body should have been. About Sufism, Sa'id said irreverently that it is a form of paganism; he used the word *shirk* ("association"), meaning a mistaken attribution of reality, by which the soul is barred from the One.

In his ecstatic identification with God, the Sufi adept breaks a fundamental taboo of exoteric Islam. His transgression is felt to be a manifestation of insanity. The Islamic "madman" is also known as a *majzub* (sometimes spelled *majdhub* or *madzub*). Pir Vilayat Inayat Khan once commented about this religious figure, "The madzub (meaning one lost in God-consciousness) might be described as an exceptional kind of dervish. The action of the madzub is always traumatic and unpredictable."[20]

Inayat Khan referred to Shems-i-Tabriz, the teacher of the world-famous Rumi, as such a *majzub*, and related the following story about him:

> The impact of this stormy fakir with eyes like the sun upon the erstwhile scholar Moulana Jelal-ud-Din Rumi was so overwhelming that he became practically overnight one of the greatest murshids [teachers] the Sufis have ever known. Hearsay has it that, accosting the scholar riding his donkey in the precincts of the *medarsa* (academy), surrounded by his disciples, Shems snatched his manuscript out of his hand and threw it down a well. He then asked Rumi: "Would you like me to take it out of the well? It will be dry." The befuddled professor took a deep breath to pull himself together, then replied: "No!" This was the 'no' that transformed his life, by reaching beyond the mind epitomized by the book. It was this 'no' that cast the die that made him one of the greatest of Persian poets.[21]

This story is as instructive about Rumi's conversion to spirituality as it is about Shems's "mad" behavior. Grabbing Rumi's book and dropping it into a well was, conventionally speaking, bad manners at the very least. But this eccentric and presumably quite spontaneous act had a hidden purpose: to awaken Rumi the mystic. Judging from history, Shems's interference in Rumi's life was timely and successful.

During the fifteenth century, shaykh Hasan achieved unwanted fame for his holy madness. He would wander through the streets of Delhi proclaiming

Prince Nizam to be his beloved—an unforgivable suggestion that caused an enormous scandal. The prince took revenge by shoving the shaykh's head into a heated furnace. To his amazement, the shaykh suffered not the slightest injury and also demonstrated utter fearlessness. Prince Nizam thereafter imprisoned the *majzub* but, to his dismay, found his prisoner had miraculously disappeared.[22] Similarly astounding miracles are ascribed to other Muslim saints, including shaykh Ala'ul Bala'ul, a contemporary of shaykh Hasan. Large crowds in Delhi and Agra came to witness his miracles, especially his clairvoyant and prophetic powers.

Saiyid 'Ali, a sixteenth-century Sufi, was another renowned *majzub*. Sometimes he wore a Sufi's robe; at other times he dressed like a soldier. Shaykh Kamal, another sixteenth-century *majzub* and a tireless pilgrim, used to throw stones at the curious who came to witness his paranormal feats. That he was no fool, however, is evident from his insightful discussions of mystical matters. Illah-Din of Narnaul used to walk about clad in torn garments, wearing iron rings around his legs. Sometimes he was seen standing stock-still for hours on a heap of garbage. He is also remembered for freeing prisoners who had been put in the stocks and assuming their place instead.

In the seventeenth century, Miyan Abu'l-Ma'ali, who had renounced the world, leaving wife and home behind, was fond of breaking traditional Muslim laws. He was a *malamati*, one who has adopted the path of blame (*mala*). Another famous Sufi *majzub* of the same era was Muhammad Sa'id Sarmad, an Armenian Jew who had converted to Islam. A wealthy merchant, he "fell in love" with a Hindu boy named Abhai Chand. When the boy's parents repelled his advances, Sarmad began to wander the streets of Thatta naked, calling Abhai Chand his God. After several months of this, the parents acknowledged Sarmad's spiritual status and became convinced of his moral purity. They entrusted Abhai Chand to him, and the boy later achieved a measure of fame for his accomplished Persian poetry. From the time of his renunciation, Sarmad refused to wear any clothes except when he was in royal company. He explained this habit simply by referring to the prophet Isaiah, who likewise adopted nudity in his last days. One of Sarmad's poems well illustrates the principle of inversion and the shock tactics characteristic of holy folly:

> Talk not about Ka'ba and temple with everyone,
> And in the valley of doubt walk not like deviated ones.
> Learn the form of worship from Satan himself!
> Take only One as the object of worship, bend not before any other.[23]

Sarmad's eccentricity, especially his nudity, provoked much public outrage and led to his execution under Emperor Aurangzeb. When the executioner tried to cover the condemned man's eyes, Sarmad smiled at him, saying, "Come in whatever garb you choose, I recognize you well."

Thus, in Sufism, we notice an expression of crazy wisdom very similar to the orientation adopted by the holy fools in Christianity. Both types of crazy-wise practitioner pursued the "kingdom of God" without concern for the worldly opposition their self-chosen life-styles provoked. Their guiding ideals were freedom from object-dependence (often manifesting in voluntary poverty and a life of wandering) and humility, as well as a submission to the world of the spirit that was, certainly in the case of the Christian fools, frequently combined with severe asceticism. At times their disregard for secular attitudes and institutions manifested as active disrespect and social criticism. However, they did not necessarily expect their censure and prophecies to lead to a change of heart in others. They did anticipate further vilification from the countless many who, bereft of spiritual discernment, judge by appearances only and fail to see the purity of the fool's heart. In other words, these holy madmen and women almost invited accusations of immorality, irreligiosity, and insanity, because such criticism provided them with a stimulus for intensifying their practice of rigorous self-abnegation. A similarly daredevil approach characterizes the crazy-wisdom masters of Hindu India, to whom we will turn next.

# 2

## CRAZY WISDOM: RADICAL SPIRITUAL ECCENTRICS IN DIFFERENT RELIGIOUS TRADITIONS

### 1. The Avadhutas, Masts, and Bauls: India's Countercultural Heroes

India has spawned a greater diversity of religious traditions than any other country. It has also given birth to some of the most eccentric forms of religious practice on earth, together with an exceptional attitude of tolerance toward all these manifestations of religious aspiration. The spiritual genius of the Hindus, Buddhists, Jainas, and Sikhs is unquestionable. The great spiritual explorers and teachers of these traditions have made a lasting contribution to humanity's self-understanding. Not all of these great ones have been masters of the stature of Gautama the Buddha, Nagarjuna, Vardhamana Mahavira, Shankara, Ramanuja, or Nanak. Nonetheless, there have been tens of thousands of pilgrims whose bold forays into the hidden depths of the human psyche have enriched not only the lives of their contemporaries but our own modern lives as well. Among these spiritual wayfarers we must count the *avadhutas* and the *bauls* of Hinduism.

The Sanskrit word *avadhuta* means literally "he who has cast off [all concerns]." It refers to an extreme type of renouncer in Hinduism—usually male—who has "dropped out" so completely that conventional standards no longer apply to him. Often the *avadhuta* walks about naked, his nudity being an external sign of his all-encompassing inner purity, even "emptiness." He is completely unmindful of the ways of the world, even of his own bodily well-being, and in the eyes of the world he is little more than a mindless idiot. However, the *avadhuta* describes his own state as being "transmental" (*amanaska*) and exalted (*unmani*)—a description that suggests a sublime awareness rather than idiocy.

The radical spirit of the *avadhuta*'s renunciation and his chameleonlike capacities, on the basis of his identification with the transcendental Reality, are captured in the following Sanskrit verses from the sixth chapter of the *Siddha-Siddhanta-Paddhati* ("Footprints of the Adept's Doctrines"), a medieval Hindu work:

Now a description of the *avadhuta-yogin* is given. Tell me, then, who is this so-called *avadhuta-yogin*? The *avadhuta* is he who casts off all of Nature's modifications. A *yogin* is one for whom there is "union" (*yoga*). *Dhuta* is [derived from] *dhun* [meaning "to shake"], as in trembling, that is, it has the meaning of trembling. Trembling or shaking [occurs when] the mind is involved with the sense objects like bodies or bodily [states]. Having grasped [these sense objects] and then having withdrawn from them, the mind absorbed into the glory of its own Domain (*dhaman*) is devoid of phenomena and is free from the diverse "dwellings" (*nidhana*) [i.e., objects], which have a beginning, middle, and end. (1)

The sound *ya* is the seed-syllable of the wind [element]; the sound *ra* is the seed-syllable of the fire [element]. Indistinct from both is the sound *om*, which is praised as the form of Consciousness. (2)

Thus he is clearly called: He who is shaven (*vimundana*) by cutting off multitudes of bonds of suffering, who is released from all states—he is named an *avadhuta*. (3)

The *yogin* who, in his body, is adorned with the splendorous memory of the innate [Reality] and for whom [the "serpent power" or *kundalini-shakti*] has risen from the "support" [at the base of the spine]—he is named an *avadhuta*. (4)

[The *yogin* who] is firmly stationed in the center of the world, devoid of all "trembling" [i.e., free from all attachment to the sense objects], whose freedom from dejection is his loincloth and staff—he is named an *avadhuta*. (5)

[The *yogin*] by whom the doctrine is preserved like the conjunction of the sounds *sham* [designating] joy and *kham* [symbolizing] the supreme Absolute in the word *shamkha* [meaning "conch"]—he is named an *avadhuta*. (6)

Whose limit is [naught but] the supreme Consciousness, whose knowledge of the [ultimate] Object is his sandals, and whose "great vow" is his antelope skin—he is named an *avadhuta*. (7)

Whose perpetual abstention is his belt, whose very essence is his matted seat, [and who practices] abstention from the six modifications [of Nature]—he is named an *avadhuta*. (8)

Whose Light of consciousness and supreme bliss are his pair of earrings, who has ceased recitation with a rosary—he is named an *avadhuta*. (9)

Whose steadiness is his walking stick and [for whom] the supreme radiance-space (*para-akasha*) is his staff and [for whom] the innate power (*nija-shakti*) is his yogic armrest (*patta*)—he is styled an *avadhuta*. (10)

Who is himself difference and identity [of world and God], whose alms are his delight in the taste of the six essences (*rasa*), whose condition of being full of that [ultimate Reality] is his adultery—he is styled an *avadhuta*. (11)

Who moves with his inner being into the Unthinkable, the remote region within, who has that very Place as his undergarment—he is named an *avadhuta*. (12)

Who [desires] to assimilate his own immortal body to the Infinite, the Immortal, who alone would drink this [draft of immortality]—he is named an *avadhuta*. (13)

By whom is devoured the *vajri* abounding in defilements of desire and strong like a thunderbolt (*vajra*) [that is none other than] nescience (*avidya*)—he is named an *avadhuta*. (14)

Who always turns round fully into the very center of himself and who views the world with equanimity—he is named an *avadhuta*. (15)

Who would understand himself and who abides in his Self alone, who is fully established in effortlessness—he is named an *avadhuta*. (16)

Who is conversant with [the art of] supreme repose and endowed with the foundation of effortlessness, who knows the principle formed of Consciousness and contentment—he is styled an *avadhuta*. (17)

Who consumes the manifest and the unmanifest [realms] and devours completely the entire manifestation [of Nature], while being [established] in his inner being [and possessing] the Truth within—he is named an *avadhuta*. (18)

Who is firmly established in his own luminosity, who is [that] lustre of the nature of Radiance, who delights in the world through play (*lila*)—he is named an *avadhuta*. (19)

Who is sometimes an enjoyer, sometimes a renouncer, sometimes a nudist or like a demon, sometimes a king and sometimes a well-behaved [citizen]—he is named an *avadhuta*. (20)

Who is of the essence of the innermost [Self] when thus performing different roles in public, who fully pierces through to the Real in his essential vision of all doctrinal views—he is named an *avadhuta-yogin*. He is a true *guru*. Because he, in his essential vision of all views, creates a [grand] synthesis (*samanvaya*), he is an *avadhuta-yogin*. (21)[1]

The *avadhuta* tradition emerged in the post-Christian era, though its antecedents reach back into the hoary past. It is associated with the semilegendary adept Dattatreya who was deified by his followers. According to one legend, Dattatreya immersed himself in a lake and, after many years, reappeared in the company of a beautiful damsel. His disciples were quite unshaken by this, feeling sure of their teacher's perfect nonattachment. In order to test their faith in him still more, he consumed wine with the maiden—an unthinkable breach of Hindu social customs. Dattatreya failed to rouse the least doubt in his followers.[2]

Because the *avadhuta* is utterly unattached and quite indifferent to his fate in the world, he has no wife, children, home, job, social responsibility, or political obligation. Steeped in the bliss of contemplating the eternal foundation of all things, he may not even bother to care for his body. The modern sage Swami Samarth of Akkalkot, a village in Maharashtra, had to be both fed and bathed. Like so many other crazy adepts, he was also prone to frequent and inexplicable mood shifts. As his biographer has stated:

> Nobody could ever dare flout Sri Swami Samarth's wishes even though they would sometimes appear whimsical and eccentric. He used to behave like a man of whims and caprices, and was completely unpredictable in his behavior. Sometimes he was so free that one could approach him and talk freely as to a mother, but at other times he seemed unapproachable and stern. Sometimes he himself talked freely and sweetly; at others, he would keep silent, uttering not a word for several days at a stretch.[3]

Another contemporary adept, Zipruanna, roamed naked in the villages of western India. His perambulatory life-style, as we have seen in the case of the Fools for Christ's Sake, was a visible sign of the renouncer's total unattachment. He felt at home on garbage heaps and was not in the least put off by squatting in excrement. Swami Muktananda, who thought highly of Zipruanna, once asked him why he had to sit on rubbish. The adept replied, "Muktananda, inner impurities are far more revolting than this. Don't you know that the human body is a chest full of waste matter?"[4] One day, it is reported, a group of English ladies who had heard of his saintly reputation went to see Zipruanna. They were shocked to find him completely naked. Noticing their squeamishness, the adept promptly grabbed hold of his penis and shook it, asking his visitors whether this "little thing" was bothering them. Zipruanna would also often ask his visitors for a cigarette. He would then light it, take a few puffs, discard it, and ask for another and another. No explanation was offered. The adept's actions followed no logical pattern, though they can be understood to parody our "square" behavior.[5]

Neem Karoli Baba, who died in 1973, was made famous in Western spiritual circles by his disciple Ram Dass (Richard Alpert). As Ram Dass himself admitted to me, his guru was one of the more controversial crazy adepts of modern India, and some deemed him an outright scoundrel. An instance of Neem Karoli Baba's more eccentric behavior relates to one of his female devotees: A childless widow came to him and expressed her anxiety over who would take care of her now that she was old and alone. Replying that he would be her child, he promptly planted himself in her lap and began to suck on her breasts. Enough milk flowed from them, it is said, to have filled a whole glass. Apparently after that the old woman no longer regretted not having had children.[6] And Neem Karoli Baba pointed out to her that his contemporary Hariakhan Baba had done a very similar thing.

Although Neem Karoli Baba lived as a celibate renunciate, he occasionally had sexual intercourse with devotees. He believed that celibacy was necessary on the spiritual path but that this did not exclude living with a woman, since a pure woman can help one realize God in an instant. One of his female disciples recalled this incident:

> The first time he took me in the room alone I sat up on the tucket with him, and he was like a seventeen-year-old jock who was a little fast! I felt as if I were fifteen and innocent. He started making out with me, and it was so cute, so pure. I was swept into it for a few moments—then grew alarmed: "Wait! This is my guru. One doesn't do this with one's guru!" So I pulled away from him. Then Maharajji tilted his head sideways and wrinkled up his eyebrows in a tender, endearing, quizzical look. He didn't say anything, but his whole being was saying to me, "Don't you like me?"
>
> But as soon as I walked out of that particular darshan ["seeing" of the guru], I started getting so sick that by the end of the day I felt I had vomited and shit out everything that was ever inside me. I had to be carried out of the ashram [hermitage]. On the way, we stopped by Maharajji's room so I could pranam [bow] to him. I kneeled by the tucket and put my head down by his feet—and he kicked me in the head, saying, "Get her out of here!"
>
> I was unable to move for the next three days, but after that I felt perfectly well again. And I had worked through a lot of my reactions to that darshan: revulsion, confusion, and so forth.
>
> That was the first time, and I was to be there for two years. During my last month there, I was alone with him every day in the room. There was a progression of comprehension. He seemed in one way to be turning me into a Mother, helping me to understand that sex is okay. Sometimes he would just touch me on the breasts and between my legs, saying, "This is mine, this mine, this is mine. All is mine. You are mine." You can interpret it as you want, but near the end in these darshans, it was as though he were my child. Sometimes I felt as though I were suckling a tiny baby. Although he didn't change size physically, he seemed to become very small in my arms. It was a beautiful transformation.[7]

Other female devotees have reported identical occasions with this guru, which had a similar flavor of "infantile sexuality." Neem Karoli Baba would make love to them while somehow seeing in them not merely a pretty woman but the cosmic Mother. He often remarked, "See all women as mothers, serve them as your mother. When you see the entire world as the mother, the ego falls away."[8] He also believed, in keeping with the Tantric tradition, that sexual energy is a vehicle for the transmutation of consciousness to the point of God-realization.

Upasani Baba, who died in 1941, was a medical doctor before he renounced the world, at the age of forty, and began to live on a cremation ground. He caused a public outcry when he revived the ancient Vedic custom of "spiritual marriage" (*brahma-vivaha*), marrying no fewer than twenty-five virgins. He was notorious for speaking quite openly about sexuality and for using coarse language. He offered the following rationale for his unorthodox behavior:

> A Satpurusha [God-realized man] may talk sweetly or harshly, tell a decent or an indecent thing, or pat or abuse at times; but it is never the business of the devotee to doubt or interpret in his own way whatever he is spoken to by the Satpurusha. He cannot understand the real purport of Sadguru's [the true teacher's] talk or action; because his reasoning and thought are never capable of fathoming Guru's thoughts or actions. In fact human reasoning is not able to fully understand even the affairs of the world . . . The state of a Satpurusha is in complete opposition to that of a human being; and that is why all his actions are always meant for and lead to the good of the world.[9]

For a period of time, starting in 1922, Upasani Baba locked himself into a small wooden cage. From his oblique explanation of this strange act one may gather that he confined himself in this manner for fifteen months in order to expiate the sins of his devotees. It was his cross of Golgotha.

Swami Nityananda, another great Indian master, was an awesome figure even among *avadhutas*. He was the teacher of the world-renowned Swami Muktananda and also played an important role in the spiritual life of Da Love-Ananda and the latter's first teacher, Swami Rudrananda ("Rudi"). Nityananda wore nothing but a loincloth; in his early years, he had walked about naked. His nudity caused public embarrassment, and finally some villagers reported him to the local magistrate. Nityananda was taken to court. When asked why he refused to wear a loincloth, he asked, "To cover which with what?"[10] In his experience, everything was one and the same Reality. But the legal system was not prepared to accommodate the experience of nondualism. The magistrate ordered the police to tie a loincloth on him, but, reportedly, however tightly they fixed it, the cloth immediately slipped off again. Then one of his devotees, a tailor, pleaded with him to wear the loincloth, and at last the adept consented.

In those days Nityananda ate only when fed by others. He traveled freely, making his home in caves and forests. His body looked lean but radiant.

Often he was seen standing completely still in a treetop for long periods of time. Recognizing the young man's saintliness, villagers would gather under the tree, and then Nityananda would bless them with a shower of leaves. Many miracles were reported. On one occasion, a pregnant young woman passed him on the road. Nityananda rushed up to her and squeezed her breasts. Although the woman offered no resistance, the villagers came to her rescue. The young *avadhuta* walked away quickly, shouting back to the villagers that this time the woman's child would not die. She confirmed that her previous three children had all died after the first suckling. Apparently, her fourth child survived, and the village then sent out a delegation to locate the powerful saint and honor him.

On that occasion, it appeared Nityananda had a good reason for his unconventional behavior. However, on many more occasions there was no explanation for his strange actions. Thus, when he was in his twenties, he would hide behind trees, patiently waiting for a cow to come his way. The moment the animal stood to drop a cowpat, he would rush forward, scoop up the dropping in midair, and then swallow it.

On another occasion, he besmeared himself from head to toe with excrement. He sat near the lavatories, with large heaps of excrement piled in front of him. Each time a devotee passed him, he would call out, "Bombay halwa [sweets]—very tasty—want to eat? Can weigh and give you some." He sat there all day, to the consternation and utter embarrassment of his followers. In the evening, he was prevailed upon to allow himself to be washed and scrubbed. Later that night, when a clean Nityananda sat among his devotees, he held out his palms inviting them to smell them. "Fine Paris perfume," he commented. Nobody had any explanation for this bizarre behavior until some devotees owned up to having wondered whether their guru would accept excrement if they fed it to him, as they did regular food. The following morning everyone lined up to beg his forgiveness.

One of the truly great saints of nineteenth-century India was Sri Ramakrishna, who displayed some of the traits of an *avadhuta*. In his earlier days he occasionally worshipped his own genitals, seeing in them the phallus (*linga*) of God Shiva, the male aspect of the Divine. He also often dressed up as a woman, identifying with the universal Mother. His love for the Divine in its female aspect was so overwhelming that he saw the Mother in all things, and for a long time he feared losing his mind:

> Intoxicated with this liberating vision of the Mother's immanence, the orthodox superstructure of Ramakrishna's thought and action came crashing down like a bamboo shed in a typhoon. The *brahmin* who a few years earlier wouldn't touch the temple offerings in dread of caste pollution, now gathered together half-eaten scraps of *chapati* and curry from the discarded leaf plates of untouchables, relishing them as the most holy

*prasad* [gift]. He took in hand the rough, matted tangle of his own hair and used it to mop clean the huts of the poorest of the poor. If he was preparing to offer some food ritually to the idol in the temple and a cat slinked by, he would hold it out to the cat instead, imploring, "Won't You take it, Mother?" He didn't act this way to be provocative, to flaunt the petty rules of men, or to proclaim his own liberated spirituality to the world. He did it because the old and familiar universe was disintegrating before his eyes.[11]

Though married, Ramakrishna regarded sex and money as the two great obstacles to spiritual life. True to his own teachings, he lived a life of perfect sexual abstinence and renunciation, looking upon his own wife, Sarada Devi, and all other women as the divine Mother. For a period during his course of spiritual training (*sadhana*), he had a woman teacher who initiated him into Tantra. Part of his Tantric initiation was to have ritual intercourse with a female initiate. Ramakrishna was struck with fear at the prospect of having to touch a woman sexually, but he obeyed his teacher. As soon as he made physical contact with the girl during the ritual, he fell into a state of ecstatic oblivion, regaining his ordinary consciousness only at the very end of the ceremony. Later, one of his followers, who thought Ramakrishna's excessive devotionalism, constant visions, and ecstatic states were due to his repressed sexual drive, tricked the saint into visiting an apartment in Calcutta where several prostitutes were waiting to serve his pleasure. The moment Ramakrishna realized the situation, he called out the Mother's name and promptly swooned in ecstasy. When the girls saw who their customer was, they became terrified at the prospect of being cursed by a holy man for trying to seduce him and tearfully begged his forgiveness.

Before Ramakrishna, this simple temple priest, was proclaimed by the brahmin theologians of his day as a living incarnation (*avatara*) of the Divine, many people thought him mad. They were especially scared and affronted by his display of intimacy with the Goddess Kali. He would enter the temple's sanctum without prostrating and, quite unself-consciously, proceed to lie down on the consecrated couch reserved for the Goddess and partake of the food offered to her. He was also seen to ceremoniously worship his own body rather than the image of the Goddess in the temple he was serving. However, Ramakrishna managed to escape the worst rancor of those who failed to understand his inner state. One of his staunchest supporters was the Princess Rasmani, of whom this story is told:

> One day, as she was seated by Ramakrishna's side listening to his ecstatic singing, he abruptly broke off and slapped her twice on the cheeks, exclaiming, "Those thoughts even here!" The Rani [Rasmani] remained silent, but her attendants were scandalized and ranted shrilly calling for the immediate dismissal of the insolent priest. The Rani, who had been mulling absentmindedly over a pending lawsuit at the precise moment of

Ramakrishna's timely rebuke, answered them quietly, "You don't understand. It was the Divine Mother Herself who punished me and thereby illumined my heart."[12]

Not all *avadhutas* express their disinterest in conventional life by frequenting garbage heaps or by eating refuse. Some demonstrate it through the opposite extreme of indulging in luxury without showing the least attachment. The devotees of Narayan Maharaj (1885–1945) treated him like an emperor. Abandoning any aspiration of a normal life of his own, he freely turned himself over to their affections, allowing them to treat him like a living image of the Divine, to be decorated and worshipped. Narayan Maharaj ran his hermitage in Maharashtra like a kingdom. He had a large personal guard, several luxury cars, an abundance of fine garments, and a full treasure chest. He would hold court and permit devotees to express their devotion by lavishing gifts on him. They understood him to be a "superconductor" between their spiritual and devotional impulses and the Divine. In their eyes, he was God rendered concrete and visible. Yet, on occasion, they would witness Narayan Maharaj assume the role of the devotee, invoking and ardently praying to the Lord.

When we look at the *avadhutas*, past and present, we see phenomenal feats of renunciation. We also see behavior patterns that border on the psychotic, at least in terms of Western psychology. Some of the *avadhutas*, like Sri Ramakrishna, have puzzled over their own experience, wondering whether it was not at least in part "sick." They certainly cannot help behaving the way they do, regardless of whether or not their eccentric behavior is intended to be instructive to others. They have entered a new frame of reference, in which the transcendence of the conventional reality looms uppermost. They *experience* reality differently, and so they may also relate to people and things in unexpected ways. As Sri Rang Avadhoot, who died in 1968, explained:

> The world calls me mad. I am mad, you are mad, all the world is mad. Who in the world is not mad? Still they call me mad. Some are mad after name and fame. Some are mad after money. Some are mad after skin. But blessed is he who is mad after God Rama. I am a madcap of that type.[13]

Madness, or psychic imbalance, is particularly associated with another kind of spiritual madcap—the *mast*. This is an individual so overwhelmed by spiritual experience that he or she is barely able to function normally in the world. The Hindi word *mast* means something like "numskull." It hardly does justice to the rich inner world of the *masts*, who are drunk on the Divine. These God-intoxicated individuals, who roam the streets of India by the hundreds and who are at times difficult to distinguish from ordinary madmen, were "discovered" by another great Indian *avadhuta*, Meher Baba.

Meher Baba was born Merwan Sheriarji Irani in 1894 to an Indian family of Persian descent. While studying at Deccan College in Poona, he was unexpectedly initiated at the age of nineteen by an old woman saint whose gaze and embrace catapulted him into a state of sheer ecstasy that lasted for a full nine months. A year later he obtained the initiatory blessings of Shirdi Sai Baba, widely hailed as an incarnation of the Divine and as a great miracle worker. Subsequently Merwan visited the controversial Upasani Baba. As he was about to enter the sage's dwelling, Upasani flung a pebble at him, hitting him square on the forehead, exactly on the spot the old woman had kissed. Several years later, Upasani told the young man that he, Merwan, was the *avatara*, the divine incarnation of this age.

Shortly thereafter, Merwan, now addressed as Meher Baba by his students, began his spiritual work. Over the years, he attracted tens of thousands of followers. Many saw in him the *avatara* of our era. Others, perhaps misled by his physiognomy, thought of him as an impostor. His prominent hooked nose gave him more the look of a con man than a holy man. In addition, he was fond of joking—which is always unsettling for those who think that holiness and humor are incompatible. Meher Baba saw himself as an awakener rather than a teacher. He did not want to found a new religion; indeed, he spoke quite scathingly about organized religion. He wanted to point to the truth beyond all doctrinal and ritual differences; this was the principal reason for the years-long silence. Words, he said, only propel the mind into action. What he hoped to accomplish, rather, was to make people's hearts sensitive to his universal love.

In 1931, Mahatma Gandhi tried to convince Meher Baba to break his silence for the good of the world. Gandhi remarked that he intuited the Baba's inner greatness but added that he had been left unimpressed by Upasani Baba. When Meher Baba asked for an explanation, Gandhi told him that Upasani Baba had taken off his loincloth and exposed his genitals to him, saying to Gandhi, "You may be a great man; what is that to me? Why have you come here?"[14] Gandhi, known for his sexual prudishness, was shocked by the *avadhuta*'s immodesty. However, Meher Baba assured him that Upasani Baba was one of the "perfect masters."

"The breaking of my Silence," Meher Baba spelled out on his little alphabet board one day, "will be as forceful as thousands of atom bombs exploding together."[15] Meher Baba died in 1969 at the age of seventy-five, without breaking his silence of forty-three years. It became evident to many that his announcement had been meant symbolically, though some saw it as an indication that he had, after all, been duping everyone.

Although Meher Baba lived frugally, fasted often, and frequently retired into seclusion, he also went on several world tours. In 1932 he was received in Hollywood like a prince, making the front page of all the major newspapers. This aspect of Meher Baba's life is as perplexing as his work with the *masts* of India. He started to identify and contact *masts* in 1924 and continued with this work until the mid-1960s.

Masts are frequently Moslem by religion, though there are also many Hindus. They are found, [Meher] Baba explained, almost entirely in India, though there are a few also in Egypt and Arabia, and a very few in Iran and Tibet . . .

There are, of course, many false masts and sham sadhus [religious men]. Baba himself in the course of his search for masts and advanced souls visited Allahabad in February 1948 for a great fair which is held only every six years, to which thousands of sadhus come together from all over India to bathe at the confluence of two sacred rivers, the Jumna and the Ganges. At this fair, among something like a million persons, there were estimated to be 30,000 sadhus . . . In the course of a morning, Baba went around all the territories, contacting some 4,000 sadhus. He afterwards told the mandali [the inner circle of followers] that among these four thousand there were no more than seven advanced souls.[16]

Meher Baba looked up thousands of *masts* over the years and gave to each what he thought was needed for their further spiritual growth. Sometimes he had to spend considerable time coaxing them into returning to body awareness before he could even feed and clean them, much less get their further cooperation. His patience was exemplary. The *masts*, he explained, had only a weak or even no relationship to their bodies. Hence they barely managed to take care of their own physical existence. Not all of them welcomed Meher Baba's approach, presumably because they sensed that he was making a spiritual demand on them. One actually refused to meet Meher Baba, saying, "My boat will be drowned in that Ocean." Some displayed a violent temper, others were completely passive, and a few behaved like playful children. Some of those who did respond to Meher Baba were gathered in special hermitages where others could take care of them and support their quest for the Divine. Meher Baba's particular sympathy for the *masts* can in part be explained by his own experience of drowning the mind in love.

The *masts* are not merely *insane*. As the British physician William Donkin, a follower of Meher Baba, observed in his book *The Wayfarers*, the *masts* do not project an aura of psychotic disturbance but rather a feeling of love and happiness.[17]

Another type of madcap known in India is the *baul*. The Bengali word *baul* is thought to stem from the Sanskrit *vatula*, meaning literally "wind-affected," that is, "mad," or from *vyakula*, meaning "confused." Some scholars have derived the word from the Arabic *auliya*, denoting "friend," which is somewhat justifiable because the *bauls* have been influenced by Islam. However, their main cultural provenance is Hinduism.

The *bauls* are religious eccentrics who refuse to pay allegiance to any particular school of thought. They proclaim their simple love for the divine in song, dance, and music. They have no aptitude for worldly life. They are itinerants, spiritual troubadours roaming the countryside—notably in Bengal—in tattered clothes, flouting conventional life. As a group, the *bauls* originated some time in the fourteenth or fifteenth century. They belong to the great devotional (*bhakti*) movement that swept across most of medieval India. Their longing for the "man of the heart," the divine, is expressed in thousands of songs, which to this day delight and inspire the peasants of northeastern India.

> When will I find him, that man of my heart?
> He is lost. In my search I have wandered near and far . . .
> He distracts my mind. But when I find him
> at last my mind will be at peace . . .
> if you know where he is hiding, be kind—
> tell me of it.[18]

Because the *bauls* are largely illiterate or have never bothered to preserve their songs for posterity, most of their unsophisticated but touching creations have been lost. The oldest available songs date back to the eighteenth century, having been passed on by word of mouth. Whereas the introverted *masts* are solitary pilgrims on the spiritual path, the *bauls* recognize the central importance of a guru's directions. The guru sets the disciple's heart aflame through songs, until the disciple becomes divinely mad as well. Sings one anonymous *baul*:

> Mad, mad,
> we are all mad.
> Why is this word
> so derogatory then?
> Diving deep into the heart's stream
> you will find
> that no one is better
> than the one who is mad.
>
> Some are mad after wealth
> and others for glory.
> Some go mad
> with poverty,
> and others with aesthetic forms,
> the flavours of feelings.
> Some are madly in love.
> And some of those who go mad
> only laugh or cry.
> The glamour of madness is great.
>
> Mad and mad!
> Madness does not grow on the tree—
> but only when
> the fake and the fact

are meaningless—
and all, being equal,
are bitter-sweet.[19]

The *bauls* live a charmed way of life in which the quest for God takes precedence over everything else. Even those *bauls* who are sexually active follow the spiritual principles of Tantrism, in which sexual energy is experienced as a manifestation of the divine power (*shakti*), the feminine aspect of the Absolute.

A similar form of crazy wisdom that is gurucentric, largely sex-positive, and chiefly instructional rather than a means of personal self-denial as in Christianity is found in Tibetan Buddhism.

## 2. The Crazy Adepts of Tibet

The Himalayan country of Tibet, wedged between the vast interior of China and the triangle of the Indian peninsula, has produced its own distinct civilization, whose survival is now threatened by Chinese imperialism. The official religion of the ecclesiastic state of Tibet is a particular brand of Buddhism—the Vajrayana.

Tibetan Buddhism is an offshoot of Indian Buddhism, more particularly of Tantrism, or Tantra. Since Tantrism is a crucial aspect of crazy wisdom in the Tibetan context, we need to examine, at least briefly, what it is. To begin with, the Sanskrit word *tantra* means "loom" or "warp." The scriptures of Hindu and Buddhist Tantrism, which also are called *Tantras*, derive the term from the verbal root *tan* meaning "to stretch" or "to extend." They explain that what is spread out or expanded through the means of Tantrism is transcendental insight (*jnana*). Thus, philosophically, Tantrism is a form of gnosis—like Vedanta or Neoplatonism. But when we look at Tantrism from a broader perspective, we find that it is in effect a sweeping cultural movement, comprising numerous orientations and schools and straddling the great spiritual traditions of Hinduism, Buddhism, and Jainism.

From its origin, around the middle of the first post-Christian millennium, Tantrism understood itself as a new gospel. The scriptures of Tantrism proclaim it to be particularly suited for the still-current "dark age" (*kali-yuga*), which suffers from moral decline and spiritual impoverishment. In their attempt to create a viable spiritual approach for the worsening conditions of the *kali-yuga*, the adepts of Tantrism freely borrowed from a variety of existing traditions, including folk religion and magic. Thus, Tantrism is markedly syncretistic.

An important feature of Tantric syncretism is the absorption of local and tribal forms of Goddess worship. In fact, in Tantrism the feminine was elevated to a high metaphysical principle in the form of *shakti*, the power aspect of the Divine. An integral part of this reappraisal of the feminine was the reevaluation of cosmic existence itself. Whereas most preceding non-dualistic schools of thought looked upon the world as an inconsequential, if not illusory, phenomenon, Tantrism celebrates the cosmos as a divine manifestation, a play of the feminine aspect of God.

This positive evaluation of the world also includes a wholesome attitude toward the dark forces in nature. Most spiritual paths seek to cultivate higher values by strenuously shunning the shadowy side of existence. However, Tantrism regards good and evil as complementary poles of life, which cannot exist apart from each other. Therefore the *tantrikas*, or practitioners of Tantrism, also do not deny the "lower" human nature—the "demons" of the psyche: fear, anger, jealousy, lust, and so on. They view sexuality as an integral part of life and as an important lever of spiritual transformation rather than as an inevitable obstacle to liberation, or enlightenment. The metaphysical basis for this world-affirmative orientation is found in the Tantric teaching that the world of change (called *samsara*) and the ultimate Reality (called *nirvana*) are, from the enlightened viewpoint, identical. Put differently, at enlightenment transcendental truth and relative truth coincide.

This famous Tantric equation has not only led to a remarkable spiritual renaissance but, unfortunately, has also opened the doors to antinomian exploitation, notably reprehensible sexual excesses on the part of self-serving teachers and their misguided students. As John Blofeld, an initiate of Vajrayana Buddhism, has observed:

> Tantric followers have to face the fact that their attitude to life offers unusually wide scope for abuse and calumny. In judging its spiritual value, it must be borne in mind that the Tantric path is not for sinners but for saints . . . Devotees are forbidden to depart from Buddhist conventional morality unless their conduct truly proceeds from the desire to attain experientially to the voidness of opposites. They must never lose sight of their prime objective. Subject to these conditions, advanced adepts are permitted to do what seems good to them, regardless of the normal rules of conduct. To consider abiding by the rules as necessarily good or transgressing them as necessarily evil would be to tie themselves down with the dualism they have set out to transcend . . .
>
> Inevitably such conduct is open to condemnation from some quarters. Sordid people judge others by their own standards, reading crude motives into every sort of action. Hypocrites will be likely to see their own vice in every unconventional act of a man sincerely seeking spiritual advancement. It is hard to convince them that others may act from lofty motives. A true adept, however, will not be put out by misguided criticism.[20]

We will understand the appropriateness of Blofeld's comments when we come to the stories of Tibetan adepts like Marpa, Tilopa, and Drukpa Kunley. Their unconventional behavior looks highly eccentric and at times even immoral to most people's sensibilities. But as the Tibetan sources assure us, their crazy-wise actions originated not in egoic motives but in a desire to demonstrate and communicate the Tantric wisdom regarding the seamless juncture between the finite and the infinite.

The Buddhist Tantric teachings were first introduced to Tibet in the seventh century A.D., and they challenged and superseded (to some extent) the native shamanistic religion of Bön. Tibetans venerate the eighth-century Indian adept and miracle worker Padmasambhava ("Lotus-born") as the founder of the old-style Vajrayana Buddhism, calling him *lama rimpoche*, "the precious teacher." His sect is known as the Nyingmapa or Red Hat school. It has incorporated many notions and practices from the Bön religion, and its members, who are generally married, engage in an elaborate magical ritualism.

The dominant Tibetan sect, however, is that of the reformed, conservative school of the Gelugpas or Yellow Hats, which was founded by Tsongkapa in the fifteenth century A.D., but which traces itself back to the eleventh-century adept Atisha. The Gelugpa school encourages monastic discipline and book learning and discourages the kind of magical ritualism that is characteristic of most of the other sects. A third important school is that of the Kargyupas, whose teaching lineage reaches back to Marpa and his famous disciple Milarepa; this sect places a premium on strict asceticism.

In all three schools, *guru-yoga* is pivotal. This practice ranges from simple veneration of one's spiritual guide to complex visualization exercises involving meditative and even ecstatic identification with the guru (in Tibetan: *lama*), who is envisioned as the ultimate principle of existence. One's personal teacher must be experienced to be none other than the original Buddha. The guru is experienced as the source of spiritual transmission, and it is widely held among Tibetan Buddhists that liberation, or enlightenment, cannot be attained without a teacher.

As in other traditions, Vajrayana teachers come, metaphorically speaking, in all shapes and sizes. Some teach quietly, more by their own example and spiritual transmission than by verbal or behavioral instruction, while others teach by directly interfering with the disciple's life. Crazy adepts belong to the latter type. Tibetan lamas are well known for confronting spiritual aspirants with any number of fierce tests—not least personal abuse—though, perhaps in the interest of preserving their teachings, many have adopted somewhat milder manners with eager Western students. Traditionally, at any rate, the spiritual seeker could expect to pass through a period of trials before being accepted by a Tibetan adept teacher. And after his or her initiation, the disciple was subject to still more severe testing. There is no sanctuary for the ego-personality in spiritual discipleship. The teacher's function is precisely to make all egoic retreat impossible. And some gurus are more theatrical and ruthlessly surgical in performing this task than others.

The classic Tibetan story of the eleventh-century adept Marpa and his pupil

Milarepa captures the ideal of traditional discipleship, and it also illustrates the propensity for crazy-wise behavior in some Vajrayana gurus.

Milarepa ("Cotton-Clad") had earned his living as a sorcerer before he approached Marpa the Translator to be initiated into Buddhist esotericism. Since the young Milarepa was indigent, Marpa put him to hard labor to earn his keep. Even then Marpa refused on several occasions to initiate him because Milarepa had failed to come up with the appropriate ceremonial fee. Then Marpa promised him initiation in exchange for Milarepa's services as a black magician; he wanted him to curse local hill men who had been robbing some of Marpa's other disciples. Obedient to his newfound teacher's behest but with a heavy heart, Milarepa cast his spells and caused much damage among the robbers. In return, Marpa simply berated him for his evil deeds and bluntly refused to initiate him into the noble teachings of the Buddha. The next morning, however, Marpa apologized for his outburst and promised to initiate Milarepa as soon as he had built Marpa a circular house on a nearby mountain ridge.

Milarepa toiled hard to complete the structure as quickly as possible. However, halfway through his efforts, his teacher found a farfetched excuse to have him dismantle the building and return every stone to its original place. Marpa then asked Milarepa to construct a crescent-shaped building elsewhere. Midway through construction, the teacher again changed his mind. This time he asked his faithful disciple to build a triangular structure. A little while later, he berated Milarepa for wasting his time on constructing such a displeasing building and demanded again that he dismantle it stone by stone.

By now Milarepa's back was an open sore, but he did not complain. However, he did find an unexpected ally in Marpa's wife, Damema. She tried to intercede on his behalf but was rebuffed by her husband. Marpa then gave his disciple some token instruction but indicated that Milarepa was unlikely to attain to any great spiritual heights. A few days later, renewing his promise of more profound initiation, Marpa asked Milarepa to build a quadrangular building on the original spot. Milarepa had reached the second story when Marpa came by to inspect his labors. He noticed a particularly large boulder as one of the cornerstones and asked how Milarepa could possibly have lifted it. The young aspirant explained that several fellow disciples had, in jest, brought it there for him. Marpa grew furious and demanded that the boulder be removed at once, knowing full well that this could be accomplished only by dismantling the entire structure. Milarepa pleadingly reminded his guru that he had promised not to order the demolition of this last building. Angrily Marpa pointed out that he *was* keeping his promise perfectly; he was merely asking for this one boulder to be removed. So again, Milarepa set about to undo his labors, even managing to shift the giant boulder on his own. Single-handedly he rebuilt the house to a height of seven stories.

Milarepa was now certain he would receive the coveted initiation and

instruction. Alas, Marpa had another cruel test in store for him. He was
willing to initiate his disciple, he said, but he still insisted on his proper fee.
Marpa even struck Milarepa, dragging him by the hair and flinging him out
of his house. The following day, he ordered his dejected disciple to build an
annex to the house, promising initiation for sure. Silently Milarepa set about
his task; he had almost completed the structure when an initiation ceremony
was scheduled. In the hope that his guru would acknowledge his commitment, Milarepa approached him once more for instruction. When Marpa
asked again for the fee, Milarepa offered various items that Marpa's wife had
secretly procured for him. At this Marpa became violently angry and literally
kicked his disciple out of the house.

At this point Milarepa was feeling suicidal. The skin on his hands and legs
was cracked, and innumerable bruises and sores covered his body. Hopelessness descended upon him like a black cloud. Seemingly unperturbed by his
disciple's agony, Marpa came to him the next day, asking him to complete the
annex. Milarepa resumed his work, but his battered body was unable to
continue. Then Damema, angry with her husband for treating the heroic
young man so unfairly, tried in various ways to get Milarepa initiated. Her
efforts, however, were in vain.

Believing that his teacher would never instruct him in the higher teachings
without a fee, Milarepa stole away. Damema provided him with a faked letter,
purporting to be from her husband, which would secure Milarepa initiation
at the hand of one of Marpa's other disciples. So it came about, but because he
had achieved initiation by stealth, Milarepa's spiritual life bore no fruit at all.
Marpa, who had found out the truth from his wife, asked his wayward
disciple to return. Milarepa willingly came back to his guru, but Marpa
dismissed him furiously and would not allow him into his presence for days.
At long last, however, Marpa's mood changed; with tears in his eyes, he
praised his beloved disciple and even proffered an explanation for his irascible
behavior: Sacred anger, he explained, is different from worldly anger. It has
the purpose of filling the disciple's heart with sorrow so that he may repent
and grow spiritually. Marpa also confessed that if he had succeeded in plunging Milarepa into utter despair one more time, the student would have been
certain of instant enlightenment. He blamed the fact that his disciple had not
been cleansed of all his sins on his wife's misplaced pity for Milarepa. Marpa
then promised to initiate him properly so that he could gain enlightenment
still in this lifetime.

Milarepa, as is well known, went on to become Tibet's favorite *yogin*-saint.
Unlike his teacher, who was a householder and a great scholar, Milarepa was
fond of the solitary life of a cave-dwelling hermit, and though he composed
exquisite poetry, he had no time for book learning. Having mastered the six
great yogic practices of Naropa, Milarepa survived the icy winters of the
Himalayas clad only in a thin cotton garment, often shedding even this

modest covering. His biographer recalls that when Milarepa's sister visited him and begged him to cover his nakedness, Milarepa replied that he felt not the least shame for having been born and discovered the path of Truth as a man. Still, he took the blanket she had brought him and made separate coverings for his genitals, fingers, toes, and head. When his sister returned, she reprimanded him for his frivolousness and for ruining a good blanket. Milarepa explained that since he could not cut off his genitals simply because she felt ashamed at their sight, he had consented to cover them. At the same time, he continued, he had decided to cover his other limbs as well, because they too are part of the same body. Then, bursting into poetic song, he instructed her that no trace of shame is attached to the body and that the only shameful thing is a dirty mind—defiled by concupiscence, deception, theft, and meanness. Unperturbed by his sister's materialistic bent of mind and moved by great compassion, he entreated her to stay with him for a while so that her heart might be turned to spiritual ideals, which she did. Milarepa's punishing discipleship under Marpa had worked miracles.

That Marpa was a hard taskmaster with his other disciples as well is borne out by the story of Ngokton. He asked Marpa for initiation into particularly secret teachings and had to offer up all his possessions in payment. Marpa even made him return to his home province in order to bring an old lame nanny goat that had been left behind. In his traditional Tibetan biography, Marpa is described as having been a rather boisterous child who was easily angered. Even his own family feared his fierce temper and they sent him away from home to study with a distant teacher. No doubt, the same aggressive drive supplied the energy for Marpa's many spiritual accomplishments and his final liberation at the age of eighty-eight.

Marpa's own discipleship had not been easy. Failing to obtain the Tantric teachings in his native country, he learned Sanskrit and other Indian languages and undertook the difficult and dangerous journey from Tibet to India in order to apprentice under the renowned adept Naropa. After welcoming Marpa and giving him some teachings, Naropa sent him on a further journey to the adept Kukkuripa. This teacher had attained enlightenment through his love for a stray dog for which he had given up the delights of paradise, though, as the legend tells us, the dog turned out to be the Goddess herself. Kukkuripa is venerated as one of the eighty-four great adepts (maha-siddhas) of Northern Buddhism.

Two weeks later, Marpa arrived at Kukkuripa's place but saw no sign of the adept. He did, however, spot a human figure under a tree. The man had his head tucked under one arm, and he was covered from toe to crown with feathers. When Marpa asked the strange figure about Kukkuripa, he received nothing but abuse. He was told that no Kukkuripa lived around there. Gradually it dawned on Marpa that the crazy birdman was none other than the great adept himself, and he approached him reverentially and mentioned that Naropa had sent him for instruction. Then Kukkuripa started to mock the young disciple and Naropa as well, saying that renowned Naropa's learning was utterly laughable since he had no experience at all in higher meditation. Marpa was consternated and not a little put off by the insults hurled at his beloved teacher. However, he continued to show respect to the crazy adept. Quickly Kukkuripa changed his tune, admitting that he was only joking about Naropa, who was indeed to be venerated as a great spiritual master and who himself could easily have initiated Marpa into the teachings he desired.

Marpa made three journeys to India in all. In between, he busied himself with acquiring enough gold to return to Naropa and his other secondary teachers, prepared to offer up his hard-earned wealth for further instruction. Only during his last pilgrimage was he given the highest initiation. When he arrived in India he learned that Naropa had left his earthly body. Marpa could not accept this; he went in search of his teacher, guided by visions of him. At last, Naropa appeared to him in physical form. The adept refused to take Marpa's offering of gold, but when the disciple insisted, Naropa indifferently scattered it in the forest. He then instructed Marpa one last time and installed him as his successor, sending him back to Tibet.

If we are touched by Milarepa's trials and impressed by Marpa's many years of hardship, the staggering tests that Naropa had to endure as a disciple of Tilopa are positively mind-boggling. Although Naropa's story is more edifying fiction and inner biography than genuine history, its deep symbolism is nevertheless paradigmatic of the type of instruction referred to as crazy wisdom.

Naropa (A.D. 1016–1100) was a famous Buddhist scholar. For eight years he served as abbot of the renowned university of Nalanda; then, at the age of fifty-one, he suddenly renounced scholarship and worldly honors. Wholeheartedly dedicating himself to spiritual life, he went in search of his teacher, Tilopa, who had been revealed to him in a vision. As if in a daze and guided by other visions, Naropa traveled the countryside. Finally, in a mood of utter despair, he resolved to end his life on the spot. In that moment of suicidal crisis Tilopa appeared.

Now Naropa's trials began in earnest. His traditional biography describes how Tilopa set him twelve tasks that amounted to Herculean acts of self-denial. Each deed contained its own form of instruction about the voidness of existence, and each left Naropa with either a shattered body or a broken heart, but Tilopa always resurrected his beloved disciple. Without thinking twice about his teacher's commands (which were always cleverly couched as an option), Naropa jumped off a roof and leaped into a fire; had himself half beaten to death for begging among the same people twice; almost drowned in the process of building an impossible bridge over a freezing pond; had his skin badly scorched and lacerated by burning sticks that Tilopa pressed into him while gently asking how he was feeling; chased after an imaginary man, conjured up by his teacher, until he was near death from exhaustion; had himself beaten almost unconscious for manhandling a minister and his new bride and later for repeating the same folly on a prince and even on the king and his queen; and castrated himself when his teacher reprimanded him for having sexual relations with a girl, even though Tilopa had asked him earlier to do just that. Later his spiritual commitment was further tested when Tilopa claimed the girl for himself and beat her severely for wanting to be with Naropa instead. Finally, the legend has it, Naropa dismembered his own body to form a sacred circle (*mandala*) at his teacher's behest. He is said to have won the highest realization through Tilopa's grace. Both Naropa and Tilopa became assimilated into the Tibetan pantheon of eighty-four *maha-siddhas*.[21]

Also among these *maha-siddhas*, or great adepts, were Saraha, Kanha, and the handsome Kalapa, who, having grown tired of people staring at him, withdrew to the cremation ground and became a holy madman. There were also four female adepts in this illustrious group, notably Lakshminkara and Manibhadra. The former was a princess who may have lived in the seventh or eighth century A.D. An initiate of Buddhist Tantrism, she was on her way to her husband-to-be when the great mood of renunciation overcame her. She gave away all her belongings, locked herself in a room, discarded her clothes, and besmeared her entire body with oil and coal dust. From then on the royal household treated her as insane. She slept in the cremation ground and lived off refuse. After seven years, she attained enlightenment. Her greatness was discovered when the king, her father-in-law, lost his way during the hunt and chanced upon Lakshminkara's cave. He found her sitting in perfect stillness, her body radiating light.

Manibhadra, the other female adept, was initiated by Kukkuripa, whom we have already met. While still a young girl, living in her parent's home, she sneaked out one night to join Kukkuripa at the cremation ground and returned seven days later, duly initiated into the Tantric mysteries. She was received by her parents with a thrashing, which she calmly took. Then Manibhadra announced that she had found her guru and would henceforth dedicate herself to realizing liberation in this lifetime. Her parents were at a loss but accepted the situation. A year later, her fiance arrived to take her to his home; to everyone's surprise, she followed willingly and became a model wife. Then, one day, on the way back from the stream, she tripped and broke her pitcher. Something in her shattered in that moment as well. For hours she stared fixedly at the broken pieces and did not even hear her husband's concerned words. Then, at the end of the day, she arose, radiant, having won perfect enlightenment—twelve years after Kukkuripa had initiated her. The story is of course intended to spell out that the highest realization of *nirvana* is by no means closed to wives fulfilling their domestic role. However, it also illustrates that even the most ordinary-seeming *sadhana*, or spiritual disci-

pline, contains an element of unconventionality. Thus, Manibhadra's "madness" manifested in a relatively quiet way at the beginning of her spiritual
life—the seven days with Kukkuripa and the year of abstracted contemplation
in her parent's home—and then again for the few hours preceding her final
awakening.

Saraha, some of whose fine didactic "songs" (*dohas*) have survived, lived in
the South of India during the late thirteenth and early fourteenth centuries.
He was a brahmin by birth but was initiated into the mysteries of Buddhist
Tantrism and acquired the monastic name of Rahula. One day, the wives of
his four brothers offered him a cup of beer. After protesting for a while, he
gulped down the beer, whereupon he had a vision of a *bodhisattva*, who asked
him to visit a certain local arrowsmith, a woman. Rahula went to see the
woman at once and watched her skillfully prepare an arrow and then aim it at a
target. When he asked her whether she was a professional arrowsmith, she
responded in a cryptic way, saying that the Buddha's teachings could be
understood only through symbols and actions, not through words and books.
Her communication was duly empowered, so Rahula instantly comprehended the inner meaning of her remarks. He had irrevocably entered the
stream toward enlightenment. It was because of his penetrating understanding of reality that he eventually came to be called Saraha—from the Sanskrit
words *sara* ("arrow") and *han* ("to slay"), signifying "he who has released the
arrow into the target."

For a while Saraha stayed with the woman and caused no end of gossip in
the villages. During their Tantric rituals, he openly sang and feasted. The
scandal soon reached the royal court, and the king sent a delegation to Saraha,
headed by his four brothers, to persuade him to abandon his outrageous
ways. Saraha responded by singing to them sixty verses in praise of the
immaculate mind that perceives the ultimate Reality in the midst of *any*
action. Next, the ladies of the royal household came to plead with Saraha, and
he responded to them also by singing verses of instruction. In the end, the
king himself arrived to set matters straight, and again Saraha explained his
position through song, converting the ruler and his entire entourage.

> There's nothing to be negated, nothing to be
> Affirmed or grasped; for It can never be conceived.
> By the fragmentations of the intellect are the deluded
> Fettered; undivided and pure remains spontaneity. (35)
>
> . . . . . . . . . . . . . . . . . . . . . . . . . . . . . .
>
> What has been done and where and what in itself it will
> become
>
> Is nothing: yet thereby it has been useful for this and that.
> Whether passionate or not
> The pattern is nothingness. (39)

> If I am like a pig that covets worldly mire
> You must tell me what fault lies in a stainless mind.
> By what does not affect one
> How can one now be fettered? (40)[22]

According to legend, Saraha even proved his innocence to the king by plunging his hands into boiling oil without singeing a hair and by drinking a cup of molten copper without scorching his mouth. The king concluded that no ordinary mortal could accomplish such feats and that if indeed Saraha were transgressing Hindu law by consuming alcohol as his accusers insisted, he should be permitted to do so forever. Saraha later took a fifteen-year-old maiden as his consort and retired to a secluded place to pursue his spiritual practices, unhindered by the interferences of puritanical people.

The legend of the adept Kanha, who lived perhaps in the eleventh or twelfth century A.D., is of interest here primarily because of the role played by one of his teachers, a weaver who was also a Tantric master. The story is also instructive because it indicates the persistence of violent emotions and magical curses in the higher stages of spiritual life: a warning that even advanced initiates are by no means paragons of virtue. Like Kanha prior to his entry into *nirvana*, they may not even have particularly trustworthy or likable personalities—an important fact in considering practitioners of crazy wisdom who are not yet enlightened.

As a young man, Kanha practiced a particular discipline for twelve years before he was rewarded with a vision of Hevajra. He thought he had achieved final liberation and was puffed up with self-importance. A female deity appeared before him scolding him for confusing a preliminary manifestation with the ultimate state. Duly chastened, Kanha returned to his disciplines. However, he could not resist testing his spiritual achievement periodically; each time, the female deity reappeared and chided him for his folly and impatience.

Then, one day, upon emerging from deep meditation, Kanha found seven royal canopies floating above his head. The air was filled with the sound of seven drums. He now felt sure that he had become enlightened, and he marched to the city with a host of disciples. Even before they reached their destination, Kanha could not resist the temptation of showing off his newly won power. He raced toward the river and, to the astonishment of his disciples, skipped across the surface of the water. Haughtily he announced that even his guru, the great adept Jalandhara, was unable to perform such a miracle; as soon as the words had left his lips, he sank like a stone and nearly drowned.

He was still coughing up water and sand when he heard the uproarious laughter of Jalandhara, who was levitating above him. Filled with shame, Kanha made obeisance to his guru, and Jalandhara ordered him to seek out another of his disciples, a weaver by trade. When Kanha had found the man and begged him to instruct him in the ultimate teaching, the weaver made him promise to obey his every order implicitly. Then he took the proud young man to the cremation ground and ordered him to eat a piece of a corpse. Suppressing his revulsion, Kanha knelt down and cut into the corpse with a knife. The weaver yelled at him, saying this was not the way to do it. Instantly he transformed himself into a wolf and gorged himself on the corpse.

Next the weaver defecated in front of Kanha, picked up a piece of his own excrement, and asked the young man to eat it. But Kanha refused. Then the weaver gave a feast that lasted for seven days, and Kanha and his disciples made gluttons of themselves, eating the food that miraculously manifested in their bowls. Finally, disgusted and ignoring the weaver's warnings, Kanha left town. After wandering for hundreds of miles, one day he spotted a lichee tree with ripe fruit. He asked a young maiden seated under the tree for some of the fruit. When she refused, Kanha angrily plucked some fruits off the tree by the sheer power of his will. No sooner had the lichee fruits fallen to the ground than they bounced up and reaffixed themselves to the branches. In his fury, Kanha did not realize that the girl was a female deity, and so he cursed her all too hastily.

The maiden started to bleed profusely. People gathered around and condemned Kanha for his heartless curse. When he came to his senses and removed the malicious spell, it was already too late; the girl had uttered her own death-bringing curse. Kanha tumbled to the ground, vomiting and bleeding. The curse on him could not be lifted, and he died after seven days. However, this final experience helped him break through to the unconditional Reality, and today he is remembered as a great *siddha*. In one of Kanha's songs, he speaks of himself as "sporting in the city of his body in nondual form." He describes himself as a "skull-bearer" (*kapalin*), with a body besmeared with the ashes of his passion and wearing the necklace of supreme liberation. In another song, Kanha sings about his murder of his mother and other relatives—all symbolic statements about his severing of social ties and his spiritual attainment of flawless identity with Reality.

Thus far we have seen instances of crazy wisdom in the context of a formal teacher-disciple relationship. But Tibet is also known for its maverick adepts, the "mad lamas" (*smyon-pa*), who roam the countryside and play the role of spiritual tricksters to any- and everyone. The best-known crazy-wisdom wildmen of this type are Dbus, Gtsang, and especially Drukpa Kunley (also spelled 'Brug-pa Kun-legs). John Ardussi and Lawrence Epstein, in their study of Tibetan mad saints, have identified the following six principal characteristics of the *smyon-pa*:[23]

First, a general rejection of customary behavior, particularly a rejection of the monastic tradition, with its ornate liturgies and ecclesiastic hierarchy: Since their spontaneous wildness could not be accommodated in the monastic setting, they were generally forced out of the monasteries or, mostly, left of their own accord.

Second, a penchant for wearing bizarre clothes, or none at all.

Third, what Ardussi and Epstein call "a disregard for the niceties of interpersonal behavior": They generally ignored a person's social standing or spiritual status, or if they chose to notice either, it was usually in order to mock and teach a lesson. They tended to be especially harsh to ecclesiastic snobs.

Fourth, an apparent scorn for book learning: They favored self-reliance and personal experience above all else, arguing, as did Milarepa, that intellectual knowledge fades as the mind ages and is only burdensome anyway.

Fifth, the employment of popular modes of communication such as poetry, dance, songs, mime, and storytelling: One crazy-wisdom adept, Than-stong-rgyal-po, invented the Tibetan opera, and Drukpa Kunley is remembered for his quick wit and poetry.

Sixth, the use of obscene acts and scatological language: Drukpa Kunley, who excelled in both, could be unbelievably crude to both men and women, peasants and dignitaries alike. He, like his fellow *smyon-pas*, wanted to startle, shock, and provoke personal change.

To Ardussi and Epstein's analysis we may add, as a seventh characteristic, a fondness for laughter, humor, joking, and comedy: The mad lamas' verbal and occasionally physical attacks on individuals and institutions that were bogged down in conventionality were always infused with a dose of good humor—the liberating laugh of the awakened being. They did not take even their own criticism of conventional life too seriously.

Drukpa Kunley, who is revered in Tibet, Bhutan, and Nepal as an enlightened adept, lived in the fifteenth century A.D. Having achieved buddhahood at a young age, Drukpa Kunley adopted the life of an itinerant spiritual "clown," using all kinds of popular devices, not least sex, to drive home his spiritual message. Keith Dowman, the translator of Drukpa Kunley's Tibetan biography, remarks about this madcap figure:

> Care-free renunciation, an excess of compassion, total lack of inhibition, skilful use of shock-therapy, tears and laughter, are the specific characteristics of the divine madman . . . If insanity is defined as deviation from a psychological norm, the divine madman is truly crazy; but if a spiritual ideal is used as a yardstick, undoubtedly, it is the vast majority of us who are insane.[24]

Commenting on the typically ribald nature of the stories told about Drukpa Kunley, Dowman goes on to preface his translation with these cautionary remarks:

> A word should be said here on behalf of the Tibetan people. Please do not delude yourselves that they are a bawdy bunch. Although they have few

neurotic obsessions regarding sex, they have a strong sense of shame.
Tibetan women will blush at the mention of sex and look askance at the
"liberated" western girl. Likewise, monks are inordinately embarrassed
by even the milder of Drukpa Kunley's jokes.[25]

In other words, Drukpa Kunley was an embarrassment to his fellow
Tibetans; nonetheless, they were and still are greatly respectful toward this
eccentric adept, no doubt because they sense his spiritual authenticity. It is an
open question whether Western readers of his biography will bring the same
sensitivity and faith to it or whether they will see in Drukpa Kunley a
misguided, arbitrary individual, perhaps even a dangerous psychopath.

The biography starts out with an explosive anecdote that could well be
based in truth and that immediately tests the reader's moral convictions.
Shortly after discarding his monastic robes and taking to the road, Drukpa
Kunley visited his mother, who promptly failed to see his newly won spiritual
freedom. She nagged him about his halfhearted commitment to spiritual life,
suggesting that he get himself a wife instead of going about half-naked as a
mendicant. The young adept, no longer bound by any vow of celibacy, took
her advice and went to the marketplace to find himself a wife. He picked out a
toothless old hag and, since she was too frail to walk by herself, carried her all
the way home. When she saw whom he had chosen for his bride, his mother
was shocked and told him to return the woman to where he had found her,
adding that she herself could perform a wife's duties better than the hag.

Drukpa Kunley did as he was bid, but when night came, he went to his
mother's room carrying a blanket. When she asked what he wanted, he
reminded her calmly that earlier that day she had said she could perform
wifely duties better than the hag. Enraged by his suggestion that she commit
incest, his mother scolded him. But Drukpa Kunley would not leave. In the
end, his mother softened somewhat, expressing her fear of what other people
might think when they found out. When he promised that he would keep it a
secret, his mother finally and foolishly yielded to his stubborn bidding. In
that instant, the adept stormed out of the room. In the morning, he went to
the marketplace and proclaimed for everyone to hear that anyone can seduce
his own mother if only he persists. The biographer adds that in this way
Drukpa Kunley cleansed his mother of her sinful desire and that she then lived
to be 130 years old.

There is little doubt that Drukpa Kunley would have broken the incest
taboo if he had thought that this might serve his mother's spiritual growth,
just as he did not hesitate to have what would conventionally be considered
affairs with married women. In fact, judging purely from the number of his
sexual exploits—his biographer mentions five thousand women—he was a
Casanova of sorts. However, Drukpa Kunley did not bed women indiscriminately, as is shown by the story of the group of five women who flirted
with him on the street. He had told them he was looking for a particular girl,

Samchuk, who was a *dakini*, a superhuman female, with "a fair complexion and soft, silky, warm flesh, a tight, foxy and comfortable pussy, and a round smiling face."[26] Then he described the nine types of *dakini* to them, after which the girls were eager to know what kind of a *dakini* he thought they were. Drukpa Kunley's response was characteristically blunt. "You are greedy but poor, and sexually frustrated but friendless," he said. "Even if you do find some idiot to couple with you, no one will gain anything from it."[27]

Samchuk, the girl for whom he had traveled hundreds of miles, was a virgin in the employ of a chieftain. Drukpa Kunley posted himself in front of the chieftain's house and spontaneously sang to the maiden. His song was about the glory of enlightenment, but also about how he wanted to make love to her. Samchuk saw the wandering adept leaning against the prayer-flag pole outside and was stirred by his song. She sang back to him her desire to achieve buddhahood. Soon the chieftain overheard their singing and wanted to know what was going on.

The girl concocted a plausible story on the spot and succeeded in sending her master on a wild-goose chase into the mountains to look for free meat. She then invited Drukpa Kunley into the house, and they wasted no time in making love. Afterward Drukpa Kunley ate his fill and prepared to leave. Samchuk begged him to take her along with him, fearing an inevitable beating from the chieftain. The adept refused, warning her that a *yogin's* mind is "as inconsistent as a madman's babble" and "like a whore's bum." In the end, he agreed to let her stay with him for seven days—walled up in an isolated cave. He advised her to meditate on him continuously. Scared but full of faith in the adept, the girl had herself immured. On the fourth day of her voluntary incarceration, the story goes, she gained the enlightenment she so fervently desired.

According to another story, Drukpa Kunley met a sixteen-year-old Buddhist nun on the street. She told him she was going into town to beg for alms. Seeing in a vision that the girl would bear him a son, he told her that she must give herself to him. Shyly she answered that she did not know how, having been a nun from childhood on. The adept took her by the hand and made love to her three times by the side of the road. In due course she gave birth to a child. When the abbot discovered who the father was, he declared that no sin had been committed. Now the other young nuns became quite envious; looking for an excuse to experience sexual pleasure of their own, they conspired that they would simply name the saintly Drukpa Kunley as the father of any child that was born from their illicit relationships. And so it passed, a year later, that the monastery was filled with the sound of newborn infants.

When questioned by the horrified abbot, all the young monastic mothers blamed Drukpa Kunley. Finally, the gossip reached the adept's ears. He went to the monastery himself and announced to the assembled nuns that he would completely care for any children that were truly his, but that he would feed all others to the Goddess. Then he grabbed his infant son by one leg and, invoking the Goddess, hurled him into a field. In that instant, deafening thunder exploded. The child was, of course, unharmed. But the nuns who had falsely accused Drukpa Kunley of fatherhood swiftly fled with their illegitimate babies.

On another occasion, Drukpa Kunley was the guest of a couple who lived in a shack. Although the husband was a half-wit, the wife clearly had spiritual potential. The adept wasted no time suggesting to her that they make love or, as he put it in song, "Come and enjoy the goodies in uncle's pocket." The woman readily agreed, and through intercourse the spiritual impulse in her was awakened. When Drukpa Kunley left, she insisted on coming with him. After three days of traveling, he explained that her husband was still looking for her and that she had accumulated guilt by abandoning him. He agreed, however, to instruct her in meditation and subsequently sent her to meditate on her own in a cave. A year later, when he inquired about her at a local monastery, he was told that she was probably dead because an avalanche had closed off the entrance to her cave long ago. Drukpa Kunley trekked to the cave and found the entrance cleared. Although the girl had had only three days' rations with her the year before, to his great joy he found her alive and well—an accomplished meditator. For three days he instructed her further, and after a short period of time the girl attained buddhahood.

In another adventure, Drukpa Kunley's song to the lady of the house did not go unnoticed by her husband; in an outburst of anger, the man hurled his sword at the adept. Accomplishing the impossible, Drukpa Kunley dexterously caught the sword with one hand while grasping the husband by the neck with the other. The man was overawed and realized that he was dealing with no ordinary wanderer but an adept. He fell at Drukpa Kunley's feet and asked the adept to accept him as a disciple. He also renounced all claims to his wife. According to oral tradition, the husband also announced that he would build a chapel dedicated to the Goddess Tara, to which Drukpa Kunley is said to have responded, "You like religion and I like cunt. May both of us be happy!"[28]

Drukpa Kunley's sexual exploits are presented by his biographer as initiatory events, not momentary weaknesses of the flesh. However, they did fly in the face of custom and propriety. His sex-positive attitude is consonant with both Buddhist and Hindu Tantrism, but especially with the left-hand schools. Tantric metaphysics regards the human body as a potential temple of the ultimate Reality. Sexuality is viewed as a manifestation of the energy aspect of that Reality. Whereas the right-hand schools make use of the powerful dynamo of the sex drive by sublimating it through ascetical practice, the left-hand schools actually employ intercourse to augment sexual energy before harnessing it for the spiritual purpose of self-transcendence.

Drukpa Kunley's unconventionality expressed itself not only in his sexual antinomianism but also in his intrepid criticism of the religious establishment. He felt free to point out and ridicule empty forms and corruption wherever he encountered them. He never hesitated to go beyond the bounds of conventionality and morality whenever he thought he could administer a useful spiritual lesson.

In one instance, such a lesson included premeditated murder. Drukpa Kunley thrust a sword into an old woman disciple whose hour of death he judged had come. People who witnessed the incident were understandably outraged and denounced him as a violent murderer. Yet because of his saintly reputation they agreed to his suggestion that they keep the woman's body in cold storage for a week. At the end of the week her son peeped into the room just as the corpse was becoming transformed into a body of light. Now, it can be argued that we are dealing here with only a legend. But what is instructive about this story is that for centuries many Tibetans implicitly believed in the possibility of such a bodily transmutation. Also, the very fact that this sacred murder—a form of euthanasia—is reported by the biographer without further comment suggests that although an eventuality of this type may be extraordinary, it is not considered, at least by Tibetan ecclesiastics, unjustifiable. Other similar stories from Buddhism and Hinduism underscore this conclusion. The underlying assumption, however, is always that the "murderer" is a fully cognizant enlightened adept, whose spiritual motives are beyond doubt.

Drukpa Kunley's avowed aim was "to free the human spirit's divinity from slavery to religious institutions, and moral and ritual conventions, that had originally been designed to support spiritual endeavour."[29] From the viewpoint of Buddhist esotericism, his anarchism was a manifestation of his boundless compassion for his fellow beings, whose spiritual awakening he had at heart. This distinguishes him from that other well-known Tibetan philanderer Aku Tompa (Akhu sTon-pa), "Uncle Tompa," whose lewd exploits are the favorite theme of tavern raconteurs. Whereas Aku Tompa is an entirely fictional character, a projection of conventional sexual fantasies, Drukpa Kunley is recognized by Tibetans as a saintly figure whose enlightenment made him incapable of evil while liberating him from the moral preoccupations of his contemporaries.

## 3. The Zen Masters of China and Japan: Traditional Shock Therapists

When Buddhism arrived in Tibet in the seventh century A.D., it was quickly transformed by the beliefs and practices of the native shamanistic Bön religion. Buddhism underwent a similar transformation in China, largely under the influence of both philosophical and religious Taoism. The Taoist tradition dates back to the sixth century B.C. and represents a development analogous to the gnosis of the Upanishads in India. The classic philosophical-spiritual work on the teachings of the "Way" (*tao*) is the *Tao Te Ching* of Lao Tzu, who is believed to have lived before the third century B.C. The *tao* is both being and nonbeing, the differentiated cosmos and the unqualified essence of the universe. For Lao Tzu, finite existence is cyclic in nature, a notion that is best captured in the polarity of *yin* and *yang*, the feminine and masculine principles.

The *tao* cannot be comprehended by reason but can be responded to only intuitively. Taoism favors an ethics of spontaneity, which is expressed in the ideal of inaction in action (*wu wei*). However, this spontaneity is not mere willfulness; it must be based on an intuitive apprehension of the eternal Reality. The Taoists are wary of the accumulation of knowledge, since knowledge tends to stifle spontaneity. They recommend the approach of becoming progressively ignorant, or unself-conscious. Thus, by stepping beyond the framework of the mind, the spiritual practitioner achieves enlightenment, which consists in identifying with the *tao*. In the enlightened disposition, all thoughts and actions flow naturally and smoothly from the center of one's being. Such spontaneity was, however, often equated with inactivity, and this gave rise to fatalism. By contrast to "philosophical" Taoism, popular "religious" Taoism, which took shape in the third century B.C., has as its avowed goal the attainment of physical immortality. It is thus a form of spiritual alchemy, not unlike Indian *hatha-yoga*, which it appears to have influenced.

So—when Buddhism was introduced into China sometime in the first century A.D., it met with a fertile spiritual and magical environment. To simplify a rather complex process of mutual osmosis, the Chinese learned from the Buddhists the fine art of metaphysical speculation and of controlling the passions through strict moral conduct. The Buddhists, in turn, were inspired by the down-to-earth practicality of the Chinese, and they also learned something about spontaneity. Because of apparent doctrinal and practical similarities, the two traditions were often confused with one another in people's minds, not least the minds of Taoist-Buddhist practitioners themselves. In later periods, however, Buddhism asserted its independence from Taoism and even heartily condemned certain of the latter's magical and shamanistic practices. The Taoists, in turn, started to claim that Lao Tzu went to India and became the Buddha.

Despite these squabbles and various attempts to suppress Buddhism, the Buddhist tradition flourished in China. It was at its height when the Indian monk Bodhidharma arrived in A.D. 520 (or A.D. 526) in the north of China. He is hailed as the founder of the Dhyana or Ch'an school of Chinese Buddhism.[30] Tradition has it that for nine long years Bodhidharma sat determinedly in front of a wall in meditation until he attained enlightenment, but he also lost the use of his legs through gangrene. He is always portrayed with a fierce, glowering look that brooks no nonsense. One of his disciples, it is said, had to cut off an arm before Bodhidharma would even acknowledge his existence. According to a probably more credible source, the disciple lost his arm in an encounter with bandits. Nevertheless, the first version epitomizes the spirit of Bodhidharma's crazy-wisdom approach to enlightenment, which is characteristic of much of Ch'an and its Japanese development—Zen.

For example, the ninth-century Ch'an master I-hsuan, better known as Lin-chi (or Rinzai in Japanese), instructed his disciples to slay everything that stood in their way of enlightenment (*wu*)—including the patriarchs and the Buddha himself. The Lin-chi branch of Ch'an is famous for its spiritual shock therapy. In order to awaken practitioners from the sleep of habituated life, the masters of this branch use a variety of "surprise" methods—including sudden shouting, physical beatings, paradoxical verbal responses, and riddles (called *kung-an* in Chinese or *koan* in Japanese).

Lin-chi was famous for his shouts and liberal use of blows. He himself had been dealt with in the same fashion by his teacher, Huang-po (Obaku in Japanese), who beat him with a staff even before Lin-chi was able to open his mouth. At a loss to understand this persistent and strange treatment, Lin-chi prepared to leave. But then his teacher (*roshi*) sent him to another master, Tai-yu (Daigu in Japanese), and Lin-chi promptly experienced *satori* during their very first encounter. When he returned to Huang-po, his teacher listened carefully to his account of what had happened. Then he observed that he would have to give Tai-yu a good thrashing on his next visit to Huang-po's monastery. To this Lin-chi spontaneously responded, "You needn't wait for Tai-yu to come; you can have a thrashing right this moment!" He gave his teacher a good slap on the shoulder, thus expressing his own illumination. Huang-po asked how Lin-chi dared "play with the tiger's whiskers," to which his pupil responded with a loud "Ho!" Huang-po then called for his attendants to carry the "lunatic" to his cell.

The Japanese Zen master Gutei had the habit of raising one finger in response to any question whatsoever. One day, a visitor asked one of Gutei's disciples to explain his master's essential teaching. In imitation of his master, the young disciple held up one finger. When Gutei heard of the incident, he confronted the young man and swiftly sliced off the disciple's finger. Screaming with pain, the acolyte ran away. Gutei called after him; when the disciple looked back, the master flashed his famous single finger. The young man's mind stopped, and he was suddenly enlightened.

This story combines three shock techniques—a *koan* (the familiar one-finger gesture, which Gutei had learned from his own teacher), an act of physical aggression (the severing of the finger), and the shout that captured the disciple's attention in a moment of extreme mobilization of psychic energy. The inner tension that had undoubtedly built up in the disciple over a prolonged period of time was abruptly released, and his consciousness was catapulted into the state of *satori* (*wu* in Chinese).

In another story, a spiritual seeker, Yun-men, once knocked on Master Mu-chou's door hoping to ask him for instruction. Periodically the adept opened the door, peered at his visitor, and then slammed the door shut again. On the third day, the Yun-men managed to slip into the house before Mu-chou could shut the door. Mu-chou grabbed hold of him and yelled, "Speak, speak!" Yun-men was so surprised that his words stuck in his throat. The adept promptly kicked him out, managing to slam the door on Yun-men's leg so hard that he broke the seeker's shin—and enlightened him in the process.

Such violence tends to alienate Western observers, even though they may be sympathetic toward Eastern traditions. However, the British Buddhist Christmas Humphreys had this to say:

> What can the wise, experienced, deeply compassionate teacher do to help the pupil in the hell of effort which was his own not all that time ago? . . . The violence may do what years of gentle encouragement had failed to do. Again and again, we read of passionate seekers flung out of the monastery itself by a "furious" Roshi, and told to seek Truth elsewhere. The seeker seeks, elsewhere, and years may elapse before he returns, bearing his triumph with him. To complain of the Master's treatment? No, to thank him for the violence which sent him back into the deeps of his own mind. Where encouragement may only sap the will, the fierceness of a Bodhidharma may rouse it to final victory. [31]

In a frank account of his experiences in a Japanese Zen monastery, Janwillem van de Wetering relates the story of a Zen practitioner who was given the koan "Stop the intercity train coming from Tokyo." [32] After many years of failing to solve the riddle, the aspirant jumped on the railroad track one morning and sacrificed his bodily life to the oncoming intercity train. This suicide was almost certainly an act of sheer desperation. However, there is always the remote possibility that, in the split second of the impact, the Zen practitioner actually became illumined.

From the enlightened point of view, the body is only one among myriad forms that no longer bind consciousness. Enlightenment means identification with the undifferentiated transcendental "body," or the dharma-kaya of Buddhism. Is suicide, then, justifiable as a means of achieving spiritual liberation? Certain schools of Jainism seem to think so. And there are numerous stories of adepts who, for various reasons of their own, have decided to die by an act of will. But these were adepts who had achieved a high level of spiritual realization, if not full enlightenment. This means that they had already ceased to identify exclusively with the physical body prior to their "autoeuthanasia." So, they could be certain of their destination after the suicide, which they accomplished by will rather than by any implements. In the case of a desperate aspirant, however, the option of suicide seems not only foolhardy but also a cop-out that can hardly be condoned.

In his book, van de Wetering relates a second story, which portrays holy madness at its wildest. It describes an excessively conceited and cantankerous contemporary Zen student.[33] One morning, when this man was perhaps especially insufferable, his teacher beat him hard with a stick and actually killed him. The incident was reported to the police, but no action was taken against the Zen master because the relationship between master and disciple was considered sacrosanct and subject to different laws. Regardless of whether this story is true or not, the critical question is whether murder is ever justifiable, even if the intention behind it is to enlighten the victim. Although the ancient traditions tend to be ambivalent on this point, most Westerners find brutality and manslaughter unacceptable in the context of spiritual practice.

This extreme case of crazy wisdom is by no means typical of Ch'an or Zen. However, the masters of the "sudden school" are all thoroughly iconoclastic. They flout abstract speculation, pale logic, icons, idols, doctrines, scriptures, gods, and other religious paraphernalia. Lin-chi admonished his disciples not to think of the Buddha as the ultimate Reality but to regard him as the peephole in the latrine. The eighth-century master Tan-hsia burned a statue of the Buddha to keep himself warm, and the adept Te-shan spoke of the Buddha as a "piece of shit."

In his *Dokugo Shingyo*, the Japanese Zen master Hakuin (A.D. 1685–1768) commented on different passages from the sacred canon of Mahayana Buddhism.[34] His commentary is a masterpiece of Zen humor and instructional brinkmanship. For instance, he honors the well-known formula "Form is emptiness, emptiness is form" with these words: "Trash! What a useless collection of junk! Don't be trying to teach apes how to climb trees! These are goods that have been gathering dust on the shelves for two thousand years." On the sentence "O Shariputra, all things are empty appearances," he has this to say: "Like rubbing your eyes to make yourself see flowers in the air. If all things don't exist to begin with, then what do we want with 'empty appearances'? He is defecating and spraying pee all over a clean yard."

The line "No wisdom, no attaining" receives these comments: "Setting up house in the grave again! So many misunderstand these words! A dead man peeping bug-eyed from a coffin. You can shout yourself hoarse at Prince Chang painted there on the paper, you'll not get a peep out of him!" The phrase "His mind is unhindered; as it is unhindered, it knows no fear, and is far removed from all delusive thought" triggers this response in master Hakuin: "Nothing extraordinary about that. Supernatural powers and wondrous activity are just drawing water and carrying fuel. Lifting my head, I see the sun setting over my old home in the west." And on the statement "And reaches final nirvana," he observes: "This is the hole pilgrims all walk into; they fill it up year after year. He's gone off again to flit with the ghosts. It's worse than stinking socks! The upright men of our tribe are not like this; the father conceals for the sake of the son, the son for the sake of the father."

Hakuin was not merely a sour critic or cynic. His iconoclastic commentary has rare depth, and he was indeed a great Zen master, as is borne out by the following story. Once a girl in his neighborhood got pregnant; pushed for a confession by her parents, she named the saintly Hakuin as the father of the unborn child. Outraged, the parents confronted Hakuin, whose only comment was, "Is that so?" When the child was born, it was handed over to him, and the now much-maligned adept took great care of it. A year later, the girl finally confessed the truth. Greatly ashamed, the parents returned to Hakuin to beg his forgiveness. Handing the child back to them, he laconically said, "Is that so?"

Suiwo, a gifted disciple of Hakuin, once gave a visiting student the famous *koan* "Hear the sound of one hand clapping." After three years of trying desperately to solve this *koan*, the student appeared tearfully before Suiwo and asked to be released so that he could return to his home province in shame. Suiwo talked him into staying for another week, and another, and another. The student was unable to break through, however, and wanted to leave. Finally, Suiwo asked him to meditate for only three more days, but added that if he failed to solve the *koan* at the end of this period, he should kill himself. The student's illumination occurred on the second day.

Stories like this have been collected by the hundreds over the centuries. Each can be understood from various points of view, but there is one overwhelming message from all of them: that Ch'an, or Zen, is utterly this-worldly, down-to-earth, direct and practical. As D. T. Suzuki, scholar and Zen master, noted:

> What Zen dislikes most is mediation, deliberation, wordiness, and the weighing of advantages. Immediacy is impossible as long as we are onlookers, contemplators, critics, idea-mongers, word-manipulators, dualists, or monists. All these faults are corrected and Zen is revealed when we abandon our so-called common-sense or logical attitude and effect a complete about-face, when we plunge right into the working of things as they move on before and behind our senses. It is only when this experience takes place that we can talk intelligently about Zen-consciousness from which the Zen-incidents or Zen-dialogues making up the annals of Zen are produced.[35]

Irrationality, or more accurately, transrationality and this-worldly spontaneity are hallmarks of Ch'an or Zen. But the most characteristic symbol of this tradition of "sudden" enlightenment is laughter—the laughter that prevails when all "golden calves" of the mind have been melted down, when the personality has been stripped of all its pretenses—worldly and otherworldly. This is the laughter of liberation, the laughter of the being who has recovered authenticity, or innate buddhahood. It is the kind of laughter that shook the belly of madcap Han Shan, who was too eccentric for the monasteries of his time and was thrown out by the monks more than once. Han Shan ("Cold Mountain"), who is thought to have lived from A.D. 627 to 749, came to be venerated as an incarnation of Manjushri, a transcendental *bodhisattva* who symbolizes unsurpassable wisdom.

According to Zen mythology, the "secret transmission outside the scriptures" commenced with Gautama the Buddha himself. During one congregation of his order, he silently held up a golden flower; of all the assembled monks, Kashyapa alone broke into a smile. The teaching had been transmitted from heart to heart, and Kashyapa had become enlightened through the Buddha's simple gesture.

The future Buddha Maitreya, prophesied in Mahayana Buddhism, underwent an interesting metamorphosis in China. He became Mi-lo-fo, the Laughing Buddha. He can be found in most Chinese Buddhist temples as a potbellied figure with jovial features. He is popularly regarded as a god of luck. However, his original significance goes far deeper, as was made clear by M. Conrad Hyers in his path-breaking book *Zen and the Comic Spirit*:

> At every level of manifestation, humour spells freedom in some sense and to some degree. Humour *means* freedom. This is one of its most distinctive characteristics and virtues. Here, however, the freedom to laugh which moves within the conflicts and doubts and tensions of life— the freedom, therefore, which is still relative to bondage and ignorance—becomes the freedom to laugh on the other side (the *inside*) of enlightenment. He who is no longer in bondage to desire, or to the self, or the law, he who is no longer torn apart by alienation and anxiety, and who is no longer defined and determined primarily by seriousness, can now laugh with the laughter of little children and great sages.[36]

In the context of spiritual practice, laughter is a sign not of gleefulness but of victory over the shadow side of the human psyche. The fierce expression on Bodhidharma's face is a put-on. Behind it lurks a gargantuan smile. Only the aspirant, who is perpetually troubled, takes everything seriously. For him or her, the Buddha's or the teacher's belly laugh is a puzzle, an affront, something to be envious about—in short, a problem. He or she has not yet tasted the "madness" of enlightenment, which has "ravaged" the brains of the great masters of the Ch'an or Zen tradition. The seeker still experiences life as a tragic event, but the Buddha's laughter and Kashyapa's smile are a signal that, in the end, all is well with life and death. The crazy-wisdom methods of Zen are designed to make that point over and over again.

# 3

## THE FEATS AND FOIBLES OF CONTEMPORARY CRAZY-WISDOM ADEPTS: FROM RASCAL GURUS TO SPIRITUAL CLOWNS

### 1. Gurdjieff: The Rascal Guru

All great men remain enigmatic to some degree. The controversial Russian teacher Georgei Ivanovitch Gurdjieff had a special gift for cultivating his own mystique. Next to nothing is known about his early years. Whatever autobiographical information he proffered may or may not have been subject to his considerable penchant for confabulation and contradiction. The reports about his later years show an individual with astonishingly chameleonlike qualities, who delighted in wearing different guises. A disciple of his, editor Gorham Munson, recollected:

> His humour was Rabelaisian, the roles he played were dramatic and the impact he made on all who came near him was staggering. Sentimentalists expected to find in him the pale figure of Christ as portrayed in literature; they went away swearing that he was nothing but a practitioner of black magic. Some among the unbelievers are asking themselves still if he didn't know more about Relativity than Einstein.[1]

It appears that Gurdjieff was born at Alexandropol, near the border between Russia and Iran, perhaps in 1877. He left his village at a young age and traveled in the Middle and Far East for the next twenty or twenty-five years, in search of higher knowledge. He wrote about this odyssey in his book *Meetings with Remarkable Men*, although the work is more parable than autobiography. According to one of his disciples, Rom Landau, Gurdjieff did indeed live in Tibet for many years—as a tutor to the Dalai Lama and as the chief secret agent for Russia.

In 1914, Gurdjieff returned to Russia, looking for suitable disciples among the intelligentsia of Moscow and St. Petersburg. Shortly thereafter he started a small esoteric school, the Institute for the Harmonious Development of

Man. Because of the Russian Revolution, the school was finally relocated in 1922 at a chateau near Fontainebleau, France, under the protection of the eminent French mathematician Jules Henri Poincaré. The "strange man" from Russia quickly attracted well-known students from Europe and the United States. Among them were architect Frank Lloyd Wright, painter Georgia O'Keeffe, author J. P. Priestley, physiologist Moshe Feldenkreis, physicist John G. Bennett (a student also of Einstein), the British literary critic A. R. Orage, and the eminent writers Aldous Huxley and Arthur Koestler. And then there was journalist P. D. Ouspensky, whose role vis-à-vis Gurdjieff has been compared to that of Plato.[2]

However, Gurdjieff's popularity in intellectual circles was also tied up with scandal. In 1924, the death of writer Katherine Mansfield at the chateau started a wildfire of rumors about the bizarre and dangerous goings-on in the Gurdjieff group. Gurdjieff's work continued to thrive, regardless. He took the occasion of public flurry over Mansfield's untimely demise, which was due to consumption, to visit America, where he was quite successful.

After Gurdjieff survived a terrible motor accident in 1934, his work entered a new, more public phase. A growing number of members were recruited, and their training was undertaken by instructors, with minimal supervision by the master himself. He also allowed the publication of some of his writings. Louis Pauwels, best known as the coauthor of *Dawn of Magic*, observed about that period:

> He scattered his secrets to the wind and went so far as to choose confusion; he allowed the good and the bad to run their course together, with an increasing contempt for the consequences and a deliberate bias towards the negative side of his work. Nietzsche said: "I must put up a fence around my doctrine to keep out the swine." Innocent words! Gurdjieff, with a laugh louder than Zarathustra's, pulled down the fence in order that, in his domain at least, the confusions and misunderstandings of his time should reach their climax.[3]

When Gurdjieff died, in 1949, he calmly stated to the disciples gathered around his deathbed, "I am leaving you in a fine mess." To create chaos and turmoil in his disciples seems to have been a central aspect of his teaching. Another disciple epitomized this by speaking of Gurdjieff as God Shiva—the destroyer in the Hindu trinity. Gurdjieff would make frequent use of shock tactics in order to interrupt habit patterns in his disciples. A smoker would be deprived of cigarettes; a fastidious teetotaler would be asked to consume alcohol; a strict vegetarian would be fed hefty meat dishes; an intellectual would be sent to clean out the stables or toilets; a proud student would frequently meet with a barrage of abuse, and so on. All of his immediate disciples were expected to live rather spartan lives, constantly being pushed and pulled to work harder, sleep less, and give more of themselves. He had his students dig trenches one day, only to order them filled the next. To visitors, the chateau gave the appearance of a work camp.

The two communal meals every day tended to be particularly trying, if also amusing, for both disciples and unprepared guests, because Gurdjieff would ritually lavish on them not only food and drink but also his own special brand of humor. His humor involved not only the systematic ridiculing of the ego personalities present but also the paying of compliments to spiritual practitioners who had the courage to face themselves and work out their destiny in a conscious fashion. He would typically offer toasts to all the "idiots" with whom he was sharing the meal. According to his "Science of Idiotism," everyone who took up the task of working on himself or herself was an idiot, in the ancient sense of truly being oneself and thus of looking mad to all others. Fritz Peters, who had fond memories of Gurdjieff from when Peters was a young boy, made these pertinent comments:

> His sense of humor was often very subtle, in an oriental sense, but also had a broad, crude side, and he was a very sensual man.
>
> He manifested this side of himself particularly when he was alone with the men and boys—in the Turkish bath or, during the summer, at the swimming pool . . . When everyone had stripped, Gurdjieff would, inevitably, begin to joke about their bodies, their sexual prowess, their various physical habits. The jokes were usually what would be called "dirty" or at least "lewd" and he found all such stories highly amusing, whether he told them or whether they were told by the other men who were quick to join the spirit of such joking. One of his favourite amusements or diversions at the swimming pool was to line all the men up facing in one direction and then compare their sunburns. This became the ritual of what Gurdjieff called the "white ass" club . . . He would then make us all turn around and make additional comments on the size and variety of male genitalia exposed to him.[4]

There have been rumors of Gurdjieff's sexual escapades with some women disciples. While these stories may or may not be true, John G. Bennett had this to say in his autobiography:

> I was especially bewildered and even outraged by all that Gurdjieff said in public, and advised me in private, about the subject of sex. He spoke of women in terms that would have better suited a fanatical Muslim polygamist than a Christian: boasting that he had many children by different women, and that women were for him only means to an end. The general impression that Gurdjieff produced shocked those accustomed to regard the sex relation as sacred—even if their private behaviour might be anything but sacred. Gurdjieff always showed the worst outwards and kept the best hidden.
>
> Sometimes young women would come to Paris to visit him. He would then flirt outrageously with them, and invite them to come back to the flat late at night when everyone had gone. Often thinking that this was

some kind of mysterious test, or just frankly curious, they would go. In all cases that I heard of, Gurdjieff would open the door, look astonished and say: "Why you come now?" give them a handful of sweets and send them away. It was, however, inevitable that the worst interpretation should be placed on his actions . . . Nevertheless, I am bound to say that the advice that he gave older men and women resulted in many irregular relationships being formed. The whole atmosphere among those who surrounded Gurdjieff was impregnated with a feverish excitement that made it hard to tell what was right and what was wrong.[5]

Rom Landau recollected the following noteworthy incident, which illustrates that Gurdjieff was certainly not above playing with fire. The incident occurred in a restaurant. Landau, who was shortly to have his first meeting with Gurdjieff, was dining with a lady friend. The conversation inevitably turned to the master, who happened to be seated at a nearby table. Landau pointed him out to her. Gurdjieff noticed their glances and all of a sudden began to breathe in a peculiar way. Landau's friend turned pale but recovered momentarily. When Landau asked her whether she was all right, in reply she whispered to him that the moment Monsieur Gurdjieff had caught her eyes, she felt as if something had struck right through her sexual center. She warned him to be careful.[6]

Visitors to the chateau described the disciples as terrified and dumbstruck in front of their teacher. Understandably, the pupils did not want to attract his attention, lest they should be saddled with insults and further tests and responsibilities. A number of outside observers and ex-disciples also noted the rather solemn and even dour demeanor of Gurdjieff's disciples—a trait that is not uncommon in other converts to gurucentric cults.

These crazy-wise treatments were meant to break down personal limitations and free the disciple's attention for the spiritual process, which consisted in acute self-observation and harmonization of the personality through a series of disciplines, including exercises and dancing. When the personality—which Gurdjieff treated as a machine—was thus put in order, it became capable of further evolution. Alas, it appears that the harmony promised by the master was not realized by his disciples. Paul Serant, an ex-disciple and author of the novel *Ritual Murder*, explained:

It is evident that if one holds the view that all men are machines, but that one is oneself beginning to be no longer a machine, a dangerous temptation arises: if others are machines, why not use them as such? Duplicity then becomes a quite legitimate means to an even keener consciousness of self.

It is then that a kind of spiritual inversion takes place that is infinitely more dangerous than *immorality acknowledged as such*.[7]

Gurdjieff was an imposing, fascinating, and powerful personality, with leanings toward Oriental despotism and, some claim, a touch of self-aggrandizement. He inspired a certain awe even in those who were otherwise immune to his charisma and mystagogy. When asked whether there was a God, Gurdjieff replied, "Yes, and Gurdjieff's relationship with him is that of a somewhat independent, obstinate and touchy minister with his King."[8]

How much of Gurdjieff's changeable style of self-presentation was integral to his character and how much was role-playing is difficult to say. Kenneth Walker, a well-known surgeon, described the way Gurdjieff was able to manifest terrible anger one moment, only to resume a conversation quite normally the next. Walker commented:

> I am convinced that Gurdjieff followed the dictates of his conscience and that when he sinned he sinned only against the moral code which 'has the unique property which belongs to the being bearing the name of chameleon'. When he offended conventional morality he did so openly for no person cared less for his own reputation than he . . . As I looked at him for the last time and thought of all he had achieved in the course of his long life and how much I owed him, the oddities in his behaviour which in the past had puzzled and even troubled me were forgotten.[9]

Bhagwan Rajneesh (Osho), to whom we will turn shortly, once remarked approvingly about Gurdjieff's angry outbursts:

> When Gurdjieff gets angry it is beautiful. When you get angry it is ugly. Anger is neither ugly nor beautiful. When Jesus gets angry it is sheer music—even anger. When Jesus takes a whip in the temple and chases the traders out of the temple, there is a subtle beauty to it. Even Buddha lacks that beauty; Buddha seems to be one-sided.[10]

Gurdjieff was a man of immense willpower, and he sought to instill the same virtue in his disciples. His teaching offered a path to God that was paved with hard work, endless self-exertion, astute self-knowledge, submission to the teacher, and the cultivation of powers, or what in India are called *siddhis*. It included, however, very little compassion or love.

Psychologist Charles Tart has hailed Gurdjieff as a genius, adding that "if he were alive today, I would try to accept him as a teacher (I know I would have many personality clashes!) and want to study in a group under his direction."[11] Judging from what we know of Gurdjieff, he did not tolerate personality clashes but expected complete obedience and surrender from his disciples. How long, one wonders, would Tart's neatly rational approach have held up under the onslaught of a guru like Gurdjieff? Curiously, Tart warns others against joining cults, including Gurdjieff groups, that invest a great deal of power in a charismatic leader—as if Gurdjieff himself and his circle of disciples had escaped this particular fate. Tart recommends that, ideally, one should seek out a teacher who is "completely awake," representing the highest stage of human evolution. The question is whether Georgei Ivanovitch Gurdjieff was such a teacher. Regardless of our answer, we may conclude, in the words of Claudio Naranjo, that "Gurdjieff's place in the world of spiritual teachings and teachers is mysterious, intriguing and definitely very important."[12]

## 2. Aleister Crowley: The Mad Magus

Aleister Crowley, a contemporary of Gurdjieff, was just as much an eccentric. However, unlike Gurdjieff, Crowley's eccentricities caused such an uproar that negative media attention overshadowed his genuine magical as well as spiritual experiments. Yet he was more influential during his lifetime than Gurdjieff, whose fame started to spread only after his death. He certainly belonged with the most advanced magi to emerge in the West—with occultists like Giuseppe Balsamo (Count Cagliostro) and Count Saint-Germain in the eighteenth century, and Eliphas Levi and Madame Blavatsky in the nineteenth century.

The reasons for Crowley's notoriety were undoubtedly his voracious, promiscuous sexuality, his liberal advocacy of drugs, and his declared antinomian (Tantra-like) philosophy. The news media and some biographers made him out be a depraved monster—an image he seems to have encouraged. The Swiss writer Henri Birven said of Crowley, "The life of this 'magus' is a tragicomedy of great proportions, which can only be appreciated by very few connoisseurs."[13]

Israel Regardie, who served as Crowley's secretary for several years, until 1934, offered a different verdict, however, despite the fact that he too broke with his mentor, as did all who valued their health and sanity. According to him, Crowley "had considerable greatness as a teacher and writer. . . . If I had to describe him in only one phrase, I'd say he was a Victorian hippie."[14] This characterization romanticizes Crowley's far more aggressive antinomianism. He was not merely a dropout who turned himself on through drugs (although he did that as well) but also an often ruthless power seeker who succeeded in wrecking more than one life.

Crowley was born in 1875, in the year of Eliphas Levi's death. He later came to consider himself a reincarnation of Levi, and also of Count Cagliostro before him—both truly outstanding magi in the history of Western occultism. He was brought up as one of the Plymouth Brethren, a Christian fundamentalist sect founded in 1830. By the age of eleven, he had succumbed to his fascination with the dark powers. It was his outraged mother who first called him "the Beast," an appellation he unhesitatingly adopted. He, in turn, regarded his mother as a "brainless bigot."

> In a way, my mother was insane, in the sense that all people are who have watertight compartments to the brain, and hold with equal passion incompatible ideas, and hold them apart lest their meeting should destroy both.[15]

As an undergraduate at Trinity College, Cambridge, the highly gifted Crowley started to write poetry and erotica but did not bother to sit for a degree. Having independent means made it easy for him to pursue his personal interests. He thought himself superior as a poet (and no doubt as a man) to W. B. Yeats, one of the leading figures in the Order of the Golden Dawn, which Crowley, in due course, would join, influence, throw into confusion, and leave.

In 1897, Crowley had a spiritual experience that revealed to him the futility of all ordinary human aspiration and endeavor, and it created in him a desire to work on something more permanent. He continued to write and publish literary works and excelled in climbing mountains around the world, but he also began to make a name for himself with his Faustian spiritual explorations. In 1898, Crowley joined the Hermetic Order of the Golden Dawn, which had been founded ten years before, and quickly rose to a high rank. He was personally tutored by Allan Bennett (alias Iehi Aour), whose fame in occult circles matched that of MacGregor Mathers, the head of the order. As the Golden Dawn was only the outer order of the Great White Brotherhood, Crowley aspired to much more. In March 1904, while on a visit to Cairo, he received from his invoked guardian angel Aiwas, over a period of three days, *The Book of the Law* (*Liber Legis*), which was to change the rest of his life. Colin Wilson, who has written a highly readable account of Crowley's life, remarks:

> Another commentator on Crowley, Jean Overton Fuller, suggests that Aiwas was actually some demonic entity sent to tempt Crowley, and points out that the voice came from over Crowley's *left* shoulder—the left-hand path being the path of black magic. But it seems just as likely that Aiwas was the voice of Crowley's own unconscious mind (a suspicion reinforced by Aiwas's use of *'pari passu'*—not a phrase one would expect from an ancient Sumerian deity).[16]

Crowley saw in the publication of this book the purpose of his entire life: The book brought him, and everyone else, a new ethic, expressed in the maxim "Do what thou wilt shall be the whole of the Law." This has frequently been misinterpreted to mean "Do as you wish." But the commandment is more in keeping with the Hindu injunction, as epitomized in the teachings of the *Bhagavad-Gita*: "Follow your inner law (*sva-dharma*) and inner nature (*sva-bhava*)."[17]

Crowley noted that he was at first "bitterly opposed to the principles of the Book on almost every point of morality."[18] Gradually he began to appreciate this revealed piece of esoteric knowledge as a guide not only to spiritual evolution but also to practical politics. Every human individual has a right to fulfill his specific purpose in life. For Crowley, this ideal embodied the acme of democracy. In this new morality, which debunks all convention, the individual reigns supreme. "In the New Aeon, each man will be a king," declared Crowley prophetically.[19] He realized that the biggest battle to be fought in this war of true individualism would be over sex, and he wrote with untrammeled optimism:

> Mankind must learn that the sexual instinct is in its true nature ennobling. The shocking evils which we all deplore are principally due to the perversions produced by suppressions. The feeling that it is shameful and the sense of sin cause concealment, which is ignoble, and internal conflict, which creates distortion, neurosis, and ends in explosion. We deliberately produce an abscess, and wonder why it is full of pus, why it hurts, why it bursts in stench and corruption. When other physical appetites are treated in this way, we find the same phenomenon. Persuade a man that hunger is wicked, prevent him satisfying it by eating whatever food suits him best, and he soon becomes a crazy and dangerous brute. Murder, robbery, sedition and meaner crimes come of the suppression of the bodily need of nourishment.
>
> The Book of Law solves the sexual problem completely. Each individual has an absolute right to satisfy his sexual instinct as is physiologically proper for him. The one injunction is to treat all such acts as sacraments. One should not eat as the brutes, but in order to enable one to do one's will. The same applies to sex. We must use every faculty to further the one object of our existence.
>
> The sexual instinct thus freed from its bonds will no more be liable to assume monstrous shapes. Perversion will become as rare as the freaks in a dime museum.[20]

Pursuing his own inner law, Crowley broke away from the Golden Dawn in 1906. After founding his own order of the Silver Star (Argenteum Astrum) a year later, he delved heavily into sexual magic, which included anal homosexual intercourse. In 1914, he journeyed to the United States, where he spent the next five years, before returning to Europe in 1919. At the "Sacred Abbey of Thelema," an ashram-type school in an isolated village in Sicily, he endeavored, with a group of disciples, to translate the philosophy of the *Liber Legis* into action. Orgies were an integral part of the daily ritual. Crowley kept a changing harem, whose members could be relied upon to do his every bidding in the sexual magic he designed. They took drugs without regard for their physical and mental well-being, and several disciples went mad. One died, possibly of food poisoning rather than magic.

In 1921, by which time Crowley was penniless and stranded with two mistresses and several children, he achieved, by his own testimony, the highest initiatic level—that of Ipsissimus, the adept beyond good and evil. As he claims in his autobiography, he "crossed the Abyss," or rather was unwittingly hurled into it, uniting his individual awareness with the cosmic Mind.[21] In the opinion of most occultists, the magus had in fact failed to accomplish this, and his self-delusion and hubris set the stage for his subsequent spiritual tumble. Crowley himself was prudent enough not to publicize his "deification," and his claims remained a secret until his complete autobiography appeared posthumously, many decades later.

Crowley was aware that the police had been keeping watch on him since 1907. Some of his followers' houses were raided. He was harassed and detained abroad and evicted from various countries. By the early 1920s, the news media had stereotyped him as "the wickedest man in the world." Expelled from Mussolini's Italy in 1923, he wandered about, hoping for disciples and trying to shake his heroin addiction. He saw himself as the messiah of the new age, bringing a new religion to replace what he deemed a defunct and intolerably repressive Christianity.

Crowley's Rabelaisian brinkmanship was extraordinary in the context of European society, which, unlike Indian society, has no acknowledged models for "spiritual" dropouts, especially not for sexually oriented adepts. The inherited image of the guiding spiritual master of Christendom, Jesus of Nazareth, is an entirely desexualized one. Few Christians ever wonder whether Jesus was married or sexually active, or why the Bible is silent on this point. Christ's image, which is essentially antisexual, tends to be applied to all who wear the mantle of spiritual teacher. If they are found wanting, as in the case of Crowley, their authenticity is immediately called into question.

Crowley, in turn, despised Christianity for its antisexual bias. He apparently had an insatiable sexual appetite and in his memoirs confesses that even short periods of sexual abstinence would give him a headache and curtail his creative energies. Writing about his days at the University of Cambridge, he remarked:

> My sexual life was very intense. My relations with women were entirely satisfactory. They gave me the maximum of bodily enjoyment and at the same time symbolized my theological notions of sin. Love was a challenge to Christianity. It was a degradation and a damnation. Swinburne had taught me the doctrine of justification by sin. Every woman that I met enabled me to affirm magically that I had defied the tyranny of the Plymouth Brethren and the Evangelicals. At the same time women were the source of romantic inspiration; and their caresses emancipated me from the thraldom of the body. When I left them I found myself walking upon air, with my soul free to wing its way through endless empyreans and to express its godhead in untrammelled thought of transcendent sublimity, expressed in language which combined the purest aspirations with the most majestic melodies. [22]

Crowley was an adept of what in India would be called *vama-acara*, or left-hand Tantrism. His magical approach revolved around the manipulation of the sexual energies in order to achieve altered states of consciousness. There was something daring but also something desperate about him. Sex and power proved his big stumbling blocks. This failure is a recurrent theme in the history of Eastern and Western adepts.

Crowley lived at the brink of madness, daring to walk where angels fear to tread, unleashing enormous creative *and* destructive forces in and around himself. His charisma was great, as was his ego. His life story graphically illustrates the failure and jeopardy of an individual who succeeds in unlocking the gates to the hidden dimension of existence without first having become grounded in such universal values as love and compassion. He had all the drive of a Doctor Faustus but lacked the *bodhisattva* impulse, and hence was destined to fall. The higher realizations of spiritual life cannot be coerced; rather, they presuppose the shedding of the power motive. The great *siddhi* of enlightenment emerges only when the hankering after the many *siddhis*, or psychic abilities, of the lesser *yogin* has been eclipsed. Crowley's life is crazy wisdom gone awry. Dramatic in its ultimate miscarriage, it can serve as a useful yardstick against which to measure the relative success or failure of other crazy-wise adepts.

This intrepid, if ultimately misguided, explorer of the inner world died a recluse and a heroin addict in England in 1947, at the age of seventy-two. In the 1960s, the LSD-hooked countercultural movement rediscovered Crowley, and his successors succeeded in recruiting new members after a long period of stagnancy. His work has also influenced contemporary witchcraft groups. Another descendant of Crowley's movement is the Church of Satan, founded in San Francisco in 1966, which claimed a membership of some 25,000 people in the mid-1970s, though it probably ran no higher than a few hundred. In the spirit of Crowley, the church celebrates self-centered individualism.

### 3. Bhagwan Rajneesh (Osho): The God-Man of Subterfuge

Bhagwan ("Lord") Rajneesh was born Rajneesh Chandra Mohan in 1931 in a small village near Jabalpur, India, and died in his homeland in 1990.[23] The eldest in a family of seven brothers and five sisters, he was brought up by his wealthy maternal grandparents, who spoiled him. His religion at birth was Jainism.

His grandfather's death left Rajneesh devastated, and he became a loner, shying away from intimate contact. Later he would make this telling admission, "I have never been initiated as a member of society—I have remained an individual, aloof."[24]

Rajneesh claimed to have had his first experience of ecstatic consciousness (*samadhi*) at the age of seven. He also stated that his full enlightenment occurred in 1953, when he was only twenty-one, on the day of the spring equinox. After that "explosion," as he referred to it, he was not in his body. "I am hovering around the body," he explained many years later. "Each moment I am surprised: I am still here? I should not be. I should have left any moment, but still I am here."[25]

This event did not, however, interrupt his academic career. He attended Saugar University and took a master's degree in philosophy in 1957. Subsequently he taught philosophy for nine years, resigning his professorship only in 1967 in order to devote himself solely to the ideal of regenerating humanity's spiritual life. During a lecture series at the Bharatiya Vidya Bhavan in Bombay, Rajneesh announced to a shocked audience steeped in Hindu puritanism that sex was natural and divine. It was here that the seed for the opposition to his teaching work in India was planted. A year later, Rajneesh made himself still more unpopular when he launched a spirited attack on the saintly figure of Mahatma Gandhi, whose centenary year was being celebrated. He referred to Gandhi as a masochist, a Hindu chauvinist, and a pervert, the latter referring to one of Gandhi's quirkier habits: having naked girls sleep next to him to test and prove his sexual continence.

After a period of traveling, Rajneesh settled down with a small cadre of spiritual seekers. Most of them had been recruited from India itself, with only a few Westerners taking the vow of renunciation (*samnyasa*). In 1971, Rajneesh began to call himself "Bhagwan"—the incarnate God. A new phase in his teaching work began in 1974 after he moved to the newly built school in Poona. By 1979, the thriving ashram had about 200 permanent residents, the overriding majority of whom were foreigners. But the ashram also had its share of difficulties, not the least of which was overcrowding. In 1978, the Rajneesh Foundation in India attempted to purchase a small valley to relocate some of the Poona renunciates, but the Indian government blocked the purchase. A year later, the foundation rented a sixteenth-century castle in the same region that could accommodate 250 disciples. The 3,000-foot pipeline they built to supply the castle with water led to local protest. The owners of the castle asked them to vacate the property, whereupon representatives of the foundation threatened violence, including blowing up the castle.

In 1981, Rajneesh announced that his work was now entering its ultimate stage and that henceforth, after giving hundreds of talks, he would observe silence. This development coincided with his secret move to the United States. He entered that country, which he had previously dismissed as "the home of charlatans and false gurus," on a visitor's visa, but with the intention of making America his new home. To secure residency, he married a Greek millionaire's daughter, who was a U.S. citizen.

The foundation acquired a 64,000-acre farm near Antelope, Oregon, which was at that time a village of forty people. Plans for the furtive construction of a city, "Rajneeshpuram," were set in motion and aggressively pursued. Some $120 million was poured into this gargantuan project. Soon the new ashram housed about 300 residents, but the guru's utopian vision was of an incorporated city of 50,000 *samnyasins* (or *sannyasins*) who would change the world. The ashram's ambitions in local politics combined with an increasingly blunt militaristic demeanor and certain criminal activities finally led to investigations by police, the FBI, and immigration officials.

In 1984, Rajneesh broke his vow of silence and resumed his frequent talks to devotees. But something had changed. One commentator described it thus:

> Bhagwan's face lost its balance and luminosity, his eyes lost their timelessness and depth, his discourses (when he began them again) lost their fire, originality, and grace, and his creation of Rajneeshism lost him all those who had loved him for his once eloquent disregard for all "ism's." An absurd number of Rolls Royces were bought for him . . . armed guards appeared, paranoia accelerated, work became known as "worship," . . . and Bhagwan, looking more and more drugged, appeared to be oblivious to it all.[26]

A year later, he began accusing his right hand and chief executive Ma Anand Sheela and "her gang" of a wide range of crimes. The accusations included attempted murder. He denied any knowledge of, and rejected all responsibility for, Sheela's numerous wrongdoings. On September 16, he declared the end of "Rajneeshism," leaving thousands of followers disoriented and disappointed; this was the same man who, only a few years earlier, had stepped off the airplane and proudly declared, "I am the Messiah America has been waiting for."

Sheela fled to Switzerland, where she was later arrested and sentenced for attempted murder, assault, arson, and wiretapping. Rajneesh himself was briefly jailed, given a ten-year suspended sentence, and finally expelled from the United States. Immediately after the court hearing, during which Rajneesh told the judge that he never wanted to return to America, he left for India, where he died in January of 1990.

What had gone wrong? Any answer to this question must take into account the immense complexity of the situation. First, there are the contradictions within Rajneesh's own life to be reckoned with: Here we have a guru who, by his own admission, was not in his body; who declared that he did not wish to create followers, yet for years served as the spiritual head of thousands of men and women, demanding their exclusive devotion; who presented himself as a renunciate but hated having photographs taken because of his baldness; who favored the rich and influential and encouraged the acquisition of a fleet of 93 Rolls Royces; who claimed to be fully enlightened yet felt the need to regularly use nitrous oxide and compulsively watch videos to dispel his boredom; and who permitted a group of power-hungry women to run his large organization and his own life.

Then there is Rajneesh's avowed antinomian philosophy and moral anarchism, based on Tantrism and epitomized in the following quotes from his works:

> Morality is a false coin, it deceives people, it is not religion at all.[27]

> You may have murdered, you may have been a thief, a robber, you may have been a Hitler, a Ghenghis Khan, or somebody, the worst possible,

but that doesn't make any difference. Once you remember yourself, the light is there and the whole past disappears immediately. [28]

Even sin is beautiful, because sin gives depth to your saintliness. [29]

A man of real understanding is neither good nor bad, he understands both. And in that very understanding he transcends both. [30]

You need lies just like children need toys . . . And if there is compassion, the person who has deep compassion is not going to be bothered whether he tells a lie or the truth . . . All Buddhas have lied. They have to because they are so compassionate . . . The whole truth will be too much. [31]

It is hard to believe that Rajneesh, although he claimed ignorance, did not know anything about Sheela's machinations—especially considering the fact that the ashram was armed to the teeth with submachine guns and that Sheela herself had started to wear firearms openly—or that many of his *samnyasins* were smuggling drugs and engaging in prostitution in order to finance his expensive tastes and imperial dreams. More likely, in keeping with his own antinomian philosophy, combined with a curious personal indifference, he simply allowed events to take their course. "Don't accept, don't reject," as he would say. Then, when the tornado finally caught up with him, he expressed his indignation and, to all appearances, became depressed and embittered over what had happened.

Another factor responsible for the fiasco in Oregon was unquestionably Rajneesh's own authoritarian treatment of devotees. In his Indian days, Rajneesh was a voracious reader, and he is known to have devoured all of Gurdjieff's and Ouspensky's books. In fact, Gurdjieff seems to have served him as a kind of role model in his interaction with devotees. He periodically turned his own ashram into a labor camp with incessant demands for further effort and greater submission, leaving many devotees exhausted, sick, weary, and unable to make sound judgments. A disturbing number of them committed suicide. Numerous others were wondering just where it was all going to lead. One ex-devotee stated:

As we later discovered, Bhagwan was continuously experimenting on us by first starving and then feasting us. Teertha [a prominent institutional figure in the Rajneesh organization] explained how the hardships we were enduring were character building, and constituted trial by ordeal. Surrender to our master in all things was being tested, and the weakest would naturally not be able to stand it. [32]

Like so many gurus past and present, Rajneesh demanded that his devotees turn themselves over to him completely, vanquishing all doubt.

If the disciple is so receptive that he has no mind of his own—he does not judge whether it is right or wrong, he has *no* mind of his own, he has surrendered his mind to the Master, he is simply a receptivity, an emptiness, ready to welcome whatsoever is given unconditionally—then words and symbols are not needed, then something can be given.[33]

I am here and I am trying to talk to you, but that is secondary. The basic thing is that if you are open I can pour myself into you . . . and unless you taste me, you will not be able to understand what I am saying.[34]

When one devotee expressed his fears about being turned into a zombie, Rajneesh readily agreed that devotees had to become perfect zombies so that they would be open to his spiritual transmission. In Rajneesh's own words:

You become idiotic. You look like an idiot! People will say that you have become hypnotized or something, that you are no longer your old self. That is true; but it is a kind of shock. And good, because it will destroy the past . . . That is the whole meaning of sannyas [renunciation] and discipleship: that your past has been completely washed away—your memory, your ego, your identity—all has to go.[35]

After the collapse of Rajneesh's religious empire, many *samnyasins* found themselves in a deep psychic crisis, realizing that they had lived like automatons. As Hugh Milne, an ex-Rajneeshee, admits, "The guru-discipleship . . . is not an easy addiction to kick."[36] He goes on:

When I cut myself off from Bhagwan's energy source I found it very difficult to become part of the ordinary world again. I had lost the support of an enormous world-wide family, and there was precious little to replace it with.[37]

Discipleship in *guru-yoga* involves a profound emotional bonding with the teacher. When this bond is broken, for whatever reason, the result can be disastrous for the disciple, often requiring a prolonged period of readjustment to ordinary life and perhaps even outside help. The matter is complicated when, as is typical, the disciple is emotionally immature and has been unable to go beyond the childish image of the guru as father figure. Then again, from a spiritual point of view, any crisis is to be welcomed, since it intensifies the seeker's desire to transcend his or her neurosis.

To Rajneesh, as for Da Love-Ananda and many other spiritual teachers, the ordinary individual was essentially neurotic. Neurosis is the end product of the socialization and education process that is the fulcrum of civilization. As Rajneesh observed, the ordinary individual cannot be at ease; he or she is always self-divided. "The hell is always there," he remarked pithily.[38] The whole point of the spiritual process is to extricate us from that experience of hell, by making us whole.

But in order to become whole, the spiritual seeker must pass through his or her own private hell or, as Carl Gustav Jung would say, he or she must encounter the unconscious, the shadow. This is a frightening and potentially dangerous event, because it brings the seeker close to the threshold of insanity. But to live dangerously was Rajneesh's definition of a *samnyasin*. Praising the work of the maverick psychiatrist R. D. Laing, Rajneesh observed, "Those who repress their neurosis become more and more neurotic, while those who express it consciously get rid of it. So unless you become 'consciously insane,' you can never become sane."[39]

Elsewhere Rajneesh remarked:

> Watch a madman, because a madman has fallen out of the society. Society means the fixed world of roles, games. A madman is mad because he has no fixed role now, he has fallen out: he is the perfect drop-out. A sage is also a perfect drop-out in a different dimension. He is not mad; in fact he is the only possibility of pure sanity. But the whole world is mad, fixed—that's why a sage also looks mad. Watch a madman: that is the look which is needed.[40]

Rajneesh's explanations indicate a full-fledged crazy-wisdom approach to teaching that was based on the metaphysics of Tantrism. As Rajneesh stated very clearly, "Unless Tantra becomes the foundation of the whole human mind, man will not be complete—because no other vision accepts man in his totality."[41]

We have encountered Tantrism, or Tantra, in preceding chapters. It is India's most radical contribution to spirituality. The underlying idea of Tantrism, which exists in both Hindu and Buddhist versions, is that even the most mundane occurrence can serve as a signal and a means of transcendence. Therefore, in Tantrism the female gender, so widely denigrated in the spiritual traditions of the ancient patriarchal cultures, is elevated to a positive symbol for the spiritual practitioner. Sex itself is no longer feared as a spiritual trap but is employed as a gateway to heaven, to the Divine. Rajneesh stated:

> Tantra has a very very beautiful thing to say to you, and that is: First, before you start serving anybody else, be absolutely selfish. How can you serve anybody else unless you have attained your inner being first? *Be absolutely selfish!*[42]

Here we have a faithful echo of Aleister Crowley's law of *thelema*—"Do what thou wilt." To be absolutely selfish does not mean to be uncontrollably selfish but to be Selfish, to fulfill one's own spiritual destiny, which is to realize God. However, this injunction can be misunderstood all too easily by overzealous, tunnel-visioned disciples who, in their simpleminded devotion to the guru, abandon the native gift of mental discrimination and take the guru literally rather than metaphorically. What then results is hedonism and power games, of which there was plentiful evidence in the Rajneesh movement and, to some extent, in Rajneesh's personal life as well.

To put devotees in touch with their emotional blocks, meaning their resistance to the guru, Rajneesh developed a variety of therapy intensives designed to bring about a catharsis, followed by the desired metanoia, or transformation of consciousness. Some of these intensives stretched over several days and involved verbal abuse, group sex, and physical violence. Those who refused to participate in the orgies were considered self-centered, frigid, and antisocial. Subtle and less subtle coercion was rampant. The weak-willed typically collapsed under the ostracism and, against their better judgment, exposed themselves to experiences for which they were neither emotionally nor morally suited.

For many women devotees, the intensives were not the only test that they were obliged to endure. There was also the "Lord's" personal interest in them. One of his former students, a psychotherapist, reported that she would go to his private rooms in the evening, where he would use her as an instrument of transmitting psychic energy to other devotees:

> It was ice cold. I took off my clothes and knelt before him, facing Vivek [Rajneesh's longtime companion]—I think he used me to "charge" Vivek. He would manipulate my genitals, masturbate me, but it was also as if he was rewiring my circuits . . . When the lights were out [during formal meditation occasions], he sometimes touched our genitals, our breasts, stimulating our lower chakras.[43]

Rajneesh cultivated such female "mediums," selecting them himself on the basis of their breast size. Only large-breasted women could hope to join this elite group. "I have been tortured by small-breasted women for many lives together, and I will not do it in this life!" he once announced to a large gathering.[44]

Yet Hugh Milne, who served Rajneesh as one of his most trusted devotees for ten years and who witnessed his teacher's decline with deep regret, proffers this sobering insight into his former guru's Tantric demeanor:

> Though Bhagwan placed so much emphasis on the physical side of sex, he was by all accounts hardly the world's greatest lover himself . . . Many of the women Bhagwan slept with told me that far from practising what he preached and making sex last for an hour or more, it was often all over in a couple of minutes. He would, I was reliably informed, get on top of a woman in the traditional missionary position, enter her, then come almost immediately. Most of his sexual pleasure seemed to lie in foreplay and voyeurism rather than in active performance.[45]

Unsavory incidents like these led to accusations of abuse and brainwashing both by outside observers and by Rajneeshees who had managed to defect. Voyeurism is clearly not Tantrism. When practiced by a spiritual teacher on his trusting disciples, it is not holy madness but an unforgivable transgression. While Rajneesh's positive influence on thousands of hopeful spiritual seekers cannot be denied, there can also be no doubt that his lack of discrimination and his personal idiosyncrasies and wiles caused considerable damage to many individuals. More important, of all the contemporary gurus, Rajneesh bears perhaps the greatest responsibility for warping the Western public's image of the guru–disciple relationship in particular and of crazy wisdom and Eastern spiritual traditions in general.

Rajneesh's "Lordship" invites comparison to claims of the American evangelist Father Divine, whose divinization made headlines in the 1930s. Stephen Zwick has noted about the eccentric preacher, "Father Divine may not have been God, but he was certainly a great man who deserves far more attention than he has received from American historians."[46]

Will posterity say the same of Rajneesh? It is more than doubtful, I think, even when the dust of disillusionment and angry opposition has settled.

## 4. Chögyam Trungpa: The Prowling Tiger of Crazy Wisdom

Chögyam Trungpa was born in Tibet in 1939 and died in the United States at the age of fifty. His extraordinary life was packed with adventure, loneliness, tragedy, fame, and notoriety.[47] Chögyam's birth in a tent village in rugged mountain terrain is reported to have been associated with all kinds of auspicious signs—a rainbow was seen and a water pail was found to be mysteriously filled with milk. When he was only eighteen months old, Chögyam was recognized and enthroned as the reincarnation (*tulku*) of the recently deceased abbot of Surmang monastery. He was to be the eleventh *trungpa* of the Karma Kagyupa branch of Tibetan Buddhism. Several objects had been placed before Chögyam, and he had picked up only those belonging to his predecessor, the tenth *trungpa*. This was a traditional test for identifying a *tulku*'s reincarnation.

When he was five, his education was formalized, and he proved an exceptionally able and eager student. At the tender age of eight years, Chögyam Trungpa took his monastic vows and entered a month-long meditation retreat. Only six years later he conducted his first full initiation ceremony, stretching over a period of six months, in which he imparted secret teachings to monks who had come from far and wide. Later Trungpa described his years as a student of Buddhism as follows:

> In my education, I was constantly criticized . . . Every time I did something right—or I thought I was doing something right—I was criticized even more heavily. I was cut down constantly by my tutor. He slept in the corridor outside my door, so I could not even get out. He was always there, always watching me . . . I had no idea what it was like to be an ordinary child playing in the dirt or playing with toys or chewing on rusted metal or whatever. Since I did not have any other reference point, I thought that was just the way the world was. I felt somewhat at home, but at the same time I felt extraordinarily hassled and claustrophobic . . .
>
> Then, very interestingly, I stopped struggling with the authorities, so to speak, and began to develop. I just went on and on and on. Finally that whole world began to become my reference point rather than being a hassle—although the world was full of hassles. At that point, my tutor

seemed to become afraid of me; he began to say less . . . My tutors and my teachers were pushed by me instead of my being pushed by them.[48]

Trungpa had become a "prowling tiger," as he put it in one of his poems composed in 1969.[49] In the poem he describes himself as a tiger with a confident smile, the smile resulting from his knowledge of having escaped the lion's jaw, meaning the lion of spiritual ignorance and thus death. A prowling tiger is a ravenous beast in search of prey. The image suggests merciless destruction, which is reinforced by another image in the same poem where he speaks of himself as a hailstorm that cannot be confronted by anyone. This is again a somewhat unfortunate metaphor as it reminds one of Milarepa's days as a hailstorm-invoking sorcerer rather than the compassionate activity befitting a spiritual adept. Though of indifferent literary merit, the poem provides us with valuable glimpses into its composer's psyche. We encounter not only accomplished self-assurance but also a sense of Trungpa's own presumed invincibility, which was to prove fatal.

In 1959, twenty-year-old Chögyam Trungpa led a group of three hundred Tibetan refugees across often treacherous mountains into India. There, in exile from the Chinese communists who were occupying and ravaging his homeland, he learned English and formed the idea to come to the West to teach. In 1963, he arrived in Oxford, England. Six years later, a tragic car accident—the car careened into a joke shop—left him paralyzed on the left side of his body. He had been feeling ambivalent about teaching in the West, but this crisis helped to make up his mind. Not only did he resolve to throw himself unreservedly into bringing the Buddhist *dharma* to eager Westerners, but he also decided to give up his monastic vows.

In 1970, Chögyam Trungpa and his new wife, an Englishwoman, arrived in America. The Americans were shocked by his appearance and demeanor. He had divested himself of his robes and other exotic accoutrements; he ate what he liked, consumed any quantity of alcohol, smoked, and freely joined his new friends in ingesting psychedelics. He understood his own crazy-wise conduct as a counterpoint to the widespread disease of "spiritual materialism," which is the trick of surreptitiously fortifying the ego while appearing to practice spiritual life. Trungpa wrote:

> Ego is able to convert everything to its own use, even spirituality. For example, if you have learned of a particularly beneficial meditation technique or spiritual practice, then ego's attitude is, first to regard it as an object of fascination and, second to examine it. Finally, since ego is seeming solid and cannot really absorb anything, it can only mimic. Thus ego tries to examine and imitate the practice of meditation and the meditative way of life . . . At last is created a tangible accomplishment, a confirmation of its own individuality.[50]

At first, everything was rather informal, but gradually Chögyam Trungpa introduced a tighter regimen. He gave his students a taste of the discipline that

he had had to endure during his own pupilage. He was preparing his students
for the higher teachings of Vajrayana. All the while, his behavior remained
completely unpredictable and incorrigible. He was regularly late, by an hour
or more, for his lectures and often arrived inebriated. Even while lecturing, he
would frequently down some beers. During meditation, he was occasionally
seen to nod off, but on other occasions he would sneak up on unsuspecting
meditators to squirt water at them with a toy pistol (a prank that Da Love-
Ananda also acted out around the same time).

> Boisterous parties often followed long meditation sessions, and students
> with purist attitudes found themselves swept like so many autumn leaves
> into the chaos. But the parties and social life were mixed with a growing
> sitting practice and close intellectual study of basic Buddhist principles.
> No matter how outrageously some nights might end, the next morning
> everyone woke to the sound of the conch, and it was back to the medita-
> tion hall, back to "square one," as Trungpa put it, "the place where you
> actually were the morning after, and not where you thought or imagined
> you ought to be."[51]

Then there were Trungpa's sexual relationships, apparently with students
of either sex. In this respect, he was something of a modern Drukpa Kunley.
Allen Ginsberg, who was both a student and Trungpa's "poetry guru," once
offered to sleep with his teacher; Trungpa is reported to have replied, "I think
that would be interesting if there's ever time—and space—to explore those
feelings."[52]

Despite his crazy-wise capriciousness, Trungpa was deeply conservative,
which was borne out by his formal and deferential treatment of the Karmapa,
the spiritual head of the Kagyupa school of Vajrayana. His conservatism was
also evident in the organizations he created. Later, this was poignantly criticized by Peter Marin:

> The Naropa Institute embodies a feudal, priestly tradition transplanted
> to a capitalistic setting. The attraction it has for its adherents is oddly
> reminiscent of the attraction the aristocracy had for the rising middle
> class in the early days of capitalistic expansion. These middle-class
> children seem drawn irresistibly not only to the discipline involved but
> also to the trappings of hierarchy . . .
>   If there is a compassion at work here, as some insist, it is so distant, so
> diminished, so divorced from concrete changes in social structure, that it
> makes no difference at all . . . Behind the public face lies the intrigue and
> attitude of a medieval court.[53]

Marin went on to condemn Trungpa's "implicit conservatism," which, he
felt, was damaging not only to his students but to those less fortunate than the
middle class—the poor and disenfranchised—whose well-being depends on
social change and on the exercise of compassion rather than the pursuit of

elitist goals. "Sometimes the entire institute seems like an immense joke played by Trungpa on the world," Marin wrote, "the attempt of a grown child to reconstruct for himself a simple world."[54]

In 1973, Chögyam Trungpa finally began to initiate disciples into the esoteric practices of Vajrayana (Tantric) Buddhism. He warned his disciples that "working with the energy of Vajrayana is like dealing with a live electric wire."[55] He might have added, and probably did, that working with a Tantric adept is actually touching that live wire with one's bare hands. The predictable result is a terrific jolt that can wreck a person for life, or at the very least cause emotional trauma. This was to be the experience of poet W. S. Merwin.[56]

Merwin participated in a three-month intensive seminar in 1975, which covered the three principal traditions of Buddhism—Hinayana, Mahayana, and Tibetan Vajrayana. Although Merwin lacked the necessary preparation and was not even one of Trungpa's students, the crazy-wisdom adept yielded to the poet's insistent request to be admitted. At the beginning of the course on Vajrayana, Trungpa interrupted the seminar with a Halloween party. He himself arrived drunk late that evening when the party was in full swing. He stepped up the excitement by asking people to undress, explaining that this was to be understood as a general demasking. He divested himself of his own clothes, and two students paraded him around the room on their shoulders. Those who were reluctant to follow suit were "assisted" by Trungpa's guards.

When Merwin and his wife arrived, they quickly decided that the party had gotten out of control and went to their rooms to pack their suitcases. Trungpa sent a message for them to join him and the others, which the couple refused. Displeased, Trungpa sent an ultimatum. When the couple switched off their lights and locked themselves in, a crowd of inebriated disciples unleashed their anger, kicking in the door and breaking the window.

In a state of panic, Merwin broke bottles on several attackers, injuring them. But when he saw that he had wounded a friend, he gave up the struggle. Both he and his wife were dragged, none too gently, before the Tantric master. An argument ensued, during which Trungpa insulted Merwin's Oriental wife with racist remarks and threw a glass of sake in the poet's face. Trungpa next asked the Merwins to take off their clothes and join the celebration. When they refused, he had them forcibly stripped in front of everyone. One student was courageous enough to oppose the mob mentality, but his pleading was rewarded by a punch in the face from the master. The assault continued until the poet and his wife stood in the middle of the room, stripped of their clothes and their dignity.

That incident more than any other greatly damaged Trungpa's reputation, and some feel that it also damaged the cause of Buddhism in the West. It certainly disadvantaged Trungpa's promising organization, which was subsequently refused grants and support and started to decline. Four years later, after the *Boulder Monthly* published a belated exposé, the outrage felt by the poet's friends and admirers caused a surge of paranoia and suspicion in the wider public, which was still stunned by the horrible massacre in Jonestown, Guyana, toward the end of 1978.

Strangely enough, the morning after the humiliation, Merwin and his wife elected to continue to participate in the seminar, perhaps because they were too traumatized to think clearly. Trungpa apparently never apologized for his and his students' behavior, which was widely condemned even in Buddhist quarters and not least among his own students. From Trungpa's perspective, Merwin had insisted on venturing into the lion's den, and he got what he deserved. Years before, the adept had once been asked the question "What if you feel the necessity for a violent act in order ultimately to do good for a person?" Trungpa's answer had been self-assured and clipped, "You just do it."[57] Perhaps if Merwin—a convinced pacifist—had known of this response and thought about it for a moment, he might not have allowed his thirst for knowledge to get the better of him.

Another infelicitous move on Trungpa's part was the appointment, in 1976, of his favorite American disciple, Thomas Rich (Ösel Tendzin), as his successor. Ösel, a former disciple of Swami Satchidananda, once explained that the only reason for his appointment was his singular lack of ambition. If true, this trait was matched only by Trungpa's lack of judgment. The tragedy of Trungpa's decision came to light only recently when Ösel, who had allegedly continued his teacher's practice of having sexual relations with many male and female students of his order, was diagnosed with AIDS.[58]

There can be no question in anyone's mind that Chögyam Trungpa abandoned himself to the stream of life with a daredevil attitude characteristic of crazy-wisdom adepts. Most of those who knew him personally would even concede that he remained true to his *bodhisattva* vow to the end: to help suffering humanity and guide his fellow beings to the Clear Light. The questions and criticisms that continue to trouble former students and interested observers concern his ability to combine wisdom (*prajna*) with skillful means (*upaya*). The doubts surrounding this issue are especially nagging when one knows that Trungpa apparently died from complications resulting from his alcohol addiction.

In his curious book *Waiting for the Martian Express*, Richard Grossinger reminds us that "the gods have chosen to be tricksters first, authorities never." Then he notes:

Many Buddhist masters, Da Free John and Chögyam Trungpa included, have been assailed for their so-called crazy wisdom. Trungpa had disciples carry him around naked at a party; broke antennas off cars on a city street and handed them to a student; spent days speaking in spoonerisms. Assuming that the ego, the programmed mind, will subvert any material it is given—even the most shocking prophecies and pronouncements—these masters attempt to wake people through extreme behavior which challenges the basis of daily reality. While the New Age guru imposes a narrative on our lives and offers change through dramatic, cosmic events, the "crazy wisdom" teacher interrupts the mindflow of self-image and social role; even a visit from the Martians would be less radical and disruptive.[59]

Grossinger appears less troubled by crazy wisdom than he is by the escapades of a Jimmy Swaggart, whom he roundly denounces on the same page. A possible explanation for his naive acceptance of crazy wisdom may be that he has recently become a student of a crazy-wisdom teacher. But this may be either cause or symptom of an apparent disinterest in inspecting the moral issues involved in crazy-wise behavior, which, after all, could be merely aberrated. A questioning attitude is healthy. So is keeping an open mind.

## 5. Lee Lozowick: A Spiritual Clown

One of the quirkier figures of contemporary spirituality is Lee Lozowick. His inclusion here is warranted not so much by his influence or the number of his disciples, which is few, but because he combines in a single person the deliberate self-deprecation typical of the holy fool for Christ's sake and the audacity of the crazy-wise teacher.

Lozowick, who recently started to refer to himself as "Mr. Lee," was born in Brooklyn, New York, in 1943, the only son of a middle-class Jewish family of Russian descent. His grandfather was a zaddik, and his father is a renowned East Coast artist. Lozowick made his fortune as a coin and stamp dealer. For several years, he was a leading figure in the Silva Mind Control movement. One morning, in 1975, he claims to have woken up from a sound sleep and found himself permanently changed—enlightened. This was also the year in which he "awakened to his teaching function." Lozowick understands his enlightenment as being on a par with that of Da Love-Ananda, with whom he assumes a special relationship. Yet he admitted once in conversation with a former student that he was still in the process of integrating his enlightenment with the rest of his life.

For Lozowick, we must note, enlightenment is simply "the knowledge that all experience is transitory, including enlightenment."[60] As we will see in a later chapter, this definition of enlightenment falls short of the traditional understanding, in which enlightenment is not considered an experience at all but the transcendence of all states of knowledge. One of Lozowick's ex-students remarked to me:

> I believe that Lee had some kind of a *satori* experience. But I think he is deluding himself when he claims to be fully enlightened. He has something going for himself. I found his clarity and presence attractive. He wasn't into playing social games. During the first year of my involve-

ment with him, I frequently experienced all kinds of blissful states in his company and would often lose the sense of being a separate consciousness. I also had any number of spontaneous movements, *kriyas*. It took me a long time to sort myself out after leaving his community, but I don't think he is a harmful person. I felt ripped off, naturally. But I can't blame him. After all, it was my choice to become his disciple and to stay for so many years. I do, however, feel that he is operating under false pretenses.

It is part of Lozowick's self-presentation that he oddly echoes the somewhat more prominent and controversial American adept Da Love-Ananda, to whom we will turn in the next chapter. The striking similarity between his teaching and that of Da Love-Ananda has been repeatedly pointed out by readers of Lozowick's works and has even given rise to the accusation of plagiarism. Either Lozowick remains oblivious to the fact of his heavy borrowing, which is hard to believe, or he chooses to deny it.

In a conversation with an ex-student of Lozowick's, Bhagwan Rajneesh once called Lozowick a fraud who had been a student of Da Love-Ananda but had deserted his teacher to set himself up as a master in his own right.[61] Incidentally, he condemned Da Love-Ananda in a similar fashion. Rajneesh's verdict about other teachers is not the issue here, since he had similar judgments lavished on him by others. Many gurus do not appear to be above games of one-upmanship. What is of interest is Rajneesh's opinion that Lozowick is a former disciple of Da Love-Ananda, which was meant to explain the curious resemblance between the respective teachings of these two crazy-wisdom *gurus*. Lozowick has always denied this connection.

Lozowick is essentially a self-made spiritual teacher of the crazy-wisdom variety, though he regards the South Indian saint Ramsuratkumar as his "spiritual father." Yogi Ramsuratkumar was a disciple of Aurobindo, Ramana Maharshi, and Papa Ramdas, and apparently still has a following of some 10,000 people in South India. Lozowick met Ramsuratkumar only four times. On his first visit to India in 1976, when he found Ramsuratkumar living on a garbage heap, he recognized that the saint was his teacher and that he had been instrumental in Lozowick's spiritual awakening the year before. On the second visit, Ramsuratkumar told Lozowick that his life was to be in the world, but on the third visit, in 1986, the saint ignored him and appeared not even to recognize him.

Lozowick's most recent pilgrimage was in 1988 for the Ramsuratkumar's seventieth birthday celebration. This time he was welcomed with traditional pomp by the saint's devotees as a Western spiritual master. Lozowick described his relationship to the saint as being primarily internal. "Instead of filling my heart with wonderful things he broke my heart," he explained in a short but dramatic speech to Ramsuratkumar's devotees.[62]

Lozowick thinks of himself as a spiritual fool and of his Hohm Community as a "school of beggars." The concept of beggary is important to him. He understands it as an equivalent of the traditional religious attitude of self–humiliation among the saints.

> We conventionally think of beggars as worthless or helpless people who are trapped by circumstances. In the mystical traditions, the beggar is the only one who is free of circumstances. Because a beggar has no home or possessions to speak of, he travels lightly. He has no resources save his own ingenuity to rely on. He has no status, and no hope of gaining status, so he is free of self-importance . . .
>
> But a beggar is not a bum. He is a fool only to the conventional observer. The esoteric beggar is like the occasional street person one meets with a real fire in his eyes—not just the fire of aggression or insanity, but of a lust for life. The esoteric beggar is always right where he is; he cannot afford to daydream or let his attention slip. He is useless to the world, but he never misses an opportunity . . . He is full of life.[63]

Lozowick consciously links his efforts and his community to what he calls the "Western Baul Tradition." As we learned in the preceding chapter, the *bauls* are madcap spiritual troubadours, traveling like beggars from village to village and singing their songs in praise of God. Lozowick sees himself as such a *baul*, and his disciples are likewise "fools" and "beggars." This is reflected in the appellations given to the various levels of involvement in his community, which comprise the Order of Ordinary Fools, the Order of Divine Fools, the Order of In-Between Fools, and the Order of Mandali (his intimate devotees, who number about twenty-five men and women). A former student sheds this light on Lozowick's crazy-wise demeanor:

> I remember many times when I would just cringe at his behavior. He was especially outrageous toward newcomers. Imagine a group of older, rather conservative women being told that all women secretly want to be raped! During public gatherings he would constantly use four-letter words, ramble on about sex and anal fixations, and generally behave and speak in a totally asinine way.
>
> I think he started to teach before he knew what he was doing. Later, he didn't want to admit his mistake and so began to cover up his ignorance by clowning. But that's just my opinion. Anyway, he went out of his way to come across as a fool.

Whatever Lozowick's ultimate motives for spiritual clowning may be, we cannot avoid noting an element of adolescent rebelliousness in certain of his actions. Thus, in 1985 he put together a mock issue of *Crazy Wisdom* magazine, the official publication of Da Love-Ananda's Free Daist Communion. Lozowick titled this elaborate satirical imitation *Lazy Wisdom*, thereby hinting at what he believed to be the largely infantile attitude of Da Love-Ananda's followers. His intention, it appears, was to bring constructive criticism, and many of his observations seemed appropriate enough. However, his cynicism got in the way and managed only to deepen the alienation between him and The Free Daist Communion. Ironically, much of his criticism of the cultic attitude among devotees of Da Love-Ananda can be said to apply to his own following as well. As one writer has pertinently observed about Lozowick, "His belief that all his own actions are God-motivated leaves him an excuse for everything—contradictions, irritability, anger, even some seemingly irresponsible behavior."[64]

In the early days of his teaching work, Lozowick tended to be more autocratic, or, as one ex-disciple put it, "he was king." Later, however, he started to develop a somewhat more democratic form of interaction with his disciples. Despite his insistence on the value of what he calls "spiritual slavery," he is said to permit a measure of questioning and dissent, which is healthy. This does not mean, however, that he has not had his share of disciples who left the community critical of him and his teaching. In contrast to some other contemporary gurus, who live isolated lives and insist on a baroque formality in their interaction with devotees, Lozowick has a relatively straightforward relationship to the world. He is approachable, makes his own phone calls, and handles his own correspondence. He even periodically tours the world with his own rock band. He supplies the lyrics for the songs and does not mind making a fool of himself as a singer. Writing in the school's magazine, one student has observed enthusiastically:

> Lee is as powerful as any Teacher who has come along, but he recognizes the liabilities of using that power. What's-his-name-Da would be an example of the opposite approach . . . Da gives Americans what they want, what they are impressed by, what one would expect from a spiritual Master who is real. But all that has a price, which is that his students get fascinated with power, with slickness, with appearances. They set up hierarchies that actually obstruct Da's influence . . .
>
> Lee, on the other hand, seems like a loser. No one in the Community has failed to see the extent of his power, but it's almost as if that's an accident. Lee's approach is usually to play the fool, to stay in the background. He makes recommendations, and gripes when people don't take them, but he never really puts his foot down. He is a Master of Understatement.[65]

Although Lozowick likes to refer to himself as "Just Mr. Typical American," this label hardly describes him. At any rate, his life-style is strikingly different from the stark asceticism of his adopted teacher, Yogi Ramsuratkumar. Lozowick is married and has six children. While he recommends monogamy, and even celibacy for some disciples, he is reported to have, or have had, several consorts himself. For a number of years, his extramarital relationships were kept a closely guarded secret even among his own followers. At one point, however, he decided to clear the air. He explained that a spiritual master could imbue objects—including living persons—with his own energy. This philosophy of spiritual cloning is widespread and by no means confined to Tantric teachers only. Even gurus of a more ascetical bent have been found to cohabit with their female devotees, giving them the standard explanation that sexual intercourse with the guru is a form of grace. Later, some of these women came to feel that they had allowed themselves to be abused.

Whatever one may think about Lozowick's claim to enlightenment or his abilities as a spiritual guide, he is, in the words of one of his former disciples, an odd rather than a dangerous spiritual figure on the contemporary New Age scene. Or at least he is no more dangerous than any other crazy-wise teacher: The interference by a guru is always hazardous to the ego-personality.

# 4

## THE MANY FACES
## OF DA LOVE-ANANDA (DA FREE
## JOHN)

### 1. The Early Years

"On November 3, 1939, at 11:21 A.M., in Jamaica, New York, I was born Franklin Albert Jones."[1] With this prosaic sentence begins one of the most fascinating autobiographies of our time. Its author, who now goes by the name of Da Love-Ananda, is revered by his followers as an *avatara*, an incarnation of the Divine. They and some readers of Da Love-Ananda's works see in him a genuinely enlightened adept—perhaps even the first fully enlightened being to appear in our Western civilization. They share Alan Watts's sentiment, as expressed in the foreword to the autobiography, that "he has simply realized that he himself as he is, like a star, like a dolphin, like an iris, is a perfect and authentic manifestation of the eternal energy of the universe, and thus is no longer disposed to be in conflict with himself."[2] Yet even for those who remain skeptical about Da Love-Ananda's authenticity and stature as a spiritual teacher, he is a larger-than-life figure. David Christopher Lane, who is critical of many of Da Love-Ananda's actions, has made this comment:

> There are very few spiritual teachers in the 20th century who could be termed religious geniuses. Da Free John [Da Love-Ananda] is one of them. Since the beginning of his formal ministry in 1972 in southern California, Da Free John has produced a body of work which is unparalleled amongst western philosophical thinkers for its radical insight, comparative depth, and force of expression.[3]

The first page of Da Love-Ananda's autobiography, enigmatically titled *The Knee of Listening*, already makes it clear that the life revealed to the reader is as extraordinary as that of any hero in the mythical past. We are told:

> The sign of my birth is Scorpio, marked by the images of Spirit and of Sex, the eagle and the crab. It is the sign of internal warfare, the problem

and perfection. I have played in the dilemma of my natural alternatives, but from my earliest experience of life I have enjoyed a condition that I would call the "bright."

As a baby I remember crawling around inquisitively with an incredible sense of joy, light and freedom in the middle of my head that was bathed in energies moving freely down from above, up, around and down through my body and my heart. It was an expanding sphere of joy from the heart. And I was a radiant form, a source of energy, bliss and light.[4]

This preindividual conscious condition, Da Love-Ananda explains, began to recede in his second or third year, and he became aware of himself as an individual facing an objective world. It was this loss of the "bright," which the adept later equated with *nirvikalpa-samadhi*,[5] that motivated him throughout his earlier life to recapture the paradisiacal state of wholeness. From the time of his undergraduate studies at Columbia College, New York, where he majored in philosophy, he was preoccupied with finding a way back to the primal condition he had enjoyed in his infancy. As he desperately tried to understand the psychic mechanism that blocked the experience of the "bright," he began to see that the ego itself is a process of psychosomatic contraction, by which Reality is constantly kept at bay. He linked this idea to the image of Narcissus, the self-adoring youth of Greek mythology.

Da Love-Ananda experienced a temporary reawakening in college. Then, while engaged in graduate work at Stanford University, where he produced a master's thesis on Gertrude Stein, he had a series of additional psychic and spiritual experiences and formative insights. These led him, at the end of his graduate studies in 1964, to Swami Rudrananda ("Rudi"), a disciple of the famous Swami Muktananda. From other students of Rudi we know that Da Love-Ananda submitted himself to his new guru in exemplary fashion. At Rudi's request, he cleaned up his life, got a regular job, and later even studied at a Christian seminary, though he had no interest in doing so. Yet after several years of diligent practice and wholehearted application to *guru-yoga*, he found Rudi's "muscular" way of teaching *kundalini-yoga* too limiting.[6] He consequently turned to Rudi's teacher, Swami Muktananda.

During his very first visit to Muktananda's *ashrama* in India in 1968, which lasted only four days, Da Love-Ananda experienced the state of objectless ecstasy (*nirvikalpa-samadhi*) for the first time in his adult life. This experience was confirmed in a letter from the Swami that was handed to Da Love-Ananda on his second visit, in 1969, in which he was given the initiatic name "Kriyananda" and was formally empowered to teach in his own right. In later years, Da Love-Ananda made much of this letter, having it repeatedly translated by different linguists, perhaps because this document sets the record straight: Although his teaching is in many respects innovative, Da Love-Ananda is not, as has been suggested, a self-proclaimed teacher. Rather, he comes out of the lineage of what is known as *siddha-yoga*.

On returning from his first visit to India, he separated from Rudi, who apparently failed to understand Da Love-Ananda's inner development. From then on he regarded Swami Muktananda as his guru. His second pilgrimage to India consolidated his yogic attainments, and when he returned a third time, in 1970, he did so on the assumption that henceforth he would be living as a renunciate in Muktananda's ashram. But again his own inner development dictated a different course. While meditating one day, he had a powerful vision of the Virgin Mary, to which he, by then an unchurched Protestant, had a peculiar reaction. In his own words:

My first impulse was huge laughter. I had spent years of total non-sympathy for Christianity. I felt I had paid my religious dues. I saw that whole religious tradition as merely a symbolic and ritual communication for what were really matters of direct consciousness, pure self-awareness, and Vedantic conclusions about reality. Now, as if I were faced with a cosmic joke, I stood in the living Presence of Christ's Mother![7]

Da Love-Ananda understood the Virgin to be a manifestation of the cosmic feminine principle (*shakti*). It became apparent to him that he had to drop all attachment to an external teacher, and so he left Muktananda's ashram. For several months, his visions of the Virgin guided him to various holy sites in Europe and then back to the United States. Specifically he was drawn to the Vedanta Temple in Hollywood, which he recognized as a potent site of the Mother-Goddess.

Now the visions of the *shakti* progressed into the experience of her permanent inner presence. And, in a final ecstatic climax, he realized his perfect identity with the cosmic creative principle. As he put it:

Then I felt the Shakti appear against my own form. She embraced me, and we grasped one another in sexual union. We clasped one another in a fire of cosmic desire, as if to give birth to the universes. Then I felt the oneness of the Divine Energy and my own Being. There was no separation at all.[8]

When next he meditated in the temple, he fully expected the same mystical fireworks, but nothing happened. He found that there was no meditative process even. He simply was aware of himself as pure Consciousness.

I simply sat there and knew what I am. I was being what I am. I am Reality, the Self, and Nature and Support of all things and all beings. I am the One Being, known as God, Brahman, Atman, the One Mind, the Self.
There was no thought involved in this. I am that Consciousness . . . Then truly there was no more to realize. Every experience in my life had led to this.[9]

From that moment on, we are told, Da Love-Ananda's sense of identity underwent a permanent shift, from conditioned ego to transcendental Self.

He referred to this state as *sahaja-samadhi* or the "ecstasy of spontaneity." In Hinduism, this state is also known as the "Fourth"—the transcendental plateau condition beyond the phenomenal states of waking, sleeping, and dreaming—beyond even temporary peak states of consciousness.

Da Love-Ananda's account, as given in the original published version of his autobiography, has the ring of authenticity and can be appreciated as a remarkable mystical document. As Alan Watts, who was not known for his generosity toward other teachers, remarked: "It is obvious from all sorts of subtle details that he knows what IT's all about . . . a rare being."[10] Later autobiographical presentations, regrettably, tend toward mythologization, as does indeed Da Love-Ananda's entire self-presentation in recent years.

When enlightenment occurred in September 1970, Da Love-Ananda's odyssey as a spiritual seeker had come to its successful conclusion. Little did he know, however, that enlightenment does not signal the end of spiritual evolution. He learned later that the destiny of the enlightened being continues to unfold. Da Love-Ananda felt compelled to communicate his newly gained inner freedom and wisdom to his teacher. But Swami Muktananda was less than receptive to his disciple's ideas. Judging from the transcripts of the clinching conversation between them, he was in fact elusive and not a little petulant.

Da Love-Ananda believed that his guru was settling for less than the ultimate, while Muktananda dismissed Da Love-Ananda's disclosures and arguments as pretentious. As so often happens, a breach between guru and disciple occurred that was never formally healed. However, there is some evidence that Muktananda never bore any real grudges against his former disciple. As for Da Love-Ananda, he continued to criticize Muktananda's position in talks and in various publications, while at the same time acknowledging his own indebtedness to that formidable *siddha*.

Da Love-Ananda began to teach shortly after his enlightenment. At first, he met relatively informally with whomever expressed an interest in spiritual life. Gradually, however, he insisted on certain formalities, including abstinence from illegal drugs, as well as certain dietary and health disciplines. Casual visitors became rarer as the conditions for seeing and meditating with him became tighter. He opened his own school (ashram) in 1972, complete with elevated chair, carpets, and an abundance of flowers—the style adopted by most Indian gurus. This was also the inaugural year of his church, The Dawn Horse Communion, which is now known as The Free Daist Communion. In the beginning, he was addressed as "Franklin," but after his visit to Swami Muktananda in the summer of 1973, he asked to be called "Bubba Free John."[11]

As "Bubba" he enacted the role of spiritual friend toward his growing group of disciples. However, at that time his "friendship" was already interlaced with formality—a formality that would, in the course of time, grow into a somewhat stilted and almost formulaic affair, making a simple, personal approach to him virtually impossible. He felt that his Western contemporaries had little or no understanding of the role of the spiritual teacher and, step by step, had to be taught the fine art of *guru-yoga*, submission to the Divine by means of surrender to the teacher.

## 2. Crazy Wisdom and the Futility of Experience

In December of 1973, Da Love-Ananda's teaching work acquired a new dimension. After demanding from his students strict adherence to a fairly ascetical life-style, he suddenly initiated a cycle of "celebrations." One devotee recalls:

> They used the traditional intoxicants, such as alcohol and cigarettes, meat, and "junk" food—all the things they had rigorously avoided for so long. Bubba [Da Love-Ananda] participated freely in these things, even after what had been a prolonged period of natural abstinence. He and his devotees drank and sang and danced—and suddenly, in the midst of these festivities, Bubba unleashed his spiritual Power with awesome effect. While his devotees were relaxed from rigid concern and self-discipline, he spontaneously raised them all into higher states of psychic and mystical awareness.[12]

These celebrations were comparable to Tantric feasts, where a small group of initiates, always under the guidance of the guru, break major taboos of the traditional Hindu society as part of a ritual intended to bring about a change of consciousness in the participants. From my many conversations with longtime devotees, it appears that for several months Da Love-Ananda did indeed use his yogic abilities to affect the psychic lives of literally hundreds of students in often very dramatic ways. They experienced visions, spontaneous body movements known as *kriyas*,[13] bliss states, heart openings, and *kundalini* arousals.[14] Several were ostensibly drawn into the mystical unitive state or even into temporary *sahaja-samadhi*.[15] This important phase in Da Love-Ananda's teaching history is recorded in a long-out-of-print book entitled *Garbage and the Goddess*.[16]

The book's title was meant to epitomize the specific lesson of that period: that everything in the finite realm is "garbage," and that even the most elevated mystical experiences must be surrendered. So long as there is an experiencing ego, unreality persists. Enlightenment, by contrast, can no longer be called an experience, because the gap between subject and object that haunts the ordinary mind is fully bridged. Da Love-Ananda told his devotees:

> I spend a lot of my time packaging your garbage, trying to get you to recognize it. You'll throw it away as soon as you see it. You can't surrender something that you don't recognize to be garbage. You intuitively hold on to it. So you've got to recognize it.

But I'll tell you right now—it is all garbage! Everything the Guru gives you is garbage, and he expects you to throw it away, but you meditate on it. All of these precious experiences, all this philosophy . . . None of them is the Divine. They are garbage.[17]

Da Love-Ananda here equated experience with the Goddess, the feminine or dynamic principle of existence. He noted:

Everyone succumbs to the Goddess on one level or another . . . So, the Guru's perfect function is to undermine all this, to make the world show itself. He makes the Goddess pull down her pants, and then you see her asshole. I shouldn't be saying these things.[18]

The pivot of Da Love-Ananda's "way of radical understanding" is to recognize the "Goddess" in and as all experiences and to develop the cool disposition of nonattachment toward everything that has been recognized as a manifestation of the Goddess. In his view, the traditional orientation is to worship and surrender to the Goddess. He argues that this is all nonsense but occasionally concedes, tongue in cheek, that he may just be mistaken. In his own words, which flowed easily from his lips in a state of ecstatic inebriation during one of his celebrations:

What do I know? This could just be an aberration. Must be. No one agrees with me . . . They all tell me that I'm mad, that I'm undeveloped . . . Muktananda used to say, "Yield to the Goddess," and that is not the principle. The Goddess used to say, "Yield to me," and I fucked her brains loose. I've never listened to anyone. Perhaps I should have![19]

However, the Goddess is not all vacuous pomp and circumstance. By Da Love-Ananda's admission, she is also the instrument by which we learn to turn to the suprapersonal Divine and thereby become enlightened. In Jungian terms, she serves the function of an archetype. But while we may accept and respond to an archetype, we do not surrender to it. As Da Love-Ananda put it graphically, "The true way is not grasping onto the bangles of the Goddess and letting her lift you up into her crotch through the spine until you realize God. The true way is to realize God in Truth."[20]

In other words, for Da Love-Ananda, self-surrender must always occur in relation to the ultimate Reality, which he calls the Divine, God, or the "Radiant Transcendental Being."

An important manifestation of the Goddess is sexual experience, the play between the sexes. This lies at the opposite pole from mystical experience. However, these two extremes of human experiential possibility are not as separate as they might seem. At any rate, in Da Love-Ananda's teaching, they are simply experiences and as such deserve to be transcended. Hence, appropriately, during the "Garbage and the Goddess" celebrations, his devotees were not only exposed to the upper end of the experiential scale; they were also obliged to inspect and confront their sexual and emotional fixations in very concrete ways.

In March of 1974, in what has come to be known as the "Saturday Night Massacre," Da Love-Ananda initiated a consideration about sexuality, marriage, and emotional attachment that left his disciples reeling for months, sometimes years. Commenting that relationships like marriage are generally entered into in order to create a sense of security and immunity for the ego-personality, he called on his students to disrupt their cultic association with one another. In particular, he challenged them to break through their marriage cults and discard their sexual attachment and jealousy. "One of the 'secrets' of spiritual life," he observed, "is continually to violate your own contracts."[21] True to the logic of his radical argument, he also asked devotees to desist from turning him into a "golden calf." Instead, he invited them to participate in his freedom and humor—an invitation that exceedingly few of his followers have accepted over the years, perhaps because they got caught up in the web of hierarchical formality surrounding the adept.

He reminded them that the guru is, by virtue of his function, a "dangerous person."[22] He has reiterated this caveat many times during his teaching career. The danger of the guru lies in his or her commitment to the disciple's radical psychospiritual transmutation. The guru is forever on the disciple's case. As Da Love-Ananda explained:

The *Guru* is a kind of irritation to his friends. You can't sleep with a dog barking in your ear . . . The *Guru* is a constant wakening sound. He is always annoying people with this demand to stay awake, to wake up . . . Therefore, he doesn't satisfy the seeker. Those that come to be satisfied are offended, they are not satisfied.[23]

When he first started to teach, Da Love-Ananda good-naturedly but naively presumed that others would attain enlightenment simply by grasping and applying his teaching argument and by occasionally being exposed to the spiritual presence of his own awakened body-mind during *sat-sanga*.[24] Gradually he acknowledged that few people possess the necessary qualifications for this shortcut and that most are in need of a prolonged period of intense preparation in which they must learn to discipline their attention and energy. Thus, partly in consideration with his students, he developed an entire way of life, comprising physical exercises, sexual practices, meditation techniques, religious rituals, and much more.

Most of the time, his cultural innovations were presented as recommendations, but, of course, they always had the considerable weight of his charismatic leadership behind them. This was certainly the case in 1974 when he started his "sexual theater," involving the switching of partners, sexual orgies, the making of pornographic movies, and intensified sexual practices—

all of which led to the temporary or, in some instances, the permanent breakup of relationships. As "contracts" were voided, emotions ran high in the community. Some people were unable to handle this emotional roller coaster and left; a few still bear the wounds today. Most stayed and braved the upheaval, and subsequently learned to live with their traumas or, perhaps more rarely, truly go beyond them.

Da Love-Ananda, who is no mere theoretician, was often found in the thick of the tumult. He had come fully alive in his crazy-wisdom function. That he was not made of the stuff of saints should have been clear to anyone who had read his spiritual autobiography carefully. Already, in *The Knee of Listening*, he had told his readers how, in his student days at Columbia, he had explored all possibilities "high and low." In his own words:

> No experience posed a barrier to me. There were no taboos, no extremes to be prevented. There was no depth of madness and no limit of suffering that my philosophy could prevent . . . Thus, I extended myself even beyond my own fear. And my pleasures also became extreme, so there was a constant machine of ecstasy. I could tolerate no mediocrity.[25]

More important, Da Love-Ananda also mentioned that he went to Swami Muktananda's ashram with his wife, who is now legally divorced from him (at his instigation) although still a devotee, and another young woman, who has not been a formal student now for several years. The trio raised eyebrows in the ashram, but Muktananda apparently never made any comments to his disciple about this unusual living arrangement.

During the "Garbage and the Goddess" period, Da Love-Ananda "married" numerous female devotees, leaving their husbands or lovers to sort out their wild emotions and confusion. These quasi marriages were by no means all platonic. On the contrary, his disciples encountered their teacher as a passionate man. Many of them understood for the first time the full significance of his description of the "man of understanding," the enlightened person, at the end of *The Knee of Listening*:

> He is a seducer, a madman, a hoax, a libertine, a fool, a moralist, a sayer of truths, a bearer of all experience, a righteous knave, a prince, a child, an old one, an ascetic, a god. He demonstrates the futility of all things. Therefore, he makes understanding the only possibility. And understanding makes no difference at all. Except it is reality, which was already the case.[26]

These words, written in 1971/72, were really a self-portrayal. Da Love-Ananda is a man with many faces, many roles, many masks, and many moods. His chameleonlike play is, as he insists, for the sake of his devotees. He claims he wants to give them nothing to cling to. As David Christopher Lane notes:

Da Free John [Love-Ananda] is, without question, the most iconoclastic teacher I have encountered. Not that his fundamental teachings change (they haven't), but that he continually upsets every model/label that he assumes. Da Free John is literally like a Cracker Jack surprise in the religious world. Just when you think that he has run out of new guises, Da Free John comes up with some bizarre clothing to startle you.[27]

Even some of his closest disciples have been constantly baffled by Da Love-Ananda's trickster nature, and they continue to be mystified by the strangeness of his life. This, however, appears to be one of the marks of a good crazy-wise adept: to be able to surprise, startle, bombshell, or shock his disciples. So the theory goes: In those moments when we are jolted out of our complacency, we can inspect the whole structure of our conventional existence and open ourselves to something greater.

There are countless anecdotes about Da Love-Ananda's Zen-like shock tactics. Often these maneuvers revealed as much about his students' self-limitations as they did about their beliefs, especially their preconceptions about what a guru is or is not. One longtime student proffered the following account in 1975:

[When I first met Da Love-Ananda,] Bubba appeared almost cold and businesslike to me. I felt crushed and disappointed . . . My growing contact with Bubba continued to frustrate and disappoint me. I had expected that he would at least be "holy," but this hope was dashed when he instigated a series of wild parties which were to last for over a year, providing me with some of the most outrageous and uproarious experiences of my life, and undermining both my expectations of him and my own sense of propriety . . .

About three months after my first meeting with Bubba, he invited me to join his household as his cook and chauffeur. Murderous rages would grip me as I stood chopping vegetables. It required steely control to refrain from running amok in the house with the meat cleaver . . . If I had well-bred (read "fearful") ideas about politely paying whatever price a seller asked, Bubba would force me to bargain relentlessly, far below the price at which the poor man could even save face. If I had commonsensical (again read "fearful") notions about what it meant to have a good time through moderate and sensible celebration, Bubba would take me on a six-week drinking binge, starting every day with a triple Bloody Mary before breakfast and settling into really serious drinking around noon, all the while devising an inexhaustible variety of games, escapades, practical jokes and general outrages.[28]

Another disciple of Da Love-Ananda, who has since left, related this incident to me:

A bunch of us were washing dishes in the kitchen when Da Love-Ananda sneaked in and started to squirt devotees with the water pistol he often carried around with him in those days. Most ducked or ran off. For some reason, one girl squirted him back. He laughed but then he returned with a container filled with water, pouring it over her. Now everyone began to participate and take sides. Soon things got out of hand. Everyone tried to find the biggest containers around.

At one point, Da Love-Ananda was trying to fill a five-gallon container, and I playfully turned the tap off. He pushed me out of the way, but I persisted. Laughing wildly, he suddenly picked me up and deposited me on top of the stove. Before I knew it, he had lit all the burners. I seem to have sat there speechless, looking in amazement at the flames below me. Miraculously, I didn't get burned.

From then on, this hilarious skirmish escalated quickly into an outrageous food fight in which every single food item in the kitchen—from mustard to sauerkraut—was sacrificed, leaving the place and us in a disgusting mess. I didn't get harmed in any way, but the incident left me completely stunned. I knew I was dealing with a "crazy" adept, who really pulled out all the stops to teach one a lesson. We always put limitations on everything. For him, it has always been no holds barred.

One devotee, now in his middle age, wrote about a moment when, while hugging Da Love-Ananda, he felt as if he were tumbling into the void—an experience that is not uncommon among devotees. That voidness, the absence of all conventional reference points, appeared to this student as a form of madness.

When I opened my eyes, the thing I recognized when I looked at Bubba was that he is totally mad, absolutely mad—but that madness is absolute freedom. I realized that he could and would do *anything*, absolutely *anything!* I laughed uproariously and called him a madman. "You shapeshifter! You madman! I've been busting my ass doing all these disciplines, and they have nothing to do with Truth! It's all futile!" I said, "What do we do now?" And he said something like, "Stay here and eat till we die."[29]

The "Garbage and the Goddess" period ended on July 7, 1974, leaving in its wake a debris of emotional confusion. This is how Da Love-Ananda explained that period of teaching theater and his participation in it:

What I do is not the way I am, but the way I teach. What I speak is not a reflection of me, but of you. People do well to be offended or even outraged by me. This is my purpose. But their reaction must turn upon themselves, for I have not shown them myself by all of this. All that I do and speak only reveals men to themselves.[30]

Da Love-Ananda then charged his devotees with using the lessons learned during the preceding years and assuming responsibility for themselves individually and collectively. He declared his intention of retiring from his teaching work; he said he hoped that his disciples had the maturity to make use of each other and the cultural disciplines he had given them and to resort to his spiritual presence rather than crave his physical company.

Da Love-Ananda has apparently from the beginning felt some ambivalence about teaching. He has explained that the "guru function" came alive in him of its own accord, and he has made many attempts since then to withdraw from his responsibilities and obligations as a teacher, longing to be simply present as a spiritual beacon or transmitter. However, again and again, what he has perceived to be the needs of his disciples have pulled him back into his teaching mode. In practice, this has often meant entering into what he called "emotional-sexual considerations" with his disciples. Thus, the sexual theater enacted during the "Garbage and the Goddess" period was repeated on many other occasions, though never again on such a large scale nor with the flashy demonstration of yogic powers. For the most part, these sexual considerations, which were never merely theoretical, were confined to the inner circle of practitioners. But occasionally some relative newcomers were included. This happened to one couple; the husband provided the following extensive account of a fascinating incident that occurred in 1982:

I had been a formal student for only a few months when, one night, my wife and I were invited over to Da Love-Ananda's home. Both of us felt an inner need to make personal contact with him, since we had only seen him in quite formal situations. So we were understandably very excited about the invitation, but also a bit terrified, because we knew that our teacher was a "difficult man" and we could expect to be tested by him.

I found my spiritual hero sitting on his big bed, holding a glass of beer in one hand and a cigarette in the other. He was enveloped by a cloud of cigarette smoke. My heart sank. In that moment a cherished image in me was destroyed: my ideal of the guru as a gentle, Jesus-like helper.

We all bowed, and I awkwardly placed a small blossom near him on the bed. No sooner had we sat down before him than I was handed a can of beer. I politely refused. I had done without alcohol for years, and I figured I wouldn't start drinking beer now. Da Love-Ananda playfully teased me about it. I noticed myself getting uptight and in an instant saw that my refusal was simply an egoic program. So, I chucked my resistance and had a beer. And another. And another.

Meanwhile Da Love-Ananda was talking to us, puffing cigarette after cigarette, and downing one drink after another. His conversation got increasingly animated, amusing, but also barbed. He had his talons in me. I knew this was to be "my" evening. I answered his various questions respectfully but guardedly, listened to his barrage of good-natured criticism, told my story in as humorous a way as possible, laughed with him and at myself, and even risked quibbling with him a few times, but all the while stayed carefully defended. Despite large amounts of beer, I remained relatively sober.

As the evening progressed, and everybody got more inebriated—

except myself—Da Love-Ananda heated things up a little. Perhaps he had done whatever "damage" he wanted to do in his conversation with me, and so he had someone put pop music on. Then we all started to dance, with him rhythmically swaying to the blaring sounds. The psychic energy in the room was phenomenal. It seemed to increase whenever he raised his arms. I began to feel an incredible wildness inside me, which was scary. There was a strange inner drama unfolding between him and me. He wanted to break down my walls, and I badly wanted them up. Yet, there was something deep within me, a still observer perhaps, that wanted to see them crumble as well.

I found myself in a real crisis. The music and movement kept on hammering in on me, while strange waves of energy welled up inside my body, threatening to explode my mind. I was feeling manipulated and feared that I had become involved in a terrible cult. Yet, the voice of reason in the back of my mind always convinced me just in time that these feelings were all nonsense, products of my paranoia. Each time I talked myself into hanging in just a bit longer.

In our earlier conversation, he had asked me many times what it was I was after, and I had repeatedly told him I wanted to attain enlightenment. His response had been to call me a benighted individual and to remind me of the rareness of such an eventuality. But I had persisted. Now that I had made my choice, he felt free to really teach me a lesson.

In front of me, my wife was being sexually prepared for the guru. I coped with my violently irrational feelings by going into emotional numbness. Happily, I did not have to witness my teacher bedding my wife. We were all asked to leave the room. I was sent to a different building where I sat for several hours in the dark, dealing with the emotional hurricane that had been unleashed in me. Finally, I got a handle on my feelings. I realized that one of my greatest attachments was to my wife, and that the guru was doing radical surgery on me for that. I had asked him, indirectly but loudly and clearly, to help me in my struggle for enlightenment. That night he was doing just that.

The day after my personal massacre, Da Love-Ananda got into my wife's case for a while and then he returned to me, presumably because I was the more defended. This traumatic episode left both of us raw for several months, but it also proved a valuable initiation. We both had been skinned to our bones and were allowed to look into niches of our respective characters that we previously had chosen to leave in the dark. We were also very clear on another point, namely that our guru meant business. He was no mere cosmetic surgeon; his knife cut deep.

I have often wondered whether that crazy-wisdom episode was really necessary, or whether I could have learned the same lessons in another way. There is one thing that has *persistently* bothered me about the incident, and that was the pressure on me to drink alcohol in an attempt to get me drunk. I still feel I was being manipulated on this count. I also never quite understood why we were asked to keep the whole incident quiet. In the aftermath of the experience both my wife and I would clearly have benefited from talking to our close friends about it. Also, this secrecy smacked of elitism and hypocrisy, because while we were busy partying, the rest of the community was living a fairly strict daily discipline of diet, exercise, meditation, and service.

Tantra-style encounters of this kind occurred periodically and more or less secretly certainly until the end of 1985 and led, in 1986, to a renewed outbreak of legal difficulties with "dissident" students. Da Love-Ananda has always been well aware of the perils of teaching in the crazy-wisdom mode and of teaching Western spiritual seekers in general, since they tend to have little preparation or understanding of the guru–disciple relationship. He once commented:

> My life is a little bit like going into the world of enemies and dragons to liberate somebody who has been captured. You cannot just sit down and tell a dragon the Truth. You must confront a dragon. You must engage in heroic effort to release the captive from the dragon. This is how I worked in the theatre of my way of relating to people, particularly in the earlier years, and in the unusual involvements of my life and Teaching. You could characterize it as the heroic way of Teaching, the way of identifying with devotees and entering into consideration in that context and bringing them out of the enemy territory, gradually waking them up.[31]

## 3. Crazy-Wise Chaos and the Community of Devotees

Burned out by months-long partying, during which he dealt with the "shadows" of his disciples' psyches, Da Love-Ananda suffered a sudden collapse at the beginning of 1986. On January 11, he underwent what he described as a literal death experience. This was one of many experiences of this kind that he has undergone since his days in college. However, this particular incident has subsequently been greatly elaborated and invested with special significance, and it continues to shape his relationship with devotees into the present.

We have Da Love-Ananda's description and interpretation of the occurrence, which is now referred to in the official literature of The Free Daist Communion as his "Divine Emergence." In a talk given at the end of February 1986, he explained that on that eventful morning in January he had spoken to his close devotees of his grief, sorrow, and frustration at the seeming futility of his teaching work. He had told them that he could no longer endure their rejection and abuse and that he wished to die quickly. Apparently, the death process was initiated almost immediately. He experienced numbness in his arms and spine, followed by convulsions. Then his consciousness faded from his body. Doctors worked feverishly on resuscitating him, and finally their efforts bore fruit. This, in his own words, is what happened next:

Eventually, I began to reassociate with the body, although I was not aware of the room exactly, nor of who was there. I began to Speak of My greater concerns and impulses and of My great sorrow for the four billion humans and the rest of the beings everywhere. I cannot endure such sorrow very well—I have never endured it very well. I have had to bring My Self very deliberately to this Work. And in this Event, I was drawn further into the body with a very human impulse, a love-impulse. Becoming aware of My profound relationship with all My devotees, I resumed My bodily state.[32]

Da Love-Ananda further explained that most adepts are only partially present in the body. In his own case, his consciousness prior to the "death event" had been associated more closely with the body but had still only been more like a "shroud" surrounding it (a statement that seems to contradict what he has said elsewhere). According to his testimony, the "death event" changed all that. He descended fully into the body, becoming utterly human, yet without forgoing his enlightenment. Da Love-Ananda understands this as a great victory, which holds greater importance for him than even the event of his enlightenment in 1970. As he sees it, his body has become a perfect vehicle for spiritual transmission, so that it is now sufficient to contemplate, or tune into, his bodily state in order to participate in his body's enlightenment. This does not really differ substantially from the views he expressed in his spiritual autobiography shortly after his enlightenment two decades ago.

Da Love-Ananda's larger-than-life explanations of this event, like so many of his comments about the inner workings of his mind and life, are fascinating but less than illuminating. They give one the impression of a quite extraordinary individual who, nonetheless, is overly preoccupied with his own evolutionary mystery. From childhood on, Da Love-Ananda has had a flair for drama, and he has been successful in keeping the attention of a few thousand people focused on his dramatic life for a good many years. This certainly is one way in which the alchemical process of *guru-yoga* can be made to work. But it is evidently not a way that holds an attraction for larger numbers of spiritually motivated people.

The "death experience" had far-reaching repercussions in Da Love-Ananda's spiritual community. As one community member described it to me:

No one was quite sure what that death event meant. I am still not altogether clear. Love-Ananda himself wasn't right away aware of all its implications either. What became clear as time went on was that he had changed dramatically. His demand for us to take responsibility for our own spiritual practice became almost overwhelming. He just wouldn't stand for a halfhearted response any longer. He started to criticize everyone and everything even more fiercely than usual. He tore into the community and the institution, bringing it to the brink of bankruptcy with his demands. He had become a formidable Shiva the Destroyer, causing tremendous chaos in our lives. He was "cult-busting."

It was almost as if he wanted all old forms and attitudes in the community to die as he had died, so that they could be reborn in a new way. In fact, things became so chaotic that I and many of my friends just fled. I am actively involved again as a student, but for over two years I kept my distance because I was unable to face the craziness of it all.

One of the casualties of Da Love-Ananda's iconoclasm in that year was the *mandala* of nine women who had composed the innermost circle of his devotees. Ruthlessly he began to dismantle this elite group, which had been inviolable until then. Five of these women devotees and longtime lovers— spiritual and sexual—of Da Love-Ananda were asked to leave his hermitage in Fiji. One of them was his former wife, who was also his very first devotee. From then on he focused on working with the remaining four women renunciates, who are now reported to be in advanced spiritual states.

Such female *mandalas*, which act almost as protective circles around the guru, have been associated with a number of adepts, past and present. The esoteric explanation for their existence is that such groups of devoted women serve as conduits for the adept's spiritual transmission in the world. We have also seen, in the case of Bhagwan Rajneesh, how such *mandalas* can be channels of political power, corruption, and destructiveness. Many students took the dismantling of Da Love-Ananda's *mandala* as a promising sign.

Unlike some modern gurus, Da Love-Ananda never concealed from his students the fact that he is sexually active. For many years he was married, and he also has three children (by different women). In various books, he has reiterated that his attitude to spiritual life is entirely sex-positive. At different times he has openly discussed the option of polygamy with students, usually recommending against it. Yet, being an intensely private person, he has understandably discouraged publicizing his own polygamous relationships.

For many years, members of The Free Daist Communion have suffered from feelings of guilt and shame about their experiments and excesses during the "Garbage and the Goddess" period. Many have felt especially embarrassed by their guru, as Da Love-Ananda himself has noted on many occasions. This became apparent when, in 1985, a lawsuit was brought against The Free Daist Communion by a group of disaffected members, which caused sensationalistic and disruptive media attention. Members were at a loss about how to deal with the situation emotionally and politically, and many stepped back or left.

For years, community representatives did their best to clean up Da Love-Ananda's talks before printing them, and in general they tried to tone down the crazy aspect of his behavior and teaching. Da Love-Ananda, on the other hand, constantly criticized them for presenting a distorted public image of him; he wanted to be portrayed as the wild man he is, despite the possible dangers resulting from such a public image. He wanted to be free to teach in crazy-wise fashion and he felt that people approaching his community were entitled to know that he is no mild-mannered teacher but, as he once put it, a "conflagration," in which the ego inevitably gets scorched and consumed. He likes to compare his work to the crazy-wise teachings of some of the great adepts of the East. In particular, he once remarked "I am Drukpa Kunley. This is exactly what I am in your time and place."[33]

It is difficult and superfluous to determine what might have happened if his followers had chosen to represent him more faithfully over the years. It certainly would have been fairer at least to give newcomers more of a sense of the crazy-wise ways of their chosen guru. Instead, there were and presumably still are many marginal friends of the community and even formal disciples of Da Love-Ananda who have no concrete idea of the precise nature of his past crazy-wisdom exploits. Many students do not really want to think about them, preferring to remain ignorant of the details lest they should prove too upsetting.

The current policy of the community's representatives is to affirm that Da Love-Ananda has definitely retired as a crazy-wisdom teacher and that he is now engaged only in "universal blessing work." But this asseveration may be founded in the same kind of deep denial that has proven so destructive to the community in the past. Regardless of his own explanations, which are known to be less than final, Da Love-Ananda continues to interact with disciples. So long as this is the case and so long as men and women relate to him as devotees, they must expect him to interfere with their lives, and this is bound to cause real tempests and problems on occasion.

It is positively naive to assume that Da Love-Ananda's crazy-wisdom days are over. For instance, his continuing production of an ornate spiritual litera-ture of gothic proportions can be seen as the elaborate play of a crazy adept. In fact, to assume anything else would leave us with only one alternative expla-nation, which is quite unsavory and tragic in its implications: that he has lost his sense of humor and is beginning to mistake his own mythology for reality. Why should his present role-playing be the last word? If there is any certainty in his work with disciples it is that nothing around him stays the same for very long.

Most recently, Da Love-Ananda's irrepressible holy madness has surfaced in a new name change, with all its attendant shifts of emphasis in the Free Daist institution and community. This time he appears as the *avatara* "Da Kalki." Kalki is the prophesied future tenth incarnation of God Vishnu. He is supposed to arrive at the end of the present dark age, the *kali-yuga*, riding on a white steed and swinging his sword to bring down all his enemies. He is perhaps the most fundamentalist of all the incarnations of Vishnu. That Da Love-Ananda should have chosen to make Kalki his symbol is significant. He could have opted for Maitreya, the prophesied reembodiment of the Buddha.

But Maitreya represents compassion rather than divine justice, as does Kalki, and compassion does not play an important role in the theology of Da Love-Ananda, nor does it seem to be an ethical practice emphasized by him or his community.

There are several other ways to read this latest addition to Da Love-Ananda's long string of self-bestowed names. We can see it as a specimen of the peculiar crazy-wise sense of humor by which he thumbs his nose at his disciples and the world. As he must know, Kalki is not due to come for another 129 million years or so, according to Hindu computations. Like some of his other names and titles, the name Kalki is another straightforward adoption from Indian sources, with the added twist that it is quite anachronistic. Surely there is great humor in this, providing it is understood as not a literal but a metaphoric statement.

Many critics would undoubtedly proffer a different analysis, namely that the name change is yet another indication of an inflated personality and perhaps a symptom of growing self-delusion. If the latter is the case, his disciples are truly imperiled. Da Love-Ananda tells them that he can do no wrong, and they, in all seriousness, see in him God incarnate. History is replete with instances of such claims and the dire consequences when they are taken literally by a sufficient number of people. The self-delusion of a charismatic leader tends to infect his or her following with the same disease; the resulting closed worldview regards the surrounding world as inimical to the purposes of the charismatic leader, and hence as enemy. From there to active aggression is, as we have witnessed in the case of the Rajneesh movement, a dangerously small step. Or, as in the case of the People's Temple of Jim Jones, the aggressive instinct may be turned inward, leading, in that instance, to enforced mass suicide.

Da Love-Ananda is a born shape shifter, the proverbial protean man, who is his own caricature. He has at one time or another assumed all conceivable roles of a crazy-wise adept. He has acted as a loving friend, a belligerent madman, a boisterous clown, a sorrow-stricken individual, a smitten and jealous lover, a peremptory king, a remorseful confessor, an oracle of doom, an arrogant dilettante, a drunkard with slurred speech, an inspired poet filled with wonder, a proud father, a stern disciplinarian, an incorrigible imp, a solemn sage, an uplifting minstrel, a sexual obsessive, a perceptive philosopher, a childlike person, a decisive businessman, a frail mystic, a tormented writer, a tireless preacher, a man of immeasurable faith and confidence, a ruthless critic, a wiseguy, an enlightened beast, a generous giver, and a formidable *avatara*. At times, he has switched from one role to another so quickly that devotees found themselves in trouble because they failed to notice the change in his mood.

Yet, somehow, behind all these theatrical masks of his persona one can sense the irrepressible Promethean impulse to teach. Even in his most drunken moments—perhaps especially in those moments—Da Love-Ananda has been known to burst into sublime eulogies on the Divine or gripping exhortations to his students to be compassionate, forgiving, and loving. It is his identity with the incommensurable Being that he has always consistently affirmed beyond all his countless roles. He has likened his existence to a screenplay, which has no consciousness in and of itself. The play itself, his activity, is the argument. As he put it on one occasion:

> The conventional sense of identity is in some way inoperable in me. It does not have the force it has in your case. It is very much like having been beheaded . . .
> I am the headless horseman. If you put me on the Dawn Horse, I will hold my hat in the air because there is nothing above my collar but the evening.[34]

This lack of a stable human identity permits Da Love-Ananda tremendous flexibility in his roles and his crazy-wise behavior. He has often remarked on his "madness." Here are two characteristic comments:

> I have always been Crazy, from the moment of my birth. I have been Crazy my entire life. This is the only way that the Great One can intervene in your midst, you see, because you all get very serious about all of the bullshit of your appearances.[35]

> I have always been insane since the day I was born, mad with this Formless Condition that is only vaguely associated with my body-mind . . . God is crazy just like me. In fact, God is crazy just like *you*.[36]

The "madness" of the Divine is a recurrent theme in Da Love-Ananda's metaphysics. He uses this radical concept as a counterpoint to the Judeo-Christian Creator-God, the heavenly "father," who is essentially benign and protective. For him, the Divine is the utterly incomprehensible and unpredictable totality of existence, which ultimately does not favor the conventional ego-personality but forever seeks to supplant it. From the point of view of the finite human mind, therefore, the Divine is a threatening chaos, or madness. The only way to meet that universal madness is by consciously sacrificing the ego-illusion, which gesture is madness in itself. For Da Love-Ananda, God-realization is the ultimate madness because it involves the complete renunciation of the ego-identity.

The function of an adept, as Da Love-Ananda affirms, is to break the spell of conventional consciousness, which is constantly building protective walls around itself, trying to ensure its own immortality. Since convention's magical spell over the conditional personality is so profound, adepts have historically resorted to particularly drastic measures. As Da Love-Ananda has stated:

Everyone is enchanted with unreality, enchanted with the conventional appearance of every moment, and merely talking to them does not break the spell. Talk is not sufficient because they are not merely thinking wrongly. They are altogether associated with this moment in a fashion that renders them incapable of being Awake to their actual Condition. In effect, you must cut them in half with a big sword! You must blow their minds. You must shake them loose. You must wholly divert them. You must trick them. To truly Enlighten human beings you must be wild.[37]

Elsewhere he said:

My Work takes many forms, but the import of it is to drive everyone Mad. It is not to make them clinically insane—that is a devastating, subhuman disorder. Clinical insanity is not Craziness, is not Wisdom, is not the Awakened State . . .

Thus, the fundamental Work of the Adept is spell-breaking. It is a wild, paradoxical exorcism of Narcissus, a terrible Interference in your life, and it must be understood, valued, and appreciated.[38]

Ever since his Columbia days, Da Love-Ananda has had strong leanings toward Hinduism; hence his attraction to Rudi and Muktananda. Over the years, but especially since his death experience in 1986, his teaching has become increasingly Hinduized. Many of his disciples have found this turn of events difficult and alienating. Da Love-Ananda's literature and community jargon brim with Sanskrit and Hindi terms—or highly idiosyncratic versions of them—and many of his numerous self-bestowed names and titles are directly derived from the Hindu tradition.

From the outside, all of this seems needlessly obfuscating. From the inside, however, these curiosities provide students with a never-ending stream of diversion. Their own lives are, on the whole, as dull as the routine existence of most people. But then, spiritual practice is not meant to be entertaining. So the guru's life and deeds hold an all-absorbing fascination for devotees; they live vicariously through him. Each event in Da Love-Ananda's life is greeted as a moment of historical magnitude. While he does not mean to entertain his devotees, he certainly has every intention of holding their attention, because that is how, in *guru-yoga*, the process of spiritual osmosis is thought to take place. However, instead of using the adept's spiritual transmission to duplicate his Awakening, disciples generally end up merely imitating him.

Robert Augustus Masters, the iconoclastic "guide" of the Xanthyros community in Canada, has harshly criticized this attitude among the students of Da Love-Ananda:

Da Free John . . . is a lucid wonder of a man, effortlessly radiant, overflowing with sublime intelligence and heartfelt wisdom, teaching through his example the transcendence of all reactivity. Nevertheless, he sits at the center of a hive abuzz with rabid earnestness, misguided loyalty, and fetishistic preoccupation with him and his every move. He has eloquently criticized such foolishness again and again over the years, but to little avail; his devotees are far too busy telling themselves how wonderful he is, and how wonderful it is to have a Master like him, to really face their cultic obsession with him . . . They compulsively and almost constantly express, or intend to express, their gratitude for him with incredibly naive sincerity and disgusting adulation, robotically convincing themselves that they are doing the right thing, rarely noticing that they're just making real estate out of a moment of light.[39]

In all the excitement that Da Love-Ananda's constant shape shifting provides, his disciples regularly miss the point: Instead of understanding the play between guru and disciple as a metaphor that is meant to disenchant, they take it literally and thus are enchanted by it, possibly sinking deeper into the morass of egoity from which they are so desperately trying to escape. Captivated by the latest emphasis, they typically fail to see that Da Love-Ananda's teaching has from the beginning been the same. *Plus ça change, plus c'est la même chose.* Translated into the language of holy folly, this means: "The more housebroken the adept appears to be, the greater is the wildness that lurks beneath his placid exterior."

Da Love-Ananda has created an entire cultural apparatus for which he reluctantly but persistently functions as the perpetual motor. Everything revolves around him, which is the gist of traditional *guru-yoga*. He once described himself as the queen bee in the hive of devotees. He is nourished by all of them and in return gives life to the hive. This is a horrifying vision to anyone who values his or her independence. But for Da Love-Ananda and his devotees, independence is ultimately illusory and therefore constantly to be undermined. Yet, as Masters rightly points out, *guru-yoga* tends to lead to a dependence that is equally neurotic—simply the obverse of egoic independence.

In his somewhat mistitled book *The Way of the Lover*, Masters wonders out loud why adepts of obvious integrity, like Da Love-Ananda, seem to permit and even encourage guru-devotion to the point where it flips over into mere adulation. Masters rightly notes that most people need to play out the guru-devotee drama in terms of the father-child archetype before they can proceed to a freer and less neurotic form of interaction. But then he remarks:

Unfortunately, Da Free John [Love-Ananda] doesn't use devotionalism in this light, but rather encourages its continuation far past the point where it ought to have served its purpose, instead of employing it as a psychotherapeutic purification. He denounces cultism, yet tacitly supports it, letting himself be surrounded by ritualized guru-worship . . .

To make wise use of someone like Da Free John, whatever his failings, we must not submit to devotional fervour, nor simply stand back, taking notes. We must feel him, empathize with him, receive him, give to him,

losing face without losing touch, giving our love without giving ourselves away. We must remain centered yet not impermeable, strong in
our very vulnerability.[40]

Masters's observations are for the most part astute. We may, however,
question his statement that we can love "without giving ourselves away."
Self-surrender is, after all, the quintessence of the spiritual process and of
love. Probably what Masters means is an immature self-denial through an
idealized love. At any rate, Da Love-Ananda's apparent encouragement of
cultic devotionalism is indeed puzzling, given his periodic trenchant criticisms of cultism. But this is only one of numerous puzzles confronting both
the outside observer and the faithful devotee. Da Love-Ananda is an enigma,
a paradox, for which there may be no solution other than the nonsolution of
enlightenment itself.

# PART TWO
## THE CONTEXT

# 5

## SPIRITUAL PRACTICE: THE PATH BEYOND ALL PATHS

### 1. The Long Search

The conventional mind entertains all kinds of misconceptions and biases about spirituality. These wrong ideas often lead to false approaches to spiritual practice on the part of those who dare to venture beyond the seemingly safe ground of exoteric religion. These misconceptions are certainly a major hurdle in adopting the life of discipleship under a guru, especially a crazy-wisdom teacher, since they prevent neophytes from relating to their teacher rightly. Most seekers travel with a great deal of ideological excess baggage. In fact, one of the heaviest pieces of surplus gear is the notion of traveling, or seeking, itself. Few appreciate the Sufi saying "Those who voyage are not saved."[1]

A person's conception of himself or herself as a spiritual "seeker" is a profound obstacle in the way of authentic spiritual practice. The mode of the seeker is the mode of the ego-personality. And to equate spiritual life with the search is to tacitly presume the persistence of the ego in the spiritual process. As the British poet Lewis Thompson put it with characteristic succinctness, "The most direct evasion is to search."[2] The quest, then, is the easy option. However, the very essence of genuine spirituality is to transcend the quest and the questing ego.

Self-transcendence is diametrically opposed to the search, which is the mood of the ego. Self-transcendence is coessential with enlightenment itself. Thus enlightenment is not the end product of self-transcending practice; it is its very foundation. *Vade in pace*, "walk in peace," quoted Meister Eckehart from Luke 7:36, explaining that we live in peace to the degree that we live in God: Such peace does not accrue from seeking it but from *being* at peace in every moment.[3]

In this notion, as in many others, Eckehart parallels the Eastern mystical

schools of "sudden" enlightenment, which Karl Potter called "leap" philosophies, as opposed to the "progressive" schools of thought.[4] The latter revolve
around the notion of a gradual progression from imperfection to perfection,
or from bondage to liberation, an idea that is based on popular spatial
metaphors that require only a small leap of the imagination. The typical
seeker conceives of spiritual life as a cumbersome ascending path along which
he or she is progressing in discernible stages. This conception is almost
archetypal and has the weighty endorsement of the majority of the world's
religious traditions.

This idea entails a strong dualistic component: Through toilsome application to specific methods, so the story goes, we can step by step elevate
ourselves from our "lower," instinctual nature to realize our "higher," spiritual essence. This notion cannot be entirely dismissed, since many obviously
look upon spiritual practice in this manner. Yet it is an unnecessarily limiting
ideal, and it also represents a self-fulfilling prophecy: Spiritual life lived on the
basis of this ideal usually turns out to be a circuitous and troublesome path. It
may even conceal the pernicious attitude of "spiritual materialism" spoken of
in Chapter 3. As Da Love-Ananda once wryly declared, "Many so-called
spiritual seekers are just Narcissus in drag."[5] Stated differently, much that
goes under the name of spiritual practice is in effect a form of self-deception.
Chögyam Trungpa put it insightfully:

> We might attempt to imitate certain spiritual paths, such as the American
> Indian path or the Hindu path or the Japanese Zen Buddhist path. We
> might abandon our suits and collars and ties, our belts and trousers and
> shoes in an attempt to follow their example. Or we may decide to go to
> northern India in order to join the Tibetans. We might wear Tibetan
> clothing and adopt Tibetan customs. This will seem to be the "hard
> way," because there will always be obstacles and temptations to distract
> us from our purpose.
>
> Sitting in a Hindu ashram, we have not eaten chocolate for six or seven
> months, so we dream of chocolate, or other dishes that we like. Perhaps
> we are nostalgic on Christmas or New Year's Day. We have struggled
> through the difficulties of this path and have become quite competent,
> masters of discipline of some sort. We expect the magic and wisdom of
> our training and practice to bring us into the right state of mind.
> Sometimes we think we have achieved our goal. Perhaps we are com-
> pletely "high" or absorbed for a period of six or seven months. Later our
> ecstasy disappears. And so it goes, on and on, on and off . . .
>
> I am not saying that foreign or disciplinary traditions are not applicable
> to the spiritual path. Rather, I am saying that we have the notion that
> there must be some kind of medicine or magic potion to help us attain the
> right state of mind. This seems to be coming at the problem backwards.
> We hope that by manipulating matter, the physical world, we can achieve
> wisdom and understanding.[6]

Lama Trungpa had Western seekers in mind, but his words apply in principle equally to seekers throughout the world and throughout all ages. They—we—tend to make the choice of adopting a "difficult" path only to avoid having to make the simple gesture of self-transcendence in every instant, or what Trungpa called the "real gift," which includes giving up the hope of getting something in return. While we strive after enlightenment, or liberation, we place ourselves in self-made shackles. We prefer to deceive ourselves, in other words. "Ego," stated Trungpa, "is always trying to achieve spirituality. It is rather like wanting to witness your own funeral."[7]

The ego-personality, however, is only toying with the idea of its own demise. This is a morbid preoccupation, since typically seekers do not really want to face mortality but rather subconsciously attempt to defer it by clinging to the notion of a progressive path toward enlightenment. They prefer to fight imaginary windmills rather than bravely stare the dragon of their own unconscious in the eye. They are scared of the sacred.

Historically speaking, the notion of spirituality as a path or journey is a dowry of what the Swiss cultural philosopher Jean Gebser called the "mental structure of consciousness."[8] This constellation of consciousness emerged after the waning of the great prepatriarchal cultures and reached its culmination at the time of Pythagoras, Socrates, and Plato in Greece, Gautama the Buddha and Mahavira in India, and Confucius and Lao Tzu in China.

Psychologically speaking, the ideal of the gradual approach to enlightenment is a clever device to keep the ego enthroned for as long as possible. The average seeker excuses himself or herself with the argument that the sudden or radical approach is "too difficult." The idea of the gradual path has been nurtured by any number of teachers, though for a different reason. They understood that most spiritual practitioners are not prepared to become fully awakened in this instant and that most need to be teased into self-transcendence. Nevertheless, it is a fact that the "easy" route of the typical seeker characteristically turns out to be the more difficult. As Da Love-Ananda has observed:

> To be absorbed in Communion with the Absolute [corresponding to the radical approach] is not what is difficult. What is difficult is to move attention up and to force it into subtle realms, separating yourself from the natural bodily attention—that is difficult. Arranging a benign future in the midst of experience, controlling your attention to yield beautiful destinies—that is difficult. To be a saint or a yogi is difficult.[9]

However, that does not imply that spiritual life—lived radically—is an easy affair. Da Love-Ananda calls it a "sacred ordeal" and a "hard school," and for very good reasons. Yet seekers seldom appreciate that something simple can demand great application. In one sense, their ignorance is bliss, since few would embark on their spiritual journey if they knew what lay ahead of them.

From a different angle, however, their lack of comprehension of the demand that spiritual life represents is a serious handicap. All too often, neophytes suffer from the delusion that spiritual practice is supposed to be fulfilling. They expect to be made happy, to be relieved of their basic existential sense of dilemma, by their own efforts or by their teacher.

Their hope for spiritual fulfillment, which is really a need to be comforted, is inevitably thwarted. Spiritual life consists in stripping the ego of its accoutrements, until the clench that is the ego itself vanishes. The ego is like an invisible man whose presence is revealed by the clothes he wears; as he undresses, he ceases to be visible. When the ego's myriad projections, which create the illusion of being separated from reality, are all dispelled, there is no one behind them. And the ultimate illusion that is dispelled upon enlightenment is the ego itself. To quote Lewis Thompson again, "This ego has no part in any real world: our grave decorates an abstract landscape."[10]

So long as spiritual practitioners identify with the seeker who is on a "vision quest," they merely experience the great search, not Reality. Instead of freeing them from their suffering, consternation, unfulfillment, and sense of dilemma, their pursuit only aggravates their condition. They unwittingly oppose the spiritual process that is always trying to come alive in them. This situation is predictably compounded by the assumption of typical seekers that spiritual life is relatively easy. In this, they think and behave out of the same frivolous mentality that largely defines their secular existence.

## 2. The Snare of Pop Spirituality

So many practitioners are merely "spiritual" consumers. Philosopher Jacob Needleman has invented an image that fittingly describes consumers in general:

> It is as though within man there were a thousand animals each seeking its own food and comfort. . . . No sooner is one fed than another appears, hungrier than ever, and sometimes hungry for the very food that has just been given his predecessor—and is therefore no longer available.[11]

Transferred into the spiritual domain, this quick-fix consumer mentality is particularly pernicious. Journalist Robert Greenfield has rightly depicted the contemporary scene as a "spiritual supermarket," though his coverage of it suffers from the shallowness and glibness that the mass media, serving consumer needs, tend to perpetuate.[12] The consumer embodies the psyche that has not grown beyond childish dependence and that still relates to life as mother's nipple, the unfailing supplier of inexhaustible goods. It is this mindset, to be sure, that is currently ruining our planet and that keeps billions of people alienated from each other and from their own essential being. The same mentality is responsible for the widespread religious fascism witnessed today, just as it is responsible for the slow diffusion and growth of genuine spiritual values and attitudes in our civilization.

The shelves of the popular "spiritual supermarket" display a surfeit of garishly displayed wares—wares that are only the worthless castoffs of the authentic spiritual traditions, which have been ransacked by unscrupulous popularizers to gratify the common seeker. As Lama Trungpa expressed it:

> Our vast collections of knowledge and experience are just part of ego's display, part of the grandiose quality of ego. We display them to the world and, in doing so, reassure ourselves that we exist, safe and secure, as "spiritual" people.
> But we have simply created a shop, an antique shop.[13]

Exoteric religion, by and large, caters to the consumer mentality. It is a concession to the will-o'-the-wisp of the ego. Spiritual life, however, is founded in the contrary principle. It makes no concessions to the separative self. Aspiring spiritual practitioners must consequently drop the consumer's pose and assume a disposition of self-surrender, or self-transcendence. Their spiritual maturation depends on how quickly they can readapt.

One of the severest critics of "pop spirituality" has been Da Love-Ananda. He has excoriated New Age proselytizers and their clientele for their misrepresentations of spiritual life, their romanticism, and their inveterate competitiveness. In an outburst of eloquent passion he once declared:

> All of these street wars of religion against religion, dull idea against dull idea are nothing but the muscle of stupidity, sheeplike ego clashes (socking macho hornheads as if competing for a rut), the separate junk piles of the past all hurled at one another for the angry sake of power, whizzing between minds that are mucked in self, hardened by fear, defined by the resident passions of birth, and utterly oblivious to the Truth and the Wide Wise significance of our bleeding worried lives.[14]

Alas, much of his criticism also applies to the community he himself founded and which he continues, if seemingly reluctantly, to shepherd. Serious as the popular misrepresentations of spirituality are, still more damaging, in his view, is the widely entertained feeling that the mighty intuitions, insights, and ideals of humanity's great spiritual geniuses are little more than ideas. As ideas, of course, they can safely be talked about, perhaps briefly scrutinized, and finally dismissed. "Ego is able to convert everything to its own use, even spirituality," observed Chögyam Trungpa.[15]

Another way of dealing with the challenge of enlightened communications is by making them the object of belief. This is possibly even more destructive, because the communications of the spiritual adepts are thereby converted into exoteric religion, which is intrinsically in conflict with authentic spirituality. The fate of the teachings of the great adept of Nazareth is a striking example of such distortion at the hands (and minds) of those lacking, in the language of the gospels, "eyes to see and ears to hear."

To understate the premise, belief is not an appropriate response to the teachings and the presence of the adepts. The adepts want to be understood and heeded, not imitated. Chögyam Trungpa insisted that the "knowledge" passing from teacher to disciple is not handed down like an antique that can be collected.[16] Rather, the guru inspires the disciple by his or her own realization. For this reason, Trungpa went on, the teachings should not be labeled "ancient wisdom," for they are always up-to-date, infused with the living spirit of the adept.

The same point is made in the story of the Zen master who once summoned his students to attend a lecture. When they had all gathered before him, he simply sat there in absolute silence. Later, when he was asked about the meaning of his unusual behavior, he remarked that there was nothing to be explained, that there was no problem, and that, besides, other teachers and their commentators had already said it all.

Belief belongs to the realm of ideas, to the techniques by which the ego seeks to massage itself, whereas the adepts' teachings are about the transcendence of ideas and the ideating ego-personality. Modern humanity is, however, largely incapable even of genuine belief. We no longer enjoy the naïveté of our ancestors. Their minds were not ruffled by the anxious mood of doubt instilled in us by our scientistic-materialistic culture. Our more immediate forebears were, like us, what Paul Tillich called "unbelievers,"[17] people bereft of real faith. But at least they were relatively uncomplicated about their acceptance of their religious heritage, and this gave them a modicum of peace and tranquility. Faith is a commitment of the whole being. Belief, on the other hand, is nowadays seldom more than intellectual make-believe—a self-conscious, anaesthetized ideology. It consists of rationalizations, not realizations.

Faith is what the adept seeks to awaken in others. Faith is bodily commitment to life. In depth, it is conscious participation in Reality—enlightenment. Faith presupposes understanding and transparency. The significance of faith is recognized in some schools of Mahayana Buddhism. In the Mahayana scriptures, faith—in Sanskrit, *shraddha*—is often likened to a massive mountain or an immovable rock. It is fundamental trust in the spiritual order of existence, the affirmation of the Buddha nature. In the Mahayana schools of "sudden enlightenment," faith and illumined insight are one and the same; there faith consists in the deeply felt conviction "I *am* the Buddha," as opposed to the conviction "I can *become* the Buddha," which is upheld by those who follow the progressive path to enlightenment. The difference is made clear in the famous exchange between Shen-hsiu and Hui-neng.

Looking for a successor, Hung-jen, the Fifth Patriarch of Ch'an, which is a historical offshoot of Indian Mahayana Buddhism, invited his monks to write verses that would reflect their spiritual maturity. Shen-hsiu posted the following verse in the monastery:

> The body is the Bodhi tree,
> The mind is like a mirror bright.
> At all times we must strive to polish it,
> And not let the dust alight.

The Fifth Patriarch felt the verse did not quite express the enlightened disposition. The young monk Hui-neng promptly posted his own response:

> Bodhi originally has no tree,
> The mirror also has no stand.
> Buddha nature is always clean and pure,
> Where is there room for dust?[18]

With these impromptu lines, Hui-neng secured for himself the spiritual office of Sixth Patriarch. Hui-neng's poetic "solution" to Hung-jen's *koan* revealed his own enlightenment. Obviously, exceedingly few spiritual practitioners are capable of such a spontaneous, radical response. Most practitioners appear to be enthusiastic seekers but hesitant disciples.

Typical seekers come to spiritual life and the teacher with open hands but a closed heart, expecting to be given something without giving something (i.e., themselves) in return. The simile of the vessel brimful with water is pertinent here: However much water is poured into the vessel, the liquid will simply spill over. Full of self, seekers remain unchanged. They remain empty of Reality, and therefore they are constantly "driven to fullness."[19] To recall Ken Wilber's term, the "Atman project" keeps pushing the seeker along.

## 3. The Paradox of Discipline

From the viewpoint of enlightenment, there is no path; the notion of an ascending spiral that leads to gradual recovery of one's innate freedom and bliss is an illusion. However, this state of no-seeking is distinctly not the experience of the unenlightened individual. Many teachers have, therefore, consented to talk about the spiritual process in terms of a stairway to heaven, a path, a journey, an odyssey, a pilgrimage, or a steep climb. This metaphor for the spiritual process undoubtedly has its usefulness, provided the spiritual traveler does not succumb to the fallacy of thinking that enlightenment is a distant goal. It helps practitioners to see their failure to realize the enlightened disposition *now*, and it encourages them to read the signposts along the way, reminding them that their true nature, Reality, is in principle accessible in every moment.

The great awakening, or enlightenment, is always sudden. In an instant, the familiar clench of the ego-personality is released, the practitioner finds himself or herself experiencing the world from within an entirely different context. There is no sense of separation from that which is experienced. Most esoteric schools agree, however, that there can and indeed must be preparation for this event. This is the paradox of spiritual life: Enlightenment cannot be brought about by force, since it is unconditional. Yet, it also cannot occur unless we are ready for it. And there are ways and means by which we can prepare our body-minds for the eventuality of illumination.

Few of us are born with the right frame of mind to realize enlightenment spontaneously. Great sages like Ramana Maharshi, who enjoyed a sudden and permanent awakening at the age of sixteen, are very rare. Traditionalists refer to this felicitous predisposition as good *karma*. I sometimes think of it as a peculiar genetic advantage—a quirk of Nature—that produces a spiritual virtuoso, a "freak."

In most cases, however, before enlightenment there is a marked need for preparation, which means discipline. Alas, this need is not always recognized. All too often, especially in New Age circles, people are so fascinated with the idea that enlightenment lies in the pathless "here and now," that they remain deaf to the countless traditional tales of struggle engaged by spiritual practitioners prior to their awakening. It is tempting and convenient to think that because *nirvana* (ultimate Reality) and *samsara* (conditional reality) are identical, we are already enlightened in our deepest nature and therefore need do nothing more, except perhaps to gossip about it.

The ego does not want to know that the spiritual process, simple as it is, consists of a patient ordeal, a sometimes "bloody" rite of passage, in which, ultimately, the ego is sacrificed. Thus the ego skillfully romanticizes spiritual life. This is aptly illustrated in the story of the mysterious trans-Himalayan country of Shambhala, popularized as Shangri-la in James Hilton's novel *Lost Horizon*.[20] According to medieval Mahayana scriptures, Shambhala is a land of wise rulers and powerful mystics, situated somewhere in the hinterland of Mongolia. It is stated that this mystical country, concealed by a ring of mountains from the prying eyes of unwelcome intruders, is the place of origin of the esoteric Kalacakra teachings.

Over the centuries, many Tibetans and Indians have journeyed the frozen vastness of the Himalayas in search of Shambhala, as the Christians once went in pursuit of the Holy Grail. There are numerous stories of pilgrims whose quest was successful, but many more stories of unprepared "tourists" who met with failure, catastrophe, and death. Shambhala may or may not have existed once as a flourishing society that adhered to the Buddha's highest teachings. But for generations, it has served the followers of North Indian Buddhism as an inspiring symbol of the "paradisiacal" condition of enlightenment, and the arduous pilgrimage to the hidden valley has come to stand for the spiritual process of self-purification, which establishes the basis for enlightenment.

Basically, spiritual consumers want to be titillated while remaining unchanged. They fear the pain of inner transformation. They like to dream of becoming beautiful butterflies but are quite unwilling to go through the caterpillar and cocoon stages. Thus, they escape into thought, neglecting action and bodily commitment. Many times I have heard that the spiritual journey is "so wonderful" or "so beautiful." This has not been my own experience, nor has it been that of any of the major or minor practitioners on record. Spiritual life is, on the contrary, an extremely difficult ordeal. The sacred is an inversion of all the attitudes and expectations of the ordinary individual; it is, as Rudolf Otto reminded us, the *mysterium tremendum et fascinans.*[21] And it is the ego's ultimate horror, because in it the ego correctly sees its own extinction. Genuine spiritual practice is hence a potentially frightening process. It is a direct onslaught on that which, empirically, we hold most inviolable: our egoic identity.

A contemporary Tibetan lama has told the story of a disciple who once asked his teacher whether it would be possible for him, the disciple, to go to Shambhala. The teacher promised him success in this aspiration, providing he practiced certain meditation techniques for several weeks. The disciple left with his teacher's blessings and began seriously to meditate in the way he had been told. At the end of the specified period, he suddenly died . . . and was promptly reborn in the mystical land of Shambhala.[22] The disciple's death is symbolic of the ego "death" that must occur for enlightenment to be possible.

The teacher's function is to stimulate in disciples the necessary condition for this symbolic death. The adept constantly seeks to provoke in them a spiritual crisis, and he or she does so by putting them in touch with their present state of suffering, which the Buddhists call *duhkha* (in Pali, *dukka*). This Sanskrit word means literally "having a bad axle-hole": A chariot with a bad axle-hole is unable to run smoothly, or to run at all. It is a wagonload of trouble, and so is ordinary life, which is lived out against the backdrop of the pain of birth, the confusion of adolescence, the competitive strife of adulthood, the awareness of aging, the loss of what we treasure, the experience of toil and sickness, and the barely admitted inevitability of our own demise. All these experiences leave their scars on us.

We need not be melancholy pessimists to testify that for every enjoyable experience in life there is at least an equally unenjoyable one. More likely, distressful or nondescript experiences outweigh those that bring us delight. If we care to really consider the matter, we realize that even our best moment is just that: a moment, a minute fraction of eternity. Most important, even when we are seemingly at our happiest, there is still, deep down, this nagging sense that one day all will be lost. We react to it mostly by denial. But the fact is, we could not possibly sustain a continuously high feeling. Life is made up of mountains and valleys; if we dare to see clearly, there appear to be more valleys than mountains, and often the mountains are little more than hills. Besides, human civilization operates on the basis of a strong taboo against total ecstasy.

There comes a point in life when we have to ask ourselves: What is it all about? Who am I? Where will I go? It can come early in life, but it is almost certain to come as part of the mid–life crisis that affects modern Westerners with predictable regularity. Some people manage to find glib answers to these questions and simply get on with life as if nothing has happened. But then there are those who, once the questions have announced themselves, cannot go to sleep again. Consensus reality has become questionable for them. These are the spiritual seekers, the existential neurotics, who devour the classics of Eastern and Western mysticism and who come to the guru for help.

According to Bhagwan Rajneesh, who voiced the view of many spiritual teachers and not a few psychologists, all people are neurotics. As he put it:

> Neurosis is the "normal" condition of man because every man passes through a training, a conditioning. He is not allowed to be just whatever he is. He has to be molded into a particular pattern. That pattern creates neurosis . . . He cannot be at ease; he cannot be silent; he cannot be blissful. The hell is always there. And unless you become whole, you cannot be freed from this hell.[23]

The spiritual seeker is always a troubled individual. He or she has become aware of the element of suffering in human life. The source of all this suffering is, of course, the ego, the sense of being a circumscribed, contracted identity. The seeker hopes, secretly or openly, that the teacher will somehow alleviate that sense of dis-ease. But this hope will inevitably be frustrated. The guru may fill his or her disciples' minds and hearts with wonderful alternatives and even initiate them into all kinds of esoteric practices. But if the teacher is genuine, he or she will do nothing to remove the disciples' deep-seated aggravation about life. Indeed, the adept will, in numerous subtle and not-so-subtle ways, do his or her absolute best to fan their fire of frustration.

Gurus do this not because they are warped sadists who want to inflict pain on their disciples, but because they want disciples to understand that all their suffering is of their own making. They want disciples to bring real understanding, wisdom, to the situation. They want them to see that their spiritual quest is for the most part little more than a desire to escape from themselves, and they want them to begin to stand in place, to meet themselves face on.

Spiritual seekers are constantly trying to hide from themselves, from the teacher, and from reality. This disposition is expressed in the well-known Christian hymn "Rock of ages, cleft for me / Let me hide myself in thee." These lines capture the spirit not of authentic self-effacement, or self-transcendence, but of the ego's desire to achieve perfect security and thus to survive in perpetuity, which is an impossible dream. Knowing the disciples' liabilities, the teacher will find any number of ways to pull off their many masks. In a sense, he or she must be crazier than the disciples, and shift shape more than they.

A story is told of poet Allen Ginsberg, a former student of Chögyam Trungpa.[24] In 1971, the poet visited his guru while the latter was staying in a hotel in Berkeley, California. Lama Trungpa, who was quite drunk, looked at Ginsberg and, in a challenging tone, asked him why he was wearing a beard. He wanted to see the face behind the beard. Ginsberg promptly procured a pair of scissors and neatly trimmed his beard. But this gesture left his teacher unimpressed. He wanted the beard to go. Trungpa was due to give a lecture in a short while, and Ginsberg reminded him of it, hoping to get out of this tight spot. His beard was part of his carefully cultivated media image. But Trungpa, after downing some more drinks, insisted on immediate action. Ginsberg convinced him that they should leave for the lecture and that he would shave his beard backstage, which he did. When he emerged clean-shaven, Trungpa called out, "He took off his mask!"

A student of Da Love-Ananda has related a similar incident:

> On my first sitting with Da Love-Ananda, which took place under a bright, sunny sky, I sat toward the back. I didn't want to be pushy and sit right in front, I told myself. But, in fact, I didn't want to be noticed by him. I wanted to be at a safe distance. The group consisted of about thirty or so people, and I hoped I would be invisible. He picked up on that. After the sitting, he sent me a message asking me why I was hiding behind my moustache. He had seen me, and had hit the nail on the head. I shaved off my moustache and sent the shavings to him in an envelope. Apparently, he was amused by this.
>
> A day or two later, we had another sitting in the same bright open space. This time, I ventured to sit in the front row. After the session, I got another message, asking me why I was wearing sunglasses during a *darshan* [sighting of the *guru*] occasion. Didn't I know I was supposed to make eye contact with him? Why was I hiding behind my sunglasses? His analysis of the situation was right, of course. But now I wasn't quite as amused as I had been about his first communication. On one level, I was thrilled by the attention he paid to me; on another level, I dreaded it. I knew he was on my case.
>
> During the next session, I wore neither moustache nor sunglasses, again sitting in the front row. I looked him in the eyes, as I had been instructed to do. I felt a certain awkwardness about it, but was proud to have come out of hiding—or so I thought. Well, it didn't take long for me to receive the next set of notes: Why, he asked, was I hiding behind my mind? The question penetrated me deeply, and I felt the truth behind it. I became quite angry and defensive.

As the Zen teachers are fond of saying and demonstrating to their students, the mind is the great barrier to spiritual realization. It is the seeker's final hideout. Spiritual life involves self-risk. It is easier for most of us to give up our possessions, or even to lose our lives, than it is to abandon our intellectual acquisitions—our illusions about reality.

## 4. The "Heat" of Spiritual Discipline

To be sure, spiritual practice is not engaged in order to inflict suffering on oneself. Rather, its whole point is to recognize that, so long as we identify ourselves as ego-personalities, we are in a condition of suffering. As Zen teacher Albert Low has phrased it:

Life is founded on suffering and suffering underlies all we do. We suffer because we are hungry and we suffer because we are full; we suffer because we have and we suffer because we lack. We suffer because of love, in fear that we shall lose what we love, and we suffer when we hate. There is a constant cycle of fear, hate, greed, boredom, hope . . . Pain, we believe, is an accident, an intrusion, the bungling of an unthinking fate. We are like people waiting at a railway station for a train that will never come. [25]

Spiritual discipline—in Sanskrit *sadhana* or "means of realization"—simply puts us in touch with our human situation. It is true that various religious traditions have at times fostered the mistaken belief that salvation can be achieved by increasing the disciple's pain and suffering. But the error of this view is amply demonstrated in the craze that swept across late medieval Europe where thousands of people, during the semireligious Feast of Fools, walked the streets flagellating each other and themselves until they drew blood. This annual procession, celebrated for twelve days following Christmas, predictably ended in nocturnal orgies. [26] Instead of being a goad to self-transcendence, pain manifestly proved a whip to self-indulgence.

This kind of institutionalized masochism has led philosopher Ben-Ami Scharfstein to conclude wrongly that the mystics "must be cruel to themselves." [27] In authentic spirituality, pain is never deliberately sought. Yet if a person's practice is real, it always contains an element of self-frustration, of resistance to his or her egoic programs or habit-patterns. This is what is meant by discipline: the voluntary harnessing of energies, thoughts, and behavior.

Spiritual discipline can thus be characterized as the renunciation of the "old Adam," implying a reversal of one's usual way of going about the business of life. Renunciation does not mean that one should live in an inaccessible cave or jungle. A troglodyte's existence does not guarantee a renunciate disposition. A lonesome cave dweller, if spiritually immature, will find ways to evade awareness of his or her basic suffering as readily as will the busy urbanite.

One form of escape is, of course, the solitary mystic's inward-and-upward flight into the Disneyland of the nervous system. Instead of succumbing to the gross pleasures of city life, the caverned mystic falls prey to the flashy attractions of his own consciousness. In this respect, the mystic can be as much a victim of his peculiar habit of attention as is the urbanite who dwells on money, possessions, sex, and entertainment.

Genuine spiritual practice goes beyond the approach of both the typical mystic and the ordinary world-enmeshed individual. It revolves around the transcendence of the process of attention itself. Instead of permitting attention and therefore the whole being to become fixed on a specific experience, whether external or internal, practitioners simply understand all their impulses toward experience and knowledge. They rest, to the degree that they are capable of it, in the awareness that is prior to the play of attention.

Spiritual life unravels itself in the tension between abiding in pure awareness, or the intuition of Reality as it is, and observation of the obsolescent but still persisting tendencies of attention. This is the trajectory along which suffering is no longer passively endured but rather actively inspected and transcended. This process has been widely typified as a sweeping catharsis of the disciple's being.

But purification burns. It is painful to see one's robotic nature acting out senseless behavior over and over again. It is also difficult to muster the willpower necessary to override the mechanism of the mind and change course. Hence Da Love-Ananda has often spoken to his disciples of the "heat" of practice. One of his students explains:

During the early days of my involvement, I often wondered just what Da Free John [Da Love-Ananda] and my fellow disciples were referring to when they mentioned experiencing the "heat" of practice, or the "crunch." For the first few weeks all I was feeling was a constant elation. I had no explanation for this. Perhaps I was just really happy to have found my guru. I don't know. Because of my happiness I was, frankly, even a bit suspicious of my friends' frequent references to "the heat." I thought they were simply mystifying their resistance to spiritual life. Anyway, I grew more and more curious about this phenomenon. Gradually, I began to suspect my own apparently happy condition. I recognized that, even though my elation was real enough, I was caught up in it, indulging in it, and not really applying the principles of the teaching to my situation. I realized just how green a beginner I was and wanted to be more real about my practice.

Shortly after I had come to this insight, I had my first opportunity to sit in formal meditation with my guru. As I bowed to him on entering the hall, I mentally laid down my search and asked for his help in my fumbling efforts at practicing his way of radical understanding. I actually asked for some "heat" in my life. Believe it or not, seconds later, I understood exactly what all my friends had been talking about! I felt a strange pressure on my being. I was all of a sudden in touch with my fundamental suffering as an egoic being. At the same time, I was curiously able to witness, with equanimity, my own state.

For a while I was rather intrigued by this paradoxical state, seeing the great possibility in it. But my fascination soon gave way to frustration: I got caught up in feeling rather than witnessing my own unhappiness. In the end, I further complicated my predicament by trying to resist the "heat" I was feeling. I had been given a glimpse of real spiritual practice, but found myself unable to assume responsibility for it. The condition abated at the end of the day, but it was the first visitation of many similar moments. By now that peculiar spiritual experience is a familiar feature of my life.

The "heat" of spiritual discipline is a phenomenon that is by no means unique to followers of Da Love-Ananda. It is essential to all spiritual practice.

For instance, in Hinduism the earliest designation for "spiritual practice" is *tapas*. This ancient Sanskrit word means quite literally "heat" or "glow." The Sanskrit scriptures point out cosmic parallels to the practitioner's ardor and psychic candescence. Thus, according to the archaic *Aitareya-Brahmana* (V. 32.1), the Creator Prajapati fashioned the world by "boiling" himself through a course of most severe asceticism (*tapas*). He "sweated" out the cosmos. As Mircea Eliade noted, the motif of producing heat by magical or religious means is common to the psychocosmologies of many Indo–European peoples.[28] The motif itself, I venture to suggest, did not originate in mere theoretical speculation but in the actual religio–spiritual experience of early humanity.

Throughout history, spiritual practitioners have resorted to the metaphor of heat or fire to describe the process of transformation that leads to enlightenment. Fire affords the most vivid example of an agency for the transmutation of forms, and it is also strongly reminiscent, Eliade pointed out, of the mystical experience of light as an aspect of the ultimate Reality. In describing an experience that overwhelmed him on November 23, 1654, Blaise Pascal was reduced to choppy phrases; the only physical description he noted down was "Fire."[29]

The "fire" of realization is prefigured in the fieriness of the process leading up to it. Spiritual discipline is a constant fiery demand to go beyond what we appear or tend to be. The frustration this causes is considerable, and a good many beginners turn back after a while. "Zen," said Kyogen, "is like a man hanging in a tree by his teeth over a precipice."[30] This applies to any spiritual discipline. Practitioners everywhere hang on to the tree of life by the skin of their teeth, and yet a mysterious impulse has come alive in them that compels them to let go of the branch. They must dare to drop into the gulf of the unknown and unknowable in order to enjoy true freedom. This is the formidable challenge of self-transcendence, or self-surrender.

A diary entry made by philosopher Sam Keen captures the agony of the spiritual seeker in very moving terms:

> God, but I want madness!
> I want to tremble, to be shaken,
> to yield to pulsation,
> to surrender to the rhythm of music and sea,
> to the seasons of ebb and flow,
> to the tidal surge of love.
>
> I am tired of being
> hard,
> tight,
> controlled,
> tensed against the invasion of novelty,
> armed against tenderness,

afraid of softness.
I am tired of
directing my world,
making,
doing,
shaping.
Tension is ecstasy in chains.
The muscles are tightened to prevent trembling.
Nerves strain to prevent trust, hope, relaxation.

Surrendering,
giving in to the involuntary is:
madness (idiots tremble),
ecstasy (being out of my skin, what am I?),
bliss (love is coming together and parting),
grace (dancing with the whole spirit).

Surrendering,
giving in to the involuntary is:
insanity (which voices are mine?),
terror (now, who am I?),
torture (aliens are fighting in my brain),
being possessed (by a god or a demon, or both).

Which:
madness or insanity,
trembling or being afraid,
enthusiasm or possession?
The path is narrow to the right madness.
Be wary of trembling in the wrong places!
The demons often disguise themselves as gods.
And vice versa.

Surrender is a risk no sane man may take.
Sanity never surrendered is a burden no man may carry.

God, give me madness
that does not destroy
wisdom,
responsibility,
love.[31]

Alas, as is clear from a subsequent entry, Sam Keen immediately romanticizes this spiritual impulse. He declares his secret desire to be as carefree as Zorba, the Greek who will "allow no lonely woman to remain comfortless." He settles for philosophy, which he acknowledges to be both "my dis–ease and my medicine." This last observation has its parallel in spiritual practice. On the one hand, spiritual practice is rooted in existential neurosis; on the other hand, it is its own cure.

The means to wholeness is *metanoia* and surrender, by which we transcend the source of all confusion, alienation, and suffering—our ego-identity. On this all spiritual traditions agree; they differ only in their prescriptions and explanations. *Metanoia* is comparable to switching rails: a relatively simple procedure, yet with far-reaching consequences. By pulling a lever (or nowadays by pushing a button), the railway worker rearranges the track so that an entire train gets rerouted in a matter of seconds. Surrender is the disposition of letting go once this profound reorientation of one's whole being has occurred. Through the relinquishment of the ego-position, we reroute our life's train in the direction of God, Self, or *nirvana*.

Unfortunately, unlike in the railway system, our inner rails snap back into their previous position again and again. Hence, the act of surrender has to be repeated endlessly, until the surrendered disposition becomes the permanent, "ordinary" state of being—an event that coincides with enlightenment, or God-realization. Meantime, there is a certain struggle to keep pulling the lever, or pushing the button, of surrender. This is partly effected through appropriate spiritual discipline. The trick is not to turn surrender into suppression and repression. Surrender is openness to Reality, whereas suppression and repression are forms of psychic closure.

Even the radical "leap" schools, with very few exceptions, agree on the need for preparation prior to enlightenment. For them, there is no ultimate path with a goal "out there," but there are countless paths through which we can learn to exercise the muscle of surrender. As Alan Watts observed, "The child is tricked into the ego-feeling by the attitudes, words, and actions of the society which surrounds him."[32] Spiritual discipline is a full-fledged attempt to trick us out of the ego-habit, first by making us fully conscious of its existence and then by giving us the means of overcoming it. Watts went on to say:

> Don't try to get rid of the ego-sensation. Take it, so long as it lasts, as a feature or play of the total process—like a cloud or wave, or like feeling warm or cold, or anything else that happens of itself. Getting rid of one's ego is the last resort of invincible egoism! It simply confirms and strengthens the reality of the feeling. But when this feeling of separateness is approached and accepted like any other sensation, it evaporates like the mirage that it is.
>
> This is why I am not overly enthusiastic about the various "spiritual exercises" in meditation or yoga which some consider essential for release from the ego.[33]

Watts, who died in 1973 (seven years after writing those lines), was only partly right. We cannot remove the ego forcibly; rather we must come to terms with it. Watts was wildly mistaken, however, when he claimed that the ego-sensation will evaporate through mere acceptance of it. There is a real need for discipline, which Watts, by his own admission, found rather difficult.[34]

Discipline, if it is authentic, is the practice of enlightenment, that is, of magnifying our intuition of what is prior to the ego-contraction. Discipline is realizing the enlightened viewpoint under all circumstances, until that realization becomes full and permanent. As Zen master Nansen reminded his disciples: "Everyday life is the path."[35] Through discipline, we can convert every single moment into a sacred instant, in which we are attuned to what is prior to the ego-identity.

Through such discipline, we come up against our habit patterns, and this creates a sense of tension or "heat." Surrender is effective only when it occurs against the backdrop of egoic resistance. Whether we practice simple mindfulness, complicated Tantric visualization techniques, service to the guru and others, or physical exercises—the *spiritual* merit of all these practices is defined by our inner disposition of letting go, the degree to which we can transcend the self.

Spiritual life is chiefly a revelation of our failure to surrender. As we apply ourselves to our chosen discipline, we gradually see all the areas over which the ego holds dominion. That is why it is so important to accept the fact that the ego-habit will be with us until the breakthrough into permanent enlightenment, whenever it may occur. And we must also be willing to accept that this final transition may never occur in this lifetime. This thought tends to discourage the beginner who wants to be assured of "success." What he or she has to understand and learn to trust is that the enlightened disposition is animated in every moment of genuine discipline. It may not be accompanied by full inner transparency or mystical fireworks, but this is truly unimportant. What matters is that the spiritual process is aflow.

Disciplined spiritual life has often been described in terms of purification. This is essentially correct. Even if we believe that in our true nature we are pure Being or Consciousness, that is not our present realization. Rather, what we experience is a personality that suffers a basic sense of alienation from the cosmos and from itself (or, rather, from its original ground). As we engage spiritual discipline, we encounter our own suffering and the many contributory causes of it. But our spiritual endeavor, the fire of practice, also gradually begins to purify the personality, enabling us to make ever deeper gestures of self-transcendence, or surrender.

Discipline, then, is active self-purification. It is our initiative to open ourselves to that which eclipses our ego-personality. Discipline is often styled "asceticism," in Sanskrit, *tapas*. It is practice that sets one afire. Ascetics are aglow. "Without asceticism," remarked Thomas Merton, one of the great Christian contemplatives of our age, "the mystical life is practically out of the question."[36] Then he added this important proviso:

But asceticism does not need to find expression in strenuous exercises of mortification, still less in spectacular and extraordinary macerations. On the contrary, the true path of asceticism is a path of simplicity and obscurity, and there is no true Christian self-denial that does not begin first of all with a wholehearted acceptance and fulfillment of the ordinary duties of one's state in life. Everyone guided by grace will spontaneously desire to add something on his own account to the sacrifices demanded by Providence and by his state of life. But the best of these mortifications will always be the ones that are seen by God alone and do not attract the attention of other men or flatter our own self-complacency. It is very bad in practice to allow ascetics to indulge in penitential rivalries with one another, for this generally fixes their attention upon themselves and gives them a narrow outlook, depriving them of the interior liberty which is absolutely necessary for progress in the ways of prayer.[37]

According to some schools of thought, the spiritual process consists solely of passive receptivity. Other schools argue that one must work hard to purify oneself. Most schools, however, assume a middle path in this matter: There must be what, in Japanese Buddhism, is called "self-effort" *and* "other-effort"—that is, work *and* grace—for spiritual growth to occur. Grace here means the inflow of understanding and strength that is received after opening up. Without appropriate self-purificatory effort, there is no foundation to receive the gift of grace, and without grace self-effort is destined to remain barren. The two are like soil and water. Both are necessary for the harvest.

"Surrender," insisted Rajneesh, "is always total."[38] However, this is the ideal. In practice, surrender is partial, although in the moment it may seem to be all that we *can* let go. This is precisely why there is need for continued discipline. As we discover more about ourselves, we learn to recognize all those places where we hold back from total surrender. This understanding empowers us to let go more. Nevertheless, in every gesture of surrender, our *intention* must be to surrender everything, to let go of all that we are. As Meister Eckehart admonished:

> You must know that no man in this life ever gave himself up to the point that he would not find he should give himself up still more. There are few people who understand this rightly and are consistent in it. [Nonetheless,] it is an equal exchange and a fair trade: To the extent that you leave behind all things, to that extent—and no more—does God enter with all that is his, inasmuch as you completely renounce all that is yours in regard to all things.[39]

Renunciation, surrender, practice, discipline, purification—these are all ways of talking about the process by which the ego-identity is dislodged. It will have become clear by now that this is both the most difficult and the most threatening task that anyone can undertake. The *Mahabharata* (XII.300.50), one of India's two national epics, contains this stanza:

> This great path of the wise brahmins is arduous. No one can tread it easily, o Bharatarshabha! It is like a terrible jungle creeping with large

snakes, filled with pits, devoid of water, full of thorns, and quite inaccessible.

The *Katha-Upanishad* (I.3.14), a Sanskrit scripture that dates back to the fifth century B.C., compares the spiritual path to a razor's edge. Spiritual practice is, indeed, a life-and-death matter. Not surprisingly, there can be a lot of drama attached to it. Some spiritual seekers have gone mad; some have committed suicide; many have succumbed to self-delusion. But there have also been victors—those blessed men and women who have crossed the rapids and reached the "other shore," the great adepts whose testimony serves as a constant reminder that we can awaken from the dream of consensus reality.

Understandably, all traditional authorities are in unanimous agreement that only the most intrepid, determined, and qualified traveler on the road to freedom will be blessed with success. Hence they stipulate all kinds of qualifications that a neophyte should possess. These range from a tenacious self-transcending impulse to such virtues as fine-tuned discrimination, a dispassionate temper, endurance, patience, the ability to concentrate, and, not least, faith. In a sense, even the neophyte is expected to display the very aptitudes and virtues associated with the higher levels of spiritual maturity. According to some traditional descriptions, the beginner has to be a saint from the start! Da Love-Ananda captured the same paradox when he demanded of his followers, "Come to Me when you are already Happy."[40] To be happy, in the spiritual sense, means to have outgrown the conventional hunt for consoling pleasures and to have freed one's energies for the spiritual ordeal of self-transcendence.

Of course, those who approach spiritual teachers tend to be seekers who suffer from unhappiness and hope to overcome it. More than that, they typically expect the teacher to alleviate their suffering. They look on him or her as a shaman, a miracle worker, a soul doctor to whom they must surrender in childlike fashion to be miraculously made whole. This hope is utterly misplaced. Genuine teachers will always do their utmost to destroy the disciple's mental image of them as omnipotent and omniscient father or mother figures.

Naturally, when average disciples realize that the teacher not only fails to live up to their ideal but actually demands that they cure themselves, they feel betrayed, disappointed, frustrated, angry, and desperate. They predictably retaliate by blaming the teacher for their own failure to grow spiritually. They may even stoop so low as to make all kinds of wild accusations in order to get back at the father or mother figure. These dynamics between spiritual teachers and their disciples must be fully understood. They can explain part of the discontent that many people feel toward Eastern-style gurus and other spiritual guides. This is not to say there are no cases where a former disciple's complaints about a teacher are perfectly legitimate. Unfortunately, the public—goaded by the news media—has hitherto found only fault with these teachers. The media has made periodic guru-bashing into something of an international pastime. Crazy-wise teachers are especially prone to misrepresentation, and this must be taken into account in any consideration of the phenomenon of holy folly. Because of their often outrageous manner of interacting with their disciples (and sometimes even with the public), they are natural candidates for media attention and manipulation.

I will say more about the vital teacher-disciple relationship in Chapter 7. But first we need to examine more closely the nature and role of the spiritual guide, who has traditionally been thought instrumental for success on the spiritual path.

# 6

## THE GURU: LICENSE TO KILL

### 1. False Images of the Guru

The purpose of spiritual practice is to "deconstruct" our carefully constructed consensus reality so that we can recover the Reality that lies beneath, or beyond, all our signs and symbols. This process of deconstruction, in which all meaning is transcended, resembles madness. Psychologically immature individuals embarking on this path have been known to go literally mad, unable to face up to the fact that naked Reality, which reveals itself when our conceptual grids are removed, is an unimaginable richness of actualities and possibilities.

The task of the spiritual guide, the guru, is to facilitate this mind-shattering discovery. Every guru, however gentle and considerate, works toward exploding the disciple's personal universe of meaning. Holy madness, or the crazy-wisdom style of teaching demonstrated by teachers like Marpa, Drukpa Kunley, Chögyam Trungpa, and Da Love-Ananda, is simply a more radical version of the task assumed by all authentic spiritual guides.

In this chapter we will look at what the guru function is ideally intended to be and what it often is in practice. We will also examine some of the powerful misconceptions circulating in our culture that impede our understanding of the nature of spiritual authority and guidance, not least the crazy-wisdom approach of teaching. We must, first of all, note that the phenomenon of spiritual guidance is ubiquitous in all forms of religion that involve an esoteric odyssey. In the gnostic schools, for instance, the initiate is aided by the *hierophantes* ("he who shows the sacred"), just as the Christian mystical aspirant has his or her *spiritual director*. In the Eastern branch of Christendom, the role of the spiritual guide is fulfilled by the *staretz*, in Sufism by the *shaykh* or *pir*, in Hasidism by the *zaddik*, in Zen by the *roshi*, in Tibetan Buddhism by the *lama*, in Hinduism by the *guru*. What is the role of the spiritual master?

What is its significance today and in the future? It would be foolhardy to consider these questions without first addressing a striking and pervasive cultural bias.

Despite the psychedelic revolution, the occult revival, neopaganism, and the emergence of the "new religions," mainstream Western society is still deeply suspicious of all things psychic and spiritual. This bias is the product of the pseudo-religion of scientism, which debunks everything that cannot be accounted for by its own ideological scratchings on the surface reality of life. Scientific materialism has not only discarded the historically potent image of the Creator-God, but it has also destroyed the underlying magical worldview as a whole. In its zeal to make absolute, logical sense of existence, it has "demythologized" sacred lore and, in doing so, has led itself and our culture down absurd tracks.

Behaviorism, the psychology without psyche, is symbolic of the whole reductionistic enterprise of scientism. Although behaviorism has luckily gone somewhat out of fashion, it is by no means extinct, as some critics would have it. As a habit of thought, it lurks just around the corner in all scientific disciplines and all "respectable" branches of knowledge that are modeled on the hard sciences. Scientific materialism has effectively "de-psychified" life. It celebrates form while exorcising essence. It is the source of what Morris Berman has called the "disenchantment" of our life world. Scientism succeeded in breaking the spell of the ancien régime only by casting a new and potentially more tragic spell on us by tabooing a whole dimension of existence—the psyche. As Berman put it:

> The story of the modern epoch, at least on the level of mind, is one of progressive disenchantment. From the sixteenth century on, mind has been progressively expunged from the phenomenal world. At least in theory, the reference points for all scientific explanation are matter and motion—what historians of science refer to as the "mechanical philosophy." Developments that have thrown this world view into question—quantum mechanics, for example, or certain types of contemporary ecological research—have not made any significant dent in the dominant mode of thinking. That mode can best be described as disenchantment, nonparticipation, for it insists on a rigid distinction between observer and observed. Scientific consciousness is alienated consciousness: there is no ecstatic merger with nature, but rather total separation from it. Subject and object are always seen in opposition to each other. I am not my experiences, and thus not really part of the world around me. The logical end point of the world view is a feeling of total reification: everything is an object, alien, not-me; and I am ultimately an object too, an alienated "thing" in a world of other, equally meaningless things. This world is not of my own making; the cosmos cares nothing for me, and I do not really feel a sense of belonging to it. What I feel, in fact, is a sickness in the soul.[1]

That feeling of "sickness in the soul," which epitomizes the great malaise of modern humanity, arises from a blanket denial of the soul, psyche, or spirit. Even such popular spokesmen for the psyche as Carl Gustav Jung and Joseph Campbell have failed to correct this cultural imbalance, and their influence is largely confined to a certain educated segment of our Western society.

Since the psychic dimension has thus been outlawed by the ideology of scientism, it is not surprising that the figure of the psychopomp should have shared the same fate. In ancient Greek mythology, the *psychopompos* was the "guide" (pompos) who conducted the souls of the departed safely through the treacherous terrain of the underworld until they reached their destination in the realm of the ancestors. In ancient Egypt, it was Thoth who guided the diseased in their postmortem voyage. In Greece, this function fell on Hermes. In traditional China, the souls of the deceased were accompanied across the Fairy Bridge by the Jade Maiden and the Golden Youth.

In later antiquity, the eschatological figure of the psychopomp was reinterpreted along mystical-alchemical lines. Thus, the Hellenistic mystery religions and the gnostic tradition "internalized" the psychopomp, as they also reinterpreted the archetypal motifs of death and regeneration. The hermetic Deity became the "liberator" (*eleutherios*) of the spiritual aspirant who desired to cross the ocean of mundane existence. In the alchemical tradition, Hermes reappeared as Hermes Trismegistus, the god of creation and revelation, the spirit encased in matter, the philosopher's stone, the alchemist's guide and tempter, corresponding on the physical plane to the strange liquid metal quicksilver.

The figure of the guru, shaykh, roshi, lama, or spiritual director is to esotericism what the psychopomp is to eschatology and mystical alchemy. Unlike the divine Hermes or the alchemical Hermes-Mercurius, the spiritual guide is not a mere psychic projection or symbolic force. He or she is an actual, embodied being, whose guidance depends on his or her being fully incarnated. The spiritual adept's function is to conduct the seeker from the unreal to the real, from darkness to light, from the nonself to the Self, from neurotic self-dividedness to wholeness.

Such a guide cannot be understood from within the disenchanted worldview of scientific materialism. The ego-ensconced contemporary will see the esoteric psychopomp—the spiritual guide—as a mere anomaly or even as a psychopath or charlatan. By the logic of his or her nonparticipatory life-style, the ego-bound individual is obliged to explain away the existence of genuine spiritual authority, an attitude that is apparently vindicated by the appearance of the numerous rogue gurus of our day and their obsequious, duped followers.

Pluralist America, duplicating in this respect medieval Europe,[2] has had its share of gurulike figures during the two centuries of its existence. As Terry Clifford has reminded us, the Religious Liberty Act owed its passage to the fervor of the stalwarts of the pietistic revival, the "first great awakening," in the latter part of the eighteenth century—to such fire-breathing preachers as the Calvinist theologian Jonathan Edwards, leader of the Community of Saints, and the militant prophet Hugh Bryan, who camped out in the swamps of Carolina with his devotees.[3]

The "second great awakening," in the first half of the nineteenth century, was connected with the flourishing of Christian revivalist sects, spiritualism, and apocalyptic preachers. Among the more eccentric figures was the frontiersman Johnny Appleseed, who underscored his mystical message by planting apple seeds wherever he went, as a symbol of spiritual love. Equally eccentric, if more controversial, was John Humphrey Noyes, founder of the Oneida Perfectionist Community, which attracted much negative public attention by dint of its counterpuritan sexual ethics. The era also saw the birth of Mormonism and of the Adventist church, founded by William Miller, who lost many followers after his prediction of the coming of Christ twice failed to come true.

These early American gurus paved the way for American transcendentalists like Henry Thoreau, Walt Whitman, and Ralph Waldo Emerson, as well as the immensely successful Theosophical Society, under the leadership of H. P. Blavatsky and Colonel H. S. Olcott—who presented themselves as disciples of an enigmatic Brotherhood of Masters secreted in the remote Himalayas. By 1890, America was ripe for the spectacular meeting between the "heathen" East and the Christian West at the Parliament of World Religions, held as an adjunct to the Chicago World Fair.[4] The delegates included masters of the traditions of Hinduism, Buddhism, Shintoism, Islam, and Zen. Reputedly the most charismatic figure was young Swami Vivekananda, chief disciple of the Hindu saint Sri Ramakrishna. His success among the American intelligentsia, together with the industrious missionizing of the Theosophical Society, opened the floodgates to Eastern esotericism and exotericism, which led in turn to the "third great awakening" of today, with its legions of prophets, visionaries, *avataras*, ascended masters, illuminati, and risen Christs.

Despite this colorful history, the American public, like its European counterpart, remains ill informed about, and ill at ease with, the contemporary "spiritual supermarket." The widespread nervousness about so-called "spiritual" movements can, on one level, be traced back to ignorance about the psychic dimension and genuine spirituality. But on a deeper level, this apprehension can be understood as the ego's subliminal fear that these esoteric traditions actually have something important and fundamental to say about the nature and destiny of humankind.

Understandably, this fear is focused on the person of the spiritual teacher, or master. After all, he or she represents the most visible threat to the ego-personality, which seeks either autonomy or anonymity as a means of escaping responsibility and self-transformation. The ego is always either in rebellion against authority and outside influence or childishly dependent on external forces. However, even a person who displays strong childish dependence on secular authority—be it parent, superior, psychiatrist, or other figures of power—is generally loath to deliver himself or herself into the hands of a spiritual master. The reason for this is that the guru is popularly perceived as someone who stakes a claim to *absolute* authority over devotees, treating them as servile zombies. The childish adult personality wants to be saved, not enslaved by authority, and the guru is seen as an exploiter, not a savior.

The mass media feed this common image by sensationalizing cases of obvious or alleged abuse of charismatic power among contemporary hierophantic leaders. Although these exposés, when genuine, are appropriate and useful enough, the media have no interest in educating the public about the spiritual process itself. Therefore, their uncovering of the many "spiritual" wolves in sheep's clothing is lopsided. Insofar as it reinforces popular stereotypes and prejudices, it is also damaging to the cause of authentic spirituality.

With their generally adolescent (rebellious) orientation to life, the media glorify the presumed autarchy of the individual. They promote and contribute to the myth of the rightful existence of Narcissus, the egocentric personality. They celebrate the secular heroes of the mass culture—stars and starlets of the leisure industry's fantasy world, those who manage to cheat the establishment, murderers and terrorists, and nowadays also pseudo-gurus or "fallen" ascended masters. This celebration of popular heroes is seldom more than ritual slaughter. Lacking the imagination or the capacity for vice displayed by these worshipped supermen and superwomen, the conventional ego must ultimately turn them into scapegoats to satisfy its own repressed desires and unfulfilled ambitions.

At bottom, ordinary individuals do not dare to conceive of a spiritual Reality or a spiritual teacher that is genuine. They can imagine only someone like themselves—perhaps more powerful (like Superman) or more amoral (like Count Dracula) but essentially still cast from the same mold. Of course, this is true even of many spiritual seekers, who are in love with the search, not with Reality, and who substitute all manner of consoling techniques for the hard work of self-transcendence. One can identify at least four principal ways of avoiding confrontation with a real, flesh-and-blood guru.

As a first and common form of avoidance, seekers tend dexterously to replace the demanding external guru with the comforting and comfortable "inner guru." In other words, they succumb to the need to preserve their ego-identity. But as we have seen, the entire spiritual adventure is about sloughing the ego-identity. The inner guru to which so many seekers entrust their spiritual career is frequently only a figment of their imagination, a product of self-delusion.

Trying to justify this approach, they are always quick to point out that the Eastern traditions themselves speak of the "inner ruler," the guru or light within, and that finally even the external teacher must be transcended. This is correct, of course. Yet what they generally fail to appreciate is that this internal guide is coessential with the transcendental Reality, or one's authentic Identity. Therefore, to be "guided" by that Identity presupposes enlightenment. Since that Identity is not separate from the ego-identity of the unenlightened state, but is its true foundation, it is quite possible that we can have strong pre-enlightenment intuitions of it. In fact, the more attuned we are to the spiritual process, the stronger and more transparent such intuitions will be. In those moments we are indeed inspired and guided, and our conduct will be correspondingly true and spontaneous. But how easy it is to deceive oneself! The ego is inherently conservative. It always seeks to maintain its position in the world. And consequently it will receive just those intuitions and "messages" from the inner guru that it likes to receive.

I am not completely debunking the concept of the inner guru. Even the external guru must be internalized at a certain point in one's spiritual maturation, and the transcendental Identity, or Self, can indeed act as a guiding force in our lives. But we must first learn to distinguish between fantasy and reality, between our childish needs and neurotic desires and the genuine impulse to transcend the ego. Otherwise our spirituality is bound to remain a sad parody.

Not everyone is endowed with razor-sharp intelligence, a fact that was overlooked by Jiddu Krishnamurti, who, in preaching against gurus, sought to turn his numerous listeners and readers to the inner teacher. His critical attitude toward gurus, one suspects, was rooted in his own personal history; he was groomed by the Theosophical Society to be the world leader of our age but, when he was old enough, refused to assume that role. Nevertheless, when Krishnamurti died in 1986, he had a large following around the world, and he is also reported to have conducted small devotee-like gatherings over the years. His opinion about gurus, like his entire public role, was that of a maverick in the spiritual traditions.

One person who cannot be faulted for lack of critical acumen or spiritual maturity is Thomas Merton, who made these highly pertinent comments:

> If we do not let ourselves be directed by other men, who speak in His name, we cannot pretend that we are directed by Him . . . Saint John of the Cross remarks, in one of his maxims: "The soul that is alone and without a master and has virtue is like the burning coal that is alone. It will grow colder rather than hotter."
>
> Some people believe that the Catholic Church is the only one that exacts submission to teaching authority and that outside the sphere of her influence all spiritual men are free as the wind—they can believe anything they like and practice any form of asceticism they please and never

have to render an account of themselves to anybody. Actually, where the contemplative life is taken seriously, the first thing required of the novice is the willingness to submit to a master, to obey, to renounce his own judgment, to practice humility and to learn a doctrine of the interior life from a spiritual master.[5]

A second way to skirt genuine discipleship is to pick a teacher who is safely dead. The New Age craze of channeling is symptomatic of this approach. Here, conveniently "ascended" (hence no longer physically present) masters give all kinds of advice, which is usually quite innocuous and makes precious little demand for actual change. "Dead gurus," Da Love-Ananda once stated bluntly, "can't kick ass."[6] The ordinary individual in this circumstance feels understood, confirmed, and loved, and confuses these feelings with genuine spirituality. Karl Marx's castigation of religion as the opiate of the masses would seem to apply here, and this confusion is almost more tragic than a starkly materialistic denial of psychic and spiritual realities.

A third way to dodge discipleship under a spiritual guide is to hold the notion that one can find the teacher everywhere. This is not wrong in itself, because life itself *is* a great and patient teacher. Yet looking for the teacher in all things can easily become a "head trip," an excuse for a casual approach to spirituality.

The fourth ploy by which some spiritual seekers immunize themselves against the interference of a personal spiritual guide is to regard that guide as a generic model, a symbol to be imitated. This is certainly a favored intellectual device that has been used extensively by Christian theologians throughout the ages. Theologian Harvey Cox, who has sampled the commodities of the "spiritual marketplace," freely admits that he does not even want to imitate anyone. Instead, he has settled for "provisional" gurus, "partial exemplars, models not so much to emulate as to argue with, learn from and— eventually—discard."[7] In other words, Cox wants a disposable guru, fashioned in his own image. He hopes for fellow wayfarers, or what in Buddhism are known as "good friends" (*kalyana-mitra*), but will have naught to do with living buddhas, or actual adepts. While it is true that, ultimately, the figure of the guru must be transcended, this should never be a matter of casually "discarding" the guru. The guru is, after all, not a model but a living being.

Compare Cox's attitude with the one proposed by Lex Hixon, a doctor of philosophy and religion, who has studied under many different teachers:

> Every seeker should receive traditional initiation and personal guidance from at least one authentic spiritual guide. Then one no longer simply *experiments* with contemplation but *lives* contemplative practice.[8]

I am inclined to agree with Hixon on this point. My own experience, harrowing as it has been at times, has demonstrated to me the value of such initiation and guidance. However, I am bound to modify his statement somewhat, because unless a person is ready and unless he or she has found a reliable and responsible teacher with whom he or she is in basic consonance, discipleship is meaningless and can even be counterproductive. For instance, if we entertain a strong, idealized image of the teacher as a humble benefactor, we would be wise not to apprentice with an adept who teaches in the crazy-wisdom mode. Or if we have difficulty relating to the female gender, we would be foolish to seek out a woman teacher. Or if we have no inner relationship to Hinduism, we would probably do well not to attempt spiritual practice under the guidance of a Hindu adept.

Once spiritual seekers have emerged from the cul-de-sac of substitute gurus and have actually found and been accepted by a flesh-and-blood teacher, they must be cautious about the ever-present temptation to make a false approach to the guru. First, they must be wary of the tendency to mythologize the teacher, to inflate him or her to the status of a superhuman being of flawless perfection, an omniscient and omnipotent entity who dwells in eternity and uses the body as a mere sounding board for communicating with devotees. This invites only neurotic self-deprecation, adulation, irrationalism, mushy devotionalism, and, not least, cultism.

Second, seekers must avoid deflating the teacher by regarding him or her as "just one of the guys." If the adept is genuine, and especially if truly enlightened, he or she is empowered by that which is ultimately real by virtue of his or her conscious participation in, or attunement to, that Reality. In the *Bhagavad-Gita* (XI.41), a pre-Christian Sanskrit work that is to the pious Hindu what the New Testament is to the believing Christian, there is a passage in which the God-man Krishna reveals his divine nature to Prince Arjuna, his disciple. After this revelatory vision, which fills the prince with fear and trembling, Arjuna recalls with shame how not too long ago he and his friends had addressed Krishna very casually and disrespectfully. Begging the God-man for forgiveness, he salutes Krishna with heartfelt humility and devotion. That is to say, the God-realized adept is more than just the human being standing before us.

An authentic guru, even if not yet fully enlightened, amounts to much more than the eye can see or the mind fathom. The disciple should always be sensitive to this fact without, however, abandoning his or her critical faculties. As I will argue in a later chapter, there is room for both devotion and criticism in a real dialog between teacher and disciple.

## 2. The Guru Function: Broadcasting God

There are many types of spiritual teachers, all differing in their spiritual maturity, personal complexity, and style of teaching. On the simplest level, there are those who have climbed on the "ladder to perfection" just one or two rungs beyond the beginning stage. While their personal attainments may be rather modest, they can still be helpful to seekers, providing they remain humble and honest and alert to the beginner's error of wanting to play master.

Then there are those who are more advanced. Naturally, they can be of immense help to others who are still trying to find their feet on the spiritual path or who have firmly entered the stream of practice but may still need occasional encouragement, confirmation, and (especially) periodic exposure to the curious psychophysical effect of "spiritual contagion." This effect, which according to one explanation consists of an enhancement of the disciple's natural vibratory state, is particularly pronounced in the case of a fully enlightened master. Hence such teachers have always been highly valued in the esoteric traditions of the world.

Some adepts, like Ramana Maharshi or Faquir Chand, become teachers by default, because people seek out their company and spiritual help. Others choose to have a few disciples whom they can instruct in a more intimate way.[9] Yet others, like Gautama the Buddha, set out to create a whole new path and community. Some teachers prefer to be informal with their disciples, while others insist on formality. There are teachers who interfere only minimally in the day-to-day living of their disciples and teachers who prescribe and enforce a strict life-style. Some teachers are quiet and ordinary, while others, like Bhagwan Rajneesh or Sathya Sai Baba, prefer a more flamboyant style of self-presentation. Some adepts choose relative silence as a means of communicating with their disciples; others, like Krishnamurti, are forever eloquent, believing that knowledge can somehow point the way to enlightenment. Some teachers refuse to call themselves teachers, because they feel they have nothing to teach; their teaching consists in their merely being present. And so on.

Psychologist Guy Claxton, formerly Swami Anand Ageha, a disciple of Bhagwan Rajneesh, has found the image of the guru as teacher somewhat misleading. He offers these comments:

> The most helpful metaphor is . . . that of a physician or therapist: enlightened Masters are, we might say, the Ultimate Therapists, for they focus their benign attention not on problems but on the very root from which the problems spring, the problem-sufferer and solver himself. The Master deploys his therapeutic tricks to one end: that of the exposure and dissolution of the fallacious self. His art is a subtle one because the illusions cannot be excised with a scalpel, dispersed with massage, or quelled with drugs. He has to work at one remove by knocking away familiar props and habits, and sustaining the seeker's courage and resolve through the fall. Only thus can the organism cure itself. His techniques resemble those of the demolition expert, setting strategically placed charges to blow up the established super-structure of the ego, so that the ground may be exposed. Yet he has to work on each case individually, dismantling and challenging in the right sequence and at the right speed, using whatever the "patient" brings as his raw material for the work of the moment.[10]

Claxton mentions other guises, "metaphors," that the guru assumes to deal with the disciple: guide, sergeant-major, cartographer, con man, fisherman, sophist, and magician. The multiple functions and roles of the authentic adept have two primary purposes. The first is to penetrate and eventually dissolve the egoic armor of the disciple, to "kill" the phenomenon that calls itself "disciple." The second major function of the guru is to act as a transmitter of Reality by magnifying the disciple's intuition of his or her true identity. Both objectives are the intent of all spiritual teachers. However, only fully enlightened adepts combine in themselves what the Mahayana Buddhist scriptures call the wisdom (*prajna*) and the compassion (*karuna*) necessary to rouse others from the slumber of the unenlightened state. In the ancient *Rig-Veda* (X.32.7) of the Hindus, the guru is likened to a person familiar with a particular terrain who undertakes to guide a foreign traveler. Teachers who have yet to realize full enlightenment can guide others only part of the way. But the accomplished adept, who is known in India as a *siddha*, is able to illumine the entire path for the seeker.

Such fully enlightened adepts are a rarity. Whether or not they feel called to teach others, their mere presence in the world is traditionally held to have an impact on everything. All enlightened masters, or God-realizers, are thought and felt to radiate the numinous. They are focal points of the sacred. They broadcast God. Because they are, in consciousness, one with the ultimate Reality, they cannot help but irradiate their environment with the light of that Reality. This spiritual "field effect" apparently extends to all creatures and things, but is particularly felt by those who are in close proximity to the adept or who are sensitive to his spiritual transmission. The natural "aura" of the enlightened being, which has a transformative effect, obliges the world to engage in involuntary spiritual practice (*sadhana*). Da Love-Ananda once remarked about this phenomenon that "even the walls" participate in this process. How literally he meant this statement is apparent from the following account by one of his disciples:

> In the summer of 1982, I found myself unexpectedly in the personal company of my guru. I saw him enter into what everyone believed to be the condition of unqualified *samadhi* or ecstasy. All present were instantly overtaken by a powerful meditative mood. As we later confirmed to each other, everyone had the subjective sensation of the room seemingly flying apart with everything and everybody in it. *Everyone reported distinctly hearing the wooden walls and ceiling beams crackle.* There was also the sensation of a strange but distinct pressure upon the whole body, notably the front. This incident left me puzzled and excited for a long time. For me, it was a demonstration of the subtle forces that are in operation around the adept.

The same student also had this to report:

> Whenever I would sit in meditation or *darshan*[11] with my guru, my body felt as if it had been exposed to a high dose of radiation. For days and

weeks afterwards, my entire chest would burn or radiate. The focus of this sensation was toward the right side of my heart. This feeling intensified whenever I would meditate on my own. Associated with this physical symptom was an unusual emotional rawness. I felt ripped open, utterly vulnerable in my emotions. It seemed to me that my teacher had "relocated" the center of my attention from the brain to the heart, where it belongs. Through my guru's grace, my heart has been awakened.

Guy Claxton comments:

By sitting in the Master's presence, aware of him without thought or judgment, the seeker begins to imbibe and manifest the same quality of clarity and stillness. There is, as Zen says, a direct transmission outside the scriptures, heart to heart. The Master is a queen bee around which the community of seekers—in Buddhism the *sangha*—gathers to drink his essence.[12]

The spiritual "presence" of the teacher is felt as a force impinging on the body. Both Bhagwan Rajneesh and Swami Muktananda delighted in demonstrating their ability to manipulate and project this force both with individual students and in large gatherings. This was a large part of their spectacular attraction. However, a teacher need not be enlightened to muster this kind of psychophysical energy. I myself have had an interesting experience of this phenomenon. While still living in England, I meditated periodically under the guidance of Irina Tweedie, a Sufi teacher. After one session in particular, I felt my entire body and being suffused with energy. It so happened that about the same time a neighbor of mine had found out that I was a meditator and wanted to learn meditation from me. As I had never been authorized to teach meditation, I politely refused. Almost every time we would run into each other, he would ask again, quite seriously about it.

After a half dozen requests, I finally agreed to show him what to do. I specified a day and a time. To my surprise, when he arrived at my home, he was dressed in his Sunday best. He later told me that he had prepared himself as if he were going to church. I asked him to make himself comfortable on a chair while I settled down on a sofa opposite him. I began to explain to him how to relax the body as a precondition for meditation. I had barely uttered a few sentences when I felt a rush of psychophysical energy seemingly enter my body from behind and explode out toward him. My speech became slurred and my eyelids got heavy, but I kept my eyes focused on him. As the wave of energy hit him, he visibly jerked back, looking at me fearfully. Then a second wave passed through me to him, and again he startled. By the time a third rush of energy reached him, he was in deep meditation. I felt a force field connecting our bodies, and while I stayed in meditation, he too remained meditating.

We talked about the experience later, and he confirmed my own sense of what had happened. At first he had felt terror at possibly being hypnotized by me; then when the second wave of energy penetrated him, he again felt pushed back by it but started to yield to it. The third time he simply let go, allowing the energy to do its work in his body-mind. He had never meditated before. I was as surprised about this effect as he was. The same energy transfer occurred subsequently every time we got together for meditation. At one point it became clear to me that he needed to make certain changes in his life before he could benefit from further sessions.

Fortunately, since I did not consider myself a guru or even a meditation teacher, I also did not interpret this experience as something I myself was generating. Rather, I regarded it as a gift and advised my neighbor to do the same. Having had this experience, however, and also having on numerous occasions been the recipient of such energy transmission, I can readily see why some teachers might attribute special significance to this ability. The same holds true of mystical experiences. It is all too easy to read into them more than is warranted. It is also easy to see how disciples can become addicted to the "hit" of spiritual transmission from a guru and how they might confuse that ability with enlightenment, wisdom, and compassion.

### 3. Jesus and Divinization

There is no question in my mind that many gurus have genuine psychic and mystical abilities. However, as I have already stated, this does not make them enlightened. Some gurus have achieved a permanent identity-shift that one could equate with enlightenment, but this does not necessarily make them wise or consistently compassionate. Some of these adepts may even display traits that would be considered neurotic in the ordinary mortal.

At any rate, the adept's theophanic nature is a great stumbling block for the conventional intellect. How can an apparently individual entity be the ultimate Reality, or God? The question has vexed generations of theologians. It was asked almost two millennia ago about the adept whose teachings are the now mostly hidden nucleus of the world religion of Christianity.[13] Jesus himself anticipated the centuries-long christological debate about his true nature when he asked his disciples, "Who do men say that I am?"[14] When he was told some of the popular responses—negative opinions were either omitted or later edited out—he turned to them, prompting, "But who do *you* say that I am?" It was Peter who spoke, "You are the Christ." This disciple's confession of faith was, predictably, not accepted by society at large. And as the adept's work proceeded, the clerical and political authorities of his day posed the question "Who is he?" with ever greater urgency.[15] Jesus' crucifixion testifies to the utterly secular and reprehensible nature of their final conclusion. But it was precisely the adept's martyrdom and the mystery surrounding it that did much to promote the Christian cause and to spark endless speculations about the relationship between the historical person of Jesus and the "Anointed one," the "Son of God."

There are no statements in the New Testament that unequivocally indicate Jesus' identity with God, but there are phrases that speak of his union or equivalence with God.[16] Still, this sufficed to trigger ingenious philosophical ruminations. The simplest solution to the christological problem was proffered by the advocates of Docetism. Inspired by Gnosticism, they held the view that Jesus was indeed one with the Divine and that his fleshly existence was merely "apparent"—hence the name of their doctrine, which comes from the Greek word *dokein* ("to appear"). Jesus' humanity was thus not denied, but it was reinterpreted in terms of a voluntary dissimulation by the Divine for the benefit of humankind. In other words, Jesus' reported struggle with the flesh, his temptations, and his suffering on the cross all occurred in a kind of phantom body.

A different solution was proposed by the school of Ebionitism, according to which Jesus was not a projection of the Divine into the human realm but a specially graced man. Without completely denying the adept's divinity, the followers of this school diluted it by interpreting it as a special gift bestowed on him by virtue of his moral and spiritual excellence. Both Docetism and Ebionitism insisted on the utter transcendence of the Divine, thereby creating the paradox of the one God who is beyond all finitude and yet has three aspects—Father, Son, and Holy Spirit. Yet another school, the Basilidians, argued that Jesus became the Christ with his baptism, while the Alogi and Artemonites insisted on the human nature of Jesus but added that he was mysteriously energized by God.

In the fourth century A.D., the whole controversy led to the convening of no fewer than eighteen councils in a period of sixty-three years. Arius, presbyter of Alexandria, proposed a subtle distinction between *homoiousion* ("of similar essence") and *homoousion* ("of the same essence"), opting for the former to define Jesus' relationship to God. He regarded Jesus as having been created, prior to space-time, by a definite act of will on the part of God, wherefore Jesus is subordinate to the Divine and of a distinct substance. The Church settled for the "homoousion" solution, however, and Arius' position was declared a heresy.

In the fifth century A.D., the new heresies of Apollinarianism, Nestorianism, and Eutychianism made their appearance. The first-mentioned school proposed that while Jesus possesses a real human body, his soul is replaced by the *logos*. For the proponents of Nestorianism, the Christ has both a human and a divine nature, but they do not intercommunicate. Eutychianism, while adhering to the dual nature of Jesus, denied that there is no link between his humanity and his divinity. Instead, the advocates of this school argued that his human personality is completely transformed by his divine nature.

In the seventh century A.D., two more christological positions were thought through and then discarded on the heretical garbage heap— Monophysitism and Monothelitism. According to the former, Christ has only one nature, his human personality being a contingent quality of God.

According to the latter, Jesus is only one person and therefore his will is also single.

Orthodox christology, as formulated at the Council of Chalcedon in A.D. 451, maintains that Jesus is truly God and truly man, without offering a logical resolution of the paradox of such an assertion, thus keeping the christological issue alive even today. The orthodox position is unsatisfactory for the intellect that hopes to creep up on truth by binary operations. Yet that same intellect, which has created through rigorous application of the laws of logic and mathematics the wonders of modern technology, is today confronted by findings, made possible by an advanced technology, that are wholly paradoxical and truly mind-boggling.

The horizon that unfolds before the inquisitive mind of the contemporary scientist is increasingly one of a wildly paradoxical universe. More and more, we begin to appreciate the deep truth in Heraclitus' pronouncement that "everything flows" (*panta rhei*). The universe as we know it is part of a vast process that defies the mind's "still-photograph" attempts to codify it. This is brought home nowhere more clearly than in the dynamic whirls and loops of bubble chamber images, the crazy footprints of the subatomic particles that are the building blocks of our solid material cosmos. The physicist who desires to contemplate this process, Shiva's cosmic dance, is obliged to resort to multivalue logic that is tolerant of paradoxes.

I suspect that pondering the nature of the enlightened, or God-realized, adept demands no less an act of intellectual agility. If we can learn anything from the centuries of scholastic exertions in Christianity, it is that in order to understand the divinity of the adept, who is human, we must come to terms with the inherent paradox of the enlightened being. "I am before time and space, and no condition has me," exclaimed Da Love-Ananda in one of his early writings, now no longer in circulation.[17] His ecstatic confession is the testimonial of all enlightened masters, who do not experience themselves as a subject or an object. Their state is absurd.

It so happens that absurdity is a characteristic of the state of enlightenment: Even as we proudly, if uneasily, presume ourselves to be separate from everyone else, we are in fact an integral part of the same Reality, or Being, that is all things. This, of course, does not help us in coming to terms with the paradoxical and enigmatic nature of the guru. Nor *should* we come to terms with it, from the viewpoint of spiritual practice. Once the guru ceases to be a *koan* for the disciple, the unenlightened student can be sure to have deluded himself or herself. Yet the guru stops being a *koan* when the disciple has awakened to the same Reality that the adept-teacher enjoys. Then the disciple finds himself or herself in the same shoes as the Zen practitioner in the following story:

"I went to my teacher with nothing and came away with nothing." Someone asked, "Why bother to go to the teacher then?" The reply was, "How otherwise would I know that I went with nothing?"[18]

Of course, this disciple did not leave empty-handed. He was taken by his teacher to the edge of the cliff, and then he jumped—into the unfathomable Reality. He had come to his guru believing in his own unenlightenment, and he was shown the utter falsehood of this belief. Now he was free of it. The adept's gift cannot be measured or weighed. It amounts to nothing in conventional terms; it is everything on the spiritual path.

## 4. True Gurus, False Gurus, Crazy Gurus

There are many teachers, like lamps in house after house, but hard to find, O Devi, is the teacher who lights up all like the sun. (vs. 104)

There are many teachers who are proficient in the Vedas [revealed sacred lore] and the Shastras [textbooks], but hard to find, O Devi, is the teacher who has attained to the supreme truth. (vs. 105)

There are many teachers on earth who give what is other than the [transcendental] Self, but hard to find in all the world, O Devi, is the teacher who reveals the Self. (vs. 106)

Many are the teachers who rob the disciple of his wealth, but rare is the teacher who removes the disciple's affliction. (vs. 108)

He is the [true] teacher by whose very contact there flows the supreme bliss (*ananda*). The intelligent man should choose such a one as his teacher and none other. (vs. 110)

These stanzas are found in the *Kularnava-Tantra* (XIII), a Sanskrit work on Hindu esotericism dating from the eleventh century A.D. They are spoken by God Shiva, the Lord of *yogins*, to his divine spouse, Devi. But his words were intended for human ears, and they are as relevant today as they were a millennium ago, if not more so. Evidently, there are true and false spiritual teachers, or gurus. Very likely, there are many who fall between these two categories; they are neither completely white nor entirely black but come in different shades of gray.

How can one tell the genuine master from the fraudulent opportunist, whose paradoxy and holy folly simply conceal wanton inconsistency? The question is pressing but by no means new. It has been asked again and again over the millennia, and for two reasons. First, because there is no easy answer and, second, because the chaff is never far from the wheat; darkness is never far from light.

In a highly informative study on messiahs throughout the ages, Wilson D. Wallis has compiled a revealing table on the frequency of known messiahs in Judaism, Islam, and Christianity. According to his compilation, the total number of known messiahs in these three world religions is 144 plus.[19] The tabulation extends only to 1940 and excludes certified psychotics. It shows a notable increase of self-declared messiahs within Christianity for the nineteenth and twentieth centuries. The coexistence of several individuals claiming to be *the* messiah or *avatara* of the age invites instant dismissal of the whole notion. Yet this was the exact situation that Jesus of Nazareth had to face. The Hebrews were expecting the messiah, and several candidates stepped forward to fulfill the prophecy. One of them was Jesus. History as written by Christians has decided that he alone was the true messiah and that all others have been, are, and will be fakes. The Jews, however, read history quite differently. They are still waiting for the messiah prophesied in the Bible. The Muslims offer yet another historical interpretation: Jesus was one of the great prophets but Muhammad was the last in line, having the final truth.

Today we confront a situation parallel to the one that Jesus' contemporaries had to face. There are not a few gurus who profess to be, or are portrayed by their followers as being, if not *the* "Anointed one," then at least fully enlightened masters. The question of authenticity naturally rears its head. Who would deny that there are, in the words of Idries Shah, "phonies" among today's crop of spiritual teachers?[20] In addition to the fakes, there are also the self-deluded. In most other cases, I daresay, the claim to enlightenment falls far short of reality, though no intentional deception may be at work. The temporary experience of *unio mystica*, or ecstatic unification, is often confused with enlightenment. Also, some practitioners mistake the peculiar "witnessing" state for transcendental realization.

The seven-stage model of human life developed by the contemporary adept Da Love-Ananda is useful in bringing a modicum of differentiation into what generally amounts to a bewildering melee of opinions. This model views the physical, emotional, intellectual, and spiritual development of the person as an integrated process that leads from the acquisition of simple motor skills to enlightenment and the special skills and abilities associated with it. This comprehensive schema, which serves an entirely practical purpose for spiritual aspirants, is broad enough to accommodate other developmental models, such as those of Jean Piaget (stages of cognitive development), Lawrence Kohlberg (moral development), or James Fowler (stages of faith). The following is a brief summary of the seven stages of life as advocated by Da Love-Ananda:

*First Stage:* Simple biological competence, as achieved during the first seven years of a child's life.

*Second Stage:* Simple relational, or emotional-sexual, competence, which should ideally be achieved during the period from 7 to 14 years but seldom is.

*Third Stage:* Basic intellectual competence, which is the theme of the period from 14 to 21 years and which permits the integration of the biological and emotional-sexual aspects of one's being.

*Fourth Stage:* Devotional competence, which marks the beginning of spiritual life. This coincides with the awakening of higher psychic sensitivity and the capacity for heartfelt devotion, selfless service, compassion, and genuine love, involving a profound reorientation of one's life. The fourth stage characterizes the paths of *bhakti-yoga* (Yoga of love-participation) and *karma-yoga* (Yoga of self-transcending activity in the world).

*Fifth Stage:* Mystical competence, which entails the ability to focus attention on the inner (psychic) dimension of one's being and which ultimately leads to the mind-shattering experience of formless ecstasy known in Hinduism as *nirvikalpa-samadhi.*

*Sixth Stage:* Witnessing competence, which transcends the play of attention itself and which characterizes the approach of *jnana-yoga* (Yoga of wisdom) in Hinduism.

*Seventh Stage:* Enlightenment competence, which is full awakening as the transcendental Self, coinciding with permanent ego-transcendence, also known as *sahaja-samadhi* or "ecstasy of spontaneity." This stage comprises, according to Da Love-Ananda, three distinct phases: transfiguration, transformation, and translation. Transfiguration is, as in the Christian tradition, the temporary and visible manifestation of transcendental radiance in and through the physical body. Transformation consists of permanent biochemical changes in the body as it adapts to the high-energy state of enlightenment. Finally, translation refers to the event of cessation of physical consciousness on the basis of the enlightened condition. This is also known as *bhava-samadhi,* or "ecstasy of the (great) mood (of perfect oblivion in the Divine)." Sometimes, it is claimed, translation is the literal illumination of the enlightened adept, who, at the moment of death, vanishes in a blaze of light (an event that should be distinguished from the curious phenomenon of spontaneous combustion). These three phases make it clear that enlightenment is not an end state but an ongoing process.

Because Da Love-Ananda quirkishly proposes this seven-stage framework not as a model but as the true form of Reality, his followers have been quick to shove other teachers into these ready-made boxes, usually those of the first five stages. At this point, the seventh-stage box seems to be inhabited only by the Buddha, Ramana Maharshi, and the inventor of this model—Da Love-Ananda himself. Jesus, who was once described as a seventh-stage adept, has been demoted to the fifth stage, to the chagrin of not a few people, including some of the disciples of Da Love-Ananda.

When used with circumspection, however, this seven-stage model can facilitate our understanding of different spiritual teachings and, to some extent, teachers. I say "to some extent," because we can assess the spiritual maturity of a teacher only by his or her observable behavior and the larger context of his or her life, as well as the adept's teachings. We cannot know the inner man or woman unless we happen to be great *yogins* ourselves, capable of reading minds and hearts. This holds true of everyone, of course. What we can and must do, however, is to trust our own intuition about people, even if they are worshipped by a million others.

The existence of fake gurus, or gurus who are less than they claim or pretend to be, is certainly deplorable, but their fraudulence or weakness should not induce us to discard the figure of the spiritual guide as a whole. Psychologist John Welwood, who has given these issues considerable thought, observes:

> To discount all spiritual masters because of the behavior of charlatans or misguided teachers is as unprofitable as refusing to use money because there are counterfeit bills in circulation. The abuse of authority is hardly any reason to reject authority where it is appropriate, useful, and legitimate. It is possible that in the present age of cultural upheaval, declining morality, family instability, and global chaos, the world's great spiritual masters may be among humanity's most precious assets. Glossing over important distinctions between genuine and counterfeit masters may only contribute further to the confusion of our age, and retard the growth and transformation that may be necessary for humanity to survive and prosper.[21]

The American philosopher William Ernest Hocking had a similarly sagacious perspective on this matter:

> Nature makes a thousand failures to bring forth one consummate product. The existence of the genuine mystic—Bernard, Mohammed, Lao Tze, Plotinus, Eckehart, John of the Cross—however seldom he is found, is the momentous thing; sufficient to command respect for the tradition of mysticism, sufficient to justify the attention which through religious history has been focused upon these individuals.[22]

In view of the sophistication displayed by some of the more successful counterfeit gurus, the question of authenticity is an urgent one. We sense something of this problem already in the report about Jesus' asking his disciples to state who they thought he was, in contrast to the public opinion. Several centuries earlier, as recorded in the *Bhagavad-Gita* (II.54–72), the warrior-mystic Arjuna asked his theophanic guru, Krishna, about the signs by which one may recognize a truly enlightened being. How, Arjuna inquired, does the one who is "steadied in gnosis" (*sthita-prajna*) speak, sit, and move about? Krishna's response leaves much to be desired. First, it is tinged with introversionist images that do not do justice to the enlightened condition. Second, he fails to address Arjuna's question directly but speaks instead of the God-realizer's psychic characteristics—notably his ego-freedom, inner peace, and detachment. This is the approach taken in most of the Sanskrit literature. Thus, the *Uddhava-Gita* (VI.8.11–12), which is one of the many "imitation" *Gitas*, contains these stanzas:

> The sage (*vidvan*), though abiding in a body, does not [really] abide in a body, rather like one who has awakened from a dream. The fool, however, though not abiding in the body, nevertheless abides in the body, like on seeing a dream.

Thus unattached while reclining, sitting, walking, bathing, seeing, touching, smelling, eating, and hearing, etc., the sage is not bound by the "qualities" [of Nature] in any [of his actions]; although abiding in Nature, he is unattached, like sky, sun, and wind.

But how can we judge whether a teacher is truly unattached, beyond egoism, and above the play of Nature's forces? Again John Welwood makes a most valuable point:

> We cannot rely on descriptions of external behaviors alone to distinguish between genuine and problematic spiritual teachers. Developing criteria for judging a teacher's genuineness by examining external behavior alone would, for one thing, neglect the context—both interpersonal and intrapersonal—from which the behavior draws its meaning; and for another, it would tend to identify one particular model of a spiritual teacher as being ideal or exclusively valid, which would be as great a fallacy as elevating a single mode of psychotherapy to a similar position. [23]

Welwood further notes that therapists have very dissimilar personalities and employ many different styles of therapy, and, we might add, are varyingly competent. They are found to help some but not necessarily all of their clients. Similarly, not every guru is good for every disciple. The relationship between master and student is one key. The other, as Welwood points out, is the source of a teacher's authority. In the case of an awakened adept, that source is his or her enlightened attunement to Reality itself. In all other cases, which are the overriding majority, the teacher is authorized by a lesser competence, as can be gauged from Da Love-Ananda's seven-stage model.

The trouble is that an unenlightened teacher may present himself or herself as a fully awakened adept. Bhagwan Rajneesh is a good case in point. For years he proclaimed himself to be a modern Buddha, attracting tens of thousands of followers from all over the world as much by this claim as by his sex-oriented teachings. Then the tragic developments at his 64,000-acre ranch in Oregon revealed Rajneesh to be a rather manipulative individual who, if he was not directly responsible, had at least connived at any number of criminal activities carried out by his devotees—from drug trafficking to the breaking of immigration laws to systematic harassment of local villagers to the abuse of charitable funds, and so forth.

During those days, Hugh Milne, who was a member of the inner circle around Rajneesh for eight years, caught a glimpse of his master in the raw. What he saw was a "hollow shell," a man who was watching videos nonstop, driving recklessly in his Rolls Royces, and feeling monumentally bored. [24] In his book *Bhagwan: The God That Failed*, Milne describes an incident in which his guru was reclining in a $12,000 dentist chair sniffing nitrous oxide and babbling nonsensically. At one point, Milne reported, Rajneesh said, "I am so relieved that I do not have to pretend to be enlightened any more." [25]

Another very popular spiritual teacher of the 1970s and 1980s was Krishnamurti. Milne reports that he said of Rajneesh, "I have received thousands of letters from all over the world asking why I do not speak out in public against this man. But I will not, as it is not my way. The man is a criminal. You have to understand this very clearly. What he is doing to people in the name of spirituality is criminal."[26] As Milne suggests, Krishnamurti was probably referring to Rajneesh's "misuse of hypnosis and psychic powers."[27]

Blaise Pascal, who possessed one of the most capable minds of the seventeenth century, once jotted down this aphorism: *Qui veut faire l'ange, fait la bête* ("Those who play at being angels, end up as animals").[28] A fallen angel of considerable stature was the late Swami Muktananda, who like Rajneesh, had a worldwide following. The rumors of sexual exploitation that reached the public after his death did much to disenchant many of his followers and left countless others suspicious and confused. About the same time, the exploits of the crazy-wisdom master Chögyam Trungpa hit the newsstands, followed a few years later by the allegations of disaffected students of Da Love-Ananda. These latter teachers had both previously been held in high esteem by many people, but the revelations about their teaching methods caused many of their followers and readers both doubt and embarrassment.

There were several other widely respected figures, though not of the same stature as the above adepts, whose private life did not seem to be informed by the wisdom they so readily dished out to others. However, we need not pile sad news upon sad news. What is certain is that these individuals have created mistrust in a large number of genuine seekers who are now understandably cautious about teachers and altogether bewildered about the usefulness of a spiritual guide.

It is important to realize that, regardless of one's ultimate approval or disapproval, there is a clear distinction between a teacher who preaches one thing and lives another and a teacher who openly teaches in crazy-wise fashion. If, for instance, the rumors about Swami Muktananda are true (and his followers have so far declined to respond either way), then we have a case of a teacher of the first type, because Muktananda's teaching emphasized sexual abstinence as a means of spiritual growth.

Chögyam Trungpa and Da Love-Ananda belong to the second type, which does not mean that there may not be a degree of duplicity in specific instances. For example, one ex-student of Da Free John recalls an incident in 1982 involving a small private party with the adept and his most intimate circle, during which alcohol, cigarettes, and sex played a part, while—and this is the critical point—the guru's following at large lived according to a strict discipline. The ex-student and his girlfriend were enjoined not to talk to anyone about the party, even though both were in something of a state of shock afterward. They had entered the situation unprepared, although both knew that their guru was a crazy-wisdom teacher; they could, in principle, have refused to participate but were emotionally and for idealistic reasons unable to do so.

What lessons can we learn from all of this? First, the seeker must understand that spiritual teachers represent different levels of personal attainment and that enlightenment is rare indeed. Second, the seeker must acknowledge that, being a seeker rather than a master, he or she is not properly qualified to pronounce *final* judgment about any teacher's level of spiritual attainment. The editors of the widely read volume *Spiritual Choices* proffer this excellent advice:

> It is impossible for one who is lodged in mundane consciousness to evaluate definitively the competence of any guide to transformation and transcendence, without having already attained to an equal degree of transcendence. No number of "objective" criteria for assessment can remove this "Catch-22" dilemma. Therefore the choice of a guide, path, or group will remain in some sense a subjective matter. Subjectivity, however, has many modes, from self-deluding emotionality to penetrating, illuminative intuition. Perhaps the first job of the seeker would best be to refine that primary guide, one's own subjectivity. [29]

Ram Dass (Richard Alpert), who has functioned on both sides of the fence (as a devotee of Neem Karoli Baba and as a teacher in his own right), has made the following complementary observation:

> Some people fear becoming involved with a teacher. They fear the possible impurities in the teacher, fear being exploited, used, or entrapped. In truth we are only ever entrapped by our own desires and clingings. If you want only liberation, then all teachers will be useful vehicles for you. They cannot hurt you at all. [30]

This is true only ideally. In practice, the problem is that in many cases students do not know themselves sufficiently to be conscious of their deeper motivations. Therefore they may feel attracted precisely to the kind of teacher who shares their own "impurities"—such as hunger for power—and hence have every reason to fear him or her. It seems that only the truly innocent are protected. Although they too are by no means immune to painful experiences with teachers, at least they will emerge hale and whole, having been sustained by their own purity of intention.

Accepting the fact that our appraisal of a teacher is always subjective so long as we have not ourselves attained his or her level of spiritual accomplishment, there is at least one important criterion that we can look for in a guru: Does he or she genuinely promote disciples' personal and spiritual growth, or does he or she obviously or ever so subtly undermine their maturation? Would-be disciples should take a careful, levelheaded look at the community of students around their prospective guru. They should especially scrutinize those who are closer to the guru than most. Are they merely sorry imitations or clones of their teacher, or do they come across as mature men and women? The Bulgarian spiritual teacher Mikhaël Aïvanhov, who died in 1986, made this to-the-point observation:

> Everybody has his own path, his mission, and even if you take your Master as a model, you must always develop in the way that suits your own nature. You have to sing the part which has been given to you, aware of the notes, the beat and the rhythm; you have to sing it with your voice which is certainly not that of your Master, but that is not important. The one really important thing is to sing your part perfectly . . .[31]

The question of a teacher's authenticity can be answered only when we see the gestalt of his or her work with disciples. It is not important whether a teacher can go in and out of mystical states at will, or whether he or she can perform all kinds of paranormal feats, or whether he or she can jolt the disciple's nervous system through the transmission of life-force, and so forth. It does not even make any difference whether a teacher has a splendid lineage or tradition to fall back upon, or whether he or she enjoys a large following. What really matters is whether a guru, in effect, works the miracle of spiritual transformation in others. St. Matthew commented on this very issue as follows:

> Beware of false prophets, which come to you in sheep's clothing, but inwardly they are ravening wolves.
> Ye shall know them by their fruits. Do men gather grapes of thorns, or figs of thistles?
> Even so every good tree bringeth forth good fruit; but a corrupt tree bringeth forth evil fruit.
> A good tree cannot bring forth evil fruit, neither *can* a corrupt tree bring forth good fruit.
> Every tree that bringeth not forth good fruit is hewn down, and cast into the fire.
> Wherefore by their fruits ye shall know them.[32]

Maggie Ross, an Anglican solitary, writes:

> Authentic leadership elicits courage, openness, and integrity, and caretaker leadership that does not inspire is always tempted to point to itself instead of to the elusive vision from which it derives. If it does so, it no longer nurtures a community in which the vision can renew itself . . . In our immaturity we do imitate, we do project, but a wise and inspired leader can elicit and enable our maturity, our letting go these childish things.[33]

Perhaps, in order to get a true glimpse of a teacher's effectiveness, we must become his or her student. But this does not at all mean that we ought to retire our critical faculties. We should, rather, test the guru with the same rigor that the guru will apply in testing our own worthiness—if he or she is genuine. And if our chosen teacher is genuine, he or she will also grant us the right and the time to become certain of the teacher's authenticity and competence. Ram Dass offers this piece of wisdom:

> Whether teachings experienced along the way are beautiful and pleasant, or unpleasant and harsh, or even bland, all are grist for the mill of awakening. The slightest reaction reflects the subtlest clinging. It is a meaningful clue to where you are still holding on. Simply watching your reaction makes anything a teaching.[34]

# 7

## DISCIPLESHIP: SPIRITUAL CLONING OR BRAINWASHING?

### 1. The Time-Honored Tradition of Spiritual Discipleship

Since time immemorial, spiritual life has been a matter of initiation and discipleship. The primary purpose of initiation is to conduct the spiritual seeker into a new mode of being, one that involves a novel way of relating to existence. Whereas previously the seeker may have had only intimations of a different, hidden order of existence, through initiation he or she is granted a vision or a palpable sense of that "alternative" reality. Through initiation the seeker is put more directly in touch with the sacred or numinous dimension of existence, which is widely referred to as the "spirit."

The novice initiate now begins a new life. Initiation has traditionally been compared to the birth event, because the neophyte undergoes a significant transformation that reorients his or her entire life. In the *Atharva-Veda* (XI.5.3) of ancient India, the symbolism of initiatory regeneration is described thus:

Initiation takes place in that the teacher carries the pupil in himself as it were, as a mother [bears] the embryo in her body. After the three days of the ceremony, the disciple is born.

In his book *Myths, Dreams and Mysteries*, Mircea Eliade examined the initiatory symbolism and ritual of tribal societies.[1] It is evident from his discussion that initiation is always associated with an element of danger, trial, or suffering, because the initiate must sacrifice his or her former self in order to be spiritually reborn. Elsewhere Eliade made these observations:

If the novice dies to his infantile, profane, nonregenerate life to be reborn to a new, sanctified existence, he is also reborn to a mode of being that makes learning, *knowledge*, possible. The initiate is not only one newborn or resuscitated; he is a man who *knows*, who has learned the mysteries, who has had revelations that are metaphysical in nature . . . Initiation is equivalent to a spiritual maturing.[2]

Eliade continued:

In the scenarios of initiations the symbolism of birth is almost always found side by side with that of death. In initiatory contexts death signifies passing beyond the profane, unsanctified condition, the condition of the "natural man," who is without religious experience, who is blind to spirit.[3]

The spiritual seeker receives neither initiation nor esoteric gnosis gratuitously. Generally speaking, the student must first pass a variety of tests before the teacher will consent to supervise his or her spiritual rebirth. Even after initiation, the neophyte's commitment and capability continue to be monitored and probed. Discipleship is solidly based on the principle of quid pro quo. Before divulging further esoteric knowledge and practices, the teacher must ensure that the disciple is able to assimilate the teachings and use them rightly. The guru does this by demanding discipline, obedience, and service, which are the bread and butter of all authentic discipleship. Even though the disciple must "reciprocate" the teacher's spiritual gifts or *charismata*, however, in the last analysis the only way the disciple can do this is by fulfilling his or her own discipleship, by duplicating the teacher's mode of being. When the disciple has become fully awake, or enlightened, he or she can then communicate the teachings to others. This completes the self-transcending cycle of spiritual life.

It is most important to understand that initiation creates a peculiar psychic link between teacher and disciple, which forms the vital basis for discipleship. This link, which is more than a rapport, carries the disciple through the inevitable ordeal of the transformative process. It serves as an umbilical cord between teacher and disciple that should never be severed casually. The connection between teacher and disciple is easily as close as that between husband and wife. It takes great responsibility on both parts for this link to function well and serve the ultimate purpose of the disciple's spiritual awakening.

In many traditions, this teacher-disciple bond is thought to be eternal, outlasting the death of the physical body and continuing until the disciple's own awakening in some future lifetime. Even after the disciple's enlightenment, this spiritual connection remains intact, although the enlightened disciple may now be a teacher in his or her own right. Thus, in India, when a seeker is accepted by a teacher, he or she knows that discipleship means being adopted into a whole teaching lineage (*parampara*), which often extends back into the distant past. There is mystery and power in the sacred relationship between teacher and disciple. All too often this aspect is entirely misunderstood or ignored by Western seekers, as well as by Western critics of spiritual paths.

When the seeker has been duly tested and initiated, he or she is entitled to receive from the teacher the necessary instructions by which the disciple can henceforth consciously become attuned to the sacred or numinous Reality. Through such attunement, he or she can, in principle, duplicate the teacher's own state of being—a duplication that can be viewed as a form of complex cloning. But this entitlement to receive instruction must be constantly re-earned through a demonstration of obedience to the teacher and sincere application to the spiritual process. Discipleship is thus a tremendously demanding affair. Not surprisingly, few seekers are qualified for it.

Today, many of those who deem themselves eligible for spiritual life sooner or later discover or have to be told that they stand in a false relationship to it and their teacher. Psychologist Frances Vaughan has provided a useful elementary typology of spiritually motivated men and women.[4] She distinguishes between the *sycophant*, who "enjoys basking in reflected glory" but is unwilling to adopt real discipline; the *seeker*, who is "like a free-floating sponge on the spiritual path" and generally lacks commitment; the *devotee*, whose love for the teacher is so all-consuming that it leaves little room for the balanced development of his or her own personality; the *student*, who approaches spiritual life primarily through the mind and likes to engage the teacher in verbal considerations; and, finally, the *disciple*, who is serious about spiritual growth and is prepared to discipline himself or herself in light of the teaching and the teacher's demands.

The authentic disciple is possibly as rare as the genuinely awakened teacher. This is true especially in our age, which exhibits such abysmal ignorance of, and insensitivity to, spiritual life. Not a few teachers are seekers themselves who pretend otherwise. Not a few seekers are little more than unhappy neurotics in quest of self-fulfillment rather than self-transcendence. This is the flimsy stuff that many religious or spiritual cults are made of.

## 2. Individualism and Obedience

The main target of today's anticult sentiments is, however, not the immature devotee but the figure of the spiritual guide, or guru. The popular mind does not care to distinguish between genuine spiritual teachers and fakes. All the public eye beholds is spiritual authorities who exert what common sense judges to be a disproportionate and unwholesome influence on their "followers." Thus, the guru is typified as a cult leader who uses his, or more rarely her, charismatic power to dupe and exploit gullible seekers. This popular prejudice, masked as a commonsense judgment, is a formidable obstacle to genuine discipleship, which our age needs as badly, if not more, than previous ages.

Alas, common sense is frequently found to be an unreliable instrument in such matters. Common sense is widely used to communicate seemingly universal truths, but as a rule those truths are seldom more than opinions. As the Jesuit philosopher-theologian Bernard J. F. Lonergan, who is hailed by some as the Aquinas of the twentieth century, has noted:

> Common sense . . . is a specialization of intelligence in the particular and the concrete. It is common without being general, for it consists in a set of insights that remains incomplete, until there is added at least one further insight into the situation in hand; and, once that situation has passed, the added insight is no longer relevant, so that common sense at once reverts to its normal state of incompleteness.[5]

Where common sense replaces careful thought, acute observation, and self-inspection, it is no more than the voice of the mass mind of conceited egos. Over three centuries ago, René Descartes remarked on the close proximity of conceit and common sense:

> Common sense is the most widely distributed commodity in the world, because everyone deems himself so well equipped with it that those who are hardest to please in all other respects, generally do not desire to have more of it than they have.[6]

Real-life situations tend to be far more complex than common sense either permits or can handle. This is especially true of spiritual matters, notably of the guru, and not least the guru who teaches in the crazy-wisdom style. Many psychic, cultural, and historical factors converge to generate the negative image of spiritual teachers in the popular mind. To disentangle all of them would require a book in itself. Here I will mention only some of the more obvious aspects.

The first factor to be mentioned, since it is likely to be uppermost in the mind of most people, is the frequent misuse of authority, whether secular or sacred, private or institutional. We need only recall here the infamous dictatorships of recent history—from Hitler and Mussolini to Ceausescu and Noriega—or the enforced mass suicide of 911 members of the People's Temple at Jonestown (1978) and the horrifying ritualistic murders by the Manson "family" (1969–1971). There are also the injurious machinations of misguided gurus and cult leaders with imperialistic dreams which have soured public attitudes.

A second and highly significant factor in the widespread dismissal of the guru figure and the ideal of discipleship in Western countries is the general emotional immaturity of the modern adult. Our civilization seems to spawn both infantile and adolescent character traits that persist into old age. It is considered "normal" not to know what one wants and not to know what one is feeling, as well as to constantly seek self-gratification, instant if possible. Our consumer industry is, in fact, based on such a frightening normalcy. The typical infantilistic adult is bound to find the demand represented by a genuine spiritual teacher, especially a teacher of the crazy-wisdom variety, too threatening to his or her weak self-image. The guru appears to such a person as an overpowering parental figure. The spiritual teacher is always a stickler for self-motivation, actual change, and, in Freudian terms, subjection of the pleasure principle to the reality principle. It is also true that, not infrequently, the teacher's demands take the form of autocratic dicta propped up by the guru's charisma. Only the mature disciple or, at the other end of the spectrum, the blind follower can respond to such *fiat* demands. But whereas the former will see them as opportunities for self-transcendence, the latter's response is typically geared to pleasing or mollifying the teacher.

The typical adolescent adult, on the other hand, is programmed to reject authority figures of any kind, because they seem to limit his or her freedom.[7] This feeling is rooted in fearful avoidance of responsibility and self-discipline and springs from a fundamental confusion of freedom with unrealistic autonomy, an egocentric "free-for-all." It is difficult, even impossible, for adolescent adults to be vulnerable. They are bulwarked against anything that is likely to impinge on their emotional life. Although they are vaguely in search of themselves, they cannot open up to the influence of others and so deprive themselves of much wisdom. They are afraid to follow anyone. Instead, they rely on their own instincts, which, given their immature character structure, cannot be expected to be particularly sound. As Carl Jung explained:

> The modern man . . . is not eager to know in what way he can imitate Christ [read: adopt a spiritual way of life], but in what way he can live his own individual life, however meagre and uninteresting it may be. It is because every form of imitation seems to him deadening and sterile that he rebels against the force of tradition that would hold him to well-trodden ways. All such roads, for him, lead in the wrong direction. He may not know it, but he behaves as if his own individual life were instinct with the will of God which must at all costs be fulfilled. This is the source of his egoism, which is one of the most tangible evils of the neurotic state.[8]

The adolescent psyche of the contemporary adult is embedded in, and reinforced by, our culture's dominant ideology of individualism, which is the legacy of the Renaissance. In the last analysis, individualism is the ego's stance when pressing for perfect autonomy—an absurd aspiration, since we are all interdependent. The logical conclusion of the "each man for himself" philosophy is total anarchy. Sadly, it is precisely this philosophy that serves contemporary Westerners as a semiconscious charter in their struggle for survival. But instead of guiding them to enhanced freedom and psychic well-being, this unwritten charter commonly leads only to greater confusion, unfulfillment, loneliness, emptiness, unhappiness, and fear. It takes considerable self-delusion, even hubris, to strive for perfect autonomy.

Apart from a few sociopaths, most people are merely what one might call "opportunistic individualists." They settle for a convenient compromise, allowing their social and cultural needs to dictate the level of their egotism. This has created the astonishing paradox in our era of a highly developed individualism combined with an increasing acceptance of religious and secular authoritarianism. The modern individual often viciously defends his or her own individualistic posture in minor matters, yet largely experiences himself or herself as powerless and faceless in relation to the larger issues of politics, economics, technology, and science. Intimidated by the power of the state, multinational concerns, large sociopolitical movements, and bureaucracy, the "opportunistic individualist" anxiously chooses anonymity over self-expression and rationality. How ready most people are to dispose of conscience, pervert their impulse toward freedom, and slip back into infantile behavior by unthinkingly submitting to authority has been demonstrated in Nazi Germany and other similar regimes.[9] On the basis of this perspective, we may speculate that the grumbling about "new religions" and cults is little more than a displacement of the smoldering resentment against our streamlined civilization's vast authoritarianism. The cults, in other words, are made into a scapegoat.

Another paradoxical feature of the rampant individualism of our contemporary culture is the democratization of freedom, whereby the ideal of liberty is reduced to the lowest common denominator so as to justify and augment the consumer mentality. Freedom is twisted into a *nirvana* of instant gratification, which is flaunted as every consumer's birthright: the right of equal pleasure under God.

Understandably, within the purview of this democratistic worldview, which indiscriminately seeks to level differences, the asymmetric relationship between spiritual teacher and disciple seems aberrated. The guru is seen as domineering and exploitative, while the disciple is dismissed as a weak-willed masochist. What escapes the critics' notice is the fact that human life and nature itself are full of asymmetric relationships, which are nonetheless viable. Indeed, social dynamics appear to be made possible in part by such asymmetry. Inequality, to put it strongly, is as essential to social processes as is equality. Immanuel Kant might have had something like this in mind when he contended that inequality is a "rich source of much that is evil, but also of everything that is good."[10] Even in an egalitarian tribal society, there are those who, by virtue of their natural talent or great life experience, are conspicuously positioned in the social network. Inequality in itself is seldom the problem. What people make of it often is.

In the spiritual process, the asymmetry in the relationship between guru and disciple is undoubtedly more accentuated than comparable asymmetries in an ordinary social context. The most important reason for this asymmetry is simple: whereas the teacher is a repository of wisdom and experience of potentially great benefit to the disciple, the disciple approaches the teacher as someone who is in need of guidance. In all religious traditions this relationship has been formalized to one degree or another, often along paternalistic lines.

However, unlike other asymmetric relationships between adults, the guru-disciple relationship is not primarily defined by conventional transactions involving information, products, or services. The spiritual teacher does not simply impart knowledge or expect mere behavioral modification on the part of the disciple. As I have tried to show in the previous chapter, the guru's principal function is to directly and bodily "communicate" the transcendental Reality, the *numen*, with which he or she consciously identifies. The purpose of that communication is not to widen the disciple's intellectual horizon, deepen his or her belief, or even improve his or her character. Rather, the ultimate objective of spiritual transmission is to modify the disciple's very state of being, to guide him or her to the same enlightenment that the adept teacher enjoys.

But this spiritual transmission is effective only when the disciple is duly prepared and receptive to the guru's teaching and being. This receptivity has been variously called "surrender," "obedience," or "submission." It is the mood of openness that enables the disciple to listen to the teacher and to truly hear him or her, so that the disciple can duplicate the adept's state of being. In return for this gift of transmission, the guru expects and demands the disciple's open-hearted cooperation. He or she calls for a disciple who understands and fully accepts the definition of the situation: that the disciple must be willing to translate the teaching and the spiritual transmission into concrete self-transcending action, namely self-discipline and service.

The ideal relationship between guru and devotee is thus one of voluntary cooperation and synergy. The disciple is free to choose the guru's influence in every moment, just as he or she is free to reject it and to desist from cooperating with the teacher. This is, in fact, the periodic experience of all beginning travelers on the spiritual path. The disciple's refusal to respond to the teacher's gift of transmission can take many forms—from outright disobedience to a more subtle resistance.

Discipleship, if it is genuine, perpetually tests the devotee's ability to let go more of his or her self-will. This is not always immediately possible, and at times the student balks. The guru appreciates the devotee's difficulties because he or she has undergone the same process. The teacher will try to find ways to coax disciples beyond all these hurdles but cannot spare them any of the growing pains. On the contrary, the guru is constantly trying to provoke a spiritual crisis in his or her disciples—a crisis that will lead to a deepening of the disciples' commitment to the spiritual process, and one that will, it is hoped, finally allow the flowering of the enlightened condition.

Spiritual discipleship is a heroic undertaking. The devotee does what the conventional individual most fears to do, which is to risk his or her entire being in the quest for Reality. This requires a tremendous act of courage. As theologian Paul Tillich explained, the common individual reacts to his or her fundamental "anxiety of non-being" either by falling into despair or, more typically, by escaping into neurosis.[11] "Neurosis," Tillich stated, "is the way of avoiding non-being by avoiding being. In the neurotic state self-affirmation is not lacking; it can indeed be very strong and emphasized. But the self which is affirmed is a reduced one."[12] That reduced self is none other than the ego-personality, estranged from itself and the Ground of its existence.

By contrast, every act of courage, however foolish it may seem, is an affirmation of being. Tillich saw in it even "a manifestation of the ground of being."[13] What more courageous act could there be than to voluntarily submit oneself to the spiritual process of self-transformation and self-transcendence? Discipleship entails a constant confrontation with the fear of death, of non-being, while its successful completion coincides with actual "ego-death," which is the dissolution of the conventional human identity. How many religious people pray daily "Thy will be done"? I wonder whether they would make this prayerful affirmation quite so readily if they expected to be taken up on it. Psychologist Charles Tart makes this observation:

> I spend a couple of class periods on Gurdjieff's ideas when I teach my course on humanistic and transpersonal psychology at the university. The idea that we need a teacher to awaken evokes strong resistance from the students every time. They frequently get so caught up in this resistance that it blocks their access to other ideas of Gurdjieff's.
>
> A major source of resistance is our enculturation as Americans: we believe we are rugged individualists and we can do anything we want to do on our own . . . A [further] source of resistance is seldom verbalized: if you were working with a real teacher, he or she might make you actually change instead of just talk about it.[14]

In authentic spiritual discipleship, submission is immediate and concrete. The disciple's surrender is demanded and seen by the teacher. Good intentions and verbal declarations do not suffice. The guru fully expects precisely the kind of actions that the abstract God of popular devotion benignly overlooks. The ordinary individual shudders at the prospect of delivering himself or herself so completely to the mercy of another person. The common fear of submission to another being springs from the firsthand experience of egoic existence: The ego-personality is experienced as a locus of power. In its paranoid need to assert and protect itself, the ego-personality looks constantly for ways to remain in control of events. It is inherently exploitive, and social life is therefore an intricate power play. Hence the human being has been characterized as *homo potens*.[15]

The ordinary person projects this experience of himself or herself as an agent of power onto the teacher-disciple relationship. The guru is popularly viewed as a dangerous potentate, while the devotee, at the opposite pole of this asymmetric relationship, is pictured as a powerless figure. Thus, Peter Marin, while recognizing the need for occasional submission, has nevertheless eloquently debunked the idea of surrender to a spiritual teacher. He remarks:

> There are many things to which a man or woman might submit: to his own work, to the needs of others, to the love of others, to passion, to experience, to the rhythms of nature—the list is endless and includes almost anything men or women might do, for almost anything, done with depth, takes us beyond ourselves and into relation with other things, and that is always a submission, for it is always a joining, a kind of wedding to the world. There is, no doubt, a need for that, for without it we grow exhausted with ourselves, with our wisdom still unspoken, and our needs unmet.
>
> But that general appetite is twisted and used tyrannically when we are asked to submit ourselves unconditionally to other *persons*—whether they wear the masks of the state or of the spirit. In both instances our primary relation is no longer to the world or to others; it is to "the master," and the world or others suffer from that choice, because our relation to them is broken, and with it our sense of possibility. In our attempt to restore to ourselves what is missing, we merely intensify the deprivation rather than diminish it.[16]

The image of the guru as a tyrant who enslaves disciples is but a caricature, which owes its existence to those regrettable cases in which the teacher-disciple relationship has indeed been perverted. It does not, however, apply to genuine discipleship. Here the apparent power differential between guru and disciple is a provisional device, a ploy only, which remains effective only so long as the disciple accepts the definition of the situation.

The devotee's ongoing gesture of voluntary submission signals to the teacher that he or she can feel free to engage the disciple in what can be called the "game of enlightenment." The rules of the game state that the teacher is invested with the authority and power to make spiritual demands on the disciple and, if necessary, to reprimand and discipline the student. The game ends either when the disciple has attained enlightenment or when, as occasionally happens, he or she opts to step back or even to terminate the relationship with the teacher. At that point, no authentic guru would cling to the disciple and expect the game to continue. Nevertheless, the subtle psychic connection—or umbilical cord—created between an authentic guru and a disciple may not be so readily dissolved. It is quite possible that this linkage will persist long after the disciple has left the guru, not because the teacher is trying to influence him or her by psychic means but because the connection, once established, cannot easily be severed. Any seeker should be completely aware of this fact and the tremendous, lifelong responsibility that discipleship means, both for the guru and for the devotee.

### 3. Levels of Conversion

One of the most pervasive problems marring the traditional teacher-disciple relationship is the paternalistic demeanor of spiritual teachers on the one hand and the infantilistic attitude of disciples on the other. This is especially apparent in India, where the devotee is characteristically encouraged to regard his guru as father, mother, and God in one person. But a similar situation prevails in the West as well. It is likely that gurucentric traditions attract personalities that are basically dependent rather than rebellious-adolescent. As has been noted by Da Love-Ananda:

> The typical follower is childish, ultimately irresponsible, self-involved, amoral, experientially undeveloped, weak and out of balance in the dimensions of action, feeling, and thought, and irrationally attached to the enclosures of cult and belief.[17]

In terms of Frances Vaughan's framework, such followers tend to be devotees rather than disciples. Even seekers with a seemingly more independent character frequently waver between moods of rebellion and sheer childish dependence; they either condemn and blame the guru or blindly relate to him or her as their savior. However, it is only in human maturity that the spiritual process can fulfill itself. The childish, dependent character leans toward cultism, whereas the adolescent, independent character inclines toward protest and revolution. Neither attitude typifies the mature personality, which alone can hope to succeed on the spiritual path.

Authentic submission, expressed through voluntary discipline, is a great art, requiring unusual inner stability, courage, a sense of direction, and even a sense of destiny. Above all, it presupposes the event of spiritual conversion. This conversion has been an abiding curiosity for psychologists of religion, who wonder how a Saul can become a Paul. Of late the subject of conversion has been a real bone of contention among anticult critics, who prefer to use such flashy but misleading synonyms as "coercive persuasion," "snapping," "mind control," "hypnotism," and "brainwashing." Because of the popular appeal of anticult ideology, which prevents a wider understanding and appreciation of the spiritual process, it seems appropriate to say a few words about conversion here.

The British physician William Sargant, a pioneer of the brainwashing model of conversion, applied Pavlovian behaviorism to the phenomenon of "sudden" conversion, arguing that "though men are not dogs, they should humbly try to remember how much they resemble dogs in their brain functions."[18] Sargant insisted that both religious converts and researchers on conversion can learn an important lesson from Pavlov's animal experiments in operant conditioning. He wrote:

> It becomes clear from studying the whole literature of religious conversion, mysticism, the acquisition of new faiths and new beliefs, whether secular or religious . . . that two main ways exist by which new faiths,

new beliefs, and totally new outlooks may be suddenly acquired, often diametrically opposed to all the previous faith and beliefs of the individual concerned. One of the two main ways seems to be to excite the nervous system—and to overexcite it—by means of drumming, dancing and music of various kinds, by the rhythmic repetition of stimuli and by the imposing of emotionally charged mental conflicts needing urgent resolution. The brain then finally becomes overwhelmed by the imposed stimuli and conflicts imposed . . . It is then that the many interesting changes in thought and behaviour can suddenly supervene . . .

The other method seems to be one in which the same final end-point occurs, but is attained in an almost opposite way. States of abnormal brain inhibition are produced not by increasing the stimulus till inhibition finally supervenes but by starting off trying to inhibit most of the ordinary voluntary and even involuntary thoughts and activities of the higher nervous system. One tries to put oneself artificially in what is now increasingly called a state of "sensory deprivation."[19]

Sargant referred to "states of contemplation and mysticism," attained after many months or even years of self-application, as examples of the brain-inhibiting method. Thus he characterized Zen, cabbalistic magic, and Scientology as typical ways of effecting an "abnormal" cerebral condition in which a "sudden ultraparadoxical switchover," or conversion, can occur. It is in that moment, as Sargant put it, that a person typically experiences states of "possession," notably mystical union with the Divine. To be sure, so long as the medical-psychiatric worldview denies the existence of a spiritual dimension of reality, mystical experiences will be seen as no more than purely neurophysiological events in the brain with no metaphysical significance. In that case, conversion must appear to be a highly dangerous phenomenon since, by implication, it alters the normal brain functions.

This still-popular psychiatric model of conversion derives largely, as Albert Biderman has shown, from the anti-Communist "cold-war" rhetoric of the 1950s.[20] It reads the convert as a passive subject who is at the mercy of overpowering, sinister influences—a view that has increasingly been challenged by recent research. A number of investigators have demonstrated that those who join a new religion or sit at the feet of a guru are by no means all weak-willed, emotionally unstable, intellectually underendowed, or socio-economically deprived.[21]

Nor are cult members necessarily more unhappy, unwell, or otherwise disadvantaged than other people. They are, however, in doubt of their identity or are in touch with the fact that our transitional culture breeds men and women like themselves who feel peculiarly homeless. The picture that is gradually emerging is one of a "protean man," who *actively* seeks out new identities and experiences and freely *decides* to engage in experiments involving alternative life-styles and worldviews.[22] Some researchers even speak of a "conversion career," to indicate that the modern convert is typically only provisionally committed, tending to move from one group or cause to the next.[23]

In light of this evidence, the brainwashing-coercion metaphor loses its credibility. With few exceptions, converts to "cults" are not bludgeoned into conformism, mindless submission to an authoritarian leader, or unquestioning acceptance of a totalitarian belief system. On the contrary, in the overriding majority of cases they freely choose to join and remain in a particular group, as well as to adopt a particular ideology; then they just as freely choose to drop out again, only to move on to the next experiential adventure. If that is so, then who exploits whom? From a spiritual perspective, it would be more apt to describe the conventional state of mind as the result of prolonged "brainwashing." The ordinary individual is obsessed with the illusion that he or she is separate from life and hence is filled with fear. This condition is undoubtedly the result of our civilization's extensive programs of socialization and education.

At any rate, spiritual conversion is a considerably more complex matter than the simplistic anticult and psychiatric models suggest. These models fall short of reality primarily because they are anchored in a materialistic metaphysics that excludes the spiritual dimension of existence even as a possibility. Frances Vaughan addresses this issue somewhat when she observes:

> A reductionist approach to the study of new religious movements adds to the confusion by failing to make a distinction between those groups that encourage dependency and regression to pre-egoic states and those that support transcendence of ego and contribute to authentic transpersonal development. The common tendency to interpret transpersonal experience as prepersonal narcissism . . . adds to this confusion and leads to the mistaken assumption that all non-ego states are pathological and consequently detrimental.[24]

Unfortunately, Vaughan does not extend her considerations to the conversion process as such. Still, it is clear that while the current models of conversion explain much of the psychosocial mechanics underlying the conversion process, they are quite oblivious to any spiritual component. Yet without due attention to its spiritual aspect, conversion will continue to elude scientific probings.

Ken Wilber, who has piloted the philosophical consolidation of transpersonal psychology, helpfully demarcates the "born again" phenomenon of the "true believer" from the wholesome adaptation of the "person of faith."[25] The former is an explosive conversion that can be understood in transpersonal terms as a subadaptation to a prerational style of relating to the world. The latter type of conversion, by contrast, implies "transformative growth." Wilber notes that the person of faith, unlike the true believer who has all the answers, is also a person capable of doubt. And the greater the faith, the greater also the doubt. This doubt is generated by the constant confrontation with oneself vis-à-vis the intuition of the spiritual dimension that is inherently challenging the configurations of the ego–personality.

From a purely spiritual perspective, conversion involves a pincer movement. On one side, there is the "thrust" of the human personality that seeks to resolve its fundamental sense of being cut off from reality; on the other side, there is the "pull" of the transcendental Reality, the spiritual dimension. The "thrust" aspect can be comprehended substantially by means of psychological, sociological, and also neurophysiological analysis, providing one allows the existence of something like David Bakan's "urge toward the unmanifest."[26] Bakan, a professor of psychology, includes in that urge the mathematician's wrestling with the abstract (i.e., unmanifest) realm of numerical relations, the scientist's struggle for comprehension of the invisible (i.e., unmanifest) laws that govern the physical and biotic processes, the psychoanalyst's efforts to decipher the symbolism of the unconscious (i.e., unmanifest) psyche, and the mystic's quest for identification with the transcendental (i.e., unmanifest) Ground of all manifestation.

The "pull" aspect of conversion, however, completely eludes the scientific method. It is primarily a matter of personal experience and secondarily of theology. E. T. Starbuck, an early pioneer of the psychology of religion, unintentionally articulated this second aspect of the conversion process when he stated that conversion is the "larger world–consciousness now pressing in on the individual consciousness." Evelyn Underhill, who quoted this phrase in her 1911 book on mysticism, remarked that Starbuck's comments are more pertinent to mysticism than to the American Protestantism for which they were originally meant.[27] The kind or level of conversion implied in Starbuck's description presupposed, in Underhill's opinion, a basic religious conversion. In other words, she distinguished between at least two levels of conversion— religious and mystical. This idea can be further refined by introducing a third, more basic level of conversion.

First, there is what I call *ideological conversion*, which is the usually sudden conversion by which a person discovers a new "home" or identity in a lifestyle, community, or worldview that is radically different from his or her previous experience. The change is in response to an emotional-intellectual crisis and promises to meet the individual's higher expectations. Often the conversion does indeed lead to a more meaningful life, but this experience may be only temporary. Then dissatisfaction may rear its head again, leading to a new crisis. When this happens, commitment flags and the convert starts to look around for the next ready-made alternative. At this level of conversion, "defection" is a rather common phenomenon.

Ideological conversion, which comprises conventional religious conversion, involves a readaptation that is primarily sustained by a change within the belief structure of the individual. The "change of heart" that is experienced is actually more a change of mind, although there is of course also always an emotional readjustment connected with it. Essentially, ideological conversion occurs in the horizontal plane of the ego-personality. In other words, the ego-personality merely adjusts to a new *convention* of reality. No genuine self-transcendence or change of reality-perception is involved, and the convert's personality tends to be that of the childish or adolescent variety.

The second type or level of conversion, which I wish to call *authentic religious* or *spiritual conversion*, represents a true change of heart. It is not only lasting but also reinforms all aspects of the convert's personality and life. Through this more profound *metanoia*, which should be styled *metacardia* ("change of heart"), the individual becomes what Ken Wilber calls a "person of faith." For such an individual, religion is no longer a matter of belief, hope, or good intentions or actions, but the discovery of the nonmaterial, psychophysical nature of existence and a growing at-onement with the sacred or transcendental Reality.[28]

The third form or degree of conversion I propose to call *transcendental conversion*, since it coincides with the awakening of a deep and apparently irreversible impulse toward enlightenment in the higher stages of mystical life.[29] This final inner turnabout represents the fulfillment of *spiritual conversion* and itself culminates in permanent enlightenment, or transcendental realization.

Evidently, conversion is a process comprising several degrees of profundity. Therefore, the seeker who hopes for a once-and-for-all conversion that, like a panacea, evaporates all personal problems will be disappointed. Conversion implies hard work on oneself, in which new levels of realization are followed by new commitments. For the spiritual practitioner there is no ideological safety net. On every turn the path is strewn with risks and demands for greater self-transcendence. Enlightenment is itself a form of *sadhana*, with a transformative ordeal of its own.

The initiate must understand from the outset that he or she will be challenged in the extreme and must ultimately surrender the very notion of self. The seeker will inevitably be frustrated in his or her seeking, for enlightenment is the *end* of all seeking. Those who cleave to their seeking on the spiritual path provoke a counterconversion, which sucks them back into secular egoic life. These people usually end up blaming the teacher or the teaching for their own failure to grow. The ego-personality is inherently at war with the spiritual path and the teacher, and when it gets the upper hand it will complain and attack. This is the stuff that many ex-devotees of different gurus are made of. Anticult critics should be aware of this larger consideration.

The biographers of Upasani Baba, a contemporary crazy-wise adept in India, relate a story that illustrates just how irrational the ego-personality can become when confronted with the spiritual process and an authentic teacher.[30] Upasani Baba had received initiation from Sai Baba of Shirdi, modern India's greatest miracle-working saint. A number of Sai Baba's followers begrudged Upasani Baba this spiritual gift; for this reason he left the village of Shirdi and took up a fast that lasted for two and a half years. One local resident in particular was irrationally envious and hateful toward Upasani Baba and would often speak ill of him during devotional gatherings at Sai Baba's hermitage. He would even go to the length of sending Upasani Baba mock invitations to celebratory occasions.

In April 1935, Upasani Baba resolved to accept one of these invitations. He arrived at Shirdi unannounced and was received with respect and awe by the whole gathering of the late Sai Baba's disciples. They felt, as the biographers tell us, that Sai Baba himself had risen from the grave to grant them a vision of his incarnate form. When the malevolent letter writer arrived, Upasani Baba turned to him with joined palms, saying "Maharaj, I have come in obedience to your call." Overcome with shame and remorse, the formerly envious man fell at the adept's feet and asked for his forgiveness.

Perhaps it is safe to say that wherever there is great spiritual force there is also great resistance. The enlightened adepts of humanity represent a principle that runs counter to conventional life. Their very existence is a threat to the ordinary person, who has no time for spiritual matters and spiritual masters but rather seeks egoic autonomy. Let it be stated, however, that even a faithful disciple is subject to bouts of resistance, which can at times be quite dramatic. The ego-personality habitually resists transformation. Yet the disciple is committed to freeing the energy frozen in such resistance and turning it to better use. Resistance and doubt are natural on the spiritual path. Their absence is generally an indication that the disciple has fallen asleep. When the disciple begins to feel cozy, it is high time for self-examination. Discipleship and complacency are incompatible. Discipleship implies a commitment to constant alertness, which is the bedrock of spiritual surrender.

## 4. Cultism, Guru-Worship, and Freedom

The difference between genuine self-surrender in the context of discipleship and mere childish submission to the guru is subtle but crucially important. The former is conducive to both emotional and spiritual growth; the latter merely leaves intact the follower's narcissism. Unfortunately, today as in the past, childish devotees are in greater supply than mature disciples. Hence, critics of the contemporary spiritual scene are justified when they refer to the groups that have formed around most modern spiritual teachers as idolatrous cults rather than true communities. Even in groups like the Free Daist Communion, where the teacher is constantly calling for the creation of true community, there is an inveterate tendency toward cultism, or sectarianism.[31]

"Cult" has become a buzz word that is fairly indiscriminately applied to both religious and secular groups of people who share a fascination for a specific cause and pursue their interests with such exclusiveness that they may appear strange to the rest of society. As Da Love-Ananda has pointed out, however, cultic behavior is virtually a "universal constant" of the ego-personality. The conventional individual is forever making exclusive (cultic) pacts with others to safeguard his or her own survival. This extended sense of the word "cult" is a handy device for talking about any cultural or social forms that seek to preserve the ego's status quo—all the countless contracts or agreements, whether spoken or unspoken, whether conscious or unconscious, that keep the ego-personality safe from having to change, to wake up, to assume full responsibility for its destiny.

In this respect, the anticult movement itself can be labeled a "cult." It seeks to "rescue" brainwashed individuals from so-called cults and to "deprogram" them so that they can again be useful members of society. As has been shown in several studies, however, the deprogramming methods are in many ways much closer to real brainwashing than the original conversion. Many anticult activists and deprogrammers are highly conservative and informed by religious fundamentalism. In effect, they are playing out the dangerous role of countergurus. Like cultic conversion, deprogramming also has its victims.

But there are no victims of genuine discipleship. To be a victim implies a state of powerlessness and exploitation. The only "victim," or sacrificial offering, in discipleship is the ego itself, which must be transcended. Ego-transcendence is not something that can be forced on a person; it is only possible as a voluntary gesture. This gesture, however, is often misunderstood by spiritual seekers. They pervert it into mere self-denial, which can simply be a way of surreptitiously inflating the ego. In gurucentric traditions, practitioners often confuse obedience to the teacher with pleasing the teacher in order to win his or her approval or favor. Still more injurious is the confusion of ritual guru worship with guru adulation. Ritual guru worship, called *guru-puja* in Sanskrit, is a device by which the disciple honors the Divine as it manifests in and as the adept-teacher. This can be a profoundly inspiring and illuminating experience, but it presupposes considerable spiritual maturity.

The idea behind this ancient ritual is as follows: The enlightened teacher experiences himself or herself as identical with the transcendental Reality. If his or her enlightenment is genuine, the implied identity shift from the ego-personality (*jiva-atman*) to the Self (*parama-atman*) becomes effective on the level of the physical body. That is to say, the guru becomes a spontaneous spiritual transmitter. In *guru-yoga*, the disciple cooperates with this transmission by placing his or her attention on the teacher during the course of the day and also in special ritual acts of worship.

In these ritual occasions the disciple attunes himself or herself more consciously to the divine or numinous Reality embodied in the guru. In other words, he or she approaches the guru with the same sacred feelings that are normally reserved for the Divine (in the abstract). In many gurucentric traditions, in fact, the disciple is expected to treat the teacher as the Divine outside ritual occasions as well. Here is an excerpt from the Hindu literature that is characteristic of the spirit of traditional *guru-yoga*, which is built on the metaphysical foundations of nondualism:

> The scriptures declare: He who is the guru is Shiva [i.e., the Divine itself]; he who is Shiva is the guru. He who makes a distinction [between these two] is [no better than] a man having sex with the guru [or, rather, the guru's wife].

> [The disciple] should always remember the guru's form; he should ever recite the guru's name; he should obey the guru's command, and he should contemplate on none but the guru.

> [The disciple] should surrender everything to the true guru: body, senses, breath, possessions, country, family, and [even] one's wife, etc.

> There is no greater principle than the guru. There is no greater austerity than the guru. There is no greater wisdom than the guru. [Therefore] obeisance to that blessed guru.

> The universe resides at the center of the guru, and the guru resides at the center of the universe. The guru is nothing but the universe. [Therefore] obeisance to that blessed guru.

> By devotion to the guru one attains the state of liberation [even] without knowledge. For the followers of a [true] guru no discipline is necessary other than the guru's grace. [This statement is somewhat misleading, for *guru-yoga* is a form of discipline.]

> The guru is God. The guru is the law. The greatest austerity is reliance on the guru. There is nothing [that is] superior to the guru.[32]

The dangers of practicing *guru-yoga*, or guru worship, are readily apparent: The disciple may never break through to a transcendental perception of the guru but remain stuck on the pedestrian level of literal worship. In that case the disciple's *guru-puja* is no more than childish adulation and fawning. As Robert Masters puts it, rather bluntly:

> Guru-worship is fundamentally no more than spiritual laziness, just one more "solution" to a primarily problematic orientation toward Life. It is but a strategy to anaesthetize oneself to one's difficulties, a strategy to be parented and consoled to such a degree that one's troubles appear to fade, perhaps even seeming to dissolve in a kind of pseudo-bliss remarkably similar to that sought by more worldly types in their pursuit of "good" feelings, ego-reinforcement, and stress-discharge, through compulsive sexual activity.[33]

Masters compares this fetishistic devotional behavior to masturbation. Incapable of an authentic response, the seeker sentimentalizes or romanticizes the guru and transmogrifies him or her into a mini-deity who grants temporary relief from the stresses of existence. The relationship to the actual guru is thereby rendered spiritually impotent.

As history shows, *guru-yoga* has led to extraordinary triumphs—witness the biography of the Tibetan adept Milarepa—and it has also had its share of dismal failures and abuses. I suspect, although it would be difficult to document, that ruinous incidents far outnumber happy endings. Enlightened teachers who are not tempted by ingratiating students are rare, but childish seekers have always existed in abundance.

Authentic discipleship paradoxically demands a mature personality with a strong ego. The biographies and hagiographies of adepts often reveal to us highly eccentric individuals who nonetheless were capable of astonishing obedience, even if the authority to which they bowed was frequently within their own psyche rather than external to themselves. Writing about the obedience of Christian saints, Benedict Groeschel has remarked:

> A review of the authentic lives of saints reveals both a strong sense of obedience and yet a growing sense of their own individuation and personal freedom. These very ones who sought to live by obedience had their priorities well enough sorted out that they were often obedient to higher laws which their less spiritual associates could not even comprehend. Frequently, this did not lead the saints to a comfortable life. Often these most devoted Christians found themselves in deep conflict with the very authorities they believed represented the will of God for them. We see this in the conflict that St. John of the Cross and St. Teresa caused by their attempts at reform. They were both seen as disobedient, and John was condemned as a rebel. Yet their writings demonstrate a profound sense of obedience. Their conscious goal was always to be completely obedient.[34]

Even when the mature disciple appears to demonstrate obedience to the external teacher, he or she really submits to the teacher as an inner authority. In that case, the disciple experiences the teacher as an extension of his or her own conscience. This works so long as the teacher does not make demands that run counter to the disciple's innermost feelings of right and wrong. Assuming the teacher is enlightened and the disciple is a mature personality, such a clash should not occur, since both are facing in the same direction: toward the Divine. This does not mean, however, that the teacher's demands may not on occasion prove profoundly difficult for the disciple or that obedience will always be naturally forthcoming.

For the *mature* disciple it should not even matter, in principle, whether or not the teacher is fully awakened. Obedience is simply a means of actively demonstrating the self-transcending disposition that is crucial to spiritual life. In the words of Meister Eckehart:

True and perfect obedience is a virtue above all virtues, and no work, however great, can happen or be accomplished without this virtue; on the other hand, however small or minor a work may be, it is more profitably done out of true obedience, whether it be hearing or reading the Mass, or prayer, or contemplation, or whatever else you may think of . . .

Where a man moves beyond his ego and renounces what is his, there God must necessarily enter; for when someone does not will for himself, God must will for him as for Himself. When I have surrendered my will to my prelate and do not will for myself, then God must will for me, and if He should fail me in this, he would fail Himself. So it is with all things: Where I do not will for myself, there God wills for me. Now hearken! What is it He wills for me when I will nothing for myself? That when I let go of my ego, he must necessarily will everything for me that He wills for Himself, no more no less, and in the same manner in which He wills for Himself. And if God did not do that—by the truth that God is, God would not be just, nor would He be God, which it is His nature to be.[35]

We see that even within a basically dualistic tradition, it is possible to practice a form of *guru-yoga*. As is well known, Meister Eckehart was, theologically speaking, closer to Indian nondualism than most other Christian mystics. Nevertheless, his recommendation that the disciple empty himself or herself of all self-motivated will and surrender to the will of the Divine is grounded not in any metaphysical doctrine but in an exemplary attitude of faith, or trust.

In fact, the teacher–disciple relationship and spiritual life as such are unworkable without basic trust—trust in the integrity of the teacher and trust in life itself. And such trust, which does not come naturally to the twentieth-century seeker, is always an expression of personal maturity. It has therefore been said that spiritual life is part of adulthood. As theologian Daniel Helminiak observes:

Spiritual development is a properly adult phenomenon. It is the growth in authentic self-transcendence that results from the individual's taking responsibility for her- or himself. The general line of human development, according to all theorists, moves from infant, impulse-dominated self-centeredness to conformist identity with one's social group and finally to post-conventional self-determination and integration of internal and external reality.

In some sense the end product is again a kind of self-centeredness, but it is of a very different kind from that of the child. Mature self-determination accords with reality; it is realistic and responsible. Even if it appears to be—and is—spontaneous response, it is the result of long self-formation and explicit choice. It is the now "natural" activity of a self-formed individual.[36]

Authentic self-transcendence is a discipline and hence involves a measure of self-constraint, of obeying an inner authority. The disciple's (and for that matter the teacher's) responses to life present themselves as inner necessities: He or she chooses what appears to be inevitable. Yet this voluntary self-limitation is not experienced as a curtailment of inner freedom. On the contrary, a self-transcending life is accompanied by an increasingly joyous sense of inner autonomy, of relief from the mechanicalness of the ego-personality. Thus, even when the disciple (or the teacher for that matter) adopts in full awareness a passive attitude toward a particular event, that passivity is not a cop-out but an expression of the same mature self-determination that in other situations might provoke instant action. Philosopher Herbert Fingarette, who has examined the nature of spiritual life and mystic "selflessness" in some depth, proffers the following clarifying comments:

> For the relatively mature person, minor decisions are made with an unqualified subjective sense of freedom. In connection with weighty decisions in life, there is the more complex feeling that one is free and yet that, in terms of one's integrity, "one can do no other" . . .
>
> Mature individuals . . . have achieved a harmonious integration of the instinctual drives, the superego standards and restrictions, the ego perceptions and discriminative faculties, and the real possibilities offered by the environment. Thus they are at once perceptive and yet, as was noted earlier, "self-forgetful."[37]

Fingarette also cites what must be one of Meister Eckehart's most profound statements: "The truth is that the more ourselves we are, the less self is in us."[38] This paradox is pivotal to mature spiritual practice and especially to the psychology of spontaneity that underlies a fully enlightened life, particularly in its crazy-wise manifestations. Next we will examine the nature of enlightenment, or God-realization, which is the ultimate fruit of the "sacred ordeal" of discipleship.

# 8

## GOD, ENLIGHTENMENT, AND EGO-DEATH

### 1. The Loss of God and Faith

It would make no sense to talk about holy madness and spiritual discipleship without also talking about God and enlightenment. After all, the crazy-wise adepts and holy fools all understood their lives as revolving around the transcendental Reality. Often they sought to humble themselves in the face of it, and in some traditions, they identified with it. But without exception they all gave witness to it. This holds true also of contemporary spiritual tricksters and clowns. Their easefulness about transcendence stands in stark contrast to the awkwardness and discomposure experienced by most people today with regard to the sacred.

Our civilization, which is dominated by the ideology of scientism, is almost entirely uncommunicative about the transcendental Reality, or God. Friedrich Nietzsche announced defiantly over a century ago, "God is dead! God remains dead! And we have killed him!"[1] His infamous declaration was not so much a philosophical or theological hypothesis as a statement about a cultural-historical fact. By the end of the nineteenth century, God had indeed become extinct—as a leading cultural ideal. For Nietzsche, as for most of his questioning contemporaries, religion was no longer a viable option. It had, in the words of sociologist Peter Berger, become a mere "rumor of angels."[2] The ideology of scientific materialism had effectively supplanted the religious worldview that formed the unquestioned framework of the past, prior to the rise of science. Thus, Nietzsche simply articulated the loss that his era was feeling and turned it into a desperate manifesto of the coming "age of Man." He assumed the role of the mad prophet and foretold a new period in which human beings would ascend the throne of God, taking responsibility for their own existence and creating and judging their own world.

Nietzsche was right, partially. We *have* cast out the Divine from our lives and, arrogating the divine attributes of omniscience and omnipotence, appointed ourselves the makers of our own universe. Alas, for all our self-proclaimed divinity, we have not yet assumed responsibility for our lives or our newfound freedom. We have so far failed to do so because, in burying the God of the old religion, we have also entombed a part of ourselves—a part without which we cannot truly come alive as free beings. In slaughtering the archaic Creator-God, we have inadvertently mutilated ourselves: We have punctured our own hearts and lost faith and hope.

Not only did we reject our Judeo-Christian heritage but we also expunged from our cultural and psychic horizon the very possibility of transcendence and a spiritual way of life. We were not satisfied with revising our religious beliefs in light of the findings of modern science; we allowed ourselves to undermine the life-giving function of authentic faith itself. The "progress" of science and its rapid demolition of the ancient religious worldview has left us in a state of shock from which we, as a civilization, have still not recovered. The pluralism of life-styles and values that marks our era is in large part only the outward manifestation of the deep inner uncertainty and confusion that countless people are suffering.

Our epoch has rightly been characterized as "post-Christian" and even "postreligious," but it is also "*pre*spiritual." That is to say, the total "revalorization of values" envisioned by Nietzsche remains unaccomplished. The new age he heralded has yet to begin because, as a culture, we have so far failed to understand that the end of the tyranny of the old patriarchal God has set us free to find the real God, the transcendental Reality beyond religious dogmas and mere belief. We have yet to catch up with Nietzsche's intuition that "Man is something that shall be overcome."[3]

Nietzsche despised the average individual, who refuses the freedom to actualize his or her full potential and who settles for less than the highest mode of existence. He eulogized and crusaded for the "superman." But he allowed his own despair, impatient radicalism, and uncompromising rejection of religion to impair his judgment. A secular travesty of humanity's true potential, Nietzsche's superman remained a truncated being, setting the ideological stage for the absurdities of fascism. Still, Nietzsche was close to the life-pulse of our civilization when he pointed at self-transcendence as the most needed task ahead.

At the same time, however, Nietzsche conceived of self-transcendence in too limited a way, because his image of humanity was flawed by his own rejection of the transcendental. In this respect, he foreshadowed the psychologizing models of the contemporary human potential movement, which also stop short with the ideal of self-actualization: There is in them no larger Reality that eclipses the self. Transcendence, in other words, is considered possible only *within* the self-system. For Nietzsche, this was primarily a matter of human will—the human individual crashing through self-erected barriers with clenched fists and knitted brows. He branded faith a weakness of will, deriding the apostle Paul for perverting the gospel of his master, who, as Nietzsche saw it, asked not for mere faith but for duplication of his Christ condition. Of course, ultimately, Nietzsche also rejected Jesus' message, for he perceived nothing greater than the human being. In this he remained loyal to Protagoras.

Nietzsche's disregard for faith was logically consequent upon his negation of the transcendental Reality. It also amounted to an unconscious impulse toward his own psychic death. For, faith—if genuine—is a person's total response of trust in the source and context of life. Faith is a matter of the heart; without faith the individual is doomed to wither, because he or she will believe in his or her own separateness from the world-process and thus cut off life at its root. "Man is of the form of faith," states the *Bhagavad-Gita* (XVIII.3), a Sanskrit tract more than two thousand years old. There are many levels of explanation of this saying. Whichever way one may want to interpret the term *faith* (in Sanskrit, *shraddha*), it denotes an attitude of transcendence. In faith, we reach beyond ourselves, beyond a presumed insularity whose ultimate end is the kind of tragic insanity to which Nietzsche fell victim.

The scientific ideology that we inherited from the nineteenth century was originally intended as an "enlightened" reaction to the "blind faith" of medieval humanity. But by showing the irrationality of previous beliefs, it destroyed the vital premises on which generations had built their lives. In the process, it also eroded the attitude of authentic faith, creating in us the feeling of uprootedness. Sociologist Peter Berger has written:

> Modernity has accomplished many far-reaching transformations, but it has not fundamentally changed the finitude, fragility and mortality of the human condition. What it has accomplished is to seriously weaken those definitions of reality that previously made that human condition easier to bear. This has produced an anguish all its own . . . In their private lives individuals keep on constructing and reconstructing refuges that they experience as 'home'. But, over and over again, the cold winds of 'homelessness' threaten these fragile constructions.[4]

Meanwhile, scientific materialism offers itself as a total philosophy of life, in which the homeless mind can find a resting place. Like the religious tradition it deposed, it asks to be taken seriously as a basis for faith. Because of the apparent success of science and technology, the scientific priesthood has attracted countless believers. But belief is not tantamount to faith; the pseudofaith proffered by scientism engages only the head, not the heart, which remains restless. Therefore it cannot remedy the psychic and spiritual malaise of our time. It is, in fact, a great obstruction to the further evolution of humanity, which is directed toward an awareness that includes transcendence.[5]

The same criticism applies to religious provincialism.[6] Both scientific materialism and religious provincialism are oblivious to authentic faith, substituting for it the heady acceptance of beliefs (or, in scientistic language, "models" of reality). Both approaches operate with a deficient concept of the Divine, or transcendental Reality. While scientism deifies humanity, leading to a reductionistic and, in the last analysis, narcissistic ideology of humanism, religious provincialism clings tightly to antiquated and implausible ideas of God and religion. Neither is concerned with transcendental Reality or with the spiritual practice of self-transcendence that can lead to an experiential encounter with that Reality, let alone to an identification with it.

Scientistic ideology continues to undermine the pseudo faith of the dwindling congregation of religious provincialists. In an attempt to rescue what can be salvaged in their own Church, Christian theologians are busy reinterpreting the spiritual message of Jesus of Nazareth. Some have even gone so far as to omit from religious discourse all talk about God, focusing instead on the symbol of the Christ. Their audacity has only aggravated the psychic dilemma of churchgoers. As Theodore Reik observed, "most educated people do not believe in God, but they fear Him."[7] Alan Watts touched the same nerve when he said, "The Christian cosmos has vanished, but the Christian ego remains."[8] Our intellect has outgrown our religious heritage; our emotions have not. They have not, because we have not yet recovered from the shock of losing our faith. We have generated new beliefs, which are "scientifically" credible, but we have not been restored in our faith. Science has not given us a "model" by which we can live in faith. Indeed, the very program of science is founded on the presumption that its models are only provisional and constantly subject to revision.

This leaves the typical Westerner in a schizoid condition; brain and heart are split asunder. This self-division now threatens our very survival as a species. We have choked the old God to death, and now our Godlessness is choking us. Clearly, we cannot recover the lost ground. The split in our being cannot be healed by returning to the religion of our ancestors. We do, however, need to make peace with it. Pre-nineteenth-century religion, with its central image of the patriarchal Creator-God, is as alien to us now as the Hellenic pantheon of all-too-human deities. Neither can we with impunity merely return to the matriarchal Goddess of paleolithic and early neolithic times. No simple solution to our dilemma exists.

There can be no question that the Judeo-Christian world still has archetypal force in our psyche, just as the Great Mother is part of our inner makeup. Therefore, it also will not do to simply ignore these forces within us. Mere denial, like voluntary regression into past modes of religious experience, would merely exacerbate our psychic chaos. The only viable option is a life dedicated to transcendence of the self in its entire complexity. Such a life is possible because the ego, or self, does not ultimately define the human being. But such a life is never an easy road.

The possibility of an ego-transcending life is contemplated by very few.

Most people are simply resigned to a clichéd existence in which, for want of "courage to be,"[9] they indulge in make-believe ideologies of one kind or another. They scrape by on a minimal or pseudofaith, denying themselves full awareness of the fundamental meaninglessness of their lives, their neurotic anxiety, the shallowness of their relationships, and their quiet desperation and suffering.

Those who cannot help noticing their own psychic discord and hopelessness and the cultural fragmentation around them willy-nilly go on a "vision quest." Unless their quest turns into an escape into the cul-de-sac of schizophrenia, they become spiritual seekers in pursuit of a new faith. Often, however, their seeking rests content with the acquisition of a more convincing *model* of reality or more fulfilling *experiences*. The motivation toward greater experiential fulfillment is frequently cited as one of the key factors in the emergence of the "innovative" religious cults of our day.[10]

The hunger for concrete religious or "spiritual" experience remains largely unmet within the religious establishment. Religious orthodoxy is by definition conservative, and personal religious experience is of necessity threatening to monolithic institutional structures. Consequently, orthodoxy prefers a theoretical God to the living Reality and relies on simpleminded conformism, dismissing and outlawing personal experimentation. Hence, the mystic, who aspires to personal union with the Divine, has always been the scapegoat of religious orthodoxy, at least in such dualistic traditions as Judaism, Christianity, and Islam. One might presume that in nondualistic religions the psychic voyager would have a better fate, but here he or she is indirectly martyred by being glorified and swiftly deified. In this way, the mystic can safely be worshipped and milked for grace without having to be taken seriously, which would involve discipleship and the duplication of his or her spiritual state.

In India this nondualistic approach has led to the absurd situation in which every other holy man or woman is worshipped as an *avatara*, or "descent," of the supreme Godhead. Despite the rapid encroachment of materialism, the cultural climate of the Indian subcontinent is still, as it has always been, favorable to the emergence and proliferation of mysticism. But authentic spirituality—which I propose to contrast with mysticism—is a rarity even in the homeland of the *rishis*, *sadhus*, *yogins*, and *samnyasins*. It is true that God-realization, or enlightenment, was acknowledged as the supreme goal of human life by India's brahmin legislators for three millennia (until the secularization of indigenous law under the British hegemony). It is also true that God-realization has been a regular feature of the intellectual orbit of both rural and urban Indians, if only by dint of their popular mythologies, which keep talk about God and God-realizers alive. Nevertheless, actual God-realizers are few and far between, even in India. In other words, even in India, God is mostly a religious symbol, not an experiential reality.

Where the Divine *is* experienced as an actuality beyond mere conceptions, it is widely encountered as the *innermost* dimension of existence—the God within, the *atman*. This is the God-experience of mysticism, which is founded in vertical ascent through the stages of consciousness. This notion of inner divinity, or divine essence, is the mystical analogue to the conventional idea of "God out there," the Heavenly Father up above. Unlike the exoteric God, however, the mystical God is not merely a pious thought but corresponds to actual experience.

Nevertheless, the "God within" is a limiting conceptualization of an experience that, at least potentially, goes beyond all mental categories. In other words, the typical mystic tends to approach his or her own experience of *unio mystica* with a certain preconception, as if God were to be found *only* within the psyche, or soul. What this means is, as Da Love-Ananda has pointed out, that God is viewed as an *alternative* reality.[11] From an integrative viewpoint, such an alternative reveals itself to be a psychological device, resorted to by many mystics, by which to deny the transcendental Reality in its fullness.

If the Divine, or transcendental Reality, is not inside or outside or above, where is it to be found? The question itself is misleading; Gautama the Buddha, for one, steadfastly refused to furnish any answer to it. Yet it is evident from some authentic passages of the Pali canon that he did not deny such a transcendental Reality and that the occasional charge of atheism against him is quite unwarranted.[12] Da Love-Ananda, less cautious than the Buddha, has made this comment:

> God is not merely behind the world and elsewhere and up there and inside. God is Omnipresent, absolutely Present, unqualifiedly Present. Not to see God in the terms of manifest reality is to fail to Realize God.[13]

The quest for the external God (be this the patriarchal deity or the Goddess) consists of ritual worship and moral obedience in keeping with the sacred revelation. The search for the inner God, which is the way of mysticism or esotericism, is a more spectacular adventure that appeals to those who are ill at ease with exoteric conformism and the demands of the world. From the vantage point of our "comparative" era, both of these God ideals are circumscribed expressions. A more sophisticated theological language is possible: God as the totality of existence. Of course, even this notion is a mental artifact. As Alan Watts reminded us:

> *All* ideas of the universe are anthropomorphic, because they are representations of the world in terms of the human mind. Furthermore, a universe which grows human beings is as much a human, or humaning, universe as a tree which grows apples is an apple tree . . .
> To construct a God in the human image is objectionable only to the extent that we have a poor image of ourselves, for example, as egos in bags of skin. But as we can begin to visualize man as the behavior

of a unified field—immensely complex and comprising the whole universe—there is less and less reason against conceiving God in *that* image.[14]

The image of God as an infinite, universal field of inconceivable dimensions is still only an image, an *idolon*, but it is one that is not burdened by the limitations, nor the political consequences, of the other traditional God ideas. It neither implies the "jealous God" of patriarchal theism, whose commandments must be obeyed, nor the "inner Self/God" into which we must withdraw by abstracting ourselves, in tortoiselike fashion, from the world. The image of God as the *totum* of existence is implicitly world-positive, since the world, when experienced from the viewpoint of full God-realization or enlightenment, reveals itself as an aspect of the immeasurable being of the ultimate Reality.

When we examine the manifestations of holy madness in different religious traditions, it is useful to bear these distinct God images in mind. As a rule, the tendency of the holy fools of Christianity and Islam to adopt the dualistic Creator-God image has given their folly its characteristic flavor of self-abnegation. In contrast, the holy fools of India, Tibet, and China were influenced by their bias toward the mystical "God within." In only a few cases, especially in the Mahayana and Vajrayana Buddhist traditions, can we find crazy adepts whose spiritual eccentricities can be understood within the framework of a metaphysics that envisions the transcendental Reality as a field continuum, a singular whole.

## 2. Enlightenment and the Transcendence of Attention

Given our modern civilization's "Godlessness" and existential confusion, it seems almost presumptuous to put forward a definition of spiritual enlightenment. Fortunately, we do not need to concoct such a definition since we can draw one from the records of authentic spiritual traditions.

In our civilization, "enlightenment"—like "God"—means different things to different people. In the popular mind, the term may stir vague memories of the French Revolution and the rationalist enterprise of the encyclopedists, like D'Alembert, Diderot, and Voltaire. To them, enlightenment meant the illumination of the mind by rational understanding until the last trace of superstition and myth has been eradicated. They were not against religion per se but preached religious tolerance and intellectual forthrightness. However, the rationalist enterprise soon became hostile toward religion as such.

For most people the term "enlightenment" used in a spiritual sense connotes some kind of rocklike trance state for which its experiencer is, if anything, to be pitied. The popular mind cannot conceive of anything greater than itself, and so it must belittle the enlightenment of the great spiritual adepts. To assume that the adepts' illumination was anything more than a state of extreme (and, by implication, bizarre) inwardness would unhinge the drab universe of popular consent.

The New Age community, by contrast, generally understands enlightenment as a psychic acquisition, a superior form of knowledge, or gnosis, which leaves reason behind and opens up new vistas of experience. Enlightenment is thus treated as a cognitive state that comes about by following certain procedures. In a recent popular book on Neo-Tantrism, the author declares that over a hundred participants in his workshop have become so enlightened. Such claims appear bombastic and nonsensical from a traditional spiritual perspective. Traditionally, enlightenment does not stand for an experience or state of knowledge at all. It is therefore also not something that could be attained as the inevitable result of a specific course of action. Hence enlightenment *en masse* is less than likely.

According to the great spiritual traditions of the world, enlightenment represents the transcendence of all knowledge and experience. It comes about through an unpredictable breakthrough, which is generally experienced or interpreted as an act of grace, or transcendental interference. This is the meaning adopted here. I equate this transcendental condition with God-realization, the recovery of Being. Such spiritual enlightenment is not a supreme value in our contemporary secularized civilization. It is, in fact, not even a moderately prominent value. Only a minuscule minority treasure enlightenment as a goal worthy of aspiration. And even within this minority only a few seem really to understand the nature of enlightenment; fewer still are those who actually assume it as the supreme value in their lives.

But what is God-realization, or enlightenment? The contemporary adept Da Love-Ananda has furnished this tentative answer:

> The usual man or woman thinks that Enlightenment is the having of a vision. Enlightenment is the most subtle, or tacit, unspeakable understanding . . . On its basis, all kinds of radiant transformations may develop, but the Realization itself is so fundamental, so tacit, so simple, so direct, so obvious, so transcendental, that it is not identified with any phenomenon of experience or knowledge.[15]

And elsewhere he has elaborated this explanation as follows:

> Understanding itself won't necessarily have anything peculiarly dramatic about it. How dramatic is it to wake up in the morning? You don't say, "Wowwwwwwww!!!" You don't go screaming, "Fantastic! Oh, Revelation!" All you do is open your eyes and live. You just wake up. The moment of the Realization that you are not stuck in the dream has a certain pleasure associated with it, but it is not usually a fantastic sort of fireworks. It is a natural, already Happy event.[16]

We also have in Da Love-Ananda's autobiography a description of his own awakening. He was sitting in the Vedanta Temple in Hollywood at the time.

In the moment of his spiritual awakening, he simply opened his eyes and walked out into the street. He did not even describe this event to anyone for several weeks. What had occurred was a radical, final identity shift from the ego-personality to the "Self" of the *totum*. He was no longer experiencing himself as a limited body-mind but as the Whole in which all body-minds and forms emerge and vanish. To everyone else, however, it seemed that this momentous event was related to one specific historical personality, namely that of Franklin Jones (alias Da Love-Ananda). In general, that is also the experience of the historical personality for whom this great breakthrough occurs.

The inherent simplicity of enlightenment contrasts starkly with the complexity of the ego that tries to understand the enlightened condition. Enlightenment has no meaning; meaning is a function of the egotropic mind, which is transcended in the event of enlightenment. To the unenlightened mind, everything is obscure and in need of explanation. It translates the simple mystery of existence into sets of questions and answers, which then dictate the whole adventure of human life and civilization. Who am I? Where am I? What is reality? How did the universe originate? When did it begin? Is there a God? Will I survive the death of my body? Why is there evil in the world? What is the right way of living? Is there a right way? How can I become happy? Why me?

Most people ponder these questions only occasionally, usually in moments of crisis. Nevertheless, they and a host of other similar existential questions form the inevitable "background noise" in all our lives. We have overt or hidden answers to all of them, even when we profess our ignorance. Feeling absolutely threatened by "naked" reality, we cocoon ourselves into layers upon layers of meaning, as if our mind-born conventions could protect us from the apparent chaos of existence. But our own mortality signals to us that our conceptual bulwarks afford us no ultimate security. It is precisely the inevitability of death that we fear and seek to shut out through our elaborate constructions of significance—the entire architecture of cultural life with its religions, philosophies, ideologies, methods of self-fulfillment, moral prescriptions, theories about humanity and the universe, beliefs, symbols, hypotheses, assumptions, opinions, judgments, prejudices, dogmas, doctrines, impressions, and sentiments.

Death encapsulates the ultimate meaninglessness of conditioned existence. It epitomizes, and is a constant reminder of, the finitude in which we find ourselves inserted. Having lost the consoling image of the paternal God and living in an era marked by incessant change and the menace of specieswide extinction, we feel particularly threatened by the reality of death. It undermines our illusion of self-omnipotence. Perhaps this is why we have developed a sophisticated style of prettifying death, while at the same time we are neurotically fascinated with it, so that the media feel free to sensationalize fatal accidents, murder, and the brutalities of terrorism and war.

Death, we intuit, is the termination of the mind-created illusions by which we maintain ourselves throughout life. It is the end of all meaning, because it is the obliteration of the subjective source of that meaning—the ego-personality. To face this irrevocable fact squarely is the challenge on all genuine spiritual paths. The spiritual process is inherently an attack on our patterns of meaning, our conventions about reality. It reveals to us their subordinate, even arbitrary, nature. The spiritual practitioner sooner or later comes to understand and accept that these conventions are ultimately inconsequential and must not be used as emotional crutches to justify the separative life of the ego-personality. He or she learns to regard them as practical conveniences. Nonetheless, unless the spiritual seeker has awakened from the dream of unenlightenment, he or she will again and again feel implicated to varying degrees in the maze of meaning woven by his or her own mind and the minds of others.

The transcendence of meaning in enlightenment, or God-realization, is the transcendence of the mind and the ego-personality itself. It dispels the myth of individuated existence. This is the crux of all mysticism and authentic spirituality. In conventional mysticism, however, this radical event of transcendence is only a temporary occlusion of the ego, which, after a few seconds, minutes, or hours, blithely reasserts itself. As soon as the *unio mystica* is over, the mystic's personality reconfigures itself, together with the meaning-making mind.

By contrast, full enlightenment is not merely a momentary loss of self but a *permanent* identity shift. Upon enlightenment, there is no ego to be lost in further mystical experiences or reestablished afterwards. Although the human personality of the enlightened being continues to exist in much the same way as before, inwardly there is no longer any exclusive identification with it. The enlightened being is *all* beings and *all* things. This paradoxical state, which would be intolerable to the ego, cannot be characterized as an experience, since the subject-object split is wholly transcended. As Da Love-Ananda, who has given us perhaps the most detailed "phenomenology" of this condition, has explained:

> Enlightenment is not a higher state of mind. It is not a glorified state of the inward or subjective being. Enlightenment is a bodily Condition. It is a matter of the transcendence of mind, all inwardness, and all illusions of independent existence. It is a matter of relationship, not inwardness. It is a matter of the conversion of attention from exclusive fascination with the objects, states, desires, and mental reflectiveness of the subjective disposition. It is a matter of the dissolution of attention in the Transcendental Reality, the Living God.[17]

The key phrase in the quote above is "the dissolution of attention." We cannot understand the mechanics of mysticism or what makes it different from the condition of full enlightenment and the spontaneity of crazy wisdom without having clearly grasped the nature of attention. The movement of attention is inextricably bound up with the state of egoic existence. Attention is the ego's object-relatedness. All experiences can be viewed as manipulations of attention; this includes mystical experiences. Conventional mysticism still lies within the province of attention, since it is based on a withdrawal of attention from the apparently external reality to focus on the apparently internal world. This deliberate act inevitably involves the ego, the sense of being a separate center of experience.

But the dynamics of attention does not consist of intentional acts only. The ego-personality is constantly caught up in the motion of attention placed either on an external object or on an internal referent (a feeling, a thought, a somatic sensation). In deep sleep, attention seems to be retracted into an objectless condition, giving the appearance of relative unconsciousness. Yet it has not been transcended, as in the case of enlightenment. The difference between deep sleep (called *sushupti* in Sanskrit) and the enlightened condition has been carefully examined by the adepts of Hinduism. They distinguish between three levels of awareness—the waking state, dreaming sleep, and dreamless sleep—as well as a "Fourth," which is not really a state of consciousness but transcendental Reality itself.

This "Fourth" (*turiya* or *caturtha*) is characterized as pure Awareness beyond all conscious activity. It is thus not unconsciousness but supraconsciousness or suprawakefulness. Within this supreme condition, all possible states of consciousness may arise. In other words, the enlightened being can and does still experience the play of attention in the states of wakefulness, dreaming, and sleeping, but there is no egoic fixation involved. Attention has been uprooted, as it were, and its play is no longer binding. Hence, in enlightenment there is a continuity of pure Awareness throughout all apparent states of mind.

The Hindu authorities compare the Fourth to the ocean, which remains essentially the same, whether or not gravity and wind whip its surface into waves. However, in most instances this idea is associated with the mystical God concept and the idea that attention must be internalized for God-realization to be possible. In the *Yoga-Bhashya* (I.12), an old Sanskrit commentary on the *Yoga-Sutra* of Patanjali, attention (*citta*) is likened to a river that flows either toward enlightenment or toward conditional experiences. In order for attention to flow toward enlightenment, the *yogin* must cultivate discernment between the Real and the unreal, as well as dispassion toward what stands revealed as impermanent and hence unreal. Discernment and dispassion are to be combined with the effort to stabilize attention by means of prescribed techniques of concentration and meditation.

The Yoga texts, which are representative of conventional mysticism in general, are replete with descriptions of, and prescriptions for, the internalization of attention. In these texts, the world of multiplicity is seen as the great enemy, which distracts the individual's attention. Therefore, much is made of the practice of mental one-pointedness. This is cultivated either by means of yogic concentration practices, preceded by sensory inhibition, or, as in the Hinayana Buddhist tradition, by means of mindfulness. The latter does not necessitate psychic withdrawal from phenomena. Instead, the practitioner of mindfulness develops the capacity to witness arising conditions (thoughts, breath, etc.). The yogic route, however, which operates on the different principle of acute focusing of attention, culminates in the experience of "formless enstasy" (*nirvikalpa-samadhi*). Swami Satprakashananda has described this transconceptual state, which is also known in the Yoga tradition as "supraconscious enstasy" (*asamprajnata-samadhi*) as follows:

> In nirvikalpa samadhi, contrary to deep sleep, all the features and functions of the mind, including even the ego-idea, are absorbed in unspecified, undifferentiated awareness, or Pure Consciousness beyond the distinction of the knower and the known. Whereas in deep sleep the mind is completely engulfed in ignorance or darkness, in nirvikalpa samadhi it is thoroughly suffused with the light of Pure Consciousness.[18]

Satprakashananda adds laconically, "This makes all the difference between the two states."[19] It does indeed! But his further comment that one returns from that transconceptual state as "an illumined person" is informed more by popular presumption than fact. He writes:

> An illumined person who regains body-consciousness after nirvikalpa samadhi identifies himself with the not-self in no form whatsoever. He experiences the manifold; but in and through everything he perceives Brahman as the One Self of all. He dwells in the body, but is never deluded by the ego-idea. He gets along with a semblance of the ego, being ever aware of his identity with Brahman. Though not impelled by the ego, yet the body runs its course because of the momentum of the past impressions that have caused it, somewhat like the potter's wheel that continues to revolve even after the rod that turns it is withdrawn.[20]

This is in fact a description of what is generally referred to in the Hindu scriptures as the condition of "liberation in life" (*jivan-mukti*). However, for the "zero experience"[21] of *nirvikalpa-samadhi* to lead to a *permanent* identity shift away from the ego presupposes exceptional spiritual maturity. In most cases, *nirvikalpa-samadhi* does not have such a dramatic effect. Although it is an extraordinary experience, it is not in itself equivalent to liberation, or enlightenment; it is, however, conducive to the further unfolding of the process of self-transcendence. *Nirvikalpa-samadhi* is based on a temporary ascent of attention in which, for a short period of time, self-consciousness is suspended. *Nirvikalpa-samadhi* does reveal the transcendental Reality, but this revelation is achieved by manipulating attention, not by transcending it, as in full enlightenment. For this very reason, it can only be a fleeting experience, because the deep-seated habits of the human personality sooner or later draw attention back to their play within the realm of subject-object distinctions. The ego resurfaces from its momentary oblivion and starts reorganizing the field of cognition.

The following analogy may be helpful in understanding the dynamics of *nirvikalpa-samadhi*: A balloon is inflated until the rubber skin is so thin that it becomes transparent and ambient light seemingly penetrates the now invisible structure freely. Then, all of a sudden, for no apparent reason, the balloon's elastic skin contracts again and becomes once more impermeable to light. Attention is just such a flexible casing; even though it becomes highly attenuated in *nirvikalpa-samadhi*, it nevertheless stays in place unless the balloon bursts—in the eventuality of full enlightenment.

The difference between the transient experience of *nirvikalpa-samadhi* and perpetual enlightenment is highlighted in the didactic Hindu story of King Hemacuda and Queen Hemalekha, as told in the *Tripura-Rahasya* (chapter X). King Hemacuda, so the story goes, was converted to a spiritual way of life by his wife, who, unbeknownst to him, was a fully enlightened adept. Queen Hemalekha skillfully guided Hemacuda to his own enlightenment. At one point in his discipleship, the king acquired the mystical ability to plunge into the state of *nirvikalpa-samadhi* at will. In fact, he became addicted to it because of the extreme bliss connected with the experience. After some time, Hemalekha intervened and asked him what he feared to gain or lose by closing his eyes and dropping his bodily awareness.

Still lacking Hemalekha's subtle discrimination, the king questioned why, although she had tasted the same bliss as he, she chose to live an active rather than a contemplative life. Smiling, Hemalekha pointed out to her husband that perfection could not possibly depend on activity or inactivity. She mocked him a little, saying, "What can I say about the absurd notion that your eyelid, a thumb's breadth long, can shut out That in which millions of universes exist in one corner alone!"[22] Then she remarked, "Perceive the undivided, eternal, blissful Self everywhere! Perceive the entire universe in the Self, like an image in a mirror."[23] The story has a happy ending, for we learn that Hemalekha's empowered words fully awakened the king.

The enlightenment that the adept Hemalekha and later her husband enjoyed was the "open-eyed" enstasy of spontaneity, called *sahaja-samadhi* in Sanskrit. In this condition of full enlightenment, the same Reality is recognized to be all things, both within and without. It is independent of the state of the human nervous system, or the play of attention, which is affected by such minor changes as the closing of the eyes.

An identical point is made in the *Ashtavakra-Gita* (I.15), a medieval Hindu work, which contains the following remarkable statement: "This is indeed your bondage that you practice enstasy (*samadhi*)!" Other forms of *samadhi*, as we have seen, hinge on the internalization of attention. *Sahaja-samadhi*, which is coessential with the transcendental Reality, does not. For enlightenment to be true, it cannot depend on the exclusion of any phenomenon, since all phenomena are manifestations of the ultimate Reality. In Buddhist terminology, *nirvana* equals *samsara*. *Sahaja-samadhi* is transparency.

In *nirvikalpa-samadhi*, the umbilical cord that ties the being to the movement of attention is not yet severed. This is also the case in the Hinayana Buddhist approach, described above, in which mindfulness rather than concentrative focusing is used to break away from ordinary awareness. That approach leads to the witnessing consciousness, which is commonly confused with "open-eyed" enstasy, which it closely resembles. In the previously introduced model of the seven stages of life, this represents the sixth stage, which is also styled *jnana-samadhi* or "enstasy of gnosis."

The witnessing state, which can be transient or permanent, does not exclude phenomena, as they appear against the screen of consciousness. But still it is not to be equated with full enlightenment because there appears to be a subtle element of tension in it: Although objects are not excluded, neither are they yet recognized as manifestations of the transcendental Reality. The witness disposition itself must be rendered transparent and seen as a posture, a last subtle stronghold of the ego-habit. It is a carryover, a hidden program, from the ego-personality that has been left behind. When the witness disposition is transcended, *jnana-samadhi* converts into full enlightenment, in which witness and witnessed form a universal field.

*Jnana-samadhi* is typically the fruit of a long course in applying discriminative awareness, or *jnana*, to phenomenal existence. This technique consists in dispassionately watching the emergence and disappearance of conditions in consciousness. Modern Western seekers are drawn to this method of mindfulness partly because it seems easier than yogic concentration and partly, I think, because it appeals to our well-defined sense of self and our schizoid tendency toward "self-watching." In practice, the techniques of mindfulness and "insight meditation" are just as difficult and grinding as any traditional yogic concentration exercise.

*Jnana-samadhi* must be carefully distinguished from the *technique* of witnessing, the admonition to "Be here now," that was popularized in the 1970s. The discipline of present-mindedness is a practice engaged by the unenlightened individual. The witnessing in *jnana-samadhi*, however, is a high-level spiritual process that occurs quite spontaneously. It is distinct from full enlightenment only because of the preprogrammed attitude toward the witnessed phenomena. In this connection, Chögyam Trungpa made the following observations:

> Enlightenment is being *awake* in the nowness. For instance, animals live in the present and, for that matter, an infant child lives in the present; but that is quite different from being awake or enlightened . . . In the case of an infant or animal, it is being in the nowness but it is swelling upon the

nowness. They get some kind of feedback from it by dwelling upon it, although they may not notice it consciously. In the case of an enlightened being, he is not dwelling upon the idea—"I am an enlightened being"—because he has completely transcended the idea of "I am." He is just fully being. The subject–object division has been completely transcended.[24]

In the Zen tradition, the *satori* experience represents a momentary flash of illumination, or *jnana-samadhi*, that offers a glimpse into the heart of Reality, without the interference of the individuated self. *Satori* can be of varying duration and depth. It is genuinely enlightening but should not be confused with full enlightenment (which is called *bodhi*). Because the *jnana* approach transpires in the context of the ordinary waking state, the insights accruing from it are likely to be more swiftly and deeply integrated than those arising from the experience of *nirvikalpa-samadhi*. In fact, I know of cases where a person has apparently experienced genuine *nirvikalpa-samadhi* without its having led to any major change in perspective or noticeable transformation of the personality.

Nevertheless, experiences like *nirvikalpa-samadhi* tend to have a strong "halo effect." In the unprepared individual, this "afterglow" will last for a short while before consciousness settles down to its "consensus trance."[25] However, in the mature practitioner, the halo effect sets the stage for a future encounter with the transcendental Reality. He or she uses this extended moment of grace to fortify discipline and obedience. The Sufis speak of this post–enstatic phase as the "sobriety of union."[26] But the heroes of the inward odyssey also know the painful condition in which they greatly suffer the subsequent absence of the bliss of enstasy or ecstasy and the afterglow of unification. The Christian mystics have called it the "dark night of the soul." Both the elevation felt on returning from the inner sojourn and the aridity and depression that result from one's incapacity to maintain communion with the Divine are signs of the persistence of the ego, the continued locomotion of attention.

Most mystics—East and West—agree on the need for outdistancing the ego.[27] Nevertheless, in practice, the ego is seldom transcended, and many *yogins* and saints settle for its temporary submergence in one or another higher state of consciousness. Thus, they never truly face the abyss that separates the knowable universe from the mind-transcending plenum that is the transcendental Reality.

## 3. A New Life Through Ego–Death

"It is a fearful thing to fall into the hands of the living God," declared St. Paul in his epistle to the Hebrews (10:31). This fear wells up in the ego because it is programmed to survive. But ultimate liberation, or enlightenment, is synchronous with ego–death. The moment of enlightenment is the demise of the ego–personality. It is also the death of God, at least as God is conceived in deistic religions and in the introvertive mystical traditions.

The God concept, like all concepts, is a fabrication of the egotropic mind. When the ego is transcended, the mind that manufactured divisive concepts is also transcended. What remains is Reality itself, which is nondual. Some schools of thought interpret Reality as the impersonal ground of all there is, others as a suprapersonal being (*purusha-uttama*) who is the transcendental origin of the multidimensional universe. Often, to the consternation of Western scholars who like to think in tidy categories, the same tradition shuttles back and forth between both interpretations.

Ego-death, not merely the temporary eclipse of the ego in mystical states, is a literal occurrence that forms the threshold to enlightenment. This has been helpfully elucidated by Da Love-Ananda:

> People play with the conception of ego-death as if it were an extension of egoic or mystical practices. The common idea is that ego-death is a matter of mortifying one's flesh, doing without things one desires, even obliterating one's existence. But these are notions of ego-death that the ego itself projects and considers in the midst of its own efforts to survive and to defend itself. The ego is not other than the mind . . . It is not by consoling one's inner being with experiences (or states of mind) that one Realizes the Truth. Rather, it is by the transcendence of the mind, by the death of the mind, or by the overcoming of the false evaluation of the status of the mind, that the Truth is Realized.[28]

The great twentieth-century sage Ramana Maharshi, who suddenly awakened at the age of sixteen, bequeathed us this account of his own passage through the fear of death:

> The shock of the fear of death drove my mind inwards and I said to myself mentally, without actually framing the words: "Now death has come; what does it mean? What is it that is dying? The body dies." And I at once dramatized the occurrence of death. I lay with my limbs stretched out stiff as though *rigor mortis* had set in and imitated a corpse so as to give greater reality to the enquiry. I held my breath and kept my lips tightly closed so that no sound could escape, so that neither the word "I" nor any other word could be uttered. "Well then," I said to myself, "this body is dead. It will be carried stiff to the burning ground and there burnt and reduced to ashes. But with the death of this body am I dead? Is the body I? It is silent and inert but I feel the full force of my personality and even the voice of the 'I' within me, apart from it. So I am Spirit transcending the body. The body dies but the Spirit that transcends it cannot be touched by death. That means I am the deathless Spirit." All this was not dull thought; it flashed through me vividly as living truth which I perceived directly, almost without thought-process. "I" was something very real, the only real thing about my present state, and all the conscious activity connected with my body was centered on that "I". From that moment onwards the "I" or Self focussed attention on itself by a powerful fascination. Fear of death had vanished once and for all. Absorption in the Self continued unbroken from that time on.[29]

Ramana Maharshi was so gripped by fear that he was quite unable to identify with the body-mind. He was in a way driven into enlightenment. But ego-death is never anything that the ego itself can perform; it is always beyond the ego's control. Ego-death coincides with the end of all the experiential possibilities that the ego could possibly project ahead of itself.

In particular, ego-death is the embrace of the "madness"—the unfathomable complexity—of existence as such. In that moment, what we normally experience as "mind" is absolutely shattered. What does this mean? Thoughts continue to arise more or less as before, but there is no "I" to connect them. An enlightened being who was a great philosopher prior to awakening will in all likelihood be a great philosopher afterward. A great poet will probably be a great poet after the enlightenment event. If, however, the adept previously had no great intellectual or other talents, he or she will still lack these skills. Yet in each case, the enlightened being will be found to possess exceptional wisdom and compassion.

Enlightenment frees attention; this means that the enlightened being has, to use conventional language, a highly developed intuitive faculty. Disciples of such beings tell numerous stories of their teachers' uncanny ability to "read" their innermost thoughts or to take actions that astound by their sheer synchronicity with events.

Thoughts always arise automatically, but in the unenlightened person they arise as if they had a common center—the ego-personality. Poets and writers know that thoughts "just drift in" like sunbeams through a window. They emerge from the fog at the back of consciousness and take shape in us even before we notice them. We certainly do not own them, though we generally presume the opposite. Upon enlightenment, we finally make peace with the fact that all thoughts—like all things—simply arise of their own accord, governed by laws that are ultimately inexplicable. This does not negate the need for responsibility in all matters, including our thinking; we can create an internal environment that invites some thoughts rather than others to manifest in us.

In the same way, not only thoughts but also externally observable behavior occurs spontaneously, without the delay mechanism of the self-watching ego-personality. The contemporary Indian sage Nisargadatta Maharaj commented on this point:

After self-realization [i.e., enlightenment], any behaviour or actions expressed through the body of a sage are spontaneous and totally unconditioned. They cannot be bound to any disciplines. A realized sage may be discovered in an unkempt person reclining in the ashes of a cremation ground, or on the cushioned bed in a palace as a king. He may be a butcher by vocation or a successful businessman. Nevertheless, a realized one, having transcended the realm of Beingness, ever abides in the Eternal Absolute.[30]

The enlightened condition is as much transmental as it is transegoic and transpersonal. Categories like mind and world, inside and outside, personal and impersonal lose their significance in enlightenment. There is only *all there is*, and that *totum* is the Identity of the enlightened being. The association of the enlightened being with a particular body-mind, which can speak about its paradoxical condition, is no more than a historical accident. However, it is an accident that holds tremendous significance for the world. As I have suggested in previous chapters, the bodily presence of the enlightened being acts as a spiritual vortex in space-time.

The fully awakened person is known in India as a *jivan-mukta*, a person liberated while yet embodied. Huston Smith, a stalwart spokesman for the *philosophia perennis*, describes the fully awakened, liberated being thus:

> Basically he lives in the unvarying presence of the numinous. This does not mean that such a person is excited or "hyped"; his or her condition has nothing to do with adrenaline flow, or with manic states that call for depressive ones to balance the emotional account. It's more like what Kipling had in mind when he said of one of his characters, "he believed that all things were one big miracle, and when a man knows that much he knows something to go upon." The opposite of the sense of the sacred is not serenity or sobriety. It is drabness, taken-for-grantedness, lack of interest, the humdrum and prosaic.
>
> All other attributes of a jivanmukta must be relativized against this one absolute: a honed sense of the astounding mystery of everything. All else we say of such a person must have a yes/no quality. Is he or she always happy? Well, yes and no. On one level he emphatically is not; if he were he couldn't "weep with those who mourn"—he would be an unfeeling monster, a callous brute. If anything, a realized soul is more in touch with the grief and sorrow that is part and parcel of the human condition, knowing that it too needs to be accepted and lived as all life needs to be lived.[31]

Smith further states that the enlightened being is "one who is in touch with his deepest unconscious, an unconscious which . . . deserves to be considered sacred."[32] This unconscious, however, as Smith clarifies, "opens mysteriously onto the world as it actually is." So, it might more fittingly be named supraconsciousness, or what the Hindus call *cit, citi, cetana*, or *caitanya* and the Mahayana Buddhists *citta-matra* or "pure Awareness."

Understanding the relationship of the body to enlightenment is crucial to understanding the nature of full illumination, or God-realization. Whereas the conventional mystic seeks to shun the body and find means of immobilizing it, the enlightened being *is* the universal Body or field of existence. The body that is historically associated with the enlightened being is neither shunned nor sought out. We can, however, expect it to reflect that transcendental realization. Not only will the body be in direct communion with the ultimate Reality, it will also show palpable evidence of this special connection in terms of signs of transfiguration.

Phenomena of transfiguration—of somatic luminosity—are well known in mysticism, but they are not necessarily an irrefutable sign that a person is fully enlightened. It is possible there may be no such signs and that only by considering a person's life in its totality—past and present—can we arrive at an *intuitive* certainty. Be that as it may, since enlightenment dispels the conventional image of the body as a skin-encased object with which the being must identify, phenomena of transfiguration are common, if unpredictable. In these phenomena, the literal nature of enlightenment is demonstrated, for the adept's body seems to the outside observer to radiate or temporarily dissolve in light. Some adepts, like the eighteenth-century Indian sage Ramalinga Swami, are reported to have died by such mystical self-incineration. Ralph Metzner, an internationally renowned researcher of consciousness, offers the following clues for understanding transfiguration:

> "A man's wisdom makes his face to shine," says Ecclesiastes. It is a common observation that uplifting, affirmative emotions, such as joy and love, cause people's bodies and faces—their eyes especially—to "light up," to "radiate" or "shine." Conversely, moods of depression or despair cast darkening hues on a person's countenance, draining the visage of color and making the eyes appear to "lack luster." We could, of course, say that such expressions are merely metaphorical and do not have any real validity. On the other hand, there is the cogent testimony of those who report luminous energy phenomena, that is, light emissions from the body, of which present-day science is as yet unable to render an account . . .
>
> Whatever the nature and origin of this "light" may be, it is apparent that it can, on occasion, suffuse the body with such intensity that it becomes visible to others, even those who are not normally clairvoyant . . .
>
> There is a universal tendency to depict saints and enlightened beings with haloes and auras of flame and light, and mystical literature is filled with accounts of yogis and prophets who were seen to be filled and overflowing with light.[33]

The "physics" of enlightenment, of ego-transcendence, is something that future scientists can look forward to studying. Whether it will ever be fully understood in rational terms is a moot point.[34]

# PART THREE
## THE SIGNIFICANCE

# 9

## HOLY MADNESS AND THE SMOKE SCREEN OF CONSENSUS REALITY

### 1. A Test Case

Several years ago a book fair was held in the vestibule of a local Christian church attached to a seminary. A friend of mine promised that I would find a fine selection of theological titles, and so I went that Saturday afternoon. By the time I arrived, thirty or forty people were milling around from shelf to shelf. I remember feeling a little awkward about participating in this shuffle for literary nuggets; after all, we were in a consecrated building.

I was about to carry an armful of musty volumes to the cashier's desk when the door was noisily pushed open. A young man burst into the hall, shouting at us angrily. It took me a while to grasp his words, even though they were clearly audible. My mind ceased functioning for a brief moment. Later others confessed that they had experienced something similar. Curiously, not one of the people I talked to afterward had felt really threatened in that first moment of angry confrontation. The young man looked strangely harmless, although he was clearly furious. At one point he even grabbed hold of a few bibliophiles and shoved them through the door. He was not of a large build, but he seemed exceedingly strong as he pulled a large shelf down single-handedly and the books thundered to the ground. Several times he repeated for all to hear very distinctly, "This is a sacred place! Why are you defiling it? Get going and don't come back unless you want to worship!"

There was a curious authority behind his words, which compelled everybody to listen to him. Most of the people, myself included, forgot about their book purchases. We left hurriedly in awkward silence. Those who wanted to pay for their trophies risked being manhandled. But no one actually came to any harm.

People gathered outside. Some demanded that the police be informed, which someone had already done. Others remarked on the young man's bright face or commented that his anger was legitimate enough. Others just stood by silently. No one laughed. Our hearts had been touched by what we had witnessed.

Then the police arrived, and the young man allowed himself to be led away without struggle. We noticed a small group of men and women who apparently belonged with the young man. They talked to the police, identifying themselves as the young man's disciples and demanding to be arrested with him. They were, in due course, charged with disturbing the peace.

As they were all driven off in two limousines, a different mood took possession of the crowd. Some people, who had not been in the vestibule with us, started talking excitedly about the cult leader, his obvious insanity and violence, his poor, misled zombie followers, and his likely court trial and incarceration in a penitentiary or mental asylum. Some, however, dispersed quietly, perturbed by the incident and disturbed by the young man's message, commanding behavior, and deep, still eyes.

This incident never made the headlines, because it never happened. Or, more precisely, it did not happen in the way I told it. Readers of the New Testament may have recognized in my description one of the stories related about Jesus of Nazareth who, two thousand years ago, threw the moneylenders out of the temple in Jerusalem. It is not important for our purposes whether this incident has historical validity. There are hundreds of similar stories told of other adepts that I could have used here. What is significant, however, is that this particular story should be a part of our inherited image of Jesus of Nazareth.

I translated the story into modern terms in order to, I hope, elicit an emotional reaction from you, the reader. What were your feelings as you read my account? What was your impression of the young man's personality, or your judgment about his strange, unconventional behavior? How would you have reacted had you been a victim of the young man's verbal abuse, or perhaps even his bodily aggression? Would your judgment have been different if you had been told from the beginning that the hero of the story was Jesus and not a contemporary?

All these questions are justified because spiritual teachers, or gurus, have fallen into disrepute in our culture. Indeed, their function is no longer comprehended. Yet when we look into the past, we find that the figure of the religious or spiritual guide was virtually omnipresent in the ancient world and still is, in traditional societies. The reasons for our own change of attitude are rather complex. Essentially, they are the same reasons responsible for our contemporary misunderstanding of or total bafflement about all things spiritual. To get some sense of the underlying causes of our lack of comprehension and to alert ourselves to possible stereotypes and biases, we must examine more closely the nature of conventional religiosity and the Reality-concealing function of the ego.

## 2. Conventional Religion as Counterfeit Spirituality

Few people today have a realistic understanding of the nature of spiritual practice or the complex relationship between a charismatic teacher and his or her disciples. Most people look askance at spiritual authority, obedience, initiation, and the transmission that occurs between spiritual adepts and aspirants on the path. This is not completely surprising.

Authentic spiritual life has always been set apart from the bustle of exoteric religion and secular society. Certainly in the West, the era of great spiritual aspiration has long been eclipsed by the age of disenchanted reason, positivism, and moral befuddlement. We have no ready standards by which to identify genuine spirituality or authentic spiritual teachers. Our civilization instead supplies us with all kinds of stereotypes that are borrowings from conventional religion and that reflect the anxious need of the ordinary individual to maintain the status quo, even at the price of freedom and truth.

This common religious phobia, which amounts to a psychological inertia that prevents real self-transformation, can be seen in action at its worst in the anticult movement of recent years. But it is also operative even in many of the so-called "new religions"[1] themselves. Few of the groups or cults that have sprung up since the 1960s, which purport to break away from the mediocrity of mainstream religion and culture, are truly the alternative altars they claim to be.[2] In most cases, it is a matter of old wine in new, sometimes quite weirdly shaped bottles.

This is not to say that the new religions are all of the same cast, which is the simplistic view conveniently espoused by the vociferous anticult league. There are real differences between them, in terms of their origins, beliefs, goals, organization, membership, leadership, and life-styles. Nevertheless, they *tend* to share an orientation that effectively perpetuates the basic mood of the religious establishment and that is not at all concentric with authentic spirituality. That mood is one of ego-affirmation (including its inverse form, ego-denial) rather than ego-transcendence; this is also a characteristic of exoteric religion, which typically caters to the ego. As the British poet Lewis Thompson has recognized:

> The spiritual is necessarily transhumanistic. For the human balance of sense, Eros, mind, intellect and intuition, sustained in humanistic culture, having all its values and memorials in human history, the spiritual is an outrage, either chaos or terror. Religion is a compromise to avoid directly facing it.[3]

From the position of authentic, radical spirituality, what is commonly called religion—in the sense of exoteric religion—is a compromise, a bargain struck with the ego that wishes to survive in its presumed autonomy. The bargain is that the individual consents to observe certain external forms in exchange for the freedom to live life as he or she will, so long as he or she at least appears to honor the moral code of the religious community. Exoteric religion is largely consensual religion and does not call for a high degree of commitment, self-criticism, or candor. To use Gordon Allport's term, it is *extrinsic* religion because the individual uses religion—to further his or her self-interests—rather than living it.[4]

Whatever provisional merit exoteric religion may have, it is clearly also the theater of bigotry and doublethink, as recently so amply demonstrated by the fallen angels of televangelism; and it is the theater of jihads, crusades, inquisitions, and persecutions. In short, from the vantage point of authentic spirituality, conventional religion is counterfeit spirituality. This may seem to be a harsh judgment; yet it is a judgment that has a long history—among the prophets, saints, and sages.

### 3. The Mystical Ego

Exoteric religion's covenant with the ego, granting concessions to the frail will of the ordinary person, is obvious. Such a covenant is not quite so apparent in the case of mysticism, which calls for a more mature response and a greater personal commitment. Nonetheless, even mysticism—unless it is the highest form of self-transcending practice—remains within the boundaries of the ego and its projects.

The mystical ego is either attenuated or inflated, depending on how we look at the transformed (but still only internalized) consciousness of the mystic. The ego lurks behind even the more sublime mystical experiences. It may be temporarily suspended in a realization of overwhelming unity, wholeness, or voidness. But short of its perfect and irrevocable transcendence in full enlightenment, the ego is a hidden variable in all experiences, including the rarefied states of the accomplished mystic. Even while he or she swoons in ecstasy, the mystic's ego is intact as a propensity; hence, the moment the *unio mystica* fades, the ego promptly reappears as the organizing structure of the ordinary consciousness. The mystic then bemoans his or her fall from grace and aspires anew to win the favor of the impartial God.

When this occurs, the mystic, like any other mortal, conceives of existence as a problem for which he or she is trying to find a solution. This problem-consciousness in both conventional religion and mysticism has nowhere been addressed more incisively than in the works of the contemporary spiritual teacher Da Love-Ananda, whose dramatic ministry has been examined more closely in Chapter 4. He has remarked:

> At the root of the argument of many traditional religious and spiritual systems is a fundamental principle of disease, suffering, and pain, and it is the common basis for all the conventional techniques applied in the name of the religious or spiritual goal. Conventional religion and spirituality are thus part of the idealism of our disease, part of the search for

cure. They reflect our aberration, or the ego-contraction, the pain inherent in the self-contraction.[5]

Insofar as the new religious cults bypass the challenge of actual self-transcendence, of going beyond the contraction that the ego represents, they do little more than transpose the conventional perspective of the religious establishment into a more exotic setting. In this way they have, for the most part, lamentably failed to provide a general concept of, and opportunity for, authentic spiritual practice.

More than that, as we have seen, some of the more outlandish and militant religious cults—masquerading under the name of spirituality—have exacerbated the fears and suspicions of the religious (and political) establishment. In doing so, they have harmed the cause of genuine spiritual groups and retarded the infusion of authentic spiritual values into mainstream culture. Their continued antagonism toward the larger culture, of which they are necessarily a part, is threatening the peaceful and cooperative coexistence of genuine spiritual movements and society at large. Thus, these groups threaten the hard-won religious freedom guaranteed by the governing charters of liberal countries like the United States.

Although it is inevitable that genuine spirituality should run counter to many of the interests propagated in mainstream society, such opposition can and should be voiced peaceably. It certainly must never degenerate into paranoid self-protection or militant demagogy. This would not only flagrantly contradict the very essence of the spiritual approach to life but would also prove suicidal. Neither should spiritual practitioners have to hide anxiously in the closet. Rather, they should take responsibility for the context in which they live and be willing to be heard as a voice for social change.

## 4. The Humanistic Way of Self-Actualization

Under the influence of the sensationalism of the mass media, the new religions have come to be perceived by the public as problematic; thus, few of those who feel disaffected from the religious establishment are moved to actually explore the possibilities the new religions have to offer. Rather, many seekers look for a new existential home among the growing number of humanistic "therapy cults." These seem more acceptable and less threatening than religious groups because of their secular veneer. Of course, they also do not demand a high level of personal commitment.

The human potential movement, with its plethora of schools, therapies, and techniques, sprang into existence in dialectical opposition to the mechanistic models of the "first force" and "second force" in psychology—behaviorism and psychoanalysis. Humanistic psychologists broke with the earlier tradition in psychology that excluded consciousness from the study and treatment of the human personality, and they also shunned the medical model of psychoanalysis. Instead, they focused on mental health, exploring the human being's intrinsic capacity to grow beyond the achievement of mere normalcy.

Although humanistic psychology has contributed significantly to a more balanced and open-minded approach to psychic welfare, in its pioneering fervor it has succumbed to the error of advancing values and goals of human existence that properly belong to the realm of religion. Therapists have widely assumed roles once reserved for priests and religious counselors. Thus, the schools of the human potential movement have ended up as surrogate religions, without God, but with their own idiosyncratic doctrines and methods of "salvation."[6] In this role they are now, arguably, slowing down the blossoming of genuine spirituality.

There is some indication of a change, however. As Ken Wilber, the unrivaled theoretician of transpersonal psychology, has remarked to me, the humanistic psychology movement is running on borrowed time, and some of its leaders are exploring genuine spiritual possibilities outside the movement; others are at least toying with the idea.[7] This is a hopeful sign. Wilber himself is fond of Zen Buddhism and, like myself, has for many years been openly sympathetic toward the controversial figure of Da Love-Ananda and toward his teaching. Like myself, however, he has also expressed his concerns about the cultic developments around this teacher, developments that appear to stem directly from an authoritarian style that encourages the totemization of the guru in immature individuals.

It should be noted here that even the now-fashionable transpersonal psychology, which emerged from the camp of humanistic psychology, is not entirely free of the stigma of salvation mongering. Extending their conceptual net to the elusive phenomena of "transpersonal" (or psychic, mystical, and spiritual) experiences, transpersonal psychologists inevitably make judgments about aspects of existence of which they have no deeper *personal* knowledge. It is clear from the writings of their pioneering representatives that they seek to construct an overall framework capable of explaining (by way of classification) all human experience, including the realization of enlightenment. In some instances, they end up confusing the map with the actual spiritual path; their work then becomes a matter of the purblind leading the blind.

Ken Wilber has stated that one of the principal aims of the transpersonal discipline is "to render spirituality theoretically acceptable to the 'other' or 'lower' schools of psychology."[8] He added that transpersonal psychologists, insofar as they assume a quasi-therapeutic role, will also refer their clients to other specialists, including spiritual adepts. Wilber stressed, however, that transpersonal psychology is a theoretical approach and not "a total psychospiritual or completely transformative path (despite all the silly claims made by some of its less intelligent advocates)."[9]

Wilber looks upon transpersonal psychologists as "apologists for the soul, gnostic intermediaries." Yet, paradoxically, he likes to think that they "sit silent at the crossroads and point; no more, no less."[10] This is more the ideal than actual practice. In practice, transpersonal psychology is rather vocal. It aspires to a model that comprises the totality of the human phenomenon. As Wilber readily admits, it does so with all the encumbrances of an intellect that has not yet been transformed by the higher realities that are described, categorized, and therefore judged in the transpersonal model.

As in the case of most of the new religions, the humanistic therapy movement, as well as the therapeutic schools of transpersonal psychology, does not embody an adequate understanding of authentic spirituality. Self-development, self-improvement, and even self-actualization do not amount to spiritual life. In humanistic therapy, the self or ego remains intact as the guiding principle of existence, whereas in genuine spirituality it is transcended, not merely denied or negated. This all-important point must be fully appreciated.

## 5. The Ego "Illusion"

The ego is the platform on which all conventional approaches to life are enacted, because the ego is the source of all conventions. It is the axis around which spin all our hopes, fears, desires, understandings, and misunderstandings. According to the spiritual traditions, the ego is itself a convention. That is to say, the egotropic consciousness is not representative of all conscious experience. There can be experience without the intervention of the self-referential psychic function that we call the "ego." This is certainly true of very young children, whose consciousness is not yet polarized into a subject that confronts multiple objects. It is also true of the enlightened condition, in which the subject–object scission is transcended.

Admittedly, the ego is an unconscious convention or habit, but, like any convention or habit, it can be dispelled. How? By going beyond it in the moment of its activation. If you want to stop smoking, you start by simply not smoking the next cigarette, and the next, and so on. The principle is that of releasing a habit in the instant of its emergence. Transcendence of the habitual contraction that we call our self or ego is realized in the same way: We witness the habit pattern in every moment and then, instead of enacting it, we adopt a nonproblematic disposition of whole-body relaxation, a disposition that "presumes" our fundamental freedom and spontaneity.

The possibility of ego-transcendence is fundamental to all spiritual paths. This is the difference between the traditional ideal of soul care and the modern humanistic ideal of psychic cures. The former is concerned with the transpersonal, even transhuman reality—what is traditionally referred to as the soul or spirit. The latter revolves around the psyche, or personality—its healing, actualization, or integration. Authentic spirituality is always a concerted effort to rescind the ego-convention.

Not that the ego will vanish overnight! We may light a million cigarettes without ever being aware of it. The challenge and the trick is to put the cigarette out as soon as we notice that we have slipped into unconsciousness. It is only the present moment for which we are responsible.

The ego habit is powerful. It cannot be forced out of existence by an act of sheer will. Its influence in our lives will begin to wane only if we turn our attention to the Reality that transcends the ego. Again, as Alan Watts put it:

> Don't try to get rid of the ego-sensation. Take it, so long as it lasts, as a feature or play of the total process—like a cloud or wave, or like feeling warm or cold, or anything else that happens of itself. Getting rid of one's ego is the last resort of invincible egoism! It simply confirms and strengthens the reality of the feeling. But when this feeling of separateness is approached and accepted like any other sensation, it evaporates like the mirage that it is.[11]

The tragedy of egoic existence lies in the unconscious replication of our patterns. This is an utterly humorless state. Humor sets in when we begin to understand the absurd mechanicalness of our personality and life. When we recognize even a little of the ego's robotic nature, we rise above it. Humor is always a rising-above, a stepping-beyond, a not-being-captive of our momentary condition. Spiritual practice could thus be defined as the discipline of real humor: We intuit our essential freedom and simultaneously witness the comedy of our constant failure to incarnate that freedom, our repeated identification with the conditions of existence.

However, were we merely to witness our tendency to sink into oblivion, without enjoying the liberating intuition of what is prior to all this, we would inevitably fall victim to hopelessness and despair. This is in fact the unhappy disposition that Jean-Paul Sartre, for instance, sculpted into a philosophical edifice. Rejecting any reassuring divinity or higher meaning, he settled for the desert of an ultimately forlorn, Sisyphean existence. For Sartre, we are "shipwrecked animals."[12]

Believing makes it so, as Sartre should have known. After all, he espoused a subjectivist framework, according to which the individual creates his or her own existential meanings. Sartre *chose* a pessimistic reading of the human situation, because he ignored the entire thrust of the spiritual heritage of humanity and misread his own heart. We may be shipwrecked, but we are also hale. If we put our attention on the emptiness and tragedy of our lives, we remain caught in meaninglessness and apathy. If instead, we envision our ultimate potential, that is, "remember" our identity beyond the ego, we begin to break the spell by which we continuously shipwreck ourselves. Even though existentialism in the spirit of Sartre or Camus is not one of today's philosophical crazes, its central message of despair is the substance of billions of human lives.

That despair is real enough. Its source, however, is a trick of the nervous system. According to the spiritual traditions, the ego is a cognitive error. They universally insist that the sense of separation, of egoic encapsulation, that motivates our despair as much as our pleasure is something we superimpose on existence. As Alan Watts expressed it, the ego is a "social fiction," a learned response.[13] We *presume* ourselves, emotionally and intellectually, to be apart from all "others": The subject confronts objects that exist entirely outside itself. This guiding presumption of our lives is demonstrably limited, if not wrong. Gregory Bateson, possibly one of the finest minds of our century, put it thus:

> We commonly think of the external 'physical world' as somehow separate from an internal 'mental world'. I believe that this division is based on the contrast in coding and transmission inside and outside the body.
> The mental world—the mind—the world of information processing—is not limited by the skin.[14]

Bateson continued:

> The individual mind is immanent but not only in the body. It is immanent also in pathways and messages outside the body; and there is a larger Mind of which the individual mind is only a sub-system. This larger Mind is comparable to God and is perhaps what some people mean by 'God', but it is still immanent in the total interconnected social system and planetary ecology.[15]

This is the crux of radical spirituality as taught by the great adepts of the past and present: We are "larger" than we appear to be. It is only from the "viewpoint" of full enlightenment, which transcends all conventions (because it transcends the convention of the ego as such), that we can hope to penetrate the existing confusion about modern humanity's "ultimate concerns,"[16] be they of a religious or a secular nature.

We must come to see that the fundamental presumption of egoity, the "illusion" of being a separate entity defensively walled off from the whole, is at the bottom of all our other intellectual frameworks and programs of living. We must allow ourselves—again and again—to be emotionally penetrated by the realization that these frameworks and programs are essentially protective ideologies. They are mere images or models of reality by which we keep ourselves in a state of apparent security and certainty in the face of a universe that is mysterious and threatening. They are manifestations of a "false consciousness"[17] that distorts our overall relationship to the total world process.

Even as I write these lines I can feel at least some of the invulnerability that my own thinking about these matters creates in me. While I am doing intellectual labor there is a clear tendency in me to experience my conscious identity in my head, to the relative exclusion of the rest of my body and certainly to the exclusion of my environment. It is easy to see how uncon-

scious indulgence in this introvertive state of intense intellection can channel
the form of my thoughts, and how isolated (alienated) thinking lends itself to
misplaced reification in the form of fixed ideologies. To overcome the limitations of ideology and ideology-making, I must be present as the whole
body—"whole" in the sense of "entire" as well as "hale."

When I am thus present, the boundaries of my postulated ego begin to
dissolve, and "my" body presents itself as essentially undefined and un-
bounded. I suddenly remember that I exist in and as a great mystery. The
thoughts that arise in this whole-body condition are experientially distinct
from the intellectual gyrations of the typical brain worker, though undoubtedly they may lead to similar or even identical conclusions about a given
matter. But they may also lead to uncommon insights.

This dynamic concept of the ego as a process of self-contraction differs
markedly from the concept of ego proposed by academic psychology. The
latter conceptualizes the ego as the regulative structural principle of many
psychic processes, meanwhile admitting that there are whole areas of our
psychic life that appear to be independent of the ego. By contrast, the
understanding proposed here is that the ego is itself a process—a process of
recoil from the world as a whole.

The ego is an ongoing activity that arises mysteriously in the totality of
Being and *apparently* delimits that totality, evoking the experience of a finite
body-mind. The sacred texts of Kashmiri Shaivism employ the graphic
Sanskrit term *atma-samkoca*, meaning literally "self-contraction," which they
define as the nescience that creates the illusion of separation from Reality.[18]

As Da Love-Ananda has pointed out, the egoic self-contraction is first and
foremost a contraction of feeling. This realization immediately makes spiritual discipline an affair of the heart, of whole-bodily risk, rather than, as in the
case with so much of Western Zen or Vedanta practice, primarily a matter of
intellectual discrimination between what is real and unreal. Such abstraction-
ism represents the same self-defensive stance that has characterized Western
culture since the seventeenth century, when the ideology of scientism first
arose. Scientism introduced a world picture that resembled a Klee more than
a Renoir: The concrete universe was rendered increasingly intangible. Today
only a highly trained mathematician can hope to understand the quantum
mechanical model of reality. The rest of humanity is left with fragments and
confusion and, where intelligence stirs, with an abstracted (left-brained)
approach to life that is dominated by the power play of the superego.

As first formulated by Freud, the superego is a basic program for the
individual's egoic survival in a cultural environment composed of numerous
other egos competing for acknowledgment or love. It is a device that allows
us, rather mindlessly or unconsciously, to navigate the complexities of society. It thus introduces an apparent simplification into our life, but at the cost
of critical intelligence. Of course, because it is a hidden automaticity, the

superego generally turns out to be a source of tension, neurotic repression, guilt, fixations, and other maladaptations, including psychosomatic illnesses. When, in the neurotic person, the superego is objectified and turned into the Voice of God, it becomes the mainspring of religious or moralistic fanaticism, whether in the form of excessive cultism or militant anticultism.

Few people reach the psychic maturity even to want to develop a personal conscience as a way of going beyond the usual man's blind reliance on the doubtful wisdom of the superego. Whereas the prepersonal superego operates with sweeping categories or stereotypes, authentic conscience is always personal and situational. Conscience is based on critical self-inspection and self-knowledge; it is conscious participation in the processes of life. Conscience is a commitment to actively love rather than clamor for love.

## 6. The Cult of Scientism

So long as a person has not achieved a certain level of responsibility for his or her own existence, he or she is liable to fall victim to all manner of ideologies that appeal to the primary egoic need to be loved and appreciated. Ideologies can be regarded as extensions of the superego, as crutches for the ego in its unwillingness to understand and ultimately transcend itself. Thus, all ideologies tend to represent a person's continuing movement toward unconsciousness.

The extent to which this is true of contemporary humanity can be gauged from the massive influence of the ideological constellation that is scientific materialism. Omnipresent in the modern mind, this force largely determines people's responses (or, rather, reactions) to spiritual life. By "scientific materialism," or "scientism," is meant the entire ideological framework, based largely on the endeavors of the natural sciences, that espouses a one-dimensional cosmology in which consciousness (and thus all psychic, religious, and spiritual phenomena) is asserted to arise from insentient matter. By implication, if not by explicit dogma, the existence of transcendental Reality, as a metamaterial (not merely immaterial) whole in which all beings and things inhere, is denied. Religion and metaphysics are deemed, at best, an unproductive pastime.

The ego-personality (as the doubting subject who confronts a presumed, objective world) is dogmatically elevated to the status of final arbiter of human fate. Its "truth" is the objective, factual truth of material evidence, as determined by the exclusive and reductionistic "scientific method."[19] The scientific method, which has been hailed as the greatest invention of human intelligence, is in effect a self-fulfilling prescription for determining what counts as knowledge and, therefore, what is real. As such it implies a particular metaphysics—in this case, that of rationalist materialism.

Since its invention, the scientific method has come under varied criticism both from within and outside the camp of science. Indeed, it has even been called in question. Among philosophers of science, a certain skepticism is abroad about the possibility of a prescriptive methodology for the scientific enterprise. Philosopher Paul Feyerabend has roundly denounced the scientific method as a fairy tale,[20] while R. S. Scorer, a British professor of theoretical mechanics, has bluntly stated that there is no such thing as the scientific method.[21] And Roger S. Jones, an American professor of physics, has argued that science is a modern attempt at myth making, the central myth of which is that of the quantification of life.[22] But only the material can be quantified, and so science is, by its own rules, a materialist enterprise.

Scientific materialism has become, in Ernest Gellner's terms, a "mode of cognition."[23] More than that, it is nowadays the pseudoreligion of those who have lost faith in their religious heritage but who are as yet incapable of making a genuinely spiritual response. Doubt has literally become their mode of engaging the world. Scientism is the religion of the left brain, and it is also a heavily patriarchal gospel that revolves around the doctrine of the conquest of nature, a creed that has recently come under close scrutiny by ecologists, especially ecofeminists. There is no question that scientism has historically been associated with androcentrism and the suppression of the female gender. The desire to gain dominion over Nature is thus directly correlated with the impulse to control women. Both ambitions are rooted in an attitude that disregards wholeness—an incognizance that may prove fatal to all life on this planet.

The alarming degree to which the modern mind is infected by scientistic values and modes of thought can be gleaned from the hidden materialism of many, if not most, seemingly sincere spiritual seekers, including actual practitioners. I am basing this judgment on my contact over the years with adherents of a variety of serious religio-spiritual schools, as well as on self-observation. Despite numerous instances that have clearly and, at the time, incontrovertibly demonstrated to me the reality of the spiritual dimension, I am aware of a persistent habit of doubt that claims a dark niche in my own psyche. The mood of doubt acts like a strong gravitational pull on the impulse to evolve spiritually. Self-inspection can somewhat neutralize its effect, but it is nonetheless an inhibiting force to be reckoned with.

This pervasive doubt cannot be overcome by mere belief or enthusiastic affirmation of a spiritual set of values and attitudes. Only an actual *metacardia*, or change of heart, leading to a tangible awakening to the spiritual Reality will empower us to transcend in every moment this inherited mood of doubt.

## 7. Religious Provincialism

If the ideology of scientism revolves around the mood of doubt, the pinion of narrow exoteric religion—another great ideological force today—is false faith, that is, mere belief. This is religious provincialism, a narrow, hidebound view of the universe that flies under the banner of religion. Religious provincialism takes the form of exoteric cultism that is intolerant of genuine ecstasy or of the kind of attitudes and practices that are associated with a truly spiritual way of life. Hence, it is always antagonistic toward personal and informal religiosity, esotericism, and mysticism. Adepts, and anyone else who seemingly steps outside the established mold, are immediately suspect and likely to be subjected to suppression, forced recantation, ridicule, anathematization, persecution, banishment, imprisonment, or even execution.

Religious provincialism, which includes more than fundamentalist religion, seeks vindication for its existence in some sacred revelation or authority and (rightly) fears and (wrongly) discourages independent inquiry and free thinking. It values dogma above actual experience and realization, ritualism above ecstatic self-transcendence, obedience to Holy Writ above direct surrender to God, ecclesiastical survival above individual freedom. Its principle is not *metanoia*, enlightenment, emancipation, or ultimate happiness, but rather moral goodness, personal contentment, or the achievement of heaven in the hereafter through prayerful submission to one's "Maker" or "Heavenly Father," or to the "Divine Mother." In other words, religious provincialism is a surrogate spirituality that falls short of our highest spiritual potential, which is enlightenment.

In religious provincialism, the unconditional Reality is reified, "miniaturized," so that it becomes psychically manageable. As an anthropomorphized icon, God is rendered innocuous and inoperative. From a terrible living fire that burns itself into the heart of the spiritually awake individual, the Divine is conveniently transformed by the conventional mind into a static picture of a fire. The ego, in making its bid for immunity, creates the fiction of the Divine as a harmless bosom pal, who will respond to its prayerful petitions but make no demands in return. In one of his sermons, the German mystic Meister Eckehart preached:

> But some people want to see God with their eyes as they might see a cow, or want to love God as they might love a cow. You love a cow for her milk and cheese and your own use. Thus it is with all those people who love God for outer riches or inner consolation; but they do not rightly love God, but they love their own self-will.[24]

To drive home the point that the Divine, or ultimate Reality, is not identical to the images that unenlightened beings may have of it, Eckehart frequently spoke of God as a sheer nothing. This description, which is reminiscent of the concept of the void (*shunya*) in certain Mahayana scriptures, was condemned in 1329 as heretical by Pope John XXII.

Whereas scientific materialism is a product of the adolescent psyche, galvanized by rebellion against authority (the introjected father figure), religious provincialism arises from childish dependence, expressed in the mediocrity of heel-clicking conformism, a constant bowing to the imperative call of the superego. Possibly because both belief systems represent uninspected, irrational orientations, they tolerate each other and, in their struggle for monopoly, even enter into a flimsy but mutually exploitative alliance. Since modern man is curiously self-divided, this unlikely alliance can take place even in a single individual, and it frequently does. By a trick of the mind the person in question fails to notice any incompatibility, thus protecting his or her mental "mazeway," his or her ideological position and posture in the world, with all its attendant emotions and desires: in other words, the entire elaborate illusion of independence as an egoic entity.

Where previous ages celebrated the community or Nature itself, our era worships individuality and individualism. Individuation *is* a necessary phase, both in our individual psychic development and in the evolution of our species. Alas, our modern Western civilization is founded in the preposterous credo that egoification forms the apex of all human unfolding. We tend to be suspicious of anything that contests this view—from religious or spiritual authority to psychologies that talk about transpersonal dimensions of existence. Our civilization is abysmally ignorant of, and blatantly antagonistic toward, all manifestations of ego-transcending spirituality. It is particularly threatened by the work of spiritual teachers, or gurus, who actively seek to erode the ego-habit.

Perhaps this pervasive fear is the underlying reason why holy madness, or crazy wisdom, has so far not even fully entered the halls of academe. Certainly, crazy-wise adepts do not cater to the needs of the ego—particularly not the academic ego—but they will, in principle, do anything to roughhouse the innumerable bulwarks that the ego erects around itself to hold Reality at bay. Holy madness must be the ultimate nightmare of the secular humanist.

## 8. Cultural Veils over Authentic Spirituality

Spirituality, to the degree that it is authentic, cuts into all the artifices of egoic existence. It challenges every convention, every self-protective elaboration of human civilization. Ultimately it calls into question the very source of all conventions—the ego itself. Understandably, this spiritual thrust meets with resistance, both conscious and unconscious, but primarily unconscious. The inveterate misconceptions about spiritual life that circulate in our civilization and that prevent most of humankind from participating in a free, Reality-based existence are largely forms of that resistance.

What, specifically, are the erroneous notions about spirituality current in our contemporary culture? Rather than compile a tedious catalog of popular misconceptions about spiritual life, I wish to highlight two main misinterpretations that have, of themselves, spawned a host of secondary mistaken ideas. These two root errors—which must both be understood as arising against a background of scientific materialism, religious provincialism, and secular humanism—are, first, the confusion of spirituality with conventional religiosity, and, second, the confusion of spirituality with conventional mysticism. I refrain from discussing here a third cardinal misconception, one that springs solely from an exaggerated scientistic viewpoint, which is the reduction of spiritual phenomena to mere psychological or even neurophysiological processes. This one-dimensional "metaphysics" goes hand in hand with an overall rejection of a spiritual approach to life, and to counter it in a decisive manner would require a fuller consideration than is possible within the orbit of the present book.

I should warn the reader that my whole argument is developed on the basis of the premise that there is indeed a spiritual dimension to existence, and that it is real and of prime significance to human life lived consciously. Unless my readers have at least a tacit appreciation of the spiritual dimension (however it may be conceived), they will perforce write off my observations and propositions as so much hogwash. In that case, no real dialogue is possible.

The first common misconception, that of confusing spirituality with religiosity, is a most obvious instance of projecting the familiar upon the unfamiliar. Since religion means different things to different people, our reading of spirituality is colored by our own experience or understanding of the nature of religiosity. But perhaps one can extract a core image from the varying interpretations that are in circulation.

Religion, in the popular view, is associated with a recurrent cluster of concepts: a personal God, worship of that God, and a superior moral life that arises as an obligation from one's recognition of the existence of a divine Being. The emphasis lies in the moral dimension: The religiously committed person endeavors to act differently by incarnating the "good" values of his or her religious tradition. These values, given as moral commandments, are surprisingly uniform throughout the great religions of mankind. Apart from the call to love God (that is, to relate positively to the transcendental Reality), the religious moral code is meant to regulate and harmonize an individual's social relations.

Thus the five precepts that form the basis of the classical eightfold path of Yoga are representative of morality in the world's religions: harmlessness in thought, speech, and deed toward all creatures; truthfulness in thought and speech; refraining from theft; chastity in thought, speech, and action; freedom from greed. In Buddhism, an almost identical set is known as the "five virtues" (*panca-shila*). The same moral values are incorporated in the "Ten Commandments" of the Judeo-Christian heritage, and they are also found in Jainism, Islam, Taoism, Confucianism, and most other religious traditions.

Religion, as commonly understood and lived, is therefore the practice of a moral life based on the recognition and worship of the divine or transcendental Reality (however it may be pictured). The divine Being is seen as a paradigm for, or monitor of, moral action; it is the ultimate "good." This is true even of popular Buddhism, which differs from the philosophical (or esoteric) schools of Buddhism in which the ultimate Reality is conceived of as impersonal and indefinable. Religious worship calls for a personal Godhead. You cannot pray to *nirvana*, but you can open your heart to the transcendental person of the Buddha, or to other liberated beings or saints. This implies that the God of conventional religion is always God-apart, or God-as-object, or perhaps God-as-Creator. The exoteric Deity is also God-as-authority, the Super-Being who mysteriously responds to our worship and moral practice and who, possibly, punishes us for our transgressions. Without necessarily "psychologizing" God, we can see in these concepts clear overtones of the superego and of personal psychopathology.

Conventional spirituality revolves around belief, sin, transgression, and redemption through grace. By contrast, authentic spirituality neither unfolds on the basis of belief nor promotes a conception of God as an "other." It is also by no means synonymous with a moral life that includes a positive orientation to the Divine. Rather, in authentic spirituality moral disciplines are engaged as a natural outgrowth of intelligent self-understanding and commitment to self-transcendence. Spiritual practice is not pursued as a means of changing the ego (wrongly conceived as an entity) or its circumstances; nor is it undertaken to improve or develop the self or personality. Such is the approach of conventional religion; genuine spirituality goes beyond this orientation. It does not operate with a concept of existence as a "problem" for which solutions are possible. It exposes the ordinary individual's desire for self-improvement as a form of the ego-personality's struggle for survival. As I have noted before, authentic spiritual practice serves not ego-fulfillment but ego-transcendence. The misidentification of spirituality with conventional religiosity engenders a number of faulty attitudes and expectations that can lead to abortive attempts at spiritual practice, which leave people empty-handed and with a sense of failure.

The second major misconception about spiritual life, chiefly entertained by those who are indifferent to and disaffiliated from conventional (organized) religion, is the equation of authentic spirituality with mysticism. Although this identification appears somewhat more sophisticated and excusable than the previous error, it is no less wrong.

The term "mysticism" is ambiguous, because it is multivalent, but it is commonly understood to refer to an inner quest that is punctuated by certain nonsensory experiences (e.g., visions, auditions, etc.) and is meant ultimately to lead to communion with the Divine. Mysticism, like conventional religion, is also a form of the search for self-fulfillment. But unlike the religious believer, the mystic tends to place no final hope in priestly doctrines and sacramental elaborations of revelation. Instead, he or she embarks on a journey of self-discovery, looking for revelation in the depth of his or her own psyche, beyond space-time. The mystic deems outward expressions of revelation to be accidental and maybe even irrelevant. At the same time, he or she tends to belittle reason, savoring instead the nonrational joys of inner union with the object of contemplation. Not surprisingly, the religious establishment has always frowned on the mystical adventure, seeing all too clearly the potential threat of chaos posed by mystical ecstasy and strong otherworldly aspirations.

As is apparent from the history of the mystical traditions and schools, both Eastern and Western, few mystics have succeeded in truly freeing themselves from the quagmire of their own psyche. For them, the excursion into the panopticum of the mind has turned into a journey without end. They entrap themselves in the infinite possibilities of the psychic wonderland, while Reality, or God, the goal of their keenest striving, remains undiscovered.

Just as spirituality is not confined to the moral regulation of our interpersonal environment, it is also not limited to the manipulation of our intrapsychic environment. It is not concerned with developing or improving the personality; its primary purpose is the total transformation of the body-mind as a whole, a transformation that amounts to perfect and perpetual enlightenment. Spirituality is not merely an event in the brain or nervous system, a fleeting glimpse of a higher reality, a flash of light, or a shower of profound intellectual truths. Rather, it implies a total revolution in which not only the nervous system but also the objective universe as a whole is transcended, since the enlightened being's sense of identity is no longer localized but has become the Identity, the Ground of Being, underlying all things.

Clearly, such a transformation does not come about overnight or during a weekend intensive, nor does it occur by straining at different consciousness-expanding techniques, by ingesting this or that psychomimetic drug, or by wiring the brain to this or that electronic gadget. Instead, it presupposes a willingness to apply oneself to the spiritual process for an entire lifetime. And this is obviously a worthwhile undertaking only when the practitioner harbors no delusions about the spiritual process itself, when he or she has come to suspect and suspend all ideological premises and personal biases and is willing and able to listen to the whispers of wisdom, as hidden in the great spiritual traditions of the world.

Neti, neti—"not thus, not thus"—was the laconic response of the Upanishadic sages of ancient India to anyone who asked about the nature of the transcendental Reality. With this apophatic formula they meant to undermine all possible notions about Reality. We can begin in a more modest fashion: by dropping our more blatant misconceptions about that Reality and about the spiritual process in and through which it becomes transparent to us.

In retrospect, how did you relate to the story at the beginning of this chapter? How do you relate to the stories told of crazy-wise adepts and mad saints in the first and second parts of this book? In the remaining two chapters I will try to give my own answers to these questions.

# 10

## UNDERSTANDING HOLY MADNESS

### 1. Holy Madness Revisited

In Parts One and Two, we encountered many spiritual eccentrics in different religious traditions who exemplify the spirit of holy madness, or crazy wisdom. A few of these individuals appear to be fully enlightened or spiritually awake, while most others are simply travelers on the road to enlightenment, or God-realization. In some instances, they deem themselves enlightened but leave one in serious doubt about the authenticity of their claims. However, in the majority of cases—as with the tribal shaman tricksters or the Fools for Christ's Sake—the ideal of enlightenment does not even enter the picture. There is also the strong possibility that enlightenment means quite different things to different people. We can distinguish between *degrees* of enlightenment, or ego-transcendence. Full enlightenment—in which one's entire being becomes permanently diaphanous to the "light" of ultimate Reality—is, as I understand it, an exceedingly rare event in human history. What, then, are we to make of the galaxy of spiritual eccentrics and religious geniuses, some of whose colorful stories have been told in this book? Does it make sense to lump these various religious types together? Or do we run the risk of blurring important distinctions?

On the most general level, that which tricksters, clowns, mad lamas, Zen masters, holy fools, rascal gurus, and crazy-wise adepts have in common is an *active* rejection of consensual reality. They behave in ways that outwardly manifest the reversal of values and attitudes intrinsic to all genuine spirituality. Spiritual aspirants everywhere seek to live by standards that are extraordinary, that is, not the ordinary standards of daily existence. These are men and women who have turned their attention away from conventional pursuits and toward the spiritual Reality. If they have turned seriously enough, they will, as the *Koran* (II.115) has it, see the face of God in all things. For those whose turning, or conversion, is not yet complete, the "face of God" will fade in and out. Nevertheless, their intention is to see it more and more stably and fully.

The fact that spiritual aspirants have set their sights on a higher principle empowers them to live a way of life that is *eccentric* with regard to social conventions but *concentric* in relation to the Divine, or ultimate Reality. Tricksters, holy fools, and crazy adepts all share this ability, even psychic need, to be different from their contemporaries. They are dropouts, obeying different rules in the game of life.

There are, however, significant differences between these figures; these involve the motivations behind their eccentric behavior. Thus, the eccentricity of the holy fools of Christianity and Islam has the declared purpose of inviting scorn and mockery, so that they are encouraged to cultivate humility. Humility is a virtue for them, but more than a virtue it is a form of grace. It is the condition of allowing the ego-personality to subside in the Ground of its existence. Humility, or self-surrender to the larger Reality, can be cultivated but not forced; whenever it is too eagerly sought, it is merely egotism in a particularly nasty guise. Nevertheless, as St. Teresa of Avila knew, self-surrender is the foundation of the entire edifice of spiritual life.[1]

Some saints of the past have found verbal and even physical abuse useful in their attempt to reduce the "I"-sense, just as not a few spiritual seekers today enlist with teachers who employ harsh methods of ego-bashing. It is quite possible that this peculiar need to be chastised by an external agency includes an element of masochism. Saints and mystics are not beyond psychopathology, as we will see, and neither are modern seekers. Yet this does not necessarily mean that the self-debasing life, for instance, of a holy fool is no more than a symptom of a deep-seated neurosis. On the contrary, without blinding ourselves to possible psychopathological manifestations, we may see an authentic spiritual impulse at work in the self-abandoning life, leading to growth and wholeness.

While self-abnegation also plays a central role in the eccentricity of the crazy-wise adepts of Tibet, with them it has a different purpose. The mad lamas behave oddly not because they want to demean themselves in the eyes of the world, but because they want to teach their contemporaries a spiritual lesson. This intent may also be present in the holy fools of Christianity and Islam, but for them it does not have the same weight as the desire to grow in humility, or meekness, through society's contempt. The motivational distinction between holy fools and crazy-wise adepts can be seen to arise from differences in their respective metaphysics, which, in my opinion, are reflective of their general level of spiritual attainment. Thus, the holy fools typically relate to the ultimate Reality as a personal God "out there," whose voice can be discerned in the chambers of the heart. The crazy-wise adepts, on the other hand, view the Ultimate as their own essential nature. Their avowed metaphysics is clearly nondualist rather than dualist.

Though not absent from nondualist schools of thought like Tibetan Buddhism, humility belongs more properly to the "language" of dualistic metaphysics. Here the Creator-God, the Holy One, is deemed the only worshipful being that exists. His rightful worship involves acute humbleness on the part of his creatures. An aspect of such worship is to identify with, and adopt the life of, fellow creatures who are especially underprivileged and who suffer from the callousness of ordinary society—the hungry, sick, and oppressed. This attitude belongs to the fourth stage in the *scala spiritualis* elaborated by Da Love-Ananda, which I have outlined in Chapter 6.

By contrast, the Tibetan adepts and their Hindu counterparts do not conceive of, or experience, Reality as an "other." The self, or ego, is assumed to be an illusion that inexplicably arises, together with the objective universe, against the backdrop of the singular Being (*tattva*), or Void (*shunya*). The ego-personality is thus not taken seriously at all, and the notion of inviting ridicule in order to lessen the ego-sense means little in the nondualist context. The Tibetan or Hindu adepts, ideally and generally, engage their spiritual discipline (*sadhana*) with the intuitive certainty that at the deepest level of being they are *already* fully awake, or enlightened, and that this innate enlightenment will become evident in the course of their practice. The orientation of the crazy-wise adepts is characteristic of the fifth, sixth, and seventh stages of life in Da Love-Ananda's model of psychospiritual maturation—the advanced stages of psychic introversion, witnessing awareness, and full enlightenment.

The adepts' commitment to self-transcendence tends to express itself in a general disinterest in ordinary life, a penchant for the cultivation of ecstatic states, and, more rarely, in acts of active compassion. Part of their compassionate activity is teaching others the truth of radical nonduality by resorting to the kind of unconventional, eccentric means that modern Westerners find so hard to understand.

The charge has been made that the traditional crazy-wisdom approach, which is definitely at odds with our Western concept of individuality, is merely an insensitive, autocratic style of teaching that issues from massive arrogance. My response to this is that crazy wisdom can certainly be that, but it can also be a great deal more. It is always easy for ego-personalities to spot egoic motives in the actions of others, especially when those actions contradict our own cherished beliefs. We tend to see the mote in another's eye more readily than we see the beam in our own. Thus, one could just as easily dismiss the Christian holy fools as suffering from rampant egocentrism because they use others to boost their own spiritual life. This opinion would be far too simplistic, because it ignores the context. On the other hand, we must not overlook the possibility that some holy fools may have fallen prey to the temptation of hypocrisy.

To summarize, we can distinguish between three principal motives for the kind of spiritual eccentricity under review in this book:

1. To simply "drop out" of conventional society in order to be able to focus attention on spiritual matters;
2. To instigate social opprobrium for the sake of cultivating humility; and
3. To instruct others in spiritual values.

Although all three motives may be present in specific individuals, phenomenologically (and tentatively) we can say that the first motive is common to all types of spiritual eccentrics and that the other two motives may be present to a variable degree. Thus, some Hindu *avadhutas* live on garbage heaps, not because they want to make a statement or because they hope to squelch their self-sense thereby, but simply because they have left conventional society behind and identify with its much-neglected "shadow." They are spiritual hippies, having no ambition beyond realizing the Self (*atman*) or, if they have already realized it, beyond living *as* it in a world without opposition. If approached for instruction, one or another of these *avadhutas* may choose to teach seekers a lesson by throwing garbage at them. Or, possibly, he or she may throw garbage just to fend off unwelcome spectators. Another *avadhuta*, or perhaps the very same *avadhuta* on a different occasion, may spontaneously feel inclined to use his or her abject physical state as a symbol for the truth of nonduality: If there is only one Divine, then it must be present even as the garbage that is discarded and emotionally rejected by everyone but the person of wisdom (*jnana*).

Objectively speaking, the very existence of such spiritual eccentrics, whether they teach or not, is a lesson in itself. Their whole life is either a sign or a symbol. While the conventional individual will see in such a life a *sign* of personal failure or perhaps economic misfortune, the spiritually sensitive person will penetrate below the level of appearances to understand the *symbolic* import, which is to say, the spiritual message contained in the adept's eccentric life-style.

## 2. Of Holiness, Wisdom, and Ignorance

In this book, I have generally used the terms "holy madness" and "crazy wisdom" interchangeably. It is, however, possible to distinguish between them, assigning the former to such religious movements as the holy fools in Christianity and Islam, and the latter specifically to Tibetan Buddhism and Hindu Avadhutism. These latter spiritual traditions are founded in nondualist interpretations of existence and operate according to a model of the path that includes full enlightenment (*bodhi*), which is by definition beyond morality and sainthood but does not exclude them. It is also possible to apply "crazy wisdom" to a much broader range of unconventional attitudes, including those expressed in secular works of art, especially poetry, such as the "Crazy

Jane" poems of William Butler Yeats and the Fool in Shakespeare's *King Lear.*[2] While in general I wish to continue to use the two terms interchangeably, it will be useful to bear the above distinctions in mind.

Whether we speak of spiritual eccentricity generically as "holy madness" or "crazy wisdom" is irrelevant. They are essentially equivalent because both terms contain the same two ideas, namely the idea of sacredness (expressed in the words "holy" and "wisdom") and the idea of a state of mind that is nonordinary or extraconsensual (expressed in the words "madness" and "crazy"). In the following section I will examine these two ideas, which will assist us in grasping the finer lineaments of the phenomenon of spiritual eccentricity.

To begin with, what is meant by "holy" and "wisdom"? As Rudolf Otto showed in his classic study more than seven decades ago, the idea of "holiness" has been usurped by the sphere of ethics. It widely connotes a condition of consummate moral goodness. This, however, is not the original significance of holiness. In addition to this ethical element, Otto noted, the notion of "holiness" contains a "surplus," which he characterized as the *mysterium tremendum*. In his own words:

> The feeling of it may at times come sweeping like a gentle tide, pervading the mind with a tranquil mood of deepest worship. It may pass over into a more set and lasting attitude of the soul, continuing, as it were, thrillingly vibrant and resonant, until at last it dies away and the soul resumes its 'profane', non-religious mood of everyday experience. It may burst in sudden eruption up from the depths of the soul with spasms and convulsions, or lead to the strangest excitements, to intoxicated frenzy, to transport, and to ecstasy. It has its wild and demonic forms and can sink to an almost grisly horror and shuddering. It has its crude, barbaric antecedents and early manifestations, and again it may be developed into something beautiful and pure and glorious. It may become the hushed, trembling, and speechless humility of the creature in the presence of— whom or what? In the presence of that which is a *mystery* inexpressible and above all creatures.[3]

To encounter the sacred or holy is to encounter Reality in its numinous, transconceptual essence. But holiness can also be an attribute of a finite being or location—a temple or church—inasmuch as that being or location serves as a conduit for Reality. Since conduits, religious or otherwise, can be more or less open or blocked, holiness can also be considered as a matter of degree. The fully enlightened person, or *buddha*, is thought to be a perfect "channel" for the numinous Reality, because all identification with the ego-personality has ceased: The tail has stopped wagging the dog. This condition of utter wakefulness is also called *jnana*, which may be rendered as "wisdom" or "gnosis." It is not knowledge or information of any kind but a state of *being* in which knowledge and information, as well as sensations and feelings, may arise, though they are not experienced as the properties or attributes of a self-limiting subject, or ego.

*Holy* madness, or crazy *wisdom*, is a particular manifestation of sacredness. It therefore shares the elusiveness of the holy. However, it is not entirely inaccessible to rational analysis, just as the numinous mystery has been quite eloquently described by Otto and others.

Let us next ask, What is the traditional meaning of "crazy wisdom"? First, the expression was apparently coined by the late Lama Chögyam Trungpa, whose crazy-wise exploits are well known in Western Buddhist circles and beyond. Trungpa's coinage was subsequently adopted by two American-born teachers, Da Love-Ananda and Lee Lozowick. The expression is an oxymoron, composed of two concepts that on first glance appear to be mutually exclusive. How can wisdom be crazy? Common sense tells us that wisdom is the very antithesis of craziness. Craziness is a mental or psychic dysfunction, an inability to respond to a real situation in a real way. To be crazy or crazed is literally to be "cracked" or "broken"—that is, not whole, out of balance. It is a state of unhappy, loveless repetition of one's habit patterns.

By contrast, wisdom has traditionally been held to be reflective of what is real or whole. It has the power to create a higher order, or harmony. In that sense, it is superfunctional. In particular, it is an articulation of, and the means to, happiness or love. This conventional understanding of wisdom is inadequate in the present context, however. The wisdom intended in the concept "crazy wisdom" is more than what is commonly understood by the term.

Ordinarily, wisdom signifies what Aristotle called *phronesis*—practical wisdom. He used this term in contrast to *sophia*, or speculative wisdom, by which one intuitively grasps the highest metaphysical concepts. In Plato's philosophy, *sophia* figured as the first of the four cardinal virtues, the others being courage, temperance, and justice. For Plato, *sophia* meant integrative knowledge of the totality of existence. Such wisdom was not divisive or divided.

However, it so happened that Aristotle's more analytical definition was upheld by Thomas Aquinas, though he made revelation rather than metaphysical thinking the province of speculative wisdom. Thus Aristotle's notion of wisdom, called by Aquinas *sophia*, came to influence the rest of Christian (Western) thought. This was still the interpretation of wisdom when, in the seventeenth century, the Dutch optician–philosopher Baruch Spinoza formulated his monistic system of philosophy. Spinoza identified wisdom with intuitive knowledge (*scientia intuitiva*) of the universal in the particulars and regarded it as the way to live under the aspect of eternity. This may sound like Plato's concept of wisdom, but it is not. Spinoza was a staunch rationalist, and his interpretation of wisdom has a strong intellectual component. He argued that for wisdom to be wisdom, it had to be reasonable or intelligible.

Spinoza's position stands in diametrical opposition to the approach of Nicholas of Cues (Nicolas Cusanus) who, two centuries earlier, had equated wisdom with "learned ignorance" (*docta ignorantia*). By that he meant the ultimate admission that reason cannot penetrate the mystery of the Divine. The rational mind is endowed with the obvious capacity to appreciate its own finitude, while simultaneously being sensitive to the infinite Ground in which it inheres. Reason is demonstrably incapable of giving rational expression to the infinite. Therein lies our basic ignorance. However, as Nicholas of Cues further realized, the fact that we are aware of our own cognitive incapacity elevates that ignorance to the status of learned ignorance. In his own words:

> The relationship of our intellect to the truth is like that of a polygon to a circle; the resemblance to the circle grows with the multiplication of angles of the polygon; but apart from its being reduced to identity with the circle, no multiplication, even if it were infinite, of its angles will make the polygon equal the circle.
>
> It is clear, therefore, that all we know of the truth is that the absolute truth, such as it is, is beyond our reach. The truth, which can be neither more nor less than it is, is the most absolute necessity, while, in contrast with it, our intellect is possibility. Therefore, the quiddity of things, which is ontological truth, is unattainable in its entirety; and though it has been the objective of all philosophers, by none has it been found as it really is. The more profoundly we learn this lesson of ignorance, the closer we draw to truth itself.[4]

Learned ignorance corresponds to an attitude of humility and openness to the infinite. And that, according to Nicholas of Cues, is the essence of wisdom. In wisdom, the human being surpasses his or her constitution and merges with the infinite Ground. This comes close to the concept of wisdom in the crazy-wisdom schools. Psychologically and functionally, crazy wisdom is not a form of knowledge. It is, rather, what the contemporary crazy-wise adept Da Love-Ananda calls a manifestation of "Divine Ignorance." This curious usage is, perhaps, explained by the fact that he once attended a Christian theological seminary.

By contrast, Eastern spiritual authorities tend to couch ultimate matters more in terms of gnosis, reserving the term "ignorance" for the state of mind from which emancipation is sought. Thus, most Hindu and also some Buddhist teachers employ the Sanskrit words *vidya, jnana,* and *prajna* to designate mind-transcending wisdom and Reality. We may note that Da Love-Ananda, too, avails himself of this usage. His teaching is strongly syncretistic and is presented as an attempt to bridge the gulf between East and West. In effect, though, it remains locked into Eastern attitudes.

Be that as it may, it is helpful to consider crazy wisdom as Divine Ignorance in action. According to Da Love-Ananda, Divine Ignorance is unlimited, unqualified, ego-transcending "radiance," apparently diffracted by the prism of individuated consciousness, which deems itself independent from the context in which it both arises and has its final resting place. For the enlightened adept, there is no such diffraction. He or she *is* that radiant Ignorance. The world process proceeds in and through the adept without the localized swirl caused by the illusion of separateness that marks the ego. In the midst of the Heraclitean flux of events, the adept, identified with Being, stands perfectly still. There is no stress, because stress is a product of the struggling ego-personality.

To penetrate the "illusion" of the ego is to stand free of its mechanics and hence of the whole mechanics of the world. The ego posits or, in phenomenological terms, "intends" the world, that is, fills it with meaning and implication. But to stand free is to stand in the position of Ignorance, not in the posture of the ego. The condition of Ignorance is devoid of subjectivity, of knowledge, of significance.

In Divine Ignorance, the "conditioned reflex" of the ego is completely transparent and transcended in every moment. Yet this condition is not one of passive spectatorship. As the adepts affirm, the enlightened being is an effective presence, a living and radiant force. The presence of illumined adepts has an impact on the environment; they are unwitting transformers of their psychophysical surroundings—both other beings and inanimate objects. In the case of the enlightened adept who mysteriously assumes the role of the guru, that transformative function is focused and augmented through voluntary instruction of others.

Another way of looking at Divine Ignorance is that it is the upsetting of all categories of experience and knowledge. It undermines all the many models of reality by which we seek to sustain ourselves in our alienation from the ultimate Reality. From the perspective of the secular mind, this kind of ignorance is utterly unintelligible, irrational—"crazy." In fact, however, it is not *ir*rational but *a*rational, or *trans*rational. It exceeds the perimeter of the egotropic mind. Nevertheless, as rational beings we are bound to apply our mind to it. The humor of this situation must be appreciated. It is comparable to someone's insisting on emptying the ocean by scooping up water with a bucket that has a large hole in the bottom. Such a Sisyphean effort is, however, not altogether futile. Even though that person will fail to drain the ocean, the attempt itself can reveal all kinds of things about he who undertakes it.

Similarly, crazy wisdom is explained by its practitioners as unpremeditated, spontaneous action that has the purpose of illuminating others. It is, we are told, unself-conscious behavior on the part of the enlightened adept. Its function is not to communicate knowledge or information, but to transmit the transcendental condition, or Divine Ignorance. That is to say, it is intended to duplicate the adept's state of being in the disciple. Yet because crazy wisdom occurs not on the transcendental plane but in a real-life context, it paradoxically always triggers knowledge in others. That knowledge can take the form of real understanding, which in due course silences the mind and plunges us into the condition of Divine Ignorance; or it can take the form of misunderstanding, in which case it produces anger toward the adept, self-doubt, and a wide range of other negative states of mind.

Such a diversity of response is reflected in the following answers obtained from disciples of a crazy-wisdom teacher when I asked, "What is crazy wisdom?" The first response is from an elderly professional gentleman:

I'm not sure how to answer your question. When you are involved in this thing, you don't really stop to define it. Let me see. I would say that crazy wisdom is a kick in the pants, a smack in the face, a bucket of cold water poured over your head, a shrill sound that keeps you awake at all times. You might say, a right old pain in the neck. Its purpose? To help you shed all your masks and become real, to find your true self, which is divine. It is a particular way in which certain teachers express their love for their disciples, strange as it may sound. Their compassion moves them to interfere with you, to blow to smithereens your fondest ideas of how it all works and who you are. And that's pretty crazy. It's crazy of them to do this kind of thing. And it's crazy of you to hold still long enough for them to do it to you.

I don't really know why I'm doing it. All I know is I don't have any real choice in the matter. I feel I'm growing in the process. It's not pleasant, and you're constantly wondering when the next bucket of cold water will be poured over your head. But I obviously need that. I want to grow spiritually, and since I happen to have a teacher who is a crazy adept, I have come to terms with it all. I tell you one thing, though: If I had known what is involved in this, I would have thought twice about it. On this path, you're not safe or immune. There is also something exciting about that. I know my teacher won't stand for any nonsense from me. I trust he'll do what it takes to enlighten me. It may not happen this year or next year, or even in this lifetime, because I'm getting on in years. But what I am involved in feels real, and I'm convinced whatever efforts I make will not be wasted.

When I put the same question to another, younger female student of the same teacher, she responded in this way:

Crazy wisdom? Do you want a definition? I don't think I can define it. It's just a way some gurus work with their disciples. For some reason I picked a guru who is a crazy adept, or perhaps he picked me. Well, I guess, you could say that crazy wisdom is a teaching method with no holds barred. The guru will do anything to enlighten you. That means he can sometimes do quite unconventional and outrageous things. To tell you the truth, most of the time, I don't even know what's going on. Sometimes I ask myself what the point of a certain lesson could possibly be. I confess I have my doubts about some of it. But I'm hanging in, because I sense that however weird things might get, my guru has my best interest in mind.

Another woman, who had been involved with the same teacher but left, disenchanted, answered my question thus:

I think crazy wisdom is a lot of baloney. I've been through it, you know. I suffered a lot of abuse—from my teacher and the people around him. I don't think it helped me any. Well, perhaps, it made me see something about myself. It certainly showed me that I didn't want to build my life around a guru who thinks it is his mission to constantly cut down everyone. I was a raving idealist at the time. I wanted to be enlightened. And for a while I did everything that I was told to do. I took all the criticism and the abuse. But deep down I got more and more hurt and angry. I felt angry toward my teacher and everyone else. I was pretty confused. You never knew what was coming down next. Constant change. Nothing would ever last for any length of time. No peace. People would always be running around doing things, trying to meet the latest demands of the guru, trying to please him. It was just crazy.

After a couple of years of this, I knew I had to get out. People told me that I wasn't mature enough to have a crazy-wisdom guru. Well, maybe. But maybe not. Maybe those people are just deluding themselves. Not one of them has gotten enlightened yet, as far as I know. I am still interested in spiritual life, in meditation. But I've given up on gurus and certainly on crazy wisdom.

There is no telling what exposure to crazy wisdom will accomplish. People will either see its wisdom or be perturbed by its apparent craziness. Similarly, it depends on the beholder whether he or she will see in holy madness holiness or mere folly.

### 3. Holy Madness, Spontaneity, and the Chaos of Existence

In its most radical manifestation, holy madness or crazy wisdom transcends the mind and the ego-function; it is a specific expression of the disposition of enlightenment itself. Of course, not all crazy-wise teachers are enlightened, but if they are genuine, their eccentric or antinomian behavior is at least informed by their intuitive appreciation of the enlightened condition. The fact that a crazy-wise teacher may not be fully enlightened raises questions of its own, which I will not go into here. There is also a lot of confusion about the nature of enlightenment, and I have addressed this in Chapter 8. For the present discussion, suffice it to say that enlightenment is transcendental identification with the totality of existence.

That totality, or *totum*, can usefully be characterized as unqualified chaos, because it exists prior to our persistent individual and collective effort to fashion an orderly and therefore more or less predictable cosmos out of it. With the possible exception of certain gnostic schools that regard the body and the world as essentially hostile to the spirit, most religious traditions view the universe as a comparatively benign place. In doing so, they have to ignore to some extent the evidence of the senses.

It is true that the known world appears to be patterned in a certain way, so that some of its processes are intelligible to common sense and scientific reason. But it is also true that we can perceive, if we care to look around, a great deal that is inexplicable and chaotic. Both points of view need to be taken into account to avoid slipping into simplistic worldviews of either optimism or pessimism. To speak of the totality of existence as chaos is, then, a heuristic device that reminds us of our ever-present proclivity to make sense of everything, to give it form, to explain and rationalize.

Enlightenment, which in many traditions is equated with God-realization, is a meaning-transcending event or process because the total Reality, which is not to be confused with mere Nature, transcends all cognitive categories. But that totality, which most people call God, is not meaningless either. The categories "meaningful" and "meaningless" make sense only with reference to our *concept* of God. The Divine eclipses our individuality even as we conceive or speak of it as if we were separate from it. Hence, Gautama the Buddha and other wise folk recommended silence on this matter.

Despite the insidious propaganda of scientific materialism over the past two centuries, the classical theistic worldview still serves as the metaphysical framework for most people. This worldview conceives of God as the creator of the marvelous order perceivable in Nature. In a way, this notion entails its own materialistic-mechanistic bias. Despite the insights of contemporary philosophy, cosmology, and quantum physics, the general emotive picture of God is still that of the grand architect of the universe, the inventor of the elegant regularities of the material cosmos—from chemical reactions to planetary motions, from neurophysiological processes to linguistic structures.

But what about irregularities? Randomness? Chaos? Catastrophes? Death? The ordinary individual seldom ponders the inconsistencies of a presumedly orderly, God-made universe that abides by God-appointed, inexorable laws. He or she is more apt to wonder about imperfections in the sociocultural world—inequality, injustice, anomie, and uncertainty of life. For many people these tragic aspects of existence seldom raise metaphysical questions because it is so much easier to pile blame on oneself and one's fellow beings, or, safer still, to point for explanation to original sin and humankind's expulsion from paradise at the beginning of history.

Cosmologically speaking, billions of people today still live in the time of Newton and earlier. The reason for this is not hard to find. It is understandably difficult to accept that existence is indeed a wild, largely unpredictable, and crazy affair, and that we are not necessarily the beneficiaries of a benignly organized cosmos, but rather participants in, and, unless we participate consciously, victims of, the chaotic forces of life. That is not to say, of course, that existence must be equated with universal anarchy. Nevertheless, because that which *is* transcends our conceptions and intentions, it appears to be unpredictable, irrational, and disorganized to the intellect that dares to contemplate the crying inconsistencies in homespun orderly systems. We live in an unfathomable universe that no model, however ingenious, can ever satisfactorily capture.

Perhaps the model of a perfectly symmetric universe and a rational and good Creator-God is especially appealing in an era of great transformation and uncertainty such as ours. It is a way of coming to terms with the enormity of life. So, however, is the idea of an essentially chaotic world, and the latter has the advantage not necessarily of being better fitted to the facts, but of freeing us from the necessity of emotional self-immunization against the inconsistencies of any cognitive system. By liberating us from our habitual need to deny the finitude of our knowledge and understanding, the chaos model in a way frees us to engage that process in consciousness by which all our models of reality may be transcended in awakening to what is ultimately Real. The Buddhist notion of Reality as voidness (*shunyata*) has precisely the same function. It was invented to remind spiritual practitioners that existence is an indefinable vastness that cannot be contained by the mind.

Enlightenment is the shattering of all mental constructs about existence, including the notions of voidness and chaos or fullness and harmony. It is awakening from the dream in which we mistake our metaphors for the real thing. As the psychiatrist and Zen practitioner Hubert Benoit put it: "At a single stroke I have completely crushed the cave of phantoms."[5] The phantoms are the curious mental creations with which we surround ourselves and through which we live a mediated existence.

Holy madness, or crazy wisdom, exists to serve such an awakening; it has no value or purpose beyond that. Unlike conventional wisdom, it is not meant to create a higher "order," a new harmony, or a better model of reality. On the contrary, crazy wisdom has the sole function of disrupting our model-making enthusiasm. It is enlightened iconoclasm. It calls into question all of our questions and answers to life's challenges and problems. Crazy wisdom does not propose to be an answer or a solution. It is radical questioning. In this sense, the crazy-wise adept is the ultimate scientist, whose investigation is so rigorous that it brooks no conventional answer whatsoever. However, his or her "science" is the science of Divine Ignorance, which means living on the basis of the plenum-void that is Reality.

Another way of putting this is that the advanced crazy-wisdom master, especially if he or she is an enlightened adept, lives a life of sheer spontaneity. The emphasis is on the qualifying adjective "sheer"; the adept's "naturalness" must be carefully distinguished from the impulsiveness of the child or of the emotionally labile adult, as well as from the kind of spontaneity that is pursued by different humanistic therapies or Orientalizing "be here now" approaches. Of course, this sheer spontaneity does not exclude the ability to think rationally—to plan ahead or proceed in a systematic fashion. The enlightened adept may well be an accomplished philosopher and scholar, as was the tenth-century Indian master Abhinava Gupta. But even careful thought and forethought occur in such a being on the basis of ego-freedom, hence as a spontaneous flow.

The common understanding of spontaneity is that it is "authentic" behavior, free from social conditioning. Frederick Perls and his school defined it as "the seizing on, and glowing and growing with, what is interesting and nourishing in the environment."[6] It is the ability to respond to what Gestalt therapy styles the "figure-ground configuration." That is to say, conventionally spontaneous individuals experience and actualize themselves in the context of their total life situation in the moment. Their responses are both original and unique, not the repetitive behavior of the neurotic. They are in touch with situational reality. It is understood that spontaneity entails a free flow of feeling, unhampered by the usual surfeit of deliberateness. It is characterized by a sense of immediacy and concreteness. In conventional terms, spontaneous persons are, in sum, bodily present, not withdrawn in subjective states. They are fully incarnate ego-personalities.

This state of enhanced awareness and integration of the body-mind is, to be sure, a desirable and important step toward a comprehensive psychohygiene. It is not, however, equivalent to the enlightened adept's pure spontaneity, in which the "figure-ground" game is no longer relevant because the ego, or self, is transcended. The ordinary individual experiences himself or herself in opposition—however subtle—to the environment. But the enlightened being is, tradition insists, *literally* the Identity of all (internal and external) environments, and therefore the illusion of opposition does not arise. Such a one is aware of differentiation, but recognizes all differences as emerging and submerging in and as the same Being. So long as egoic consciousness is in place, however, there can be only degrees of spontaneity, corresponding to the extent to which the self is not pitched against its environment.

Pure spontaneity is coessential with the world process itself. Both medieval Hindus and Buddhists used the Sanskrit term *sahaja* to express that spontaneity. The word means literally "together born" and is generally translated as "spontaneous," "natural," "coessential," or "innate."[7] The underlying idea is that spatio-temporal phenomena are not ultimately isolated from Being-Consciousness-Bliss (*sac-cid-ananda*), which is the noumenal, transconceptual Reality itself. Only from the self-contracted position of the egoic consciousness do phenomena appear to be segregated and insular. Upon the release of the ego-spasm, the same phenomena lose their independent status; they are realized to be mere variations on the same "transcendental theme." The world is observed to be God, and the dynamic of the universe is experienced as having no ultimate significance.[8]

Both these understandings are found everywhere in the spiritual literature. However, one must not confuse talking *about* transcendental truths with realizing them. Therefore, we are free to talk about the limitations of language and of the testimonies of the great adepts because these testimonies *are*, after all, interpretations of Reality, not Reality itself. Hence we are also at liberty to express our misgivings about the metaphysical doctrine that the phenomenal world is intrinsically inconsequential.

The perennialist tradition upholds the belief that phenomena are spontaneous manifestations of the singular Reality, which some call "God." This is almost a truism, because we as individuals are indeed not in control of the world process as a whole, nor, when we examine things closely enough, even of its parts. We may decide to build a bridge or go on a hike. But "who" is it that makes the decision? There is a mystery about the human will. Causality is an idea by which we seek to explain that mystery to ourselves. Upon closer inspection, the universe turns out to be a self-governing event. Phenomena appear and disappear—our finite selves included—without our being able to stop this process by an act of will.

All the same, the conclusion that the very instability of the world process makes it inconsequential has no logical foundation; it appears to be simply a value judgment. It implies that only the permanent aspect of the Divine is valuable, whereas the impermanent, manifest universe holds no intrinsic worth, even though it is also the Divine. This is not merely an abstract metaphysical issue. It is also a profoundly important ethical concern. It ties in with the generally amoral, or transmoral, stance of nondualist or monistic mysticism, which I will address in Chapter 11. The belief that the world process as such is utterly insignificant all too easily gives rise to the attitude that anything goes. What we then face is the kind of mind-set that produced the horrors of Jonestown in 1978 or, more recently, the deplorable criminal developments in Rajneeshpuram, Oregon.

*Sahaja* is not merely random behavior. Enlightened spontaneity has nothing to do with a willfulness that disregards everything. It does, however, occur against the backdrop of the adept's personality, and so inescapably includes idiosyncratic elements, as becomes particularly apparent in the case of crazy-wisdom gurus. According to Buddhist doctrine, *sahaja* is the realization of the coessentiality of *nirvana* (the transcendental reality) and *samsara* (the world of change). But that coessentiality makes little sense from the viewpoint of the finite intelligence of the individual. Upon enlightenment, the great authorities of Hinduism and Buddhism assure us, the "twinned" nature of the noumenal reality and the phenomenal world, the perfect coalescence of transcendence and immanence, is an obvious fact. The Buddhist adept Sarahapada, who lived in the tenth century A.D., composed these lines in his "Royal Song":

> Though the house-lamps have been lit,
> The blind live on in the dark.
> Though spontaneity is all-encompassing and close,
> To the deluded it remains always far away. (vs. 3)

As a cloud that rises from the sea
Absorbing rain the earth embraces,
So, like the sky, the sea remains
Without increasing or decreasing. (vs. 5)

So from spontaneity that's unique,
Replete with the Buddha's perfections,
Are all sentient beings born and in it come
To rest. But it is neither concrete nor abstract. (vs. 6)

There's nothing to be negated, nothing to be
Affirmed or grasped; for It can never be conceived.
By the fragmentations of the intellect are the deluded
Fettered; undivided and pure remains spontaneity. (vs. 35)[9]

The ego-identity, as the reference point of adult human consciousness, creates the overpowering illusion that it is in charge of the spontaneous unfurling of phenomenal structures, insofar as the individual's body-mind is concerned. This illusion of control is reflected in the linguistic habit of speaking of "my" body, "my" thoughts, "my" sensations and feelings, or "my" movement. But upon closer examination, the processes of the body-mind are almost all "spontaneous," that is to say, automatic.

Thoughts simply arise of their own accord. We speak, then hear ourselves speaking; we are perhaps even surprised at the speed with which the stream of words organizes itself into meaningful sentences. Our fingers move over the keyboard of the piano or word processor faster than we can become conscious of the beautiful coherent patterns they are producing with relative ease. Self-consciousness is mostly a retrospective activity, and the more deliberate and self-conscious we become, the more the movements of our body-mind also tend to slow down and lose fluidity. Chronic deliberateness is synonymous with neurosis.

By contrast, the spiritual process is the gradual cancellation of the habit of (left-brained) deliberateness, not by reducing a person's level of consciousness but by surpassing it, by opening up a "new" mode of existence—the enlightened disposition. Zen Buddhism tries to achieve this state of no-mind through such paradoxical means as *koans*, which are puzzles that cannot be solved logically but require a leap of intuition. D. T. Suzuki, who not only had a first-class intellect but was also a respected Zen master, offered this explanation:

The worst enemy of Zen experience, at least in the beginning, is the intellect, which consists and insists in discriminating subject from object. The discriminating intellect, therefore, must be cut short if Zen consciousness is to unfold itself, and the koan is constructed eminently to serve this end.
On examination we at once notice that there is no room in the koan to

insert an intellectual interpretation. The knife is not sharp enough to cut the koan open and see what are its contents. For a koan is not a logical proposition but the expression of a certain mental state resulting from the Zen discipline. [10]

Suzuki continued:

All koans are the utterances of satori with no intellectual mediations; hence their uncouthness and incomprehensibility.

The Zen master has no deliberate scheme on his part to make his statements of satori uncouth or logically unpalatable; the statements come forth from his inner being, as flowers burst out in spring-time, or as the sun sheds its rays. Therefore to understand them we have to be like flowers or like the sun; we must enter into their inner being. When we reproduce the same psychic conditions out of which the Zen masters have uttered these koans, we shall know them. [11]

That is to say, *koans* are created and solved out of spontaneity. In this respect, they symbolize the spiritual process per se. All authentic spirituality seeks to realize a condition in which being, thought, and action coincide perfectly.

To recapitulate, we can distinguish three types of spontaneity. First, there is the pseudospontaneity of diminished awareness that characterizes the life-style of the ordinary individual. This consensus mind fancies itself as the norm and confuses conformism to the ideal of "I do as I please" with genuine spontaneity.

Second, there is the relative spontaneity of enhanced awareness that characterizes the individual committed to personal growth. Adam Curle has styled this "true spontaneity," which is the mode of functioning of people "who have access to the essential parts of their make-up" and are thus "able to respond swiftly and positively." It is to be differentiated from the "automatic spontaneity of unawareness," which, in his words, "may equally well be cruel, violent, or selfish." [12]

The third form of spontaneity is the "divinely ignorant" spontaneity of the enlightened being. Here the "automaticity" is, by definition, that of the world process itself, apart from any egoic intervention. It is a form of acceptance of, or submission to, life as it is. What this means is explored by Shri Anirvan, a modern Indian sage:

From that moment [of full awakening] on, everything in a flash passes before your eyes and becomes your real food. Everything is "one and the same thing in you." Then we are faced with a new task in the realm of sensation and relaxation. It becomes a question of forgetting oneself, of voluntarily obliterating the self, which is a "letting go" in a region that is very subtle and hard to discover . . . To forget voluntarily is, in fact, impossible for forgetting proceeds from a principle without any form.

When your being is invaded by a movement coming from the heart or mind you are like a vibrating bell filled by the echo of a sound coming from nowhere.[13]

Shri Anirvan cites the sixteenth-century Vedanta teacher Keshab Das, who said: "I discover that I am what I was, but between the two there are nothing but complications." Upon enlightenment, as the Zen masters are fond of saying, the trees are trees and the mountains are mountains again. But prior to enlightenment, and especially during the course of spiritual disciplines, the world looks rather complicated and the mind is quite befuddled. Life itself is experienced as a *koan*, which hammers away at the subconscious until, one day, there is a breakthrough: Then everything becomes transparent. The mind's internal dialogue ceases, the whole being relaxes, and the enlightened person knows that everything is as it should be. Now he or she can do whatever is needful in the moment, whether it is to water the flowers, build a house, construct a mathematical theorem, write a book, or do nothing at all. After enlightenment, life is no less difficult, but it is much simpler.

## 4. The Playfulness and Humor of Enlightenment and Crazy Wisdom

In human interaction with the world, three kinds or levels of play can usefully be distinguished. First, there is the unself-conscious play of the child who is completely absorbed in his or her make-believe world of toys and games. Much of the child's play can be understood as an unpremeditated rehearsal of adult roles, similar to the "play" of animals. As the child grows older, more and more of his or her play can be seen as a reaction to the propriety of the "real," adult world. In play, the child escapes into the freedom of his or her own universe of imagination, creativity, and unbridled self-assertion.

This infantile escapist play is also an important safety valve for the emotionally immature adult who, because of his or her incomplete psychic adaptation to life, is never quite at ease with the world. He or she is, therefore, in periodic need of withdrawal from the responsibilities of the real world: thus, the weekend football game, the daily crossword puzzle, or watching television.

Such a person is oblivious to the second level of play, as it is engaged by the mature, "successful" personality who tacitly or knowingly appreciates that "real" life itself is pliable and therefore playable. The player of the "game" of life recognizes, to a certain degree, the illusory nature of the social arrangements and cultural forms in which he or she is obliged to participate—in fact, the word "illusion," as Johan Huizinga pointed out, means "in play" (*in lusio*).[14] The mature adult no longer completely believes the magic spell under which the rest of humanity seems to labor. He or she has achieved a level of freedom and humor in the midst of the pressures of human existence.

At the lower end of the second-level spectrum of players is, perhaps, the "consciousness-raised" entrepreneur who uses his or her insight into the illusoriness of human life to personal advantage. On the upper end of the same spectrum we may place the rare individual who has become sensitive to the sacred dimension and who, beyond all conventional piety and pre- scribed religious behavior, attempts to live a self-transcending life. This is the man or woman of whom Plato said, in the *Laws* (VII.803), that he or she is "made God's plaything." Plato recommended that such a person should live life as a form of play, entering into the noblest games, which are different from the games that absorb most people's attention. However, the freedom of such a person is still only conditional, because he or she still plays the game of life as an ego-identity. In other words, he or she still believes in the very source of all the sociocultural magic that people reinforce in each other. So, ultimately, he or she also succumbs to the same illusion.

Only the enlightened being plays without having to create an imaginary world (as does the child or adult fleeing from reality), or adopt an alternative model of reality (as does the mature adult) by which he or she can play the game of life successfully. The God-realizer discards all substitute realities and simply abandons himself or herself to the vicissitudes of the world process, while identifying exclusively with none of the emergent phenomena. This is the third and ultimate type or level of play. In his delightful book *Finite and Infinite Games*, James P. Carse calls that ultimate level "infinite play." He remarks:

> A finite player is trained not only to anticipate every future possibility, but to control the future, to *prevent* it from altering the past. This is the finite player in the mode of seriousness with its dread of unpredictable consequence.
>
> Infinite players, on the other hand, continue their play in the expecta- tion of being surprised. If surprise is no longer possible, all play ceases.
>
> Surprise causes finite play to end; it is the reason for infinite play to continue . . .
>
> Because infinite players prepare themselves to be surprised by the future, they play in complete openness. It is not an openness as in *candor*, but an openness as in *vulnerability*.[15]

Carse also makes this all-important observation:

> Since finite games can be played within an infinite game, infinite players do not eschew the performed roles of finite play. On the contrary, they enter into finite games with all the appropriate energy and self-veiling, but they do so without the seriousness of finite players. They embrace the abstractness of finite games *as* abstractness, and therefore take them up not seriously, but playfully. (The term "abstract" is used here accord- ing to Hegel's familiar definition of it as the substitution of a part of the whole for the whole, the whole being "concrete.") They freely use masks

in their social engagements, but not without acknowledging to themselves and others that they are masked. For that reason they regard each participant in finite play as *that person playing* and not *as a role played by someone*.[16]

It should be clearly understood that the enlightened being, who is a player of the infinite variety, does not *merely* take part in the usual activities of the human species. Neither does such a being *merely* disidentify with those conditions, in which case we could expect him or her to be either an autist or a mystic in a state of introverted ecstasy or trance. Rather, the enlightened adept's simultaneous participation and nonidentification are grounded in transcendental identification with Being. He or she is the Identity in which all processes of participation or nonparticipation, identification and nonidentification occur. In the *Yoga-Vasishtha* (V.77.7ff.), a marvelous Sanskrit work of the tenth century A.D., such a being's paradoxical condition is described as follows:

He does not concern himself with the future, nor does he abide in the present, nor does he recall [i.e., live in] the past, but he acts out of the Whole. (vs. 7)

Sleeping, he is awake. Awake, he is like one asleep. Performing all actions, he "does" nothing whatsoever inwardly. (vs. 8)

Inwardly always renouncing everything, devoid of desires within and performing externally what is to be done, he remains [perfectly] equable (*sama*). (vs. 9)

Remaining perfectly happy and experiencing enjoyment in all that is expected [of him], he performs all deeds, [always] abandoning the misconception of doership. (vs. 11)

[He behaves] as a boy among boys; an elder among elders; a sage among sages; a youth among youths, and as a sympathizer among the well-behaved afflicted. (vs. 14)

He is wise, gracious, charming, suffused with his enlightenment, free from stress (*kheda*) and distress, an affectionate friend. (vs. 16)

Neither by embarking on the performance of action nor by abstention, nor by [such ideas as] bondage or emancipation, underworld, or heaven [can he be disturbed]. (vs. 19)

When the phenomenal world is perceived as the unitary [Being], then the mind fears neither bondage nor emancipation. (vs. 20)

Several key ideas touched on in this excerpt deserve exegesis. In the first stanza, the phrase "he acts out of the Whole" is found. This is another way of saying that the enlightened being acts perfectly spontaneously. The Whole is not any perceptual or cognized wholeness, or gestalt, but the totality in which wholenesses, or gestalten, appear. That Whole is, therefore, not merely a representation in the consciousness of the enlightened being. It *is* the enlightened being. In a recent issue of *Parabola* dedicated to the theme of wholeness, David F. K. Steindl-Rast relates an autobiographical anecdote that is relevant here:

> Wholeness has intrigued me ever since we boys built sand castles on the beach. You built a perfect world. You surrounded it with a moat. You looked up, and there was some incongruous beach chair, a blanket, or simply somebody's leg, out of scale and totally out of context. No way to bring this out-of-bounds reality into your wholeness. So I learned the lesson early on: Wholeness is not truly whole until it is all-inclusive.[17]

To act out of the Whole, then, means to act out of the all-inclusive Identity of existence, or the transcendental Ground of the world. This is the place or position in which there are no incongruities, in which perfect play is not only possible but actually the case. The nature of that play is hinted at in the second stanza, which speaks of the God-realizer's active life of nondoership, an idea that is further expanded in subsequent verses. Action, or process, is the mark of phenomenal existence—a notion that is conveyed in the two most frequently employed Sanskrit words for "world," *bhava* ("becoming") and its cognate *samsara* ("confluence"). Hence, complete inaction is impossible, as the anonymous composer of the *Bhagavad-Gita* (III.5) had clarified already in pre-Christian times. The real question is, What type of action can and should an individual perform, and in what disposition? Here the *Bhagavad-Gita*, the New Testament of Hinduism, recommends the spiritual approach of "action-transcending action" (*naishkarmya-karman*). How this is to be accomplished is explained in the following stanzas:

> In action alone is your [rightful] interest, never in its fruits. Let not your motive be action's fruit, nor let your attachment be to inaction. (II.47)

> Steadfast in Yoga perform actions abandoning attachment, O Dhanam-jaya [=Arjuna], and remaining the same in success and failure.—Yoga is called equability (*samatva*). (II.48)

> This world is action-bound, save when this action is intended as sacrifice. To that end, O Kaunteya [=Arjuna], engage in action devoid of attachment. (III.9)

> Hence always perform, unattached, the right deed. For, the man who performs action without attachment attains to the supreme [condition]. (III.19)

What is recommended here is an essentially paradoxical attitude in which what is renounced is the notion of "doership" rather than action itself or a certain kind of action. In action-transcending action, the actors express their transcendental identity—as pure Being-Consciousness. They pierce through

the web of their numerous projected identities and identifications with phenomenal processes. They extricate themselves from their models, which are
all forms of what the Shaiva adepts of Kashmir call *atma-samkoca*, the "collapse around the ego." Thus, action-transcendence means the transcendence
of the presumed "actor," the ego. In enlightenment, this action- and ego-
transcending movement is rendered permanent.

In enlightenment, the resolution of the limited self-sense, the ego, makes
room for spontaneity. The personality becomes suddenly malleable, truly
protean. For the enlightened being there is no "face" to be lost or to be
preserved. Like a chameleon, he or she can assume the colors of the environment. The enlightened man can be, as the *Yoga-Vasishtha* has it, "a boy among
boys," and "an elder among elders." And he alone can truly empathize,
because his psychic boundaries are infinitely flexible. To him everyone and
everything is indeed the same Whole.

Because the enlightened adept is not an "egoized" individual, he or she can
playfully embrace all beings, things, and situations. But this embrace is not
wantonness. Hedonism presupposes an egoic enjoyer, a seeker after pleasure.
As art historian Ananda Coomaraswamy observed:

> Under the sway of modern hedonism, where nothing is accepted as an
> end, and everything is a means to something else, the preconditions for
> understanding Sahaja scarcely exist. Sahaja has nothing to do with the
> cult of pleasure. It is a doctrine of the Tao, and a path of non-pursuit. All
> that is best for us comes of itself into our hands—but if we strive to
> overtake it, it perpetually eludes us.[18]

The enlightened being is neither an ascetic nor a hedonist, although his or
her life-style, for which the keynote may have been struck in the pre-
enlightenment period, could be that of a hermit with few needs, or it could be
that of a political leader, a physician, or a scientist with numerous responsibilities. (Let us remember here that not every enlightened being necessarily
has a full-fledged teaching function!)

Of course, enlightened persons are not immune to the law of cause and
effect. If they eat wrongly, their stomachs will ache. If they cut their fingers,
they will bleed. And if they misunderstand something, they will draw the
wrong conclusions. They are not omniscient, omnipresent, and omnipotent—at least not in the usual sense of these terms. Their omniscience transcends the particulars of knowledge. And the omnipresence of fully illumined
persons does not pertain to the material-sensate order. It is, rather, their
ability to be present without obstruction, to shine like a bright light to
infinity. Likewise, their omnipotence is neither physical nor mental. It is the
stream of life itself, the transcendental energy (*shakti*), out of whose inconceivable "mechanics" enlightened beings spontaneously enact whatever is
needful in the moment, as would we all without the interpolation of the ego
mechanism.

The ego chronically fears to be overpowered, to lose control. This is the underlying reason for much of the criticism of spiritual masters. It is also at the root of the widespread rejection of spiritual discipline and spiritual states of consciousness. But some form of influence by another is integral to all conditional existence, which is an interdependent process. Da Love-Ananda once observed that one can be "God-possessed," "other-possessed," or "self-possessed." In speaking of "God-possession," he did not use this phrase in a conventional sense. He clearly meant to refer to the God-realized condition, in which there is no possessor or possessed. There is only the one Being. Only from the viewpoint of the ego does its own prospective eclipse by the larger reality appear as a threat. In avoiding God, or Being, the ego-personality inevitably chooses not autonomy but self-possession or other-possession.

Some mystics, especially those who speak from within a deistic tradition such as Christianity, occasionally avail themselves of metaphors that depict the *unio mystica* as a form of possession.[19] This can be misleading, even relative to the experience of mystical unification, which I do not equate here with ultimate enlightenment. When the mystic is overwhelmed by the beatific vision, his or her self or ego is temporarily suspended. Thus, there is no subject to be possessed by an "other." Possession states may hold true of the Biblical prophets, trance mediums, and shamans. They have, however, nothing to do with enlightenment.

In the mystical state as well as upon full enlightenment, which is permanent, all opposites coincide: *coincidentia oppositorum*—the great secret of mystics and alchemists alike. This is *sahaja* or, in Buddhist Tantric terminology, *yuga-naddha* (lit. "pair-cord"). The phrase evokes the image of a strong, tightly twisted rope. The expression applies more specifically to the iconographic depiction of the sacred intercourse between God and Goddess, intertwined in ecstatic forgetfulness. In the Tibetan language, this esoteric imagery is appropriately called *yab-yum*, meaning "father-mother," and represents transcendental Consciousness and its Power respectively.

From the "frog perspective" of the unenlightened mind, the masculine (consciousness) aspect and the feminine (power) aspect of the one transcendental Reality appear to be distinct. In the enlightened condition that seeming separateness is dispelled. Then it is obvious that there is, as the Buddhist writer Advayavajra put it, "identity of emptiness and compassion" (*shunya-kripayor aikyam*).[20] To our finite logic this is barely more than gibberish. We may, however, intuit something of the great truth that is being conveyed here in paradoxical language. And such intuition is our most valuable endowment. If logic will lead us to its antipodes, where we can permit analogy and feeling to come into play, our binary intellect will have served us well. As Ananda Coomaraswamy remarked:

> The last achievement of all thought is a recognition of the identity of spirit and matter, subject and object; and this reunion is the marriage of

Heaven and Hell, the reaching out of a contracted universe towards its freedom, in response to the love of Eternity for the productions of time. There is then no sacred or profane, spiritual or sensual, but everything that lives is pure and void. This very world of birth and death is also the great Abyss.[21]

Once the individual is liberated from the burden of the scission between subject and object that is fundamental to the unenlightened state, he or she is also freed from the peculiarly human need to take play seriously—a need whose ubiquity becomes quickly apparent when one watches grown-ups and even children at play. The enlightened being is inherently blissful, relieved of the cumber that weighs down the ego. That does not mean such a being will inevitably walk about with a big smile on his or her face. A permanent smile would be a grimace. The delight of enlightenment is not an emotional state. It definitely leaves its mark on the human body-mind, but it is not *of* the body-mind. The body-mind will continue to experience typical human states, including anger, sorrow, grief, and ordinary joy or pleasure. But there is no longer any egoic identification with those states or with the body-mind as a whole. The enlightened being "experiences" himself or herself as the very Identity of *all* conditioned phenomena, while the particular body-mind with which the enlightened person has been historically and exclusively associated continues to be so associated in the eyes of the unenlightened observer.

The body-mind, carried by its own momentum, will continue to follow its course within the web of psychophysical existence. And the recognition that everything is as before, that enlightenment makes no difference—because the ego that was clamoring for the advantages of enlightenment is transcended— is an occasion for huge laughter. Just as spiritual life seems crazy to the conventional mind, mundane life, indeed all of life, appears crazy to the enlightened being. But unlike his or her unenlightened counterpart, who takes everything very seriously, the self-transcending person is not threatened by the craziness of conditioned existence. Therefore, he or she is free to see the humor of the fact that life is always out of control—the control of the self.

Enlightened humor should not be confused with mere gaiety, mirth, gleefulness, or jocosity, which tend to be self-defensive, escapist reactions. Even where genuine humor breaks through in an unenlightened individual, it is qualitatively different from enlightened humor because the latter happens outside the lattice of the ego. Enlightened humor belongs to the realm of infinite games. Unenlightened, finite-game individuals always play for keeps. They have a program, which they pursue in earnest. They have no real humor, and their laughter ill conceals their secret awareness that the game is destined to be frustrated. They know all along that, despite their pretensions at immortality, they will die.

Enlightened, infinite-game persons, on the other hand, *fully* accept their physical mortality, and through this acceptance become capable of true humor and laughter. As James P. Carse comments:

Infinite play resounds throughout with a kind of laughter. It is not a laughter at others who have come to an unexpected end, having thought they were going somewhere else. It is laughter *with* others with whom we have discovered that the end we thought we were coming to has unexpectedly opened. We laugh not at what has surprisingly come to be impossible for others, but over what has surprisingly come to be possible with others.[22]

Enlightened humor springs from the recognition that all conditioned phenomena are themselves only the playful self-manifestation of the Divine. Such humor arises whenever we are, perhaps only for a brief spell, not in dread of our own mortality, when we glimpse the larger picture. According to legend, the Zen tradition originated with Kashyapa's smile of recognition when the Buddha silently held up a sandalwood flower as a means of instruction. In that moment, Being itself was communicated between the adept and the disciple. Kashyapa's mind stood still; entering the condition of *satori*, he burst through his usual frame of reference and awakened to Reality in its nakedness.

Kashyapa, in turn, transmitted the "Buddha-Mind" to his disciple Ananda. As Zen tradition recollects, Ananda once asked Kashyapa what he had received from the Buddha besides the robe and the begging bowl. Kashyapa apparently answered with a cry, "O Ananda!" When the disciple responded with "Yes," Kashyapa asked him to take down the flagpole at the gate of the monastery. This request was enough to instantly dissolve Ananda's mind forms and plunge him into *satori*. The *satori* state is not simply a silencing of the mind; rather, it is a new state of being. The limits of the ego-personality and its characteristic body concept are shattered. In this sense, we can understand Da Love-Ananda's otherwise unintelligible observation that the adept's laughter "is one of his vague attempts to blow himself to smithereens! True laughter is shattering."[23]

If ordinary life is the humorless, serious repetition of oneself, then spiritual practice is continuous humorous re-creation, or re-orientation, by which the self and its motives and finite games are outwitted. And it is the teacher's equally humorous and seldom thankful task to reveal to the disciple when and where he or she misses the mark by playing the same old patterns and programs over and over again. As with the Corinthian king Sisyphus, the guru's toil is unending. He or she is curiously moved to liberate the world, yet knows the task cannot possibly succeed. As the modern adept Da Love-Ananda has confessed:

There is the urge to Enlighten every being, and then there comes the realization that it is impossible to do. That is the joke. The impossibility makes a joke of spiritual Teaching. Spiritual Teaching is a primal urge, like sex, you see, but it is bound to be laughed at. It must become a laughing matter so that the Teacher can go on to something else.

This Teaching is also a kind of joke, an expression of my sense of humor. I am a clown, don't you see? I do everything for the sake of good

humor. You are able to see the Brightness of God only through respond-
ing properly to his fool—in other words, by getting the "jokes" of the
Teaching of the Adept, by transcending the world in his Company. If you
do not laugh at God's fool, then you do not see God. The way to God is
through God's fool, God's clown, one who has already transcended the
world.[24]

The adept invites disciples to laugh at "God's fool." But, simultaneously,
the adept asks them to laugh at themselves and the world. The guru plays, as
Alan Watts observed, a "countergame," in which the rules of the ego's game
are turned upside down like an hourglass.[25] The logic of this countergame
demands that spiritual teachers should, on occasion, poke fun at themselves
and their teaching. Where the adept and the teaching are made into an icon
and become part of the ego's search for fulfillment and consolation, they
forfeit their value as an index of Reality. Authentic spiritual teachers never set
themselves up as a permanent monument in the disciple's mind. Rather, they
avail themselves of all kinds of ploys to crush whatever images and cultic
attitudes the disciple has created to freeze the fleeting image of the *guru*. It
behooves the teacher to disappoint the practitioner's "appointments," or still
frames of reality, especially the most treasured "snapshots" of the guru.

In order to instruct, to reflect back the disciple's self-limitation, the adept
may animate in himself or herself the disciple's character qualities, or their
opposites. Because the adept is an infinite-game player, he or she can be
anybody whatsoever and remain completely unpredictable. There is a wild-
mannered crazy-wisdom teacher in every guru, regardless of his or her
spiritual standing, for every guru has the same job: to coach the disciple
toward freedom, authentic existence, true humor.

However, the crazy-wise adept is a trickster par excellence. Such an adept
plays his or her role as "disappointer" of deep-laid conventional notions with
gusto. Using all manner of theatrical contrivances, the adept constantly
counters the normal order of things to highlight the endless ways in which
people trap themselves in modes of thought, attitudes, emotional disposi-
tions, and forms of behavior that they confuse with reality. Da Love-Ananda,
who has been more forthright about the function of the guru than many other
past and contemporary teachers, offered this comment in one of his early
works:

> Everyone is enchanted with unreality, with the conventional appearance
> of every moment. Therefore, one cannot break that spell merely by
> talking to people. They are not just thinking wrongly. They are associ-
> ated with each moment in such a manner that they are incapable of being
> Awake to their actual Condition. So, in effect, you must cut them in half
> with a big sword. You must blow their minds. You must shake them
> loose. You must wholly divert them. You must trick them. You must be
> wild to truly Enlighten people.[26]

The crazy-wisdom adepts, whose shape-shifting capacity is phenomenal, make an art out of reversal. Ideally, in their skillful hands, everything becomes a means of awakening others, of beguiling them, as Søren Kierkegaard would say, into the truth.[27] The masters of crazy wisdom expose the ordinary individual's constant trivialization of life by uninhibitedly "acting out" the desires and tendencies of the worldling, as when they take on the appearance of wine bibbers and womanizers. In this way they not only satirize the common individual, but also and above all negate the popular dichotomy between worldliness and spirituality by deliberately crossing the conventional boundary between purity and impurity. Thus, they collide with and call in question a whole range of deeply rooted beliefs and attitudes.

Despite the religious skepticism and moral stagnation of our secularized civilization, most people's sensibilities are still adjusted to a premodern morality. In general, and when it suits them, they hold to puritanical notions of good and evil, pure and impure, inherited from Victorian times. Thus even those who do not consider themselves especially religious can be quite disturbed when they find out that this or that supposedly enlightened being drinks alcohol, smokes, has sexual intercourse (possibly with more than one partner), takes drugs, lashes out in fury, curses, utters obscenities, and perhaps even blasphemes. Somehow such behavior is felt to be a rude breach of an unspoken, sacred covenant. They seldom stop to ask themselves whether that covenant is not merely a "sacred cow" of the egoic mind, which likes to keep the profane neatly separated from the sacred.

To show that all taboos are human-made and to point beyond them to Reality is the mad adept's self-appointed task. Little wonder that throughout history the fools of God have not fared too well at the hands of those they sought to instruct. They were often abused, verbally and physically, and not a few were murdered. Today, perhaps a more enlightened attitude is possible. It is natural enough that we should feel offended by some of the escapades of crazy-wisdom masters. But instead of taking the easy option of righteous indignation, wholesale condemnation, or angry retaliation for our offended sensibilities, our first obligation is to cultivate the light of understanding, including self-understanding.

In some cases, however, a crazy-wisdom teacher may well have been guilty of overzealousness and misjudgment that caused harm to another human being. This raises serious questions about the appropriateness and usefulness of crazy-wisdom teachings in our time, and also about the moral and criminal liability of teachers who work in this manner. I will examine this crucial issue next.

# 11

## HOLINESS, MADNESS, AND MORALITY

### 1. Madness and Holy Madness

Holiness and madness—like genius and insanity—have traditionally been viewed as closely associated. As we saw in Part One, every major religious tradition has an antinomian aspect that appears to the conventional mind to be madness. From the spiritual perspective of the crazy-wise adept or holy fool, however, that madness is a matter of sheer spontaneity or "divine play" (*lila*), that is, self-abandonment to the world-process (or "will of God"). Far from seeing themselves as certifiable, these spiritual madcaps have tended to understand their own eccentricity as worthy of duplication. As St. Teresa of Avila expressed it: "Let us all be mad, for the love of Him Who was called mad for our sakes."[1]

Here I propose to examine more closely the interface between crazy-wise spontaneity and the personality structure through which it is expressed. Specifically, I want to consider the possibility that holy madness may at times include components that, from a Western psychiatric perspective, could be labeled "neurotic" or even "psychosis-like." Some adepts, past and present, have unhesitatingly confessed to their own madness. I have already discussed what this means in spiritual terms. For the moment I am primarily interested in a psychological understanding of their eccentric behavior. I see the psychological and the spiritual explanations as intersecting rather than as clashing with each other. Thus, the controversial Bhagwan Rajneesh once stated, "Don't be afraid that I am going mad or something. It is impossible. How can a madman go mad again? . . . I am a little crazy. Everyone knows it so no need to worry."[2] And later he said, "But trust my insanity. The more insane I am, the closer I am to truth."[3]

Given Rajneesh's later personal history, which we have touched upon in Chapter 3, this pronouncement has import over and above its spiritual significance. Likewise the contemporary teacher Da Love-Ananda has remarked about himself, "I have always been Crazy, from the moment of my birth. I have been Crazy my entire life."[4]

For a while, Da Love-Ananda even permitted devotees to address him as "Crazy Da." Recently, a close, longtime disciple commented, "You think he is joking when he says he is mad. He really *is* mad!" In 1979, this adept surprised devotees by announcing that he was Mickey Mouse; just like himself, Da Love-Ananda said, Mickey must be understood as a transcendental icon. During one of the many evenings of celebration and inebriation in the same year, he broke into "ecstatic speech":

> I am the headless horseman. If you put me on the Dawn Horse, I will hold my hat in the air because there is nothing above my collar but the evening.[5]

Da Love-Ananda has described his extraordinary, "headless" condition in terms reminiscent of the self-reports of hallucinating schizophrenics:

> My spine tastes sour. My eyebrows are milky. My forehead is odorous and my hairs are unacceptable to me. Having seen this about my own form, I have decided to reach out and exceed the limits of my proportions and save myself with philosophy that involves the navel and the heart of life. And Light is my expression. I am a poet and dead![6]

He further elaborated that poets were once valued but are now considered rather useless—and such is the fate of gurus. He called himself "dead" because he no longer shares the values of the world. He has become a "headless horseman," that is, free from the constraints of the conventional mind. Next he advised his devotees, "You must become exaggerated and inappropriate, as I have"[7]—a suggestion that, in the hands of an immature disciple, could prove disastrous.

The contemporary Hindu *avadhuta* Vimalananda is reported to have said, "Either I must be mad or everyone else is; there are no two ways about it."[8] Robert E. Svoboda, a disciple of Vimalananda, proffers this explanation of his teacher's remark:

> Who was Vimalananda? The more I remained in his company the less I knew about him. He really was "no-body": there was no one personality present perpetually in his body which could be pinned down and categorically identified as his. He could be hard and soft by turns, alternately refined and coarse according to his environs. One memorable night we started off dining elegantly at a posh Turf Club party and ended up, as fate would have it, listening to music in the middle of Bombay's red light district. Vimalananda finally took up an instrument himself and taught the delighted prostitutes a new song, just for fun!
>
> Psychiatrists would probably classify Vimalananda as schizophrenic ... Though no psychiatrist I am a licensed physician, and, in my

opinion (an opinion shared by those who lived with him for many years
before I met him), he was far saner than the rest of the world.[9]

What does it mean when the adepts confess to being mad? How mad is
mad? Must we understand their self-declared lunacy in purely metaphoric
terms? Or could high spiritual attainments possibly be compatible with
actual psychopathological states? In other words, could a spiritually advanced
person, or even an enlightened being, suffer from neurotic or psychotic traits?
I will try to answer this question as equitably as I can. But let us first ask:
What *is* madness in psychological terms? There is no clear-cut definition of
insanity. Clinically, mental illness is labeled "psychosis"; in Freudian terms, it
is characterized as the ego's loss of control over the id (or unconscious).
Different types and degrees of psychotic breakdown are distinguished, and
the two most important are manic-depressive states and schizophrenia, which
have their own subcategories.

To begin with, manic-depressive states are generally found among persons
who, prior to the onset of psychosis, are outgoing and sociable, if moody.
Once the psychotic state is established, these mood swings become quite
dramatic. In the depressive phase, the person is suicidal; in the manic phase he
or she is highly energized, restless, and elated. In the acute state, the person
becomes impulsive, violent, and uninhibited. These symptoms are often
combined with delusions of grandeur. The psychiatrist unsympathetic to
metaphysics might detect manic elements in the adept's self-declaration that
he or she has stepped outside the orbit of conditioned existence, is utterly free
and autonomous, in fact is one and the same with God. What, for instance,
would an orthodox psychiatrist make of Da Love-Ananda's several "death"
experiences and his unpredictable outbursts of anger, which on occasion have
involved physical violence?

Schizophrenics generally belong to the sensitive, introvertive personality
type; prior to the schizophrenic breakdown, they tend to be shy and retiring,
as well as inept at social intercourse. Either their penchant for daydreaming
then gradually worsens or schizophrenia strikes them suddenly like a light-
ning bolt. Schizophrenics show flat or incongruous feeling responses. They
may show no reaction at all to pain and misfortune, or laugh and giggle
inappropriately. In contrast, pleasant experiences may cause them to burst
into tears. Feelings are thus split from events. Schizophrenics become apa-
thetic and disinterested in themselves and the world.

Schizophrenic withdrawal invites comparison with the attitude of icy indifference found in many spiritual adepts. Crazy-wisdom masters are characteristically unattached and preach indifference to the world as a noble virtue.
Although often they live in the society of devotees, they typically manifest
sublime apathy, or what the Greeks called *ataraxia*, toward everything. As
preserved for posterity in many photographs, the "bored" expression on the

face of the late Ramana Maharshi, one of modern India's most celebrated sages, is perhaps an indicator of this very inner disposition. Photographs of other gurus give one the same impression.

The paranoid schizophrenic projects his or her deep-rooted desires into voices and visions, as well as into feelings of augmented significance. This immediately suggests the mystical experiences recounted by adepts, their frequent denunciation of the world as a place of doom, and not least their insistence that the ego is a falsity that must die. For the psychoanalyst there is no Reality, or transcendental Consciousness, beyond the id and the ego. Therefore, within such a reductionist framework, the death of the ego can logically signal only the triumph of the unconscious, that is, disintegration of the personality.

A third type of schizophrenia is the hebephrenic state, in which the person behaves oddly and often indulges in fantastic notions with a religious tinge. Some psychiatrists would presumably have no difficulty in fitting elements of holy folly into this category. After all, the crazy-wise adept is an eccentric par excellence, and his or her ecstatic babbling about being identical with the blissful Self, which eclipses the ego, sounds distinctly weird to the rational, antimetaphysical mind. Often the hebephrenic individual's flighty talk includes sexual references, and this is certainly also true of some crazy-wisdom masters. Sexual metaphors, puns, and obscenities are so much part and parcel of the countless talks given by one contemporary adept that published versions of his talks have been carefully edited by devotees more sensitive to public relations than he.

At its most extreme stage, psychosis involves a splitting of the psyche into independent functional units ("multiple personalities"). This psychiatric category might be thought to include the chameleonlike ability of crazy-wise adepts to assume different characters. However, a more plausible explanation for the adept's shape-shifting capacity is provided by the psychological theory of subpersonalities. According to this theory, the human personality is composed of semipermanent and semiautonomous regions each of which can act as if it were the "I."[10] If we accept this model of psychic functioning, we can better understand not only our own complex behavior but also the rapidity with which adepts can animate vastly different responses. Hitherto such changes have been explained in terms of role-playing. But it would seem that distinct roles elicit from us different semiautonomous response patterns (or "subpersonalities"), which is why we can slide into and out of particular roles so readily and also why on-the-spot conversions are possible. However, it is up to psychologists to argue the merits of this theory. Here I am solely concerned with understanding spiritual phenomena from a psychological perspective without reducing them to purely psychological or psychiatric categories, as has all too often been the case.

The parallels between psychosis and religio-spiritual states are instructive.

As philosopher Ben-Ami Scharfstein, who refuses to take the metaphysical claims of mystics seriously, has remarked:

> I think that if the writing of admitted mystics and admitted psychotics is compared line by line, image by image, conviction by conviction, they will often not be distinguishable. Both, as we have seen, can share the feeling of the immensity and incommunicability of their experience. Both can be totally happy. Both can feel that they contain the universe or are joined with it in a surpassing union. Both can be overwhelmed by the sudden conviction that they see the truth now bare. Both can believe that they have godly wisdom and benevolence. Both can use Jehovah's self-definition and say of themselves, 'I AM.'[11]

However, Scharfstein agrees that "psychosis" and "mysticism" refer to distinct experiential syndromes. As he puts it succinctly, "The psychotic is ill with the mystic's cure."[12] That is to say, that although the mystic is hale, despite any psychosis-like manifestations or experiences, the psychotic is diseased (or, perhaps, "dis-eased"). It would therefore be foolhardy to claim that crazy-wise adepts are by definition psychotic.

We can characterize insanity as a state of diminished functioning in which the person is profoundly out of touch with reality, and in which he or she is incapable of upholding moral distinctions between right and wrong. Of course, some clinicians insist that there is no such thing as insanity at all. In the opinion of Thomas Szasz, mental illness is the name we give to a particular strategy of coping with life.[13] In his earlier career, R. D. Laing regarded schizophrenia as a "communication disease" that strikes a given family.[14] In his later writings, however, he went so far as to suggest that schizophrenics do not suffer from a psychiatric disability but are engaged in a natural process of healing themselves. Groping for a definition of schizophrenia, in *The Politics of Experience*, Laing arrived at the following pessimistic conclusion:

> Schizophrenia is a label affixed by some people to others in situations where an interpersonal disjunction of a particular kind is occurring. This is the nearest one can get at the moment to something like an "objective" statement, so called.[15]

Since Laing admitted that the schizophrenic "disjunction" is of a particular kind, it should have been possible for him to qualify his definition further. But this was clearly not his intention. As he saw it, schizophrenics are struggling toward wholeness—a process that, for Laing, had mystical overtones. In his own words:

> Rare experiences, difficult to explain socially and virtually invariant across the world, do indeed occur, in saints and sinners, geniuses, crazy people and even in otherwise apparently ordinary people. For the purpose of putting a stop to this sort of thing, it is useful to regard them as signs of disease, and to classify them as delusions and hallucinations, or what not.[16]

Laing understood the insane individual as a spiritual voyager, while the so-called normal or sane individual is really the one who is suffering, because he or she is alienated from the spiritual process of life. Therefore, he concluded, we ought not to interfere with schizophrenics by trying to bring them back to conformity. In his book *The Voice of Experience*, Laing told the story of a middle-aged woman who, after many years of unhappy marriage and growing disillusionment with life, was suddenly filled with an inexplicable love.[17] She reported love pouring into her body through the back and illuminating her. She conceived of a new purpose: to communicate to others that love was what was missing from their lives. After only a few days of this euphoric state, she was diagnosed as "manic" and was tranquilized and given electroshocks. Her sense of love was wiped out and her newly won purpose in life was extirpated. But she was "cured" and could resume her normal existence. Luckily, her experience had left her with a vague hope that one day love would return to her life.

Ten years later, she consulted Laing, who simply allowed her to talk without passing judgment on her. Then the same experience of overwhelming love recurred, on a Good Friday, and she decided to permit it, regardless of the consequences. She stripped off all her clothes and prepared a safe place for herself—a lair under the kitchen table. In her inward imagination, she became a hound, growling and prowling around the country house. On the following Easter Monday, she came back to consciousness as a naked lady curled up in a blanket under the kitchen table. She had healed herself.

There is a wonderful logic and symbolism in this rebirth, this transmutation from "insanity" to "sanity." We find a similar logic and symbolism pervading the spiritual traditions of the world, which have at their core an equally dramatic rebirth—the *metanoia* or turnabout of the ordinary individual into a being who is sensitive to the larger spiritual context. What is more, had Laing's patient been a member of a different culture, she might have been welcomed as a spiritually gifted individual rather than diagnosed as insane.

As Karen Horney has shown, a person is neurotic or psychotic only within the framework of a specific culture.[18] What is neurotic in a Euro-American context may be considered quite normal elsewhere. To some extent, we also can apply this knowledge to so-called psychotic states. What appears as a terrible breakdown of the personality *may*, from certain cultural perspectives, include elements of a genuine breakthrough. The psychosis may even reveal itself to be an authentic mystical state for which there is no separate category in our secular Western culture, with its impoverished lexicon of spiritual phenomena. However, and this is where Laing and others have gone astray in their idealism, psychosis is not necessarily an idiosyncratic pathway to wholeness. It may simply be collapse, ending in disintegration.

We would also do well to note that our "normal" everyday life is shot with psychopathological or quasi-schizophrenic conditions. There are few people who do not suffer from one mild neurosis or another, and some border on what is called the schizoid, a form of dissociation in which individuals tend to encapsulate their feelings to protect themselves against hurt from other people and the general lovelessness of our competitive society. The inevitable conclusion is that normalcy is little more than a statistical mean or an ideal standard.

To come back to our original question: Can there be psychopathological elements present in spiritually transformed personalities? Or more specifically, can we identify some of the eccentric behavior of adepts as neurotic or psychotic, as those terms are understood by Western psychiatry? The answer is yes and no. First, we must realize that a fully enlightened being cannot be straightforwardly labeled either neurotic or psychotic. Both neurosis and psychosis are "diseases" of the ego-personality, or, if we side with radical psychiatrists, they are efforts to heal the ego–personality. Since the ego is transcended in enlightenment, these labels obviously cannot apply. Yet, as we have seen in earlier chapters, enlightened adepts of the past and the present have apparently displayed behavioral traits that in the ordinary individual would be deemed neurotic, possibly even psychosis-like.

It would appear that holy fools or crazy-wise adepts are at the far end of the spectrum of what some cultures find permissible as part of religious or moral life. They are, I propose, liminal characters who travel the no-man's-land between sanity and insanity or normalcy and abnormality. The more a culture emphasizes the ego and reason, the less likely it is to tolerate crazy-wise conduct and the more likely it is that an adept teaching in this fashion will be branded insane. This, however, would be not a medical judgment but a moral and political one that has the implicit purpose of maintaining the status quo.

What would our culture make of Sri Ramakrishna, one of the best-known saints of modern India and the teacher of the world-renowned Swami Vivekananda? Ramakrishna once confessed that he had to curb his impulse toward crazy behavior in the company of his devotees. He also recollected that, when he was going through a phase of heightened spiritual craziness, he used to worship his own penis as the cosmic principle of creativity (or *linga*). Some psychologists of religion would regard this behavior as neurotic, perhaps even bordering on the psychotic. At any rate, it *is* highly eccentric. Had Ramakrishna lived in the West and been caught in the act, he might well have ended up in an asylum.

From within Ramakrishna's own definition of reality, however, his strange impulse made perfect sense: The body is a microcosmic replica of the cosmos and, at root, divine. Hence it is worthy of reverence and worship as a manifestation or expression of the greater Reality. Moreover, far from being a burden on the health-care system, Ramakrishna the madcap was destined to fulfill a positive social function in his own country. He was venerated as a saint, even as a "full descent" (*purna-avatara*) of the Divine, inspiring an entire generation of religious Hindus, and he was an influential factor in the renaissance of Hinduism in modern times and its dissemination in the Western hemisphere.

It is difficult to say whether Ramakrishna was a fully enlightened being, and opinions on this matter have clashed even during his lifetime. However, while we may credit Ramakrishna with high mystical attainments, we can still question whether some of his experiences would not have been labeled "mad" even within the context of traditional Hindu society. After all, he himself admitted to a phase of accentuated "craziness." Agehananda Bharati, an Austrian-born Hindu monk and renowned scholar of Hinduism who does not mince words, puts it this way:

> He [Ramakrishna] was a strange and unusual priest, unlike his fellows: more devout though less civilized, and perhaps even a little off his head. It is in any case not easy to draw the line between mania and trained mysticism. In fact if there had always been trained psychiatrists we should probably have far fewer mystics and holy men in our various calendars than we have now.[19]

Bharati, who incidentally is a former member of the Ramakrishna Order, does not tell his readers outright whether or not the diminution of mystics and holy men would be a loss. But it is clear from his later comments that, in his view, many of the inmates of Indian monasteries are in need of psychiatric counseling.

Early in his spiritual practice, Ramakrishna was unable to sleep for six years; his eyes refused to close. One time he tried to force them shut in front of a mirror, but failed. His hands went numb when he touched money. We can look upon these phenomena as yogic manifestations or as physical symptoms of a psychosis-like condition. Even some of Ramakrishna's own disciples were concerned about, and exasperated by, his more eccentric behavior. We need not deny Ramakrishna's spiritual accomplishments and generally saintly character to entertain the possibility of his having suffered from neurosis-type patterns—by Western and by Indian standards. The same holds true of numerous other mystics, both Eastern and Western.

To offer one more illustration: As a child, the saint Anandamayi Ma, who is widely venerated in India as an incarnation of the Goddess Kali, was believed by her parents to be retarded. The reason for this belief was that she liked to talk to plants and invisible beings. For several years, from her seventeenth year on, she would become cataleptic during devotional chanting. People thought she was possessed by evil spirits and enlisted exorcists to effect a cure, but they were either too afraid or too awed by her presence to do any good.

Anandamayi Ma would frequently become absorbed in spiritual states that left her body cold, discarded like a rag doll. Efforts to bring her back to body-awareness were futile, and she always returned to ordinary consciousness according to an inner law, sometimes after ten hours or more. On other occasions, her eyes would remain wide open with a vacant stare, and her body would give the impression of having melted against the floor. During chanting sessions, she often experienced violent muscular contractions (called *kriya* in Sanskrit), or she would roll on the ground in undulating movements in rhythm with the music, only to rise with upstretched arms, balancing on her big toes alone. Then her skin color would turn crimson and her hair would stand on end in ecstasy. She would also succumb to bouts of weeping and laughter that could last for more than an hour.

At one point, Anandamayi Ma barely took any food and ate only what was placed directly into her mouth. Devotees tried to train her to feed herself but gave up after she persistently used some food to feed others and rubbed the rest into the floor. She called her body "the doll" and did not mind her devotees treating it as an object to be bathed, dressed, decorated, mollycoddled, and worshipped. There was also a pronounced impish side to her character. Arthur Koestler commented on it thus:

> She liked to tease her devotees and to display a kittenish behaviour, though sometimes her playfulness could more appropriately be called cruelty . . . But Indians are accustomed to their cruel female deities.[20]

## 2. The Personality of Adepts: Self-Transcendence and Compassion

Arthur Koestler recollected an incident that happened while he was sitting at Anandamayi Ma's feet, admittedly not sensing any magic emanating from her and feeling rather awkward amidst doting devotees. An old woman approached the dais and begged Anandamayi Ma to intercede for her son who was missing in action after a recent border incident. The saint ignored her completely. When the woman became hysterical, Anandamayi Ma dismissed her rather harshly; this was a signal to the attendants to conduct the suppliant out of the room. Apparently, the female *avatara* had declined to show compassion or love.

Devotees are expected to demonstrate devotion and not to beg the Divine for favors. Gods and their representatives on earth clearly do not always hear their devotees' even most fervent prayers. Indeed, they may violate not only their most cherished expectations but also the rules by which people seek to relate to the sacred or to each other for that matter—the very rules that were established by divine fiat in the first place. Hence historian of religion Alf Hiltebeitel can speak of "criminal" deities.[21] These are gods who step beyond the established moral and sacred boundaries. Of course, if we regard the Divine as the transcendental per se, such "transgressions" of the moral order should not surprise us. The God who transcends space-time also transcends the moral realm. Did not the righteous Yahweh of the ancient Israelites murder and maim his enemies?

Probably most of the devotees who witnessed the incident reported by Koestler thought nothing of it. If asked, they might have expressed slight feelings of disapproval toward the old woman for making a display of herself, but it would undoubtedly never have occurred to them to question the disinterest shown by Anandamayi Ma. Because she was one with the Divine, her judgment was assumed to be infallible. Koestler, a Westerner who definitely did not share the devotees' frame of mind, was taken aback by Anandamayi Ma's indifference to the woman's suffering.

Was Koestler right in concluding that the saint was, in that moment, lacking compassion? Or should we assume that the native Hindu interpretation was correct, namely that Anandamayi Ma—as a supposedly enlightened being—acted spontaneously, out of the fullness of the Divine, and that her inherent compassion was manifested by her display of outward indifference, throwing the woman back on her own sorrow for mysterious reasons known only to the Divine? The two explanations need not, I propose, be incompatible. Another factor in the picture, which Koestler ignored, is the fact that in India, and in the East in general, individualism is not as pronounced as in our part of the world, and individual persons are not accorded the same value.

Granting for the sake of the argument that Anandamayi Ma was fully enlightened, we must assume that her life was informed by the "transcendental" motive to be a benign presence in the world, a vortex of transformation, and to draw all beings into the mind-transcending blissful condition that she herself appears to have enjoyed. The impulse to illumine others seems to be a natural concomitant of enlightenment, though it may not always crystallize in the desire to teach. In other words, not all adepts are gurus. But even gurus who do cater to the spiritual needs of disciples will not, indeed cannot, continuously channel this transcendental desire or will into concrete, recognizable acts of compassion.

Such acts are necessarily based on selective attention. For instance, an adept addressing a large gathering may not notice, or choose to notice, a specific individual. On the other hand, there are anecdotes of adepts who on occasion appear to have simultaneously interacted with *more* than one person, perhaps even with people who were miles apart. If true, these reports merely demonstrate that an adept—and indeed the ordinary person—exists on more than the physical plane. On the physical level, at any rate, the adept can focus his or her attention on only one given locus at a time.

Let us assume that a guru is displaying anger in reprimanding a disciple. If the disciple is spiritually mature, he or she will, though shaken by the teacher's outburst, still sense the guru's generalized compassion. The disciple may even believe that the teacher's shouts or blows are appropriate and necessary. However, while the teacher is thus being angry, he or she is not being *actively* compassionate toward another disciple who happens to be standing nearby. Similarly, the guru may focus his or her attention on reading or interpreting a scripture. In that moment, the adept's attention is collected in the act of reading or interpreting rather than on *actively* radiating love.

We must clearly distinguish between *generalized* and *intentional* compassion. This dualism is part of the paradox of the spiritually advanced mystic or enlightened being. Its explanation is to be found in the same paradoxicality by which mystics or adepts can, as I assert, display neurotic traits or have experiences reminiscent of psychotic states. How is this possible? The answer, I think, is relatively simple: The aptitude for spiritual experiences or states is as much a specialization of attention as, say, the capacity for high intellectual or aesthetic creativity. Mystics are spiritual geniuses. But, like intellectual, literary, musical, or artistic geniuses, they can be—and perhaps typically are—subject to psychic imbalances, which we call neuroses or psychosis-like conditions.

Here it is important to remember that, in the present volume, mystics and saintly folk are not treated as fully enlightened beings. How, then, does this consideration apply to those who have permanently awakened, in the sense that the buddhas or *maha-siddhas* have awakened to and as the ultimate Reality? Enlightenment, as has been explained, does away with the ego. It consists in the transcendence of the ego-habit, that peculiar sense of being somehow identical with the body-mind. But enlightenment, or God-realization, does *not* obliterate the personality. If it did, we would be justified in equating it with psychosis.

That the personality of enlightened beings—just as of advanced mystics—remains structurally largely intact is instantly obvious when one examines the available biographies and autobiographies of adepts past and present. Each one manifests his or her specific psychological qualities, as determined genetically and by his or her life history. Some are more inclined toward passivity; others are spectacularly dynamic. Some are typically gentle, others congenitally fierce. Some have no interest in knowledge and learning; others are great intellectuals. What the fully awakened beings all have in common is that they no longer identify with the personality complex, however it may be configured, but live on the basis of the identity of the Self. U. G. Krishnamurti, who claims to be enlightened (and who must not be confused with Jiddu Krishnamurti), has made these telling comments:

> The personality does not change when you come into this state [of enlightenment]. You are, after all, a computer machine which reacts as it has been programmed. It is in fact your present efforts to change yourself which are taking you away from yourself and are keeping you from functioning in the natural way. The personality will remain the same. Don't expect such a man to become free from anger or idiosyncracies. Don't expect some kind of spiritual humility. Such a man may be the most arrogant person you have ever met, because he is touching life at a unique place where no man has touched before.

It is for this reason that each person who comes into this state expresses it in a unique way, in terms which are relevant to this time. It is also for this reason that if two or more people are living in this state at the same time they will never get together. They won't dance in the streets hand in hand—"We are all self-realized men; we belong."[22]

The fact that the basic personality structure, or character, is essentially the same after enlightenment as it was prior to that incisive event raises the interesting question of whether enlightenment also leaves untouched traits that in the unenlightened individual might be called neurotic. As I have indicated already, my own conclusion is that this is in fact the case. An adept's psychological idiosyncracies are inextricably bound up with his or her spontaneous presentation in the world. Each adept, as Da Love-Ananda once observed, represents a particular limitation in space-time.

This is a very important point, which is too often ignored by those who place their whole life at the feet of a spiritual teacher. Even assuming that the guru is fully enlightened, the disciples' submission to him or to her frequently derives from a neurotic need to abdicate authority and have a father or mother figure make life decisions for them. What they fail to understand is that adepts, though identifying or identified with the transcendental Reality, are still incarnate. As incarnate beings, they are susceptible to making mistakes and misjudgments. *Errare humanum est.* In fact, the more adepts abandon themselves to the spontaneity arising within themselves and the less they censor their own actions, the more their behavior is apt to clash with the conventional expectations and standards of their devotees and the "factual" world. In practice, disciples will be exposed to a constant frustration of their own will and design, which is manifestly not possible for everyone. This also contains the considerable danger of violating the personal growth of some devotees.

If the guru's personality displays pronounced authoritarian traits, as is often the case, this places a heavy burden on the devotee not only to clone himself or herself in the guru's spiritual image but also to emulate the teacher's psychophysical personality. The result is a cult, with the guru as the golden calf. In that case, personal growth and spiritual maturation are only a remote prospect. Traditionally, such literal emulation has been warned against. In practice, however, it is the rule rather than the exception.

Enlightenment does not abolish ignorance, and, contrary to many traditions, the enlightened being is far from omniscient. Despite the psychic fluidity and spontaneity of awakened beings, they cannot—in their appearance in space-time—help but be themselves (as determined by their genetic and basic psychological makeup). If they are true teachers, or what the Hindus call *sad-gurus*, their overriding purpose can be expected to be the communication of the transcendental Reality. Yet their behavior is, in the final analysis, always a matter of personal style.

For example, some male adepts have demonstrated crazy wisdom by initiating numerous women through sexual contact, but they have carefully steered clear of homosexual encounters. Since the transcendental Reality is genderless (or omnigendered), this can only be interpreted as a personal predilection—however spontaneous. Devotees, of course, like to think that their ideal guru is free from whims—and that all apparent idiosyncracies must be for the sake of teaching others. A moment's reflection would show this to be based in fantasy and projection. This is not to say that even the adept's most idiosyncratic conduct may not, indirectly, serve the students' awakening. But for the teacher's conduct to be truly helpful, the devotees must recognize it for what it is. Only a realistic relationship to a guru can possibly bear benign fruit.

Some teachers have claimed that their conduct reflects the psychic state of those with whom they come in contact; that their crazy-wisdom exploits are, in other words, triggered by disciples. This may well be so. I have already commented on the chameleonlike quality of the adepts. But such mirroring still proceeds along personal lines. For instance, most gurus will not sit on garbage heaps, consume human flesh (as did the modern Tantric master Vimalananda), or meditate on corpses to instruct others, but those few who do engage in such practices might not consider training their intellect or acquiring musical skills in order to serve a disciple better.[23]

Whatever explanations a teacher may offer for his or her crazy-wise behavior, students should always remain sensitive to the fact that no adept, whether enlightened or not, is infallible or incapable of further growth. Any such claim could, in my view, be taken as a sure sign that there is either lack of self-understanding on the part of the teacher or a definite attempt to deceive. In either event, the disciple is imperiled. Contrary to popular New Age opinion, there are no "perfect masters." Ken Wilber puts it very well:

> Perfection exists only in transcendental essence, not in manifest existence, and yet many devotees consider their master "perfect" in all ways, the ultimate guru. This is almost always a problematic sign, although it is rarely disastrous. It is problematic for the devotee because, in confusing essence with concrete existence, the devotee is invited to project his or her own archaic, narcissistic, omnipotent fantasies onto the "perfect" guru. All sorts of archaic and magical primary process cognitions are thus reactivated: The guru can do anything; how great the guru is; in fact, how great I must be to be among the chosen. It is an extremely narcissistic position.
>
> Of course, the guru eventually displays his or her human side, but the devotee is devastated, disillusioned, crushed. . . . A good master might indeed be fully enlightened and divine, but he or she is also human. Even Christ was said to be one person (Jesus) with two natures (human and divine). Further, the fact that a guru has been thoroughly educated in soul and spirit does not mean he or she has been thoroughly educated in body and mind. I have yet to see a guru run a four-minute mile with his

"perfect body" or explain Einstein's special theory of relativity with his "perfect mind."[24]

In the absence of perfection in the conditional realms of existence, the peculiar eccentricity of the enlightened adepts who teach in the crazy-wisdom mode is potentially dangerous. They see themselves as not quite human; but rather, they identify with the suprahuman transcendental Reality that lacks all distinction. Their actions are, by their own statements, purely spontaneous. There is no ego to intervene. And where there is no ego-identity, we must assume that there is also no superego or conscience. Yet, clearly, they are not clinically insane. Once the premise of their nondualist metaphysics is accepted, their "rantings" and "ravings" make sense in a spiritual context. The danger lies in the fact that their mission to communicate that state of transcendental unity is inevitably filtered through a particular individual psyche (or personality), which is to be distinguished from the ego-mechanism. In other words, their spontaneity, powered by the impulse to enlighten others, intermeshes with and is overdetermined by the patterns of the finite body-mind. The enlightened adepts cannot even be considered neurotics, despite possible neurosis-like personality traits, because those particular traits appear in the context of ego-transcendence. Yet this does not rule out the possibility, as I will shortly affirm, that even fully awakened beings may still have some work to do on their own body-minds.

By extension, it is easy to see why crazy-wise adepts who are not yet fully enlightened could be potentially even more dangerous than enlightened masters who teach in eccentric ways, since their egos are not yet utterly transcended and therefore may give rise to a host of misperceptions and even delusions, as well as ulterior motives. The least danger, perhaps, is associated with adepts who, like the Fools for Christ's Sake, check their mystical impulses toward apotheosis with a healthy dose of old-fashioned humility in the face of the Divine. Of course, as we have seen, the metaphysical dualism of the holy fools has the disadvantage of generally cutting short the spiritual process. So long as the father image is projected onto the Divine, the mystic cannot completely realize the transcendental Reality, which voids the ego-personality, and which is itself experienced as the Void.

The personality of the adept is, to be sure, oriented toward self-transcendence rather than self-fulfillment. However, it is characteristically not on a self-actualizing trajectory. I understand "self-actualization" here in a more restricted sense than it was intended by Abraham Maslow: as the intention toward realizing psychic wholeness based on the integration of the shadow into consciousness.[25] The shadow, in Jungian terms, is the dark aspect of the personality, the aggregate of repressed materials. The individual shadow is ineluctably tied up with the collective shadow. The integration of the shadow into consciousness is not a once-and-for-all event but a lifelong process. Integration can occur either prior to enlightenment or subsequently. If integration is not a conscious program of the preenlightened personality, it is also unlikely to form part of the postenlightened personality, because of the relative stability of the psychic structures.

The claim has been made by some contemporary adepts that in the breakthrough of enlightenment, the shadow is entirely flooded with the light of supraconsciousness. The implication is that the enlightened being is without shadow. This is difficult to accept as a statement about the conditional personality. The shadow is the product of the near-infinite permutations of unconscious processes that are essential to human life as we know it. While the personality experiences life, unconscious content is formed simply because no one can be continuously aware of everything. The uprooting of the ego-identity in enlightenment does not terminate the processes of attention; it merely ends the anchorage of attention to the apparent center of the unenlightened body-mind, which we style the "ego" or "ego-identity." Moreover, as I have shown, the enlightened being continues to think and emote—both processes that leave an unconscious residue, even when there is no inner attachment to them. The important difference is that in the realizer the unconscious residue is not experienced as a hindrance to ego-transcendence simply because ego-transcendence has already been accomplished.

Not a few adepts have resolved this issue by admitting that there is a "phantom ego," a vestigial functional center, even after awakening as the universal Reality. If we accept this proposition, then we could perhaps also speak of the existence of a "phantom shadow" or a "vestigial shadow," which permits the enlightened being to function in the dimensions of conditional reality. In the unenlightened individual, ego and shadow go together, and we must postulate an analogous polarization between the phantom ego and the phantom shadow of the personality that functions on the basis of enlightenment.

The *yogin* is traditionally said to create *karma* that is neither black nor white—but he still creates *karma*.[26] In the *Bhagavad-Gita* (III.4ff.), the oldest known Yoga scripture, we find a clear enunciation of this principle. Here the God-man Krishna explains to his disciple Arjuna that life means action (*karma*); in other words, so long as the body-mind is animated, it is forced to be active. All actions, however, leave their traces in the unconscious. Just like life and death, consciousness and shadow are natural polarizations. They continue to inform conditional reality even after enlightenment. Despite the claims of some spiritual traditions that assert the possibility of an immortal transubstantiated body, the body-mind of the enlightened adept is just as liable to sickness and death as the body-mind of an ordinary mortal.

Even if we were to assume that enlightenment illumines and evaporates the shadow, we must still seriously question whether this illumination corresponds to integration. Integration, as I see it, is the basis for higher self-transformation. This means that it involves intentional change—change in the direction of psychic wholeness that is noticeable to others. When I examine the lives of contemporary adepts who claim to be enlightened, I do not see the evidence that such integration work is being done. One of the first indications of it would be a visible willingness not only to reflect disciples to themselves but also to have disciples be a mirror for the adept's own further human growth. However, this kind of willingness calls for an openness that is precluded in the authoritarian style adopted by most gurus.

The traditional spiritual paths are by and large grounded in the vertical ideal of liberation *from* the conditioning of the body-mind. Therefore, they focus on what is conceived to be the ultimate good—the transcendental Being. This spiritual "mono-ideism" jars the human psyche out of focus: The concerns of the psyche become insignificant and its structures are viewed as something to be transcended as quickly as possible rather than transformed. Of course, all self-transcending methods involve a degree of self-transformation. But as a rule, such self-transformation does not entail a concerted effort to work with the shadow and accomplish psychic integration. This explains, I think, why so many mystics and adepts are highly eccentric and authoritarian, and appear socially to have weakly integrated personalities.

However, we must not necessarily equate eccentricity or weak social integration with psychic dysfunction. As James Royster has argued, "before the depths of mystical experience can be fully plummeted, a certain amount of psychic health must prevail."[27] The emphasis must be placed on "*fully* plummeted," because psychotics apparently can experience conditions quite similar to, if not identical with, certain mystical states.

Integration, as understood here, occurs in the horizontal plane. It extends the ideal of wholeness to the conditional personality and its social nexus. Yet integration makes sense only when the conditional personality and the conditional world as such are not treated as irrevocable opponents of the ultimate Reality but are valued as manifestations of it. Psychologist Erich Neumann has articulated this problem very clearly. He characterizes the former, vertical attitude as "pleromatic mysticism," saying:

> It is a view of the world which has attracted a great deal of attention in our time. It involves an attempt to disregard reality in its character of existent givenness. It is "pleromatic" in the sense that the pleroma, the fullness of the divine nature as it was before the world began, when the Godhead had not yet entered into the world, is regarded as the "real" state of the world. It is mystical because relationship or relatedness with the pleroma can only be achieved in a mystical or illusory manner . . . The ego attempts to evade the problem of the darkness and the shadow side of the world and of man in an illusory way by means of a mystical,

inflationary expansion of the individual who equates himself with the pleroma, the primal spirit, the Godhead, etc., soars into the realm of the infinite and the absolute and loses his identity in the process.[28]

Neumann contrasts this pleromatic mysticism with what he labels "nihilism," by which he means positivism in the broadest sense of the term. Both approaches are essentially monistic. In the one case, the spiritual is elevated to the sole principle of reality; in the other case, matter is given ultimacy. As he went on to argue, either orientation involves the abdication of individual responsibility for the shadow in oneself and in the social body.

Responsibility is the key to any spiritual practice aimed at comprehensive wholeness. Maslow, perceptive as always, offered these germane comments:

> This matter of responsibility has been little studied. It doesn't turn up in our textbooks, for who can investigate responsibility in white rats? Yet it is an almost tangible part of psychotherapy. In psychotherapy, one can see it, can feel it, can know the moment of responsibility. Then there is a clear knowing of what it feels like. This is one of the great steps. Each time one takes responsibility, this is an actualizing of the self.[29]

As I have explained in previous chapters, spiritual practice proceeds on the basis of dissent from consensus reality, the "normal" universe of the ordinary person. But this must not lead to endless self-isolation, as is symptomatic of some forms of mysticism. Such self-encapsulation would be merely another excrescence of narcissism. Having discovered the Divine in the depths of his or her own soul, the mystic must now find the same Divine in all other beings and things. This is, in fact, the mystic's principal obligation and responsibility. To put it differently, having drunk at the fountain of life, the mystic must complete the spiritual opus and practice compassion on the basis of the recognition that everything participates in the universal field of the Divine. As the masters of Mahayana Buddhism knew, the awakened life unfolds in the creative tension between gnosis (*prajna*) and compassion (*karuna*).

## 3. Holy Folly and the Transcendence of Good and Evil

Most of us prefer our spiritual teachers to be gentle, even-tempered paragons of virtue. As we have learned in this volume, they seldom are. And not one embodies perfection, since perfection does not exist in our finite universe. Therefore, we must be wary of our idealistic projections, which can obscure the spiritual path. On the other hand, the popular stereotype of the spiritual teacher as a Jesus-like figure of surpassing benignity and sweetness does contain a sound instinct. We should expect our teachers, especially those who profess to be enlightened and who teach in the crazy-wisdom style, to demonstrate great wisdom and equally great compassion.

We should, moreover, expect them to demonstrate exceptional skill (*upaya*) in their mission to illumine us. What good are knowledgeable physicians if their bedside manners are so poor that they erect a wall between themselves and their patients? Conversely, what benefit can we hope to derive from a consultation with a physician who is congenial and charming but lacks the knowledge for a correct diagnosis and treatment? Spiritual teachers are "physicians" of the psyche in its deepest aspects. Their influence on disciples is momentous and fateful, and in some instances has even proven fatal. Traditionally, the link between teacher and disciple is said to endure beyond death. But even if we do not subscribe to this ancient belief, we can readily appreciate the profundity of the teacher-disciple relationship, which affects all aspects of the disciple's life and which involves massive responsibilities on both parts.

Spiritual life is full of risks, for disciples and teachers alike. Gurus have a thankless and near-impossible task, especially in our secular era, and they are in the same precarious position as physicians who face the constant threat of legal action by disgruntled clients.[30] Western disciples are notoriously fickle in their perception of the guru and in their commitment to the spiritual process. They are torn between the desire to catch a glimpse of Reality, or God, and the powerful impulse to affirm and assert themselves. It is difficult for them to submit to discipline and the authority of the teacher. But this difficulty has characterized seekers of premodern periods and cultures as well.

Then again, disciples of all eras have had to confront the possibility that their teacher may not be authentic or sufficiently qualified to guide them. But beyond any personal liabilities that a teacher may have, his or her very role is hazardous to the ego-personality that likes to dabble in spiritual matters but really resents and resists interference, divine or otherwise. As Da Love-Ananda has admitted, "The Guru enacts the threat of the Divine, which is an absolutely transforming and absorbing Force . . . So the Guru is a dangerous person."[31]

George B. Leonard made much the same point when speaking about the figure of the mystic, who is "most dangerous of all."[32] Even though, as Leonard conceded, mysticism has frequently given rise to rigid structures, the mystical impulse has just as often torn those very structures down again. The whole point of mysticism or spiritual esotericism is to undermine conventional reality so that transcendental Reality can shine forth. Spiritual life is intrinsically deconstructive, and in its crazy-wisdom format it is often antinomian.

As we have seen, the function of the adept is to provoke a deep spiritual crisis in the disciple—a crisis that is intended to lead to a spiritual breakthrough, and ultimately to illumination. Given this declared objective, the eccentric ways of crazy-wisdom masters may seem legitimate enough. These teachers seek to create chaos in the disciple in order to break down all these emotional-mental patterns that prevent enlightenment, or authentic being. However, in their efforts to deconstruct the normal world of the disciple, crazy-wisdom adepts have been known to far exceed the boundaries of both morality and the law. While this may have been admissible in traditional societies, in our own time it raises serious questions.

This issue has been broached in the book *Spiritual Choices*, edited by Dick Anthony, Bruce Ecker, and Ken Wilber. These authorities distinguish between authenticity and legitimacy in spiritual groups—a useful distinction that can also be applied to spiritual leaders. As Ken Wilber explains, authenticity has to do with change in the group's or institution's deep structure ("transformation"), whereas legitimacy has to do with change in the surface structure of a group or institution ("translation"). Adapting this model to our present consideration, we can say that a spiritual leader, or guru is "authentic" when he or she facilitates transformational (vertical) growth in disciples. Again, a teacher is "legitimate" if he or she facilitates integration or coherence within a given level of structural adaptation to the spiritual process. That is to say, an authentic and legitimate teacher will not only encourage disciples to grow beyond their present level of adaptation in the scheme of psychospiritual evolution, but he or she will also respect disciples' present psychospiritual status and encourage them to consolidate their present growth.

Thus, an authentic and legitimate teacher will do nothing either to shock disciples into stasis or to push them beyond their capacities. Rather, he or she will be tolerant and compassionate while persisting in the effort to encourage disciples to move beyond their present level of psychospiritual maturity. As should have become clear by now, this does not mean that the spiritual process will not include deep valleys of despair that disciples must traverse with great courage and faith. It also does not mean that the teacher cannot or should not resort to harsh means at times. But the adept's ploys to attract his or her disciples into self-surrendered life should always be appropriate and tempered by compassion. This measured approach is illustrated well in an auto-biographical account by Irina Tweedie, a modern Sufi practitioner. In her invaluable diary, she recounts numerous instances when her teacher contrived to plunge her into utter despair but then always provided her the means of resurrecting herself. He proved a hard taskmaster, yet would also demonstrate to her his unwavering commitment to her growth and not least his love for her. She recollects the following rebellious exchange with her teacher, who had once again pushed her to the limits of her endurance:

> "There are many things in your environment, your family and your way of life which I could point out as being far from perfect!"
> "I don't want to listen to you!" he hissed at me. "You don't know how to respect people like me; you never learned what respect and reverence mean! You are an ignorant, dense and stupid woman, and you try to preach to me?"
> "I am nothing of the sort!" I retorted angrily. "I have had enough of this treatment. You are an arrogant autocrat . . . For nine months now I have been pleading for help but it is of no avail."

"Did I give you your trouble? . . ."

"But it is *you* who put me into this state!" I shouted, beyond myself with fury. "All I ask is do it gently! I understand why it is done, that it is necessary, but have a heart, I am at the end of my strength."

"Nonsense!" he shouted back, leaning forward and glaring at me. "You idiot!"[33]

The apparent ill-treatment continued, and in the end, "Guru Maharaj" even threatened to expel her from his hermitage. But much later, he explained, "No, I was not angry, never angry, never. No such feelings are there for you in my heart."[34]

Chögyam Trungpa spoke of "ruthless compassion" and even recommended it to advanced practitioners of spiritual life. This prompted the following thought-provoking conversation between him and a student:

Q [student]: What if you feel the necessity for a violent act in order ultimately to do good for a person?
A [Chögyam Trungpa]: You just do it.
Q: But if you are not at that point of true compassion and wisdom?
A: You do not question or worry about your wisdom. You just do whatever is required. The situation you are facing is itself profound enough to be regarded as knowledge. You do not need secondary resources of information. You do not need reinforcement or guidelines for action. Reinforcement is provided by the situation automatically. When things must be conducted in a tough manner, you just do it because the situation demands your response. You do not impose toughness; you are an instrument of the situation.[35] . . .
Q: This ruthless compassion sounds cruel.
A: The conventional approach to love is like that of a father who is extremely naive and would like to help his children satisfy all their desires. He might give them everything: money, drink, weapons, food, anything to make them happy. However, there might be another kind of father who would not merely try to make his children happy, but who would work for their fundamental health.[36]

When asked whether ruthless compassion does not lend itself to the considerable danger of abuse through self-deception, Trungpa agreed and observed that the lawful practice of this ideal presupposes self-understanding, mature meditation, and a sense of humor. Trungpa's unqualified answer that violence is a valid means in the spiritual process is alarming. However, this belief reflects an attitude that is common in spiritual circles and is closely associated with the paternalism so prevalent in the spiritual traditions, which treats the seeker or disciple as a child. This has repeatedly led to situations of abuse.

Trungpa's endorsement of violence smacks of the radical antinomianism that has caused the downfall of teachers like Bhagwan Rajneesh who, abandoning the insight he had shown at other times, once grandiosely announced:

I am such a con-man. Even my ears are trained, they hear only what they
want to hear. My eyes are trained, they see only what they want to see.
For the simple reason that I want to live the way I want. I have always
lived according to my own way, right or wrong. I don't care. *If* there is a
God, and I have to face Him, He will have to answer to me, not me
answer to Him.

I have lived my own way. I am not answerable to anybody.[37]

The guru is a charismatic person of great power. Not to feel answerable to
anyone—not even the Divine—is a sign of hubris rather than illumination;
such an attitude bodes ill for disciples. Accountability and responsibility are
important instruments of balance in the spiritual process that takes place
between teacher and disciple. When they are scorned we find power games
and abuse, as has been amply demonstrated in recent years by the fallen angels
of spiritual and religious life in America and elsewhere.

One of the most atrocious and harmful aspects of such moral failure is the
sexual abuse of disciples by unscrupulous or irresponsible mentors. Addressing this issue, the editors of *Spiritual Choices* arrive at this conclusion:

A spiritual master who sexually exploits a trusting disciple is comparable to a parent who sexually molests a child. Erotic feelings, tensions,
and dependencies are a normal part of children's healthy development,
but the sexually exploitative parent (or master) massively compounds
these erotic tensions, failing to meet the unguarded child's (or disciple's)
critical need for a way of resolving them and severely undermining his or
her self-esteem. To be thus betrayed and used as an object by the very
person from whom one most needs deep regard, understanding, and
support, and who represents one's whole world of meaning, does great
psychological harm with long-lasting emotional repercussions.[38]

Dick Anthony and Bruce Ecker, who are responsible for the above statement, are adamant that there is no possible justification for sexual activity
between gurus and disciples. They deny that sexual intercourse could conceivably promote the disciple's endeavor to transcend the limitations of conventional morality. They even reject the traditional Tantric argument that
sexual intercourse with an adept is a form of spiritual transmission:

Most female disciples who describe the effects of sexual intercourse with
a master report not inner spiritual progress but deep psychological
wounds and spiritual disillusionment and derailment.[39]

While this may indeed be so, Anthony and Ecker's discussion is not without a certain bias. This is obvious from statements like the following:

Our own understanding of the unitive heights of spiritual gnosis is that
the fully truth-realized master has shed all limited identifications with
matter, energy, and mind and directly experiences being the infinite,
eternal, formless reality or Godhead, the true nature of all beings and

things on all planes of existence. This is a permanent state of infinite completeness, freedom, knowledge, power, and bliss . . . *Sexual desire, which is based on the duality of feminine and masculine qualities, could not exist in this fully truth-realized state* [my emphasis].[40]

Anthony and Ecker speak of this God-realized state as one of "perfection." This choice of words harbors their apparent belief that full enlightenment is exclusive of desires, especially of the sexual variety. This implicitly puritanical bias is still more evident from an interview that *Clarion Call* magazine conducted with Anthony. When asked about the relationship between morality and transcendence, he responded by defining conventional morality as "arbitrary etiquette" and then proceeded:

You have to somehow go beyond morality, but as far as I can understand, true saints never contradicted conventional morality. At the most they flouted social conventions . . . So masters have often flouted simplistic rules of etiquette in a way that offended the expectations of their superficial disciples because they were trying to force their disciples to go to the heart of conventional morality in a purer sense and to become more indifferent to social conventions and social acceptance and rejection. But I cannot find any records of them breaking serious rules involving sexual immorality, or murdering people, or any similar serious violations of conventional morality, the likes of which you *can* encounter in contemporary spiritual groups in America.[41]

Although Anthony's heart-searching is honorable, his position is untenable. The traditional biography of Drukpa Kunley, for instance, reports quite clearly serious breaches of a variety of sexual taboos, which were even at that time considered to be instances of sexual immorality. As we have seen in Part One, there are many other adepts who have used sex to instruct actual or potential disciples. Anthony and Ecker's unqualified rejection of left-hand Tantrism—or what they quirkily style "Tantric Freudianism"—appears hasty and judgmental. Their dismissal is, however, consistent with their belief that enlightenment is free of all desires. By contrast, quintessential to the philosophy of the Tantric masters is the idea that desires and enlightenment are not stark opposites. This is epitomized in the dictum that conditional reality (*samsara*) and absolute Reality (*nirvana*) are coessential. A similar orientation was articulated in the *Bhagavad-Gita* (II.70), the New Testament of Hinduism, composed long before the Tantric scriptures:

Just as the river waters enter the ocean, full and of unmoving ground, so all desires enter him who attains peace, but not the desirer of desires.

In other words, desires are binding only when they revolve around the axis of the ego-personality. Upon enlightenment, desires do not cease to arise. On the contrary, the enlightened being is filled with desires, brimming with life-force. But he or she is not controlled by any of them. Non-Tantric adepts typically adopt a more puritanical, quietistic approach characterized by the nonexercise of desires, notably the sexual urge. For the Tantric masters, however, desires hold no threat, and so they do not pursue this strategy. Instead, they give themselves tacit permission to experience all kinds of desires, acting on some and not on others out of the spontaneity of their illumination. In their experience, far from fragmenting Being, desires are mysteriously arising in and as the Divine.

This position is difficult to accept so long as one adheres to a dualistic metaphysics, viewing God and world as antithetical. The predictable corollary of such a two-tiered philosophy is that God (or the ultimate Reality) is inherently good, whereas the world (or the human being) is intrinsically evil (or sinful). Accordingly, from the dualistic point of view the Tantric outlook must be condemned as positively immoral. It cannot be denied that the radically antinomian schools of Indian Tantrism have frequently given rise to a dangerous intemperance in the service of self-gratification rather than self-transcendence. But these degenerate excesses should not be used as the sole yardstick for judging Tantrism, even its left-hand branch.

The great vision of Tantrism is, to put it bluntly, that the Divine is not without genitals—that sexuality and spirituality are not incongruous aspects of human existence. Anthony and Ecker seem to espouse a philosophy that leans toward a neutered divinity and to favor a spirituality that hinges on the ideal of moral perfection, which makes the enlightened being a sexless, desireless monolith. I have criticized this view elsewhere and so will not repeat myself here.[42]

Nonetheless, I share Anthony and Ecker's concern about the kind of antinomianism that is associated particularly with left-hand Tantrism. It is one thing to experience or permanently realize the singularity of Being, and quite another to live in the realm of conditional reality as if there were no distinctions at all. In the moral sphere, this fallacy of "misplaced dimension" always manifests as the feeling or claim that the adept and perhaps even his or her disciples are above good and evil, that they are not subject to the existing law. In this respect the Nazarene adept Jesus was wiser. He admonished his disciples to "give unto Caesar what is Caesar's and unto God what is God's" (Mark 12:17).

When this distinction is blurred, we begin to move in perilous waters in which many have drowned. The absurdity and hazard of a transcendentalizing (unilevel) attitude in moral matters is brutally demonstrated in the antisocial antinomianism of mass murderer Charles Manson. Manson, who is serving a life sentence with no hope of parole, understood his diabolical rampages as a holy war. In his eyes, he was doing his victims a huge favor. He explained his philosophy thus:

> A free mind creating thought may seem in raw form to be mad. I'm not of your school-thought. Your world's thoughts are just as mad to me as I may seem to you.[43]

I don't think in goods or bads, just ISs.[44]

Fools think in life and death circles because they are locked in fear—No one ever dies—No one ever lives—Those are two words in a left over game.[45]

I am love . . . True love casts out all fear. If you're afraid of me then there's something wrong with you.[46]

The jurors were not allowed to hear Manson's hour-long testimony lest his persuasiveness should influence them unduly. In his testimony, Manson stated, "In my mind I live forever . . . I am only what you made me. I am only a reflection of you."[47] He concluded his rambling, associative speech saying that he did not mind being sent back to the penitentiary where he had spent most of his life anyway. He finished with "Prison's in your mind . . . Can't you see I'm free?"[48]

Many of Manson's remarks could have been and actually were uttered by genuine mystics. In *Our Savage God*, R. C. Zaehner highlighted the parallels between helter-skelter "Mansonism" and the activist spirituality of the *Bhagavad-Gita*, in which the God-man Krishna admonishes his devotee Arjuna to do his military duty and not be daunted by the possibility of killing friends and relatives on the enemy's side.[49] We know that Manson had dabbled in Scientology and had also studied Masonic rituals and occultism during his earlier incarceration. His "family" indulged in what they called Tantric sex, and several of Manson's female followers claimed that he would continue intercourse until his partner had "died," that is, experienced ego-loss.

We may value the ideal of action that is not self-motivated, as expounded in the *Bhagavad-Gita* and other scriptures. We may appreciate, for instance, Prince Arjuna's nonpacifist *karma-yoga*, for sometimes it is necessary to defend the good and the just. Or we may empathize with the traditional story of the prostitute in the *Milinda-Panha*, a Buddhist scripture, who goes about her business with magnificent dispassion. According to the story, her very disinterestedness bore unusual fruit, for she acquired the paranormal power to reverse the flow of the river Ganges. But this ancient ideal has its built-in limits. Otherwise we would also have to admire the murderer who, taking his role seriously, slaughters innocent men, women, and children with the utmost aloofness. Disinterestedness alone is not enough. Alas, some gurus make just this claim and seek to justify their "transmoral" status thereby. But adepts are above good and evil only in their ecstatic realization. In their embodied condition, they are as susceptible and liable to moral considerations as the next man or woman. Otherwise we must treat them on a par with the truly insane, who are moral morons.

Similarly, the adept's transcendental motive to illuminate others is also not sufficient in itself. The teaching function that comes alive in some adepts can be compared to the essential social role of a warrior, a prostitute, or a philosopher; it is engaged with passion and yet also with sublime indifference, for adepts know full well that their voice will be heard by very few. However, their zeal to teach and uplift must be carefully calibrated to the situation. This is possible only when it is matched by an equal degree of wisdom (or discernment) and compassion (or love). In other words, in theologian Paul Tillich's phraseology, the guru-function must be tempered by what Tillich calls *kairos* ("the right moment") and *agape* ("love").[50] Translated into Buddhist language, these are *prajna* (gnosis) and *karuna* (compassion).

In their realization or experience, adepts may be above good and evil. In their actions, however, they are not. Mysticism and morality must be spliced to form a spirituality that does not sink into the morass of a bottomless antinomianism, but that still has the vitality to effectively transmute our lives.

# EPILOGUE

Adepts—masters of spirituality—come in all magnitudes of spiritual accomplishment. Many are authentic, but some are not. Many teach in a legitimate way, but some do not. Most adepts present themselves in a manner that, though inevitably in opposition to consensus reality, is sufficiently familiar as not to alienate us. A few, however, use their life as a symbol for what, from the conventional point of view, is the upside-down world of spirituality. These are the spiritual eccentrics we have discussed in this book. For the most part, they are essentially benign; yet they are always a living fire—a fire that can warm but also burn those who draw close to it. Their very being is a powerful challenge to the habits of the conventional mind and culture. They are luminous beacons signaling deep-level change.

Adepts have played this role for millennia, and in so doing have on occasion succeeded in releasing neurotic blockages not only in individuals but in the larger social body.[1] India, which is known for a fairly rigid social structure that permits little spontaneity, has yet shown enough flexibility to accommodate its own antithesis—the bohemian figure of the world-renouncer or ascetic, the spiritual dropout. Indian culture has thus been able to maintain itself in creative tension for millennia. Until the Communist Revolution, Chinese culture made similar provisions for its spiritual adventurers, and also benefited from their extraordinary explorations and viewpoints.

In stark contrast to these traditions, our contemporary Western society is forever trying to deny and repress its countercultural heroes, even though—as was clearly demonstrated in the far-reaching developments of the 1960s and 1970s—they can do much to infuse new lifeblood into the social organism. Many of the youthful rebels of those days saw themselves as the vanguard of a new humanity—at once more conscious and more caring. Although they were mostly fumbling in the dark, their protest against the status quo led to more widespread questioning. They were searching for self-knowledge in the hope of understanding the purpose of life. As Arthur Stein has argued, critics have been wrong in their wholesale dismissal of these existential probings as mere narcissism.[2] Beneath the narcissistic excesses of drugs and rampant promiscuity, we can also perceive the seeds of a genuine cultural transformation.

Today a good many of those same dropouts lead and support important movements of social change, especially those favoring environmental, feminist, and human, as well as animal, rights issues. By no means do all have what could be called a spiritual orientation. However, in their shared reverence for life, social activists are not too far removed from spiritual values; this is a healthy and a hopeful sign.

Part of the counterculture of the traditional Eastern societies is the grand ideal of liberation, or enlightenment. Our own Western society has as yet no such ideal. This is a regrettable defect and impoverishment, for without an equivalent ideal that celebrates the transcendence of the ego and consensus reality, we are condemned to a spiritual flatland. More than that, it is becoming increasingly clear that the environmental and social crises we face today cannot be overcome without a sweeping spiritual renaissance. This has nowhere been more insistently debated than in the work of the Swiss cultural philosopher Jean Gebser, who placed the whole issue in the fascinating context of the evolution of human consciousness.[3]

Gebser presented a richly documented model, which culminated in his insight that we are witnessing today the possible beginnings of a new structure of consciousness, what he called the "aperspectival-integral" consciousness. This emergent type of consciousness, or reality-perception, transcends the vacuous rationalism inherited from the nineteenth century just as it transcends romantic emotionalism. Nor must aperspectival-integral consciousness be confused with mystical states. Instead, that consciousness represents a condition of intensified wakefulness in which we become aware of the play of the psychohistorical structures that go into the making of our perceptual universe. That intensified awareness is coupled with the growing capacity to go beyond the inherent limitations of those structures and to experience life integrally. This emergent consciousness shares many of the aspects of authentic spirituality.

The big question is whether the religious-spiritual models of the past can serve our contemporary quest for self-understanding and higher spiritual adaptation. I think Carl Jung was right when he warned us against merely imitating the East and blindly abandoning our own historical roots. Yet we also cannot avoid feeling that Jung was perhaps overly impressed with the significance of the Western Judeo-Christian heritage. With the hindsight of the past two decades, we can perhaps envision a pluralistic culture that, without forsaking what is valuable in the Judeo-Christian tradition, also does not make immodest claims for it.

In order to round out the deliberations in the present book, I want to briefly consider the possible place of the spiritual teacher, notably the adept who is a divine madman, in our present-day effort to evolve a spirituality commensurate with our Western psyche. First, spiritual teachers exist, and they attract followers, but we do not at this point have a sufficiently sophisticated phenomenology to allow us to objectively evaluate their spiritual attainments and their abilities as communicators of the spiritual dimension. However, I have already given a number of helpful hints for those embarking on a course of spiritual apprenticeship. The single most important criterion is whether one experiences genuine growth as a disciple. In order to ascertain this the student must possess the emotional maturity to distinguish between reality and wishful thinking, that is, he or she must have the capacity for self-criticism.

This is especially necessary when the teacher presents himself or herself as enlightened, or when he or she teaches in highly eccentric ways. Here we must simply remember Rabbi Ben Zion Bokser's comments, which were made in a political context but which apply with equal force in the spiritual sphere:

> Tyrants, to rationalize their use of arbitrary power, have occasionally pretended to be God. They have claimed infallibility which is an attribute of God and not of man. All human claims to absolutism, as all acts of arbitrary power, are idolatrous. All power exercised by men has only relative authority. An important safeguard of freedom is, therefore, a recognition of man's fallibility . . . Man fulfills his highest self not when he conforms to others but when he finds the distinctive note his own life can play, and when he does indeed play it.[4]

Obedience to spiritual authority need not, and should not, negate personal freedom. As theologian Nels F. S. Ferre remarked, "genuine authority is for freedom."[5] And it appears that few travelers on the spiritual path can grow without guidance. Spiritual discipleship is the voluntary acceptance of constraints in order to facilitate one's own inner freedom. Thomas Merton, speaking from firsthand experience, proffered these insightful observations:

> A spirit that is truly drawn to God in contemplation will soon learn the value of obedience: the hardships and anguish he has to suffer every day from the burden of his own selfishness and clumsiness and incompetence and pride will give him a hunger to be led and advised and directed by somebody else.
>
> His own will becomes the source of so much misery and so much darkness that he does not go to some other man merely to seek light, or wisdom, or counsel: he comes to have a passion for obedience itself and for the renunciation of his own will and of his own lights.
>
> Therefore he does not obey his abbot or his director merely because the commands or the advice given to him seem good and profitable and intelligent in his own eyes. He does not obey just because he thinks the abbot makes admirable decisions. On the contrary, sometimes the deci-

sions of his superior seem to be less wise: but with this he is no longer concerned, because he accepts the superior as a mediator between him and God and rests only in the will of God as it comes to him through the men that have been placed over him by the circumstances of his vocation.[6]

Thus, obedience itself becomes a means of self-transcendence. Merton's views, which were shaped by the contemplative tradition within Christianity, can be applied to spiritual practice within non-Christian traditions as well. However, Merton's recommended attitude demands a spiritual maturity that few disciples or devotees possess. It also calls for a spiritual guide who, though he or she may err on occasion, has great integrity. Such a teacher is not readily found. Therefore, the best advice one can give to spiritual seekers is to aspire to Merton's ideal of obedience while remaining aware of the possibility of abuse. As St. Teresa of Avila said, "From foolish devotion may God deliver us!"[7] She seems to have had a no-nonsense attitude about spiritual directors. She felt a guide was essential but that "he must be a man of experience, or he will make a great many mistakes and lead souls along without understanding them or without allowing them to learn to understand themselves."[8]

My personal conviction is that, in due course, our age will develop its own characteristic spirituality and that this will give rise to a new class of spiritual guide. The traditional guru type, I submit, is generally too autocratic and paternalistic for our modern sensibilities. Hence the Eastern-style guru-centric approaches are bound to fail in the West, obliging us to look at alternatives. Those who are spiritually "musical" will look and call for new maestros—teachers who are also learners, who wear their halos lightly, and who do not mind sticking their feet in the humus of life in order to walk with their fellow beings, including those who are not of the privileged white middle class.

Certainly, the new type of spiritual teacher will have a healthy sense of humor and will be able to inspire the same in others. We need to invite the figure of the spiritual clown back into our midst, if only to ease the psychic burden of living in such troubled transitional times as our own. As theologian Harvey Cox suggested, we need the equivalent of the medieval Feast of Fools:

> The Feast of Fools flourished during a period when people had a well-developed capacity for festivity and fantasy. We need to develop that capacity again today. We cannot and should not try to resuscitate the jesters and gargoyles of the Middle Ages. But neither need we exclude medieval man entirely from our consciousness. We can benefit from the experience of that time to enrich and vitalize our own, just as we can learn from other historical epochs and other civilizations.[9]

Cox feels we need a rebirth of festivity and fantasy. He is absolutely right. He is aware that this means establishing a world that is "much more heterogeneous, messier, more sensuous, more variegated, more venturesome, more playful."[10] For the same reason, I venture to suggest, we need the religious fool, the clowning guru who can serve us as a signal of transcendence.

In these times, we need the holy fool not as an instigator of orgies and havoc but as a mediator of the sacred. This means we must look at the legitimacy of his doings, and we must be prepared to respond to his antistructure game not only with self-abandonment but also with a measure of rationality. We do not live in the past. Responsibility is necessary. Chögyam Trungpa reminded Ram Dass of this fact, and it is tragic that he failed to heed his own wisdom.

The new type of teacher-disciple relationship is likely to be more dialectical, allowing for "information"—and humor—to pass more freely between both partners of the process. Because of the weak individualism and the strictly hierarchical way of thinking of the East, few traditional gurus have permitted a dialogue between themselves and their disciples. As Jungian therapist Peter Coukoulis has noted, Ramakrishna and Sri Aurobindo were noteworthy exceptions to this rule. He explained:

> Ramakrishna encouraged and promoted a sense of kinship between his disciples and himself. He allowed some of his disciples to confront and challenge him on various occasions. He even encouraged lay devotees to become involved in a dialogue with him. He did not hesitate to admit his human shortcomings, and he confronted others daringly, relying on his psychic and spiritual insights. More than many great gurus, he paid attention to individual needs, talents and the personality makeup of his disciples . . .
>
> Accepting and dealing with the individual differences and uniqueness of each disciple was, perhaps, stressed more by Sri Aurobindo than any other renowned Eastern guru. According to him, the Divine as a Principle or Essence is involved in the process of uniting with the finite nature of man to produce an evolutionary transformation. This is a symmetrical type of relationship between the Divine or Self and ego-conscious man. In this context the Divine is the Supreme Guru and man is his disciple. The guru is only a medium to assist the disciple to become a disciple of the Supreme Guru.[11]

So, despite the misgivings expressed about traditional crazy-wise adepts and eccentric masters in this book, they can conceivably still serve a useful societal function: to act as mirrors of the "insanity" of consensus reality and as beacons of that larger Reality that we habitually tend to exclude from our lives. To the extent that they can help us free ourselves from the blinders with which we block out Reality and conceal ourselves (or our Self) from ourselves, we would do well to heed their message. At the same time, I feel, they are relics of an archaic spirituality that, sooner or later, will be replaced by a more integrated approach to self-transcendence. This new approach will be sustained by teachers, including holy fools, who place personal growth and integrity above the need to instruct, Reality above traditional fidelity, and compassion and humor above all role-playing.

# NOTES

## Foreword

1. Thomas Merton, *New Seeds of Contemplation* (New York: New Directions, 1961), p. 103.
2. W. James, *The Varieties of Religious Experience* (New York: The New American Library, 1988), p. 29.
3. A. Toynbee, *Civilization on Trial* (New York: Oxford University Press, 1948), p. 156.

## Chapter 1

1. Retold after J. Campbell, *The Hero with a Thousand Faces* (Cleveland, Ohio: Meridian Books, 1956), p. 45. Campbell got the story from Leo Frobenius's work in German *Und Afrika Sprach*, which was first published in 1912.
2. C. G. Jung, "On the Psychology of the Trickster-Figure," *The Archetypes and the Collective Unconscious* (London: Routledge & Kegan Paul, 1959), p. 261.
3. Ibid., pp. 263–64.
4. See K. Wilber, *The Atman Project: A Transpersonal View of Human Development* (Wheaton, Ill.: Theosophical Publishing House, 1980).
5. A. Low, *Zen and Creative Management* (Garden City, N.Y.: Anchor Books, 1976), p. 62.
6. Ibid., p. 193.
7. Ibid., p. 198.
8. R. Erdoes and J. Fire, *Lame Deer: Seeker of Visions* (New York: Pocket Books, 1972), p. 225.
9. M. C. Hyers, *Zen and the Comic Spirit* (London: Rider, 1974), p. 172.
10. H. Cox, *The Feast of Fools: A Theological Essay on Festivity and Fantasy* (New York: Colophon Books, 1970), p. 139.
11. Cited in G. Claxton (Swami Anand Ageha), *Wholly Human: Western and Eastern Visions of the Self and Its Perfection* (London: Routledge & Kegan Paul, 1981), p. 31.
12. This story and most of the following stories about the Fools for Christ's Sake are told in John Saward's excellent book *Perfect Fools: Folly for Christ's Sake in Catholic and Orthodox Spirituality* (Oxford, England: Oxford University Press, 1980).
13. This story is told in P. S. Hilpisch, "Die Torheit um Christi willen," *Zeitschrift für Aszese und Mystik*, n.s., 6 (1931), p. 123.

14. G. T. Peck, *The Fool of God: Jacopone da Todi* (Montgomery, Ala.: University of Alabama Press, 1980), p. 158.

15. See M. Foucault, *Madness and Civilization: A History of Insanity in the Age of Reason* (New York: Vintage Books, 1973).

16. See D. Elgin, *Voluntary Simplicity: An Ecological Lifestyle That Promotes Personal and Social Renewal* (New York: Bantam Books, 1982).

17. S. Spencer, *Mysticism in World Religion* (London: Allen & Unwin, 1966), p. 299.

18. This story and several others related in this section are found in the impressive two-volume work by Saiyid Athar Abbas Rizvi, *A History of Sufism in India*, vol. 1: *Early Sufism and Its History in India to 1600 A.D.* (New Delhi: Munshiram Manoharlal, 1978).

19. R. A. Nicolson, *The Mystics of Islam* (London: Routledge & Kegan Paul, 1963), pp. 66–67.

20. P. V. Inayat Khan, *The Message in Our Time* (San Francisco: Harper & Row, 1978), cited in *Emergence: Journal for Evolving Consciousness*, vol. 2, no. 2 (Spring 1989), p. 31.

21. Ibid., p. 31.

22. This and some of the following anecdotes are found in appendix A ("Majzubs") of Saiyid Athar Abbas Rizvi's *A History of Sufism in India*, vol. 2: *From Sixteenth Century to Modern Century* (New Delhi: Munshiram Manoharlal, 1983), pp. 470–79.

23. Ibid., p. 477.

## Chapter 2

1. The translation is my own. The obscurity of the English reflects that of the original, which is replete with esoteric notions. Several stanzas contain a wordplay on *avadhuta*.

2. One wonders whether they would have succumbed to suspicion and confusion if, in Tantric fashion, he had openly made love to the girl as well? Either they were spiritually very mature or they were what Eric Hoffer called "true believers." A true believer has made up his mind, and no amount of contrary evidence makes any difference. Everything is reinterpreted to fit the existing mind-set. This is one of the psychological characteristics of cult behavior, which is widespread even in otherwise genuine spiritual groups. It permits fake adepts to play their dangerous power games, just as it permits authentic adepts who are sexually active with their devotees to continue this behavior unquestioned. It is my contention, affirmed elsewhere in this volume, that spiritual accomplishment and moral perfection do not necessary dovetail in every case. See E. Hoffer, *The True Believer: Thoughts on the Nature of Mass Movements* (New York: Harper & Row, 1951).

3. N. S. Karandikar, *Biography of Sri Swami Samarth Akkalkot Maharaj* (Bombay: Akkalkot Swami Math, 1978), p. 208.

4. Swami Muktananda Paramahansa, *Chitshakti Vilas: The Play of Consciousness* (Ganeshpuri: Shree Gurudev Ashram, 1972), p. 97.

5. I owe this and several of the other *avadhuta* stories and many of the bibliographic references to James Steinberg, librarian of the American Trickster Library. This library, which belongs to The Free Daist Communion and is accessible only to members, contains one of the most comprehensive collections of publications on crazy wisdom.

6. This story is found in Ram Dass, *Miracle of Love: Stories about Neem Karoli Baba* (New York: E. P. Dutton, 1979), pp. 291ff.

7. Ibid., pp. 292–93.

8. Ibid., p. 295.

9. *The Talks of Sadguru Upasani-Baba Maharaja*, vol. 2, part B (Sakori, India: Upasani Kanyakumari Sthan, 1978), pp. 713–14.
10. This and the following stories about Nityananda are found in M. U. Hatengdi, *Nityananda: The Divine Presence* (Cambridge, Mass.: Rudra Press, 1984).
11. R. Schiffman, *Sri Ramakrishna: A Prophet for the New Age* (New York: Paragon House, 1989), p. 45.
12. Ibid., p. 46.
13. S. Thaker, *Songs of the Avadhut* (Kampala, India: Avadhut Parivar, 1972), p. 9.
14. Cited in T. and D. Hopkinson, *Much Silence: Meher Baba, His Life and Work* (London: Gollancz, 1974), p. 54.
15. Ibid., p. 44.
16. Ibid., p. 71.
17. See W. Donkin, *The Wayfarers* (Ahmednagar: Adi K. Irani, 1948).
18. Cited in E. C. Dimock, Jr., *The Place of the Hidden Moon: Erotic Mysticism in the Vaisnava-Sahajiya Cult of Bengal* (Chicago: University of Chicago Press, 1966), p. 261.
19. Translated in D. Bhattacharya, *Songs of the Bards of Bengal* (New York: Grove Press, 1969), p. 42.
20. J. Blofeld, *The Tantric Mysticism of Tibet: A Practical Guide* (New York: E. P. Dutton, 1970), pp. 92–93.
21. For the stories of the eighty-four *maha-siddhas*, see K. Dowman, *Masters of Mahamudra: Songs and Histories of the Eighty-Four Buddhist Siddhas* (New York: SUNY Press, 1985).
22. Translation by H. V. Guenther, *The Royal Song of Saraha: A Study in the History of Buddhist Thought* (Berkeley, Calif.: Shambhala, 1973), pp. 70–71.
23. See J. Ardussi and L. Epstein, "The Saintly Madman in Tibet," in James F. Fisher, ed., *Himalayan Anthropology: The Indo-Tibetan Interface* (The Hague: Mouton, 1972), pp. 327–38.
24. K. Dowman, *The Divine Madman: The Sublime Life and Songs of Drukpa Kunley* (Clearlake, Calif.: Dawn Horse Press, 1983), pp. 28–29.
25. Ibid., p. 29.
26. Ibid., p. 45.
27. Ibid., p. 47.
28. See Ardussi and Epstein, "Saintly Madman," p. 334.
29. Dowman, *The Divine Madman*, p. 26.
30. The Chinese term *ch'an* is synonymous with the Sanskrit term *dhyana*, meaning "meditation." The Japanese equivalent is *zen*.
31. C. Humphreys, *Zen: A Way of Life* (London: English Universities Press, 1962), p. 108.
32. J. van de Wetering, *The Empty Mirror: Experiences in a Japanese Zen Monastery* (New York: Pocket Books, 1973), p. 177.
33. Ibid., pp. 177–78.
34. Norman Waddell, transl., "Zen Master Hakuin's Poison Words for the Heart: Hakuin Zenji's Dokugo Shingyo," *The Eastern Buddhist*, vol. 13, no. 2 (Autumn 1980), pp. 90ff.
35. D. T. Suzuki, *Studies in Zen* (New York: Dell Publishing, 1955), p. 81.
36. M. C. Hyers, *Zen and the Comic Spirit* (London: Rider, 1974), p. 168. On humor and laughter in the context of Christian spirituality, see Conrad Hyers's two mature books *The Comic Vision and the Christian Faith: A Celebration of Life and Laughter* (New York: Pilgrim Press, 1981) and *And God Created Laughter: The Bible as Divine Comedy* (Atlanta, Ga.: John Knox Press, 1987).

## Chapter 3

1. Cited in L. Pauwels, *Gurdjieff* (New York: Samuel Weiser, 1972), p. 34.
2. See C. Wilson, *The Outsider* (New York: Houghton Mifflin, 1967).
3. Pauwels, *Gurdjieff*, p. 320.
4. F. Peters, *Boyhood with Gurdjieff* (Baltimore, Md.: Penguin Books, 1972), pp. 80–81.
5. J. G. Bennett, *Witness* (Charles Town, W. Va.: Claymont Communications, 1984), pp. 258–59.
6. This story is related by Pauwels, *Gurdjieff*, pp. 39–40.
7. Pauwels, *Gurdjieff*, pp. 331–32.
8. Ibid., p. 178.
9. Ibid., p. 112.
10. Bhagwan Rajneesh, *Tantra: The Supreme Understanding* (Poona, India: Rajneesh Foundation, 1975), p. 99.
11. C. T. Tart, *Waking Up: Overcoming the Obstacles to Human Potential* (Boston: Shambala/New Science Library, 1987), p. 288.
12. Foreword to K. R. Speeth, *The Gurdjieff Work* (Los Angeles: J. P. Tarcher, 1989), p. ix.
13. H. Birven, *Lebenskunst in Yoga und Magie* (Zurich: Origo Verlag, [1953]), p. 76.
14. Cited in Nat Freedland, *The Occult Explosion* (New York: Berkley Medallion Books, 1972), p. 161.
15. J. Symonds and K. Grant, eds. *The Confessions of Aleister Crowley: An Auto-hagiography* (London: Routledge & Kegan Paul, 1979), p. 387.
16. C. Wilson, *Aleister Crowley: The Nature of the Beast* (Wellingborough, England: Aquarian Press, 1987), p. 84.
17. This is in fact the very essence of the approach of *karma-yoga*, the Yoga of self-transcending action, one of the principal orientations of the Yoga tradition of Hinduism.
18. Symonds and Grant, *Aleister Crowley*, p. 403.
19. Ibid., p. 853.
20. Ibid., p. 851.
21. Ibid., p. 513.
22. Ibid., p. 142.
23. The word *Bhagwan* derives from the Sanskrit honorific *bhagavan*, meaning literally "possessor of fortune (*bhaga*)." It generally stands for "lord," as an address of the Divine but also of a notable person. "Rajneesh" comes from Sanskrit *rajna-isha* "Queen's Lord," the "queen" being presumably the feminine force, the Goddess of Tantra, as manifested in the *kundalini*.
24. Bhagwan Rajneesh, *Dimensions Beyond the Known* (Los Angeles: Wisdom Garden, 1975), p. 156.
25. Cited in Yarti, *The Sound of Running Water: A Photobiography of Bhagwan Shree Rajneesh and His Work, 1974–1978* (Poona, India: Rajneesh Foundation, 1980), p. 29.
26. R. A. Masters, *The Way of the Lover: The Awakening & Embodiment of the Full Human* (West Vancouver, B.C.: Xanthyros Foundation, 1989), p. 148.
27. Rajneesh, *Tantra: The Supreme Understanding*, p. 55.
28. Ibid., p. 61.
29. Ibid., p. 102.
30. Ibid., p. 233.
31. Cited in Yarti, *Sound of Running Water*, p. 153.

32. H. Milne, *Bhagwan: The God That Failed* (New York: St. Martin's Press, 1986), p. 102.
33. Rajneesh, *Tantra: The Supreme Understanding*, pp. 8–9.
34. Ibid., p. 69.
35. Bhagwan Rajneesh in *Sannyas* magazine (May–June 1978), p. 11.
36. Milne, *Bhagwan: The God That Failed*, p. 306.
37. Ibid.
38. Bhagwan Shree Rajneesh, *Meditation: The Art of Ecstasy* (New York: Perennial Library, 1978), p. 26.
39. Ibid., p. 28.
40. Rajneesh, *Tantra: The Supreme Understanding*, p. 39.
41. Ibid., p. 101.
42. Ibid., pp. 109–10.
43. Cited in J. S. Gordon, *The Golden Guru: The Strange Journey of Bhagwan Shree Rajneesh* (Lexington, Mass.: Stephen Greene Press, 1987), p. 79.
44. Cited in Milne, *Bhagwan: The God That Failed*, pp. 177–78.
45. Ibid., p. 118.
46. Stephen Zwick, "The Father Divine Peace Mission Movement," Senior thesis, Princeton University, 1971.
47. For an autobiographical account, see Chögyam Trungpa, *Born in Tibet* (Baltimore, Md.: Penguin Books, 1971).
48. Chögyam Trungpa, *Journey Without Goal: The Tantric Wisdom of the Buddha* (Boulder, Colo.: Prajna Press, 1981), pp. 97–98.
49. Chögyam Trungpa, *First Thought Best Thought: 108 Poems* (Boulder, Colo.: Shambhala, 1983), p. 9. The book has an introduction by Trungpa's friend Allen Ginsberg.
50. Chögyam Trungpa, *Cutting Through Spiritual Materialism* (Boulder, Colo.: Shambhala, 1973), p. 7.
51. R. Fields, *How the Swans Came to the Lake: A Narrative History of Buddhism in America* (Boston: Shambhala, 1986), p. 310.
52. Cited in B. Miles, *Ginsberg: A Biography* (New York: Simon & Schuster, 1989), p. 453.
53. P. Marin, "Spiritual Obedience: The Transcendental Game of Follow the Leader," *Harper's* (February 1979), p. 47.
54. Ibid., p. 49.
55. Trungpa, *Journey Without Goal*, p. 25.
56. Merwin's story, as related by him, is told in B. Miles, *Ginsberg: A Biography*, pp. 466–70.
57. Trungpa, *Cutting Through Spiritual Materialism*, p. 107.
58. See Katy Butler's report "Encountering the Shadow in Buddhist America," published in *Common Boundary*, vol. 8, no. 3 (May/June 1990), pp. 14–22. She relates the story of a friend who had a homosexual encounter with Ösel Tendzin. She writes: "I observed Tendzin's apparently routine transformation of a religious audience into an afternoon of drinking and sexual relations, and how casually he admitted to addictively frequent sex" (p. 14).
59. R. Grossinger, *Waiting for the Martian Express: Cosmic Visitors, Earth Warriors, Luminous Dreams* (Berkeley, Calif.: North Atlantic Books, 1989), p. 19.
60. L. Lozowick, *The Cheating Buddha* (Tabor, N.J.: Hohm Press, 1980), p. 31.
61. See Karuna, "A Master Is a Fire You Have to Go Through: Reflections on a Talk by Bhagavan Shree Rajneesh," *Tawagoto: The Sacred Foolish Song of the Hohm Community*, vol. 1, no. 1 (Spring 1988), pp. 38–41 and 81.

62. *Tawagoto*, vol. 2, no. 2 (Spring 1989), p. 16.
63. *Tawagoto*, vol. 1, no. 2 (Winter 1988), pp. 44–45.
64. M. Albert, "Enlightened Masters," *Yoga Journal* (July/August 1985), p. 34.
65. Bandhu Dunham, "Journal Entry 6/2/88," *Tawagoto*, vol. 2, no. 1 (Winter 1989), p. 55.

## Chapter 4

1. Bubba Free John [Da Love-Ananda], *The Knee of Listening: The Early Life and Radical Spiritual Teachings of Bubba Free John* (Middletown, Calif.: Dawn Horse Press, 1978), p. 9.
2. Ibid., p. 5.
3. D. C. Lane, "The Paradox of Da Free John: Distinguishing the Message from the Medium," in *Understanding Cults and Spiritual Movements* research series, vol. 1, no. 2 (1985), p. 1.
4. Bubba Free John, *The Knee of Listening*, p. 9.
5. The Sanskrit phrase *nirvikalpa-samadhi* means literally "formless ecstasy" and refers to the temporary condition of supraconsciousness without any objective referent. Typically, this advanced spiritual state is accompanied by loss of body awareness. It can last from a few seconds to several hours, though if it endures for much longer than that, reintegration with the body can become difficult and physical death may result.
6. *Kundalini-yoga*, the Yoga of the serpent-power, is an ancient Hindu tradition that revolves around the awakening of the latent psychospiritual force of the body, particularly by means of breath-control and mental concentration. The *kundalini* force is traditionally thought to reside *in potentia* at the base of the spine. The practices of *kundalini-yoga*, which is fundamental to Tantrism, are designed to activate that latent force and to conduct it along the spinal axis to the center of the brain. When this is accomplished, the state of ego-transcending, blissful ecstasy (*samadhi*) is said to result.
7. Bubba Free John, *The Knee of Listening*, p. 126.
8. Ibid., p. 134.
9. Ibid., pp. 134–35.
10. This statement appears to have been made by Alan Watts shortly before his death. It has been printed repeatedly on the back cover of *The Knee of Listening* and in the promotional literature of The Free Daist Communion and The Dawn Horse Press.
11. "Bubba" had been Da Love-Ananda's childhood nickname and was therefore not, as some authorities suggested, a bowdlerized version of the Hindi title "Baba." "Free John" was his translation of "Franklin Jones" into spiritual terms, expressing his newly found inner autonomy and capacity for acting as an agent of grace. Da Free John assumes a theological and mystical connection with the biblical St. John, whereas he has few words of commendation for St. Paul.
12. Bubba Free John [Da Love-Ananda], *The Enlightenment of the Whole Body* (Middletown, Calif.: Dawn Horse Press, 1978), p. 48.
13. The Sanskrit term *kriya* means literally "action." It refers here to spontaneous body movements, such as swaying, head rolling, eye rolling, protrusion of the tongue, etc., which are the result of heightened psychosomatic energy in the body.
14. The *kundalini*, or *kundalini-shakti* ("serpent power"), is a psychospiritual phenomenon that forms the foundation of Tantric Yoga. The activation of this subtle energy is held responsible for a variety of psychic and mystical phenomena. Some traditional authorities, like Gopi Krishna, even argue that it is at the bottom of all psychosomatic and spiritual activity.

15. *Sahaja-samadhi* is the ecstasy of spontaneity, in which there is no self-consciousness, regardless of the states of consciousness that the individual is experiencing. Strictly speaking, this term applies to permanent enlightenment, or Self-realization.

16. Bubba Free John [Da Love-Ananda], *Garbage and the Goddess: The Last Miracles and Final Spiritual Instructions of Bubba Free John* (Lower Lake, Calif.: Dawn Horse Press, 1974). The book, which was edited by Sandy [Saniel] Bonder and Terry Patten, had a second printing in the same year, but almost immediately, at the behest of Da Love-Ananda, every effort was made to retrieve all existing copies. It is, perhaps, the least edited of all the books by Da Love-Ananda and contains materials that clearly evince his crazy-wisdom style of teaching.

17. Ibid., p. 104.

18. Ibid., p. 106.

19. Ibid., pp. 106–7.

20. Ibid., p. 127.

21. Ibid., p. 20.

22. Ibid., p. 23.

23. Bubba Free John [Da Love-Ananda], *The Method of the Siddhas* (Middletown, Calif.: Dawn Horse Press, 1978), pp. 152–53. This book was first published in 1973.

24. *Sat-sanga* means literally "contact with the True" and refers to the time-honored practice of sitting in the company of an enlightened adept to absorb his spiritual transmission. Da Love-Ananda's early naivete about the sufficiency of *sat-sanga* demonstrates that enlightened adepts are by no means omniscient but are, like everyone else, engaged in a learning process. One suspects that some may even be slow learners. For instance, in the face of available evidence, Da Love-Ananda continues to assume that he can profoundly transform his devotees' lives while permitting them only scant contact with him.

25. Bubba Free John, *The Knee of Listening*, p. 12.

26. Bubba Free John, *The Knee of Listening*, p. 270.

27. Lane, "Paradox of Da Free John," p. 5. Lane's statement that Da Love-Ananda's teaching has not fundamentally changed needs qualification. While it is true that "radical understanding" is still basic to Da Love-Ananda's approach, over the years the devotional practices have been so greatly elaborated that some observers feel that they now obscure the original simplicity of his teaching. In fact, in recent years, many students have left because of this shift of emphasis, which either requires extraordinary spiritual maturity (to avoid the peril of cultic worship) or is tolerable only for those who still see in the guru a father figure; this appears to be the case with the overriding majority of Da Love-Ananda's followers. He continues, however, periodically to belabor them for their childishness, lack of true discrimination, and cultic attachment to him.

28. Peter Roberts, "Down from the Mountain," *The Dawn Horse*, no. 5 (1975), pp. 15–16.

29. Saniel Bonder, "Miracles: The Irreverent Intrusions of God," *The Laughing Man*, vol. 1, no. 2 (1976), p. 80.

30. Bubba Free John, *The Enlightenment of the Whole Body*, p. 53.

31. Da Free John [Love-Ananda], *The Dreaded Gom-Boo: Or the Imaginary Disease That Religion Seeks to Cure* (Clearlake, Calif.: Dawn Horse Press, 1983), pp. 16–17. Not surprisingly, Da Love-Ananda's various encounters with the dragon left him with not a few battle scars. Over the years, he has been sued several times by disaffected students, although his institutional representatives have so far succeeded in keep-

ing him out of court. Cases were settled by arbitration, which bled The Free Daist Communion financially. Perhaps most of these settlements could have been avoided if the alienated members had been treated with more respect by their former fellow devotees.

32. Da Love-Ananda, *The Love-Ananda Gita* (*The Wisdom-Song of Non-Separateness*) (Clearlake, Calif.: Dawn Horse Press, 1989), p. 111. According to an earlier version of this account, it was his love for a specific woman devotee that drew him back into the body. This was later declared to have been a misunderstanding.

33. From a talk by Da Love-Ananda given on September 24, 1985. In this talk he insisted that the parallels between his way of teaching and Drukpa Kunley's crazy wisdom should be truthfully communicated by the institutional representatives of his community. He also wondered whether it should not be completely understood and acceptable that when devotees come on retreat at his hermitage in Fiji they must expect him to interfere with them.

34. Da Free John [Love-Ananda], *God Is Not a Gentleman and I Am That One* (Clearlake, Calif.: Dawn Horse Press, 1983), p. 28.

35. Ibid., pp. 58–59.

36. Da Free John [Love-Ananda], *Crazy Da Must Sing, Inclined to His Weaker Side* (Clearlake, Calif.: Dawn Horse Press, 1982), p. 25.

37. Da Love-Ananda, "My Real Work Is to Drive You Mad," *The Lesson*, vol. 4 (Dawn Horse Press, no date), p. 58.

38. Ibid., p. 60.

39. R. A. Master, *The Way of the Lover: The Awakening & Embodiment of the Full Human* (West Vancouver, B.C.: Xanthyros Foundation, 1988), p. 152.

40. Ibid., pp. 154–55. Here Masters clearly expresses his appreciation for Da Love-Ananda, though he has never been one of his formal students. This makes one wonder about the motives behind his hard-hitting critique of Da Love-Ananda's disciples, of whom he has apparently met only a few. Be that as it may, his observations are largely accurate and can serve as a useful mirror for all those groups that are lavishly criticized in his book.

## Chapter 5

1. This saying is found in a little-known but remarkable allegoric treatise by Niffari, a wandering dervish who lived in the tenth century. Quoted in R. A. Nicholson, *The Mystics of Islam* (London: Routledge & Kegan Paul, 1963), p. 75.

2. L. Thompson, *Mirror to the Light: Reflections on Consciousness and Experience*, ed. by Richard Lannoy (London: Coventure, 1984), p. 48.

3. See J. Quint, *Meister Eckehart: Deutsche Predigten und Traktate* (Munich: Carl Hanser, 1963), p. 188. The sermon in question is *Populi eius qui in te est, misereberis.* The translation is mine.

4. See K. Potter, *Presuppositions in Indian Philosophy* (Englewood Cliffs, N.J.: Prentice-Hall, 1963).

5. Bubba Free John [Da Love-Ananda], *The Method of the Siddhas* (Middletown, Calif.: Dawn Horse Press, 1978), p. 137.

6. Chögyam Trungpa, *Cutting Through Spiritual Materialism* (Boulder, Colo.: Shambhala, 1973), p. 79.

7. Ibid., p. 63.

8. See J. Gebser, *The Ever-Present Origin* (Athens, Ohio: Ohio State University, 1985). For an introduction and critique of Gebser's model, see G. Feuerstein, *Structures of Consciousness* (Lower Lake, Calif.: Integral Publishing, 1987).

9. Bubba Free John [Da Love-Ananda], *The Enlightenment of the Whole Body* (Middletown, Calif.: The Dawn Horse Press, 1978), p. 112.

10. Thompson, *Mirror to the Light*, p. 75.

11. J. Needleman, *The New Religions* (London: Penguin Press, 1972), p. 11. Interestingly, the Sanskrit term for enjoyment, frequently used in contradistinction to the sacred ordeal of self-transcendence, is *bhoga*, which literally translated means "food" and "eating." It is the devouring, or consumption, of the world. The profane person, who lives for the fulfillment of his or her desires (the thousands of "animals" within), is the *bhogin* or "consumer." He or she consumes the offerings of the world, but, as the *yogin*-bard and former prince Bartrihari (seventh century A.D.) indicated in his *Vairagya-Shataka* (vs. 7), it is really the consumer who is consumed—by his or her desires. "Enjoyments are never enjoyed, but we our selves are enjoyed."

12. See R. Greenfield, *The Spiritual Supermarket: An Account of Gurus Gone Public in America* (New York: E. P. Dutton, 1975). Curiously, psychologist Charles T. Tart seems to regard the notion of "spiritual supermarket" as something positive. He even panders to the consumer mentality when he suggests that "one of the more enlightened things science could do for spiritual paths would be to develop something like a 'Spiritual Consumer Reports' " (p. 284). God forbid! See C. T. Tart, *Waking Up: Overcoming the Obstacles to Human Potential* (Boston: Shambhala, 1987).

13. Trungpa, *Cutting Through Spiritual Materialism*, p. 15.

14. Da Free John, *Nirvanasara: Radical Transcendentalism and the Introduction of Advaitayana Buddhism* (Clearlake, Calif.: Dawn Horse Press, 1982), p. 107.

15. Trungpa, *Cutting Through Spiritual Materialism*, p. 7.

16. Ibid., p. 17.

17. P. Tillich, *Systematic Theology* (London: SCM Press, 1978), vol. 2, pp. 47–48.

18. Cited after Sung Bae Park, *Buddhist Faith and Sudden Enlightenment* (Albany, N.Y.: SUNY Press, 1983), p. 23. The two verses are found in Hui-neng's *Platform Sutra*, an eighth-century work.

19. Franklin Jones [Da Love-Ananda], *The Knee of Listening* (Middletown, Calif.: Dawn Horse Press, 1978), p. 239.

20. For a beautiful and detailed account of the Shambhala legend, see Edwin Bernbaum, *The Way to Shambhala: A Search for the Mythical Kingdom Beyond the Himalayas* (Los Angeles: J. P. Tarcher, 1989).

21. See R. Otto, *The Idea of the Holy* (Harmondsworth, England: Penguin Books, 1959). First published in German in 1917.

22. This story is told in Bernbaum, *The Way to Shambhala*, p. 158.

23. Rajneesh, *Meditation: The Art of Ecstasy* (New York: Perennial Library, 1978), p. 26.

24. This story is told in Barry Miles, *Ginsberg: A Biography* (New York: Simon and Schuster, 1989), pp. 440–41.

25. A. Low, *The Iron Cow of Zen* (Wheaton, Ill.: Quest Books, 1985), p. 15.

26. See J. Cleugh, *Love Locked Out: A Survey of Love, Licence and Restriction in the Middle Ages* (London: Anthony Blond, 1963), pp. 37–45.

27. B.-A. Scharfstein, *Mystical Experience* (Baltimore, Md.: Penguin Books, 1974), p. 159.

28. On the mystical experience of unqualified light, see M. Eliade, *The Two and the One* (Chicago: University of Chicago Press, 1979), pp. 19–77.

29. The short record of Pascal's mystical experience was found on a scrap of paper that had been sewn into his doublet. The full text runs: "From about half past ten in

the evening to / about half an hour after midnight. / Fire. / God of Abraham, God of Isaac, God of Jacob, / Not the God of philosophers and scholars. / Absolute Certainty: Beyond reason. Joy. Peace. Forgetfulness of the world and everything but God./ The world has not known thee, but I have known thee. / Joy! joy! joy! tears of joy!" See F. C. Happold, *Mysticism: A Study and an Anthology* (Harmondsworth, England: Penguin Books, 1967), p. 39.

30. Cited in P. Reps, *Zen Flesh, Zen Bones: A Collection of Zen and Pre-Zen Writings* (Garden City, N.Y.: Anchor Books, n. d.), p. 94.
31. S. Keen, *To a Dancing God* (New York: Harper & Row, 1970), pp. 117–19.
32. A. Watts, *The Book: On the Taboo Against Knowing Who You Are* (New York: Vintage Books, 1972), p. 64.
33. Ibid., p. 112.
34. See A. Watts, *In My Own Way: An Autobiography—1915–1965* (New York: Vintage Books, 1973). Here Watts defended his somewhat self-indulgent life, while also staking a claim to the status of philosopher and mystic. Thus, he remarked: "I distrust people who show no sign of naughtiness or self-indulgence" (p. 257).
35. Cited in Reps, *Zen Flesh, Zen Bones*, p. 105.
36. T. Merton, *The Ascent to Truth* (New York: Harcourt, Brace & Co., 1951), p. 159.
37. Ibid., pp. 159–60.
38. Rajneesh, *Meditation*, p. 104.
39. See J. Quint, *Meister Eckehart: Deutsche Predigten und Traktate* (Munich: Carl Hanser, 1963), p. 57. The quotation is from Eckehart's "Reden der Unterweisung" (Talks of Instruction), section 4. The translation is mine.
40. See Da Free John, *The Bodily Location of Happiness* (Clearlake, Calif.: Dawn Horse Press, 1982), p. 184.

## Chapter 6

1. M. Berman, *The Reenchantment of the World* (New York: Bantam Books, 1984), pp. 2–3.
2. For an account of prophetic and messianic figures during the Elizabethan period, see K. Thomas, *Religion and the Decline of Magic* (Harmondsworth, England: Penguin Books, 1973), pp. 157–73. Apparently, multitudes flocked to these messiahs, especially during the period of the Civil War of 1642–1649, although after 1660, because of the persecution of sects, messianism waned. It did not surge up again in England until the nineteenth century.
3. See T. Clifford, "The Master List," *New Age* (May 1976), pp. 23–36. For my brief resume of American "spiritual" history, I am particularly indebted to Clifford's treatment, but I have also benefited from I. I. Zaretsky and M. P. Leons, eds., *Religious Movements in Contemporary America* (Princeton, N.J.: Princeton University Press, 1974); J. Needleman, *The New Religions* (London: Allen Lane, 1972); and R. Fields, *How the Swans Came to the Lake* (Boulder, Colo.: Shambhala, 1981).
4. See J. H. Barrows, ed., *The World's Parliament of Religions: An Illustrated and Popular Story of the World's First Parliament of Religions, Held in Chicago in Connection with the Columbian Exposition of 1893* (Chicago: The Parliament Publishing Co., 1893). 2 vols.
5. T. Merton, *The Ascent to Truth* (New York: Harcourt, Brace and Co., 1951), pp. 156–58.
6. Bubba Free John [Da Love-Ananda], *The Method of the Siddhas* (Middletown, Calif.: Dawn Horse Press, 1978), p. 225.
7. H. Cox, *Turning East: The Promise and Peril of the New Orientalism* (New York: Simon and Schuster, 1977), p. 175.

8. L. Hixon, *Coming Home: The Experience of Enlightenment* (Los Angeles: J. P. Tarcher, 1989), p. 187.
9. See, for example, I. Tweedie, *The Chasm of Fire: A Woman's Experience of Liberation through the Teaching of a Sufi Master* (Tisbury, England: Element Books, 1979). See also the unabridged version of the diary she kept during her discipleship with a Sufi teacher, entitled *Daughter of Fire: A Diary of a Spiritual Training with a Sufi Master* (Nevada City, Calif.: Blue Dolphin Publishing, 1986).
10. G. Claxton, *Wholly Human: Western and Eastern Visions of the Self and Its Perfection* (London: Routledge & Kegan Paul, 1981), p. 98.
11. The Hindu word *darshan* ("seeing") is used for the reverential act of gazing at the teacher and receiving his blessings, or spiritual transmission. This practice is an important aspect of *guru-yoga*.
12. Claxton, *Wholly Human*, p. 98.
13. To create a "true community" that would serve as the seed for a worldwide, spiritually based culture is also the ambition of Da Love-Ananda, though hitherto his efforts have been thwarted by the inveterate cultic tendencies of his followers, leaving him periodically disillusioned and frustrated.
14. See Mark 8:27.
15. See Mark 14:61.
16. See John 5:18 and 10:30; and Philippians 2:6.
17. Bubba Free John [Da Love-Ananda], *Breath and Name* (San Francisco: Dawn Horse Press, 1977), p. 159. This book is out of print.
18. Cited in A. Low, *The Iron Cow of Zen* (Wheaton, Ill.: Quest Books, 1985), p. 19.
19. See W. D. Wallis, *Messiahs: Their Role in Civilization* (Washington, D.C.: American Council on Public Affairs, 1943), p. 187.
20. See the conversation between Indries Shah and Elizabeth Hall, "The Sufi Tradition," *Psychology Today* (July 1975), p. 53: "Some [gurus] are frankly phonies, and they don't try to hide it from me. They think that I am one, too."
21. D. Anthony, B. Ecker, and K. Wilber, *Spiritual Choices: The Problem of Recognizing Authentic Paths to Inner Transformation* (New York: Paragon House, 1987), pp. 299–300.
22. W. E. Hocking, *The Meaning of God in Human Experience* (New Haven, Conn.: Yale University Press, 1912), p. 349.
23. J. Welwood, "On Spiritual Authority: Genuine and Counterfeit," in Anthony, Ecker, and Wilber, *Spiritual Choices*, p. 292.
24. H. Milne, *Bhagwan: The God That Failed* (New York: St. Martin's Press, 1987), p. 255.
25. Ibid., p. 232.
26. Ibid., pp. 275–76.
27. Ibid., p. 286.
28. The translation is Thomas Merton's. See his *The Ascent of Truth*, p. 110, where he also has this astute observation: "It is rare for an ascetic to live his whole life long as if he did not have a body. Much more common are the ones who punish themselves furiously for two or three years and then lose their morale, fall into despair, become hypochondriacs, obsessed with every fancied need of their flesh and of their spirit."
29. Anthony et al. *Spiritual Choices*, p. 6.
30. Ram Dass, *Journey of Awakening: A Meditator's Guidebook* (New York: Bantam Books, 1978), p. 126.
31. M. Aïvanhov, *What Is a Spiritual Master?* (Frejus, France: Prosveta, 1984), p. 70.
32. Matthew 7:15–20. The quote is from the authorized King James version.

33. M. Ross, *Pillars of Flame: Power, Priesthood, and Spiritual Maturity* (San Francisco: Harper & Row, 1988), pp. 50–52.
34. Ram Dass, *Journey of Awakening*, p. 126.

## Chapter 7

1. See M. Eliade, *Myths, Dreams and Mysteries: The Encounter Between Contemporary Faiths and Archaic Reality* (London and Glasgow: Fontana Library, 1968).
2. M. Eliade, *The Sacred and the Profane: The Nature of Religion* (New York: Harcourt, Brace & World, 1959), p. 188.
3. Ibid., p. 191.
4. See F. Vaughan, *The Inward Arc: Healing and Wholeness in Psychotherapy and Spirituality* (Boston: Shambhala, 1986), pp. 135–36. It should be noted that in the present book, the terms "student," "devotee," and "disciple" are used interchangeably.
5. B. J. F. Lonergan, *Insight: A Study of Human Understanding* (New York: Harper & Row, 1978), p. 175.
6. R. Descartes, *Discours de la méthode*, ed. Étienne Gilson (Paris, 1930), opening section.
7. The *puer aeternus*, the "eternal youth," is a special case of adolescent adult. When this high-flying personality type is attracted to spiritual life, teachers, or groups, it is usually because the idea of supramundane perfection sounds like a fascinating alternative to the round of daily obligations. "The tenacity with which the *puer* clings to such cults," observes Jeffrey Satinover, "stems from the price he would pay in sacrificing this attachment: fragmentation of his identity."—J. Satinover, "The Childhood Self and the Origins of Puer Psychology," in J. Adams, ed., *Reclaiming the Inner Child* (Los Angeles: J. P. Tarcher, 1990), p. 150. On the other hand, when the "eternal youth" has found his identity, he tends to drop his spiritual interests, which bears out that his involvement had neurotic roots to begin with.
8. C. G. Jung, *Modern Man in Search of a Soul* (New York: Harcourt, Brace and Co., 1933), p. 237.
9. See also the revealing experiments by S. Milgram, *Obedience to Authority: An Experimental View* (New York: Harper & Row, 1974).
10. I. Kant, *Populäre Schriften*, P. Menzer, ed. (Berlin: Reimer, 1911), p. 325.
11. See P. Tillich, *The Courage to Be* (London: Collins, 1963).
12. Tillich, *The Courage to Be*, p. 71. (In the original, the whole sentence is in italics.)
13. Ibid., p. 175.
14. C. T. Tart, *Waking Up: Overcoming the Obstacles to Human Potential* (Boston, Mass.: Shambhala, 1987), pp. 244–45.
15. See, e.g., J. H. Craig and M. Craig, *Synergic Power: Beyond Domination and Permissiveness* (Berkeley, Calif.: Proactive Press, 1974).
16. P. Marin, "Spiritual Obedience: The Transcendental Game of Follow the Leader," *Harper's* (February 1979), p. 44.
17. Da Free John [Da Love-Ananda], *Scientific Proof of the Existence of God Will Soon Be Announced by the White House!* (Clearlake, Calif.: Dawn Horse Press, 1980), p. 31.
18. W. Sargant, *Battle for the Mind* (London: Pan Books, 1970), p. 215.
19. W. Sargant, "The Physiology of Faith," *The British Journal of Psychiatry* 115 (1969), p. 510.
20. See A. D. Biderman, "The Image of 'Brainwashing,'" *Public Opinion References Quarterly* 26 (1962), pp. 547–63.
21. From the psychological-psychiatric point of view, see, e.g., J. T. Ungerleider and D. K. Wellisch, "The Programming (Brainwashing)/Deprogramming Religious

Controversy," in D. G. Bromley and J. T. Richardson, eds., *The Brainwashing/Deprogramming Controversy: Sociological, Psychological, Legal and Historical Perspectives* (New York and Toronto: Edwin Mellen Press, 1983), pp. 205–14. From the sociological point of view, see, e.g., J. A. Beckford, *The Trumpet of Prophecy* (Oxford, England: Basil Blackwell, 1975).

22. The term "protean man" was used by R. J. Lifton, *Boundaries* (New York: Vintage Books, 1969), to describe the capacity and tendency of modern Western men and women to change their self-definition with comparative ease and frequency. Like Proteus, the uncanny shape shifter of Greek mythology, many modern Westerners enjoy switching roles and identities. Lifton writes: "The Protean style of self-process, then, is characterized by an interminable series of experiments and explorations, some shallow, some profound, each of which can readily be abandoned in favor of still new, psychological quests" (p. 44). This protean capacity must be distinguished from the tendency to drift seen in the *puer aeternus*.

23. See J. T. Richardson, ed., *Conversion Careers: In and Out of the New Religions* (Beverly Hills, Calif., and London: Sage Publications, 1978).

24. F. Vaughan, "A Question of Balance: Health and Pathology in New Religious Movements," *Journal of Humanistic Psychology*, vol. 23, no. 3 (1983), p. 24.

25. See K. Wilber, *A Sociable God: A Brief Introduction to a Transcendental Sociology* (New York: New Press/McGraw-Hill, 1983), p. 69.

26. See D. Bakan, *The Duality of Human Existence: An Essay on Psychology and Religion* (Chicago: Rand McNally, 1966).

27. See E. Underhill, *Mysticism: A Study in the Nature and Development of Man's Spiritual Consciousness* (New York: E. P. Dutton, 1961), p. 177.

28. In terms of Da Love-Ananda's seven-stage model of personal evolution, described in Chapter 6, spiritual conversion belongs to the fourth stage of life. The fourth-stage individual knows how to take responsibility for his or her own development and life and is free from emotional reactivity and self-destructive behavior. This stage is the true beginning of the spiritual process of self-transcendence and higher self-transformation.

29. According to Da Love-Ananda's developmental schema, this *transcendental conversion* occurs in the sixth stage of life, which is often confused with enlightenment itself.

30. See B. S. Narsimha Swami and S. Subbarao, *Sage of Sakuri: Life Story of Shree Upsasani Maharaj* (Sakuri, India: B. T. Wagh, n. d.), pp. 182–84.

31. Da Love-Ananda's longstanding criticism of the cultic tendencies among his followers is remarkable. Equally remarkable is the stubborn persistence of those tendencies and the fact that in many ways this teacher's style of interacting with his disciples is almost designed to elicit a cultic response. Over the years, Da Love-Ananda's growing isolation from his community has led to a fairly rigid formality that makes him virtually untouchable and encourages childish behavior and power games. There are many who, while respectful of his spiritual accomplishments, feel that he is sadly out of touch with ordinary reality. Like Pope John XXIII, he has often lamented that he is being kept prisoner by his institution. He may be a victim of circumstances in some sense, but perhaps he is more a victim of his own choices, including his need to be isolated from the world and even his own community of devotees.

32. *Guru-Gita*, verses 20, 39, 52, 77, 81, 101, and 257. The rendering from the Sanskrit is mine.

33. R. A. Masters, *The Way of the Lover: The Awakening & Embodiment of the Full Human* (West Vancouver, B.C.: Xanthyros Foundation, 1988), p. 141.

34. B. J. Groeschel, "Obedience: A Practical Approach to a Difficult Dimension of the Spiritual Life," *Studies in Formative Spirituality*, vol. 5, no. 2 (May 1984), p. 208.

35. Meister Eckehart, *Talks of Instruction*, section 1. My rendering is based on the German edition by J. Quint, *Meister Eckehart: Deutsche Predigten und Traktate* (Munich: Carl Hanser, 1963).

36. D. A. Helminiak, *Spiritual Development: An Interdisciplinary Study* (Chicago: Loyola University Press, 1987), pp. 77–78.

37. H. Fingarette, *The Self in Transformation: Psychoanalysis, Philosophy and the Life of the Spirit* (New York: Harper Torchbooks, 1963), p. 316.

38. This quotation is from the English edition by R. B. Blakney, *Meister Eckehart: A Modern Translation* (New York: Harper & Bros., 1957), p. 17. The sentence is found toward the end of section 11 of Eckehart's *Talks of Instruction*.

## Chapter 8

1. O. Levy, ed., *The Complete Works of Friedrich Nietzsche* (London: Allen & Unwin, 1910), vol. 10, p. 169. This quote is from "The Gay Science."

2. This is the title of Peter Berger's excellent sociological study, in which he suggests that rather than stolidly accept that transcendence has been reduced to a mere rumor, we can always begin to follow the rumor back to its source and rediscover the "supernatural" for ourselves. See P. L. Berger, *A Rumour of Angels: Modern Society and the Rediscovery of the Supernatural* (Harmondsworth, England: Penguin Books, 1971).

3. W. Kaufmann, *The Portable Nietzsche* (New York: Viking Press, 1968), p. 124. This quote is from "Thus Spoke Zarathustra" (part 1, section 3).

4. P. Berger et al., *The Homeless Mind: Modernization and Consciousness* (Harmondsworth, England: Penguin Books, 1974), pp. 166–68.

5. For my views on humanity's spiritual evolution, see *Structures of Consciousness: The Genius of Jean Gebser—An Introduction and Critique* (Lower Lake, Calif.: Integral Publishing, 1986).

6. I have borrowed the term "religious provincialism" from the works of Da Love-Ananda, who has characterized this particular mind-set with great perceptiveness. Ironically, his acuity has not prevented him from indirectly encouraging this very attitude among his followers.

7. T. Reik, *From Thirty Years with Freud* (New York: International Universities Press, 1949), p. 122.

8. A. Watts, *Psychotherapy East and West* (New York: New American Library of World Literature, 1963), p. 83.

9. See P. Tillich, *The Courage to Be* (London: Collins, 1963). On pp. 175–76, Tillich remarked: "Every act of courage is a manifestation of the ground of being, however questionable the content of the act may be. The content may hide or distort true being, the courage in it reveals true being . . . By affirming our being we participate in the self-affirmation of being-itself. There are no valid arguments for the 'existence' of God, but there are acts of courage in which we affirm the power of being, whether we know it or not."

10. See, e.g., F. Bird, "Charisma and Ritual in New Religious Movements," in J. Needleman and G. Baker, ed., *Understanding the New Religions* (New York: Seabury Press, 1978), pp. 173–89. Interestingly enough, experiential hunger is not one of the factors adduced by D. Anthony and T. Robbins, eds., in their otherwise informed introduction to *In Gods We Trust: New Patterns of Religious Pluralism in America* (New Brunswick, N.J.: Transaction Books, 1981).

11. See Da Free John [Da Love-Ananda], *The Paradox of Instruction* (San Francisco: Dawn Horse Press, 1977).

12. See, e.g., R. Johannson, *The Psychology of Nirvana* (London: Allen & Unwin, 1969).

13. Da Free John [Da Love-Ananda], *The Transmission of Doubt* (Clearlake, Calif.: Dawn Horse Press, 1984), p. 242.

14. A. Watts, *Beyond Theology: The Art of Godmanship* (New York: Vintage Books, 1964), pp. 214–15.

15. Da Free John [Da Love-Ananda], *The Bodily Sacrifice of Attention* (Clearlake, Calif.: Dawn Horse Press, 1981), p. 128.

16. Bubba Free John [Da Love-Ananda], *The Method of the Siddhas* (Middletown, Calif.: Dawn Horse Press, 1978), pp. 171–72.

17. Bubba Free John [Da Love-Ananda], *The Enlightenment of the Whole Body* (Middletown, Calif.: Dawn Horse Press, 1978), p. 500. John White has called Da Love-Ananda's model of the seven stages of life "the most insightful and accurate brief map of reality for the contemporary spiritual seeker."—J. White, ed., *What Is Enlightenment?* (Los Angeles: J. P. Tarcher, 1985), p. 211.

18. Swami Satprakashananda, *Methods of Knowledge* (London: Allen & Unwin, 1965), p. 280.

19. Ibid., p. 280.

20. Ibid., p. 281.

21. This phrase is borrowed from Agehananda Bharati, *The Light at the Center* (Santa Barbara, Calif.: Ross-Erikson, 1976).

22. Translated from the *Tripura-Rahasya* X.20–21.

23. Translated from the *Tripura-Rahasya* X.37–38.

24. Chögyam Trungpa, *Cutting Through Spiritual Materialism* (Boulder, Colo.: Shambhala, 1973), pp. 204–205.

25. This is Charles Tart's phrase. See C. Tart, *Waking Up: Overcoming the Obstacles to Human Potential* (Boston: Shambhala, 1987).

26. See R. A. Nicholson, *Studies in Islamic Mysticism* (Cambridge, England: Cambridge University Press, 1921), p. 200.

27. Plotinus, Ruysbroeck, and Swami Turiyananda are among the more noteworthy exceptions to the generally accepted proposition that the ego can be completely transcended. See, e.g., Swami Turiyananda, "Spiritual Talks," in C. Isherwood, ed., *Vedanta for Modern Man* (New York: Mentor Books, 1972), p. 65.

28. Da Free John [Da Love-Ananda], *Scientific Proof of the Existence of God Will Soon Be Announced by the White House!* (Clearlake, Calif.: Dawn Horse Press, 1980), p. 161.

29. A. Osborne, ed., *The Teachings of Ramana Maharshi* (New York: Samuel Weiser, 1978), p. 10.

30. R. Powell, ed., *The Nectar of the Lord's Feet: Final Teachings of Sri Nisargadatta Maharaj* (Longmead, England: Element Books, 1987), p. 82.

31. H. Smith, "The Sacred Unconscious," in R. Walsh and D. H. Shapiro, eds., *Beyond Health and Normality: Explorations in Exceptional Psychological Well-Being* (New York: Van Nostrand Reinhold, 1983), p. 269.

32. Ibid., p. 266.

33. R. Metzner, *Opening to Inner Light: The Transformation of Human Nature and Consciousness* (Los Angeles: J. P. Tarcher, 1986), p. 77. See also M. Murphy, "The Body," in A. Villoldo and K. Dychtwald, eds., *Millennium: Glimpses into the 21st Century* (Los Angeles: J. P. Tarcher, 1981), pp. 77–88.

34. Commenting on this concluding sentence, John White made the interesting remark that the luminous phenomena associated with enlightened beings "prefig-

ure a distant stage of human evolution when we shall become beings of light."
This essentially gnostic notion, which has made its way into contemporary
science fiction, has very ancient roots. Einstein's discovery of the conversion of
matter into energy has made this belief somewhat less farfetched. As an evolutionary *ideal* it certainly can have a powerful directive force in our moral life.

## Chapter 9

1. The coinage "new religions" is somewhat misleading, since at least some of the
   movements so designated have their historical roots in age-old Eastern traditions.
   The Hare Krishna movement is a good example. I have retained the phrase here
   for the sake of convenience.
2. It should, however, be emphasized here that, as the authors of *Strange Gods* observed, *"there is no avalanche of rapidly growing cults"* (emphasis in the original). D. G.
   Bromley and A. D. Shupe, *Strange Gods: The Great American Cult Scare* (Boston:
   Beacon Press, 1981), p. 3. Harvey Cox, in his introduction to this volume, com-
   mends the book as "a balanced, impartial, and scholarly work" (p. xv).
3. Lewis Thompson, *Mirror to the Light: Reflections on Consciousness and Experience*, ed.
   Richard Lannoy (London: Coventure, 1984), p. 128.
4. See G. W. Allport and J. M. Ross, "Personal Religious Orientation and Prejudice,"
   in *Journal of Personality and Social Psychology*, vol. 5 (1967), pp. 432–42.
5. Da Free John [Da Love-Ananda], *The Dreaded Gom-Boo, or the Imaginary Disease
   That Religion Seeks to Cure* (Clearlake, Calif.: Dawn Horse Press, 1983),
   pp. 214–15.
6. For an intelligent critique of these salvific therapies, see M. K. Termelin and J. W.
   Termelin, "Psychotherapy Cults: An Iatrogenic Perversion," *Psychotherapy: Theory, Research, and Practice*, vol. 19, no. 2 (Summer 1982), pp. 131–41.
7. Personal communication during a meeting on July 13, 1985.
8. Ken Wilber, "What Is Transpersonal Psychology?" in *The Laughing Man*, vol. 5,
   no. 2 (1984), p. 16.
9. Ibid.
10. Ibid.
11. A. Watts, *The Book: On the Taboo Against Knowing Who You Are* (New York:
    Vintage Books, 1977), p. 112.
12. In an interview with Jacqueline Piatier, entitled "Jean-Paul Sartre s'explique sur
    'Les Mots,' " in *Le Monde*, April 18, 1964.
13. See A. Watts, *Psychotherapy East and West* (New York: Mentor Books, 1961).
14. Gregory Bateson, *Steps to an Ecology of Mind: Collected Essays in Anthropology,
    Psychiatry, Evolution and Epistemology* (Frogmore, England: Paladin, 1973), p. 429.
15. Ibid., p. 436.
16. The phrase "ultimate concern" was introduced by theologian Paul Tillich to give
    existential expression to the idea of an unconditioned Ground of Being that is the
    ultimate significance of humanity's religious quest, which is a quest for the
    meaning of our essential being. In our pluralistic society, this ultimate religious
    concern can assume a dishearteningly mundane guise, in which case it is substi-
    tuted by worldly obsessions of one kind or another.
17. The concept of "false consciousness" belongs to the philosophy of Marxism,
    where its usage is restricted to the sociopolitical dimension. However, the notion
    has profound ontological import. The falsification of reality coincides with the
    emergence of self-consciousness, the ego, and not only as a result of political
    interests (which are secondary effects of the ego-presumption).
18. See, e.g., Kshemaraja's fine commentary on the *Shiva-Sutra* (I.2). A scholarly
    translation of this important Sanskrit work is found in J. Singh, *Śiva Sūtras: The*

*Yoga of Supreme Identity* (Delhi: Motilal Banarsidass, 1979). The full practical implications of the concept of self-contraction have only recently been spelled out in the works of Da Love-Ananda, who emphasizes the need for moment-to-moment recognition and transcendence of that contraction.

19. For an astute critique of the scientific method from a spiritual point of view, see Da Free John [Da Love-Ananda], *The Transmission of Doubt* (Clearlake, Calif.: Dawn Horse Press, 1984). See also Da Free John, *Scientific Proof of the Existence of God Will Soon Be Announced by the White House!* (Clearlake, Calif.: Dawn Horse Press, 1980).

20. See P. Feyerabend, *Against Method: Outline of an Anarchistic Theory of Knowledge* (London: Verso, 1980), p. 300.

21. See R. S. Scorer, *The Clever Moron* (London: Routledge & Kegan Paul, 1977), p. 30.

22. See R. S. Jones, *Physics as Metaphor* (Minneapolis, Minn.: University of Minneapolis Press, 1982).

23. See E. Gellner, *Thought and Change* (Chicago: University of Chicago Press, 1964), p. 72.

24. See J. Quint, *Meister Eckehart: Deutsche Predigten und Traktate* (Munich: Carl Hanser, 1963), p. 227.

## Chapter 10

1. See E. Allison Peers, transl./ed., *The Autobiography of St. Teresa of Avila* (Garden City, N.Y.: Image Books, 1960).

2. See, e.g., S. Niskar, *Crazy Wisdom* (Berkeley, Calif.: Ten Speed Press, 1990).

3. R. Otto, *The Idea of the Holy* (Harmondsworth, England: Penguin Books, 1959), pp. 26–27.

4. Nicolas Cusanus, *Of Learned Ignorance*, transl. G. Heron (New Haven, Conn.: Yale University Press, 1954), pp. 11–12.

5. H. Benoit, *The Supreme Doctrine: Psychological Studies in Zen Thought* (New York: Viking Press, 1959), p. 31.

6. F. Perls, R. F. Hefferline, and P. Goodman, *Gestalt Therapy: Excitement and Growth in the Human Personality* (Harmondsworth, England: Penguin Books, 1973), p. 277.

7. *Sahaja* can be employed both as an adjective and a noun.

8. The idea that the cosmos is one with God and the notion that there is no stringent necessity for the appearance of the world are pure Vedanta. Both credos are presented by many adepts as the irrefutable intuitions of an enlightened being. They are also talked about extensively in the many publications by Da Love-Ananda, without, however, being metaphysically elaborated or philosophically consolidated. Despite Da Love-Ananda's occasional gesturing toward philosophical formulations, he has persistently denied that he is "doing" philosophy or theology; he prefers to understand his writings and talks as merely bearing witness to what is self-evident to him.

9. H. V. Guenther, *The Royal Song of Saraha: A Study in the History of Buddhist Thought* (Berkeley, Calif.: Shambhala, 1973), pp. 63–70.

10. D. T. Suzuki, *Essays in Zen Buddhism: Second Series* (New York: Samuel Weiser, 1976), p. 96.

11. Ibid., pp. 110–11.

12. A. Curle, *Mystics and Militants: A Study of Awareness, Identity and Social Action* (London: Tavistock Publications, 1972), p. 15.

13. L. Reymond, *To Live Within* (Baltimore, Md.: Penguin Books, 1973), p. 85.

14. See J. Huizinga, *Homo Ludens: A Study of the Play Element in Culture* (Boston, Ill.: Beacon Press, 1955), p. 11.

15. J. P. Carse, *Finite and Infinite Games: A Vision of Life as Play and Possibility* (New York: Free Press, 1986), p. 18.

16. Ibid., pp. 14–15.

17. D. F. K. Steindl-Rast, "The Price of Wholeness," *Parabola*, vol. X, no. 1 (Spring 1985), p. 94.

18. A. Coomaraswamy, *The Dance of Shiva: Fourteen Indian Essays* (Bombay/Calcutta: Asia Publishing House, 1956), p. 147.

19. On the basis of such statements, I. M. Lewis has felt justified to speak of ecstasy *tout court* as a state of possession. See his *Ecstatic Religion: A Study of Shamanism and Spirit Possession* (London: Routledge, 1989), p. 15: "Transcendental experiences of this kind, typically conceived of as states of 'possession', have given the mystic a unique claim to direct experiential knowledge of the divine and, where this is acknowledged by others, the authority to act as a privileged channel of communication between man and the supernatural."

20. See Advayavajra's *Yuganaddha-Prakasha* (p. 49). Sanskrit text quoted in H. V. Guenther, *Yuganaddha: The Tantric View of Life* (Varanasi, India: Chowkhamba Sanskrit Series Office, 1969), p. 135.

21. A. Coomaraswamy, *The Dance of Shiva*, p. 140.

22. J. P. Carse, *Finite and Infinite Games*, p. 25.

23. Da Free John [Da Love-Ananda], *The Transmission of Doubt: Talks and Essays on the Transcendence of Scientific Materialism through Radical Understanding* (Clearlake, Calif.: The Dawn Horse Press, 1984), pp. 394–95. Even conventional humor has a liberating function, as has been noted by Paul E. McGhee in *Humor: Its Origin and Development* (San Francisco: W. H. Freeman, 1979), p. 233: "All of us feel certain pressures to conform our behavior to the expectations held for us by certain subgroups of society. Such conformity robs us of spontaneous and flexible behavior, but humor weakens the bonds of conformity . . . Humor is liberating because of its ability to release us from such demands."

24. Ibid., p. 398.

25. See A. W. Watts, *Psychotherapy East and West* (New York: Mentor Book, 1963), p. 107.

26. Bubba Free John [Da Love-Ananda], *The Method of the Siddhas* (Middletown, Calif.: The Dawn Horse Press, repr. 1978), p. 252.

27. See Søren Kierkegaard's philosophical treatment of the role of the teacher, in which he recapitulates Socrates' insight that a teacher can only thrust a student back on himself so that he may discover the Truth of his own accord by understanding how he deprives himself of that Truth. S. Kierkegaard, *Philosophical Fragments or A Fragment of Philosophy* (Princeton, N.J.: Princeton University Press, repr. 1974), pp. 16ff.

## Chapter 11

1. E. Allison Peers, transl./ed., *The Autobiography of St. Teresa of Avila* (Garden City, N.Y.: Image Books, 1960), p. 166.

2. Bhagwan Shree Rajneesh, *Notes of a Madman* (Rajneeshpuram, Oregon: Rajneesh Foundation International, 1985), pp. 44–45.

3. Ibid., p. 103.

4. Da Free John [Da Love-Ananda], *God Is Not a Gentleman and I Am That One* (Clearlake, Calif.: Dawn Horse Press, 1983), p. 58.

5. Ibid., p. 28.

6. Ibid., p. 65.

7. Ibid., p. 87.

8. R. E. Svoboda, *Aghora: At the Left Hand of God* (Albuquerque, N.M.: Brotherhood of Life, 1986), p. 36.

9. Ibid.

10. This definition is based on the formulation of John Rowan, *Subpersonalities: The People Inside Us* (London and New York: Routledge, 1990), p. 8.

11. B.-A. Scharfstein, *Mystical Experiences* (Baltimore, Md.: Penguin Books, 1974), p. 164.

12. Ibid.

13. See T. S. Szasz, *Ideology and Insanity: Essays on the Psychiatric Dehumanization of Man* (Garden City, N.Y.: Anchor Books, 1970).

14. See R. D. Laing, *The Divided Self* (Harmondsworth, England: Penguin Books, 1965).

15. R. D. Laing, *The Politics of Experience* (New York: Ballantine Books, 1967), p. 67.

16. R. D. Laing, *The Voice of Experience* (New York: Pantheon Books, 1982), p. 39.

17. Ibid., pp. 169–70.

18. See K. Horney, *The Neurotic Personality of Our Time* (New York: W. W. Norton, 1937).

19. A. Bharati, *The Ochre Robe: An Autobiography* (Garden City, N.Y.: Doubleday, 1970), p. 92.

20. A. Koestler, *The Lotus and the Robot* (New York: Harper Colophon Books, 1966), pp. 77–78.

21. See A. Hiltebeitel, ed., *Criminal Gods and Demon Devotees: Essays on the Guardians of Popular Hinduism* (New York: SUNY Press, 1989).

22. J. Brodskyu, ed., "More Conversations with U. G. Krishnamurti," *Yoga Journal*, vol. 2, no. 3 (May/June 1976), p. 20.

23. See R. E. Svoboda, *At the Left Hand of God* (Albuquerque, N.M.: Brotherhood of Life, 1986), pp. 183–84: "Aghoris eat human flesh, but not because they have become cannibals. There is a ritual involved. I have eaten human flesh many times; even my son has eaten human flesh. I used to wait at a funeral pyre until the skull would burst—it burst with a fine "pop"—and then I would rapidly, to avoid burning my fingers, pull out parts of the brain, which would be a gooey mass, partially roasted by then, and would eat it. It was nauseating, but at that moment you must forget your nausea and everything else: This is sadhana [spiritual discipline], not dinner at the Ritz."

24. K. Wilber, "The Spectrum Model," in D. Anthony et al., eds., *Spiritual Choices: The Problem of Recognizing Authentic Paths to Inner Transformation* (New York: Paragon House, 1987), p. 258.

25. See A. Maslow, *The Farther Reaches of Human Nature* (Harmondsworth, England: Penguin Books, 1973).

26. See Patanjali's *Yoga-Sutra* (IV. 7). In this Hindu scripture, it is also made clear that the *karma* "deposits" in what we would call the unconscious, which Patanjali names the "depth memory," are infinite. This infinity is explained as resulting from the interconnectedness of all beings. See my *The Yoga-Sutra of Patanjali: A New Translation and Commentary* (Rochester, Vt.: Inner Traditions, 1990).

27. J. E. Royster, "Personal Integration and Mystic Union in Sufism," *The Journal of Religious Studies* (Patiala: Punjabi University), vol. 8, no. 1 (Spring 1980), p. 63.

28. E. Neumann, *Depth Psychology and a New Ethic* (New York: Harper Torchbook, 1973), p. 87.

29. Maslow, *The Farther Reaches of Human Nature*, pp. 48–49.

30. All new students of the adept Da Love-Ananda are now expected to sign a disclaimer several pages long, although the legality of this document is questionable.

31. Bubba Free John [Da Love-Ananda], *Garbage and the Goddess* (Lower Lake, Calif.: Dawn Horse Press, 1974), p. 23.

32. George B. Leonard, *Education and Ecstasy* (New York: Dell Publishing, 1979), p. 96.
33. Irina Tweedie, *The Chasm of Fire* (Tisbury, England: Element Books, 1979), p. 132.
34. Ibid., p. 140.
35. Chögyam Trungpa, *Cutting Through Spiritual Materialism* (Boulder, Colo.: Shambhala, 1973), p. 107.
36. Ibid., pp. 214–15.
37. Bhagwan Shree Rajneesh, *Notes of a Madman* (Rajneeshpuram, Oregon: Rajneesh Foundation International, 1985), pp. 71–72.
38. D. Anthony et al., *Spiritual Choices*, p. 90.
39. Ibid.
40. Ibid., p. 89.
41. "Spiritual Authenticity: Separating the Wheat from the Chaff," *Clarion Call*, vol. 2, no. 4 (1989), p. 63.
42. See G. Feuerstein, ed., *Enlightened Sexuality* (Freedom, Calif.: Crossing Press, 1989).
43. N. Schreck, ed., *The Manson File* (New York: Amok Press, 1988), p. 17.
44. Ibid., p. 18.
45. Ibid., p. 19.
46. Ibid., p. 22.
47. Ibid., p. 46.
48. Ibid., p. 65.
49. See R.C. Zaehner, *Our Savage God: The Perverse Use of Eastern Thought* (Mission, Kans.: Seed and Ward, 1975).
50. See P. Tillich, *Morality and Beyond* (New York: Harper & Row, 1966).

## Epilogue

1. This is strongly argued by Alondra Oubre in her manuscript *The Guru Principle in Human Evolution: The Anthropology of Transcendence and the Numinous Mind* (1988).
2. See A. Stein, *Seeds of the Seventies* (Hanover, N.H.: University Press of New England, 1985).
3. See J. Gebser, *The Ever-Present Origin* (Athens, Ohio: University of Ohio Press, 1985). See also G. Feuerstein, *Structures of Consciousness: The Genius of Jean Gebser—An Introduction and Critique* (Lower Lake, Calif.: Integral Publishing, 1986) and *Jean Gebser: What Color Is Your Consciousness?* (San Francisco: Robert Briggs, 1989).
4. B. Z. Bokser, "Freedom and Authority," in L. Bryson et al., eds., *Freedom and Authority in Our Time: Twelfth Symposium of the Conference on Science, Philosophy and Religion* (New York: Harper & Row, 1953), pp. 488–89.
5. N. F. S. Ferre, "Authority and Freedom," in Bryson et al., *Freedom and Authority in Our Time*, p. 491.
6. T. Merton, *Seeds of Contemplation* (Norfolk, Conn.: New Directions Books, 1949), pp. 117–18.
7. E. A. Peers, transl./ed., *The Autobiography of St. Teresa of Avila* (Garden City, N.Y.: Image Books, 1960), p. 145.
8. Ibid., p. 144.
9. H. Cox, *The Feast of Fools: A Theological Essay on Festivity and Fantasy* (New York: Harper & Row, 1969), p. 161.
10. Ibid., p. 162.
11. P. Coukoulis, *Guru, Psychotherapist, and Self: A Comparative Study of the Guru-Disciple Relationship and the Jungian Analytic Process* (Marina del Rey, Calif.: DeVorss, 1976), p. 105.

# BIBLIOGRAPHIC REFERENCES

## I. Select Publications Cited

Anthony, D., B. Ecker, and K. Wilber, eds. *Spiritual Choices: The Problem of Recognizing Authentic Paths to Inner Transformation.* New York: Paragon House, 1987.

Anthony, D., and T. Robbins, eds. *In Gods We Trust: New Patterns of Religious Pluralism in America.* New Brunswick, N.J.: Transaction Books, 1981.

Ardussi, J., and L. Epstein. "The Saintly Madman in Tibet." In *Himalayan Anthropology: The Indo-Tibetan Interface,* edited by James F. Fisher. The Hague: Mouton, 1972.

Bakan, D. *The Duality of Human Existence: An Essay on Psychology and Religion.* Chicago: Rand McNally, 1966.

Bateson, G. *Steps to an Ecology of Mind: Collected Essays in Anthropology, Psychiatry, Evolution and Epistemology.* Frogmore, England: Paladin, 1973.

Bennett, J. G. *Witness.* Charles Town, W.Va.: Claymont Communications, 1984.

Benoit, H. *The Supreme Doctrine: Psychological Studies in Zen Thought.* New York: Viking Press, 1959.

Berger, P. L. *A Rumour of Angels: Modern Society and the Rediscovery of the Supernatural.* Harmondsworth, England: Penguin Books, 1971.

_____, et al. *The Homeless Mind: Modernization and Consciousness.* Harmondsworth, England: Penguin Books, 1974.

Berman, M. *The Reenchantment of the World.* New York: Bantam Books, 1984.

Bharati, A. *The Light at the Center.* Santa Barbara, Calif.: Ross-Erikson, 1976.

Bhattacharya, D. *Songs of the Bards of Bengal.* New York: Grove Press, 1969.

Blofeld, J. *The Tantric Mysticism of Tibet: A Practical Guide.* New York: E. P. Dutton, 1970.

Bolshakoff, S. *Russian Mystics.* Kalamazoo, Mich.: Cistercian Publications, 1977.

Bromley, D. G., and A. D. Shupe. *Strange Gods: The Great American Cult Scare.* Boston, Mass.: Beacon Press, 1981.

Bromley, D. G., and J. T. Richardson, eds. *The Brainwashing/Deprogramming Controversy: Sociological, Psychological, Legal and Historical Perspectives.* New York and Toronto: Edwin Mellen Press, 1983.

Carse, J. P. *Finite and Infinite Games: A Vision of Life as Play and Possibility.* New York: Free Press, 1986.

Claxton, G. [Swami Anand Ageha]. *Wholly Human: Western and Eastern Visions of the Self and Its Perfection.* London: Routledge & Kegan Paul, 1981.

Coukoulis, P. *Guru, Psychotherapist, and Self: A Comparative Study of the Guru-Disciple Relationship and the Jungian Analytic Process.* Marina del Rey, Calif.: DeVorss, 1976.

Cox, H. *The Feast of Fools: A Theological Essay on Festivity and Fantasy.* New York: Colophon Books, 1970.

————. *Turning East: The Promise and Peril of the New Orientalism.* New York: Simon and Schuster, 1977.

Curle, A. *Mystics and Militants: A Study of Awareness, Identity and Social Action.* London: Tavistock Publications, 1972.

Da Love-Ananda. *See under* Free John.

Dimock, E. C., Jr. *The Place of the Hidden Moon: Erotic Mysticism in the Vaisnava-Sahajiya Cult of Bengal.* Chicago: University of Chicago Press, 1966.

Donkin, W. *The Wayfarers.* Admednagar: Adi K. Irani, 1948.

Dowman, K. *The Divine Madman: The Sublime Life and Songs of Drukpa Kunley.* Clearlake, Calif.: Dawn Horse Press, 1983.

————. *Masters of Mahamudra: Songs and Histories of the Eighty-Four Buddhist Siddhas.* New York: SUNY Press, 1985.

Feuerstein, G. *Structures of Consciousness: The Genius of Jean Gebser—An Introduction and Critique.* Lower Lake, Calif.: Integral Publishing, 1986.

————, ed. *Enlightened Sexuality: Essays on Body-Positive Spirituality.* Freedom, Calif.: Crossing Press, 1989.

Fields, R. *How the Swans Came to the Lake: A Narrative History of Buddhism in America.* Boston: Shambhala, 1986.

Fingarette, H. *The Self in Transformation: Psychoanalysis, Philosophy and the Life of the Spirit.* New York: Harper Torchbooks, 1963.

Foucault, M. *Madness and Civilization: A History of Insanity in the Age of Reason.* New York: Vintage Books, 1973.

Freedland, N. *The Occult Explosion.* New York: Berkley Medallion Books, 1972.

Free John, Bubba [Da Love-Ananda]. *The Enlightenment of the Whole Body.* Middletown, Calif.: Dawn Horse Press, 1978.

————. *Garbage and the Goddess: The Last Miracles and Final Spiritual Instructions of Bubba Free John.* Lower Lake, Calif.: Dawn Horse Press, 1974.

————. *The Knee of Listening: The Early Life and Radical Spiritual Teachings of Bubba Free John.* Middletown, Calif.: Dawn Horse Press, 1979.

————. *The Method of the Siddhas.* Middletown, Calif.: Dawn Horse Press, 1978.

Gebser, J. *The Ever-Present Origin.* Athens, Ohio: University of Ohio Press, 1985.

Gordon, J. S. *The Golden Guru: The Strange Journey of Bhagwan Shree Rajneesh.* Lexington, Mass.: Stephen Greene Press, 1987.

Greenfield, R. *The Spiritual Supermarket: An Account of Gurus Gone Public in America.* New York: E. P. Dutton, 1975.

Hatengdi, M. U. *Nityananda: The Divine Presence.* Cambridge, Mass.: Rudra Press, 1984.

Helminiak, D. A. *Spiritual Development: An Interdisciplinary Study.* Chicago, Ill.: Loyola University Press, 1987.

Hiltebeitel, A., ed. *Criminal Gods and Demon Devotees: Essays on the Guardians of Popular Hinduism.* New York: SUNY Press, 1989.

Hixon, L. *Coming Home: The Experience of Enlightenment.* Los Angeles: J. P. Tarcher, 1989.

Hopkinson, T., and D. Hopkinson. *Much Silence: Meher Baba: His Life and Work.* London: Gollancz, 1974.

Humphreys, C. *Zen: A Way of Life*. London: English Universities Press, 1962.

Hyers, M. C. *And God Created Laughter: The Bible as Divine Comedy*. Atlanta, Ga.: John Knox Press, 1987.

_____. *The Comic Vision and the Christian Faith: A Celebration of Life and Laughter*. New York: Pilgrim Press, 1981.

_____. *Zen and the Comic Spirit*. London: Rider, 1974.

Jung, C. G. *Modern Man in Search of a Soul*. New York: Harcourt, Brace and Co., 1933.

_____. "On the Psychology of the Trickster-Figure." In *The Archetypes and the Collective Unconscious*. London: Routledge & Kegan Paul, 1959.

Karandikar, N. S. *Biography of Sri Swami Samarth Akkalkot Maharaj*. Bombay: Akkalkot Swami Math, 1978.

Keen, S. *To a Dancing God*. New York: Harper & Row, 1970.

Koestler, A. *The Lotus and the Robot*. New York: Harper Colophon Books, 1966.

Laing, R. D. *The Politics of Experience*. New York: Ballantine Books, 1967.

_____. *The Voice of Experience*. New York: Pantheon Books, 1982.

Lame Deer, J., and Richard Erdoes. *Lame Deer: Seeker of Visions*. New York: Pocket Books, 1972.

Lane, D. C. "The Paradox of Da Free John: Distinguishing the Message from the Medium." In *Understanding Cults and Spiritual Movements* research series, vol. 1, no. 2 (1985).

Lewis, I. M. *Ecstatic Religion: A Study of Shamanism and Spirit Possession*. London: Routledge, 1989.

Low, A. *The Iron Cow of Zen*. Wheaton, Ill.: Quest Books, 1985.

Lozowick, L. *The Cheating Buddha*. Tabor, N.J.: Hohm Press, 1980.

Marin, P. "Spiritual Obedience: The Transcendental Game of Follow the Leader." *Harper's*. February 1979.

Maslow, A. *The Farther Reaches of Human Nature*. Harmondsworth, England: Penguin Books, 1973.

Masters, R. A. *The Way of the Lover: The Awakening & Embodiment of the Full Human*. West Vancouver, B.C.: Xanthyros Foundation, 1988.

Mertin, T. *Seeds of Contemplation*. Norfolk, Conn.: New Directions Books, 1949.

_____. *The Ascent to Truth*. New York: Harcourt, Brace & Co. 1951.

Metzner, R. *Opening to Inner Light: The Transformation of Human Nature and Consciousness*. Los Angeles: J. P. Tarcher, 1986.

Miles, B. *Ginsberg: A Biography*. New York: Simon & Schuster, 1989.

Milgram, S. *Obedience to Authority: An Experimental View*. New York: Harper & Row, 1974.

Milne, H. *Bhagwan: The God That Failed*. New York: St. Martin's Press, 1986.

Muktananda Paramahansa, Swami. *Chitshakti Vilas: The Play of Consciousness*. Ganeshpuri, India: Shree Gurudev Ashram, 1972.

Narsimha Swami, B. S., and S. Subbarao. *Sage of Sakuri: Life Story of Shree Upasani Maharaj*. Sakuri, India: B. T. Wagh, n. d.

Needleman, J. *The New Religions*. London: Allen Lane, 1972.

Neumann, E. *Depth Psychology and a New Ethic*. New York: Harper Torchbook, 1973.

Nicholson, R. A. *Studies in Islamic Mysticism*. Cambridge, England: Cambridge University Press, 1921.

_____. *The Mystics of Islam*. London: Routledge & Kegan Paul, 1963.

Niskar, S. *Crazy Wisdom*. Berkeley, Calif.: Ten Speed Press, 1990.

Osborne, A., ed. *The Teachings of Ramana Maharshi*. New York: Samuel Weiser, 1978.

Otto, R. *The Idea of the Holy*. Harmondsworth, England: Penguin Books, 1959.

Pauwels, L. *Gurdjieff.* New York: Samuel Weiser, 1972.

Peck, G. T. *The Fool of God: Jacopone da Todi.* Alabama: University of Alabama Press, 1980.

Peers, E. A., transl./ed. *The Autobiography of St. Teresa of Avila.* Garden City, N.Y.: Image Books, 1960.

Peters, F. *Boyhood with Gurdjieff.* Baltimore, Md.: Penguin Books, 1972.

Powell, R., ed. *The Nectar of the Lord's Feet: Final Teachings of Sri Nisargadatta Maharaj.* Longmead, England: Element Books, 1987.

Quint, J., *Meister Eckehart: Deutsche Predigten und Traktate.* Munich: Carl Hanser, 1963.

Rajneesh, Bhagwan. *Dimensions Beyond the Known.* Los Angeles: Wisdom Garden, 1975.

―――――. *Tantra: The Supreme Understanding.* Poona, India: Rajneesh Foundation, 1975.

―――――. *Meditation: The Art of Ecstasy.* New York: Perennial Library, 1978.

―――――. *Notes of a Madman.* Rajneeshpuram, Oreg.: Rajneesh Foundation International, 1985.

Ram Dass [Richard Alpert]. *Journey of Awakening: A Meditator's Guidebook.* New York: Bantam Books, 1978.

―――――, ed. *Miracle of Love: Stories about Neem Karoli Baba.* New York: E. P. Dutton, 1979.

Reps, P. *Zen Flesh, Zen Bones: A Collection of Zen and Pre-Zen Writings.* Garden City, N.Y.: Anchor Books, n.d.

Reymond, L. *To Live Within.* Baltimore, Md.: Penguin Books, 1973.

Richardson, J. T., ed. *Conversion Careers: In and Out of the New Religions.* Beverly Hills, Calif., and London: Sage Publications, 1978.

Rizvi, Saiyid Athar Abbas. *A History of Sufism in India.* Vol. 1: *Early Sufism and Its History in India to 1600 A.D.* New Delhi: Munshiram Manoharlal, 1978.

Ross, M. *Pillars of Flame: Power, Priesthood, and Spiritual Maturity.* San Francisco: Harper & Row, 1988.

Rowan, J. *Subpersonalities: The People Inside Us.* London and New York: Routledge, 1990.

Sargant, William. *Battle for the Mind.* London: Pan Books, 1970.

Saward, J. *Perfect Fools: Folly for Christ's Sake in Catholic and Orthodox Spirituality.* Oxford, England: Oxford University Press, 1980.

Scharfstein, B.-A. *Mystical Experience.* Baltimore, Md.: Penguin Books, 1974.

Schiffman, R. *Sri Ramakrishna: A Prophet for the New Age.* New York: Paragon House, 1989.

Shreck, N., ed. *The Manson File.* New York: Amok Press, 1988.

Smith, H. "The Sacred Unconscious." In *Beyond Health and Normality: Explorations in Exceptional Psychological Well-Being,* edited by R. Walsh and D. H. Shapiro. New York: Van Nostrand Reinhold, 1983.

Speeth, K. R. *The Gurdjieff Work.* Los Angeles: J. P. Tarcher, 1989.

Spencer, S. *Mysticism in World Religion.* London: Allen & Unwin, 1966.

Stein, A. *Seeds of the Seventies.* Hanover, N.H.: University Press of New England, 1985.

Suzuki, D. T. *Essays in Zen Buddhism: Second Series.* New York: Samuel Weiser, 1976.

―――――. *Studies in Zen.* New York: Dell Publishing, 1955.

Symonds, J., and K. Grant, eds. *The Confessions of Aleister Crowley: An Autohagiography.* London: Routledge & Kegan Paul, 1979.

Szasz, T. S. *Ideology and Insanity: Essays on the Psychiatric Dehumanization of Man.* Garden City, N.Y.: Anchor Books, 1970.

―――――. *The Manufacture of Madness: A Comparative Study of the Inquisition and the Mental Health Movement.* New York: Harper & Row, 1970.

_____. *The Myth of Mental Illness: Foundations of a Theory of Personal Conduct.* New York: Hoeber-Harper, 1961.

Tart, C. T. *Waking Up: Overcoming the Obstacles to Human Potential.* Boston: Shambala/New Science Library, 1987.

Thaker, S. *Songs of the Avadhut.* Kampala, India: Avadhut Parivar, 1972.

Thompson, L. *Mirror to the Light: Reflections on Consciousness and Experience.* Edited by Richard Lannoy. London: Coventure, 1984.

Tillich, P. *Morality and Beyond.* New York: Harper & Row, 1966.

Trungpa, C. *Born in Tibet.* Baltimore, Md.: Penguin Books, 1971.

_____. *Cutting Through Spiritual Materialism.* Boulder, Colo.: Shambhala, 1973.

_____. *First Thought Best Thought: 108 Poems.* Boulder, Colo.: Shambhala, 1983.

_____. *Journey Without Goal: The Tantric Wisdom of the Buddha.* Boulder, Colo.: Prajna Press, 1981.

Tweedie, I. *The Chasm of Fire: A Woman's Experience of Liberation through the Teaching of a Sufi Master.* Tisbury, England: Element Books, 1979.

_____. *Daughter of Fire: A Diary of a Spiritual Training with a Sufi Master.* Nevada City, Calif.: Blue Dolphin Publishing, 1986.

Underhill, E. *Mysticism: A Study in the Nature and Development of Man's Spiritual Consciousness.* New York: E. P. Dutton, 1961.

van de Wetering, J. *The Empty Mirror: Experiences in a Japanese Zen Monastery.* New York: Pocket Books, 1973.

Vaughan, F. "A Question of Balance: Health and Pathology in New Religious Movements." *Journal of Humanistic Psychology,* vol. 23, no. 3 (1983).

_____. *The Inward Arc: Healing and Wholeness in Psychotherapy and Spirituality.* Boston: Shambhala, 1986.

Wallis, Wilson D. *Messiahs: Their Role in Civilization.* Washington, D.C.: American Council on Public Affairs, 1943.

Watts, A. *Beyond Theology: The Art of Godmanship.* New York: Vintage Books, 1964.

_____. *The Book: On the Taboo Against Knowing Who You Are.* New York: Vintage Books, 1972.

_____. *In My Own Way: An Autobiography—1915–1965.* New York: Vintage Books, 1973.

_____. *Psychotherapy East and West.* New York: Mentor Books, 1961.

White, J., ed. *What Is Enlightenment?* Los Angeles: J. P. Tarcher, 1985.

Wilber, K. *The Atman Project: A Transpersonal View of Human Development.* Wheaton, Ill.: Theosophical Publishing House, 1980.

Wilber, K., J. Engler, and D. P. Brown, eds. *Transformations of Consciousness: Conventional and Contemplative Perspectives on Development.* Boston: Shambhala, 1986.

Wilson, C. *Aleister Crowley: The Nature of The Beast.* Wellingborough, England: Aquarian Press, 1987.

Yarti, Swami Anand. *The Sound of Running Water: A Photobiography of Bhagwan Shree Rajneesh and His Work, 1974–78.* Poona, India: Rajneesh Foundation, 1980.

Zaehner, R. C. *Our Savage God: The Perverse Use of Eastern Thought.* Mission, Kans.: Seed and Ward, 1975.

## II. General Reading

Brooke, T. *Riders of the Cosmic Circuit.* Tring, England: Lion Publishing, 1986.

Cammell, C. R. *Aleister Crowley: The Man, The Mage, The Poet.* London: University Books, 1962.

Chakravarti, S. C. *Bauls: The Spiritual Vikings.* Calcutta: Firma KLM Private Ltd., 1980.

Chetanananda, Swami. *The Breath of God*. Cambridge, Mass.: Rudra Press, 1988.

Chidester, D. *Salvation and Suicide: An Interpretation of Jim Jones, the Peoples Temple, and Jonestown*. Bloomington, Ind.: Indiana University Press, 1988.

Cole, W. O. *The Guru in Sikhism*. London: Darton, Longman & Todd, 1982.

Fortune, M. M. *Is Nothing Sacred? When Sex Invades the Pastoral Relationship*. San Francisco: Harper & Row, 1989.

Gold, D. *Comprehending the Guru: Toward a Grammar of Religious Perception*. Atlanta, Ga.: Scholars Press, 1988.

————. *The Lord as Guru: Hindi Sants in the Northern Indian Tradition*. New York and Oxford, England: Oxford University Press, 1987.

Green, J. *God's Fool: The Life and Times of Francis of Assisi*. San Francisco: Harper & Row, 1985.

Gurdjieff: *Views from the Real World: Early Talks in Moscow, Essentuki, Tiflis, Berlin, London, Paris, New York and Chicago as Recollected by His Pupils*. New York: E. P. Dutton, 1975.

Hartmann, T. and O. *Our Life with Mr. Gurdjieff*. San Francisco: Harper & Row, 1983.

Isherwood, C. *My Guru and His Disciples*. Harmondsworth, England: Penguin Books, 1980.

Jha, A. *The Imprisoned Mind*. New Delhi: Ambika Publications, 1980.

Johnson, W. A. *The Search for Transcendence: A Theological Analysis of Nontheological Attempts to Define Transcendence*. New York: Harper Colophon Books, 1974.

Jung, C. G. *Psychology and the East*. Princeton, N.J.: Princeton University Press, 1978.

Kakar, S. *Shamans, Mystics and Doctors: A Psychological Inquiry into India and Its Healing Traditions*. Boston: Beacon Press, 1982.

Kopp, S. B. *Guru: Metaphors from a Psychotherapist*. New York: Bantam Books, 1976.

McMullen, C. O., ed. *The Nature of Guruship*. Delhi: I.S.P.C.K, 1976.

*Mother as Revealed to Me*. Translated by G. Das Gupta. Varanasi, India: Shree Shree Anandamayee Sangha, 1972.

Nicholl, D. *Holiness*. Mahwah, N.J.: Paulist Press, 1987.

Pelletier, K. R. *Toward a Science of Consciousness*. New York: Dell, 1978.

Rajneesh, Bhagwan. *My Way: The Way of the White Clouds*. New York: Grove Press, 1975.

Robbins, T. *Cults, Converts & Charisma*. London and Newbury Park, Calif.: SAGE Publications, 1988.

Schur, E. *The Awareness Trap: Self-Absorption Instead of Social Change*. New York: McGraw-Hill, 1977.

Sennett, R. *Authority*. New York: Vintage Books, 1981.

Speeth, K. R. *The Gurdjieff Work*. Los Angeles: J. P. Tarcher, 1989.

Stark, C. A. *God of All: Sri Ramakrishna's Approach to Religious Plurality*. Cape Cod, Mass.: Claude Stark, 1974.

Stark, R., ed. *Religious Movements: Genesis, Exodus, and Numbers*. New York: Paragon House, 1985.

Symonds, J. *The Great Beast: The Life and Magick of Aleister Crowley*. London: Macdonald, 1971.

Tart, C. T. *Transpersonal Psychologies*. London: Routledge & Kegan Paul, 1975.

————. *Open Mind, Discriminating Mind: Reflections on Human Possibilities*. San Francisco: Harper & Row, 1989.

Walsh, R. N. *The Spirit of Shamanism*. Los Angeles: J. P. Tarcher, 1990.

————, and Frances Vaughan, eds. *Beyond Ego: Transpersonal Dimensions in Psychology*. Los Angeles: J. P. Tarcher, 1980.

Welwood, J., ed. *The Meeting of the Ways: Explorations in East/West Psychology.* New York: Schocken Books, 1979.
White, J., ed. *The Highest State of Consciousness.* Garden City, N.Y.: Anchor Books, 1972.
Wilson, P. L., and Nasrollah Pourjavady. *The Drunken Universe: An Anthology of Persian Sufi Poetry.* Grand Rapids, Mich.: Phanes Press, 1987.

# INDEX